A Perennial Stream

Penn Bobby Singh

A Perennial Stream © 2014 by Penn Bobby Singh
And RAJ International Inc.

ALL RIGHTS RESERVED
No part of this book may be reproduced in any form, by photocopying or by any electronic or mechanical means, including information storage or retrieval systems, without permission in writing from both the copyright owner and the publisher of this book, except for the minimum words needed for review.

First Printing, 2014-15
Edited by Janet Elaine Smith
Cover and Interior Design by T.C. McMullen

Trade Paperback: ISBN 1-978-935188-39-1
Ebook: ISBN 1-935188-40-7

A Star Publish LLC Publication
www.starpublishllc.com
Published in 2014
Printed in the United States of America

Ordering Information: Quantity sales. Special discounts are available on quantity purchases by corporations, associations, and others. For details, contact the agent at raijintl1@cox.net

Acknowledgments

I would like to acknowledge and express my gratitude to, the following individuals:

Ralf Heynen for his photo of Patwon Ki Haveli in Jaisalmer which is used in the front book cover

Janet Elaine Smith, my editor for her support and kindness

T.C. McMullen of Star Publish for her help in seeing the book come to print

Gary and Sandra Worthington for reviewing the book, providing very useful input and their support

Late Budh Singh Sb Bapna for providing oral history for this book, particularly the stories of Deoraj, Guman Chand and Zorawarmal

Late P. S. Bapna Sb for providing oral history, for this book, particularly stories of Chhogmal and Siremal

Late Ratan Kumari Bapna Sb, for providing oral history for this book, particularly stories of Zorawarmal and Chhogmal

Late Harnath Singh Sb Mehta, for providing oral history for this book, particularly the story of Chhogmal

Dr. Rodney Jones for previewing the book and providing valuable input

Craig Sager, my friend of 30 years, for his support and encouragement

Kalpana, my wife, for her unflinching belief in this book and the value of telling this story

Kaumudi Naithani, for previewing the book and providing valuable input and for her support

Nanda K Sharma Sb, renowned historian of Jaisalmer, and his **Desert Museum of Jaisalmer** for providing a picture of Salim Singh and other support

Table of Contents

Introduction 13
Chapter 1 – Indore City, Central India 22
Chapter 2 - Dev in Convalescence 43
Chapter 3 - Story of Dev - Part 1 48
Chapter 4 - Story of Osian 58
Chapter 5 - Story of Deoraj - Part 1 75
Chapter 6 - Story of Deoraj - 2 97
Chapter 7 - Story of Guaman Chand - 1 108
Chapter 8 - Story of Guman Chand - 2 132
Chapter 9 - Story of Guman Chand - 3 137
Chapter 10 - Story of Guman Chand - 4 142
Chapter 11 - Story of Zorawar Mal - 1 159
Chapter 12 - Brothers Parting 165
Chapter 13 - Story of Zorawar Mal - 2 170
Chapter 14 - Story of Zorawar Mal - 3 178
Chapter 15 - Story of Zorawar Mal - 4 189
Chapter 16 - Story of Chhogmal 198
Chapter 17 - Story of Siremal 218
Chapter 18 - Story of PS 244
Chapter 19 - Story of Dev - Part 2 258
Chapter 20 - Story of Dev- Part 3 287
Chapter 21 - Story of Dev - Part 4 305
Chapter 22 - Story of Dev - Part 5 317
Chapter 23 - Story of Dev - Part 6 327
Author's Notes 358
Glossary 367
Bibliography - Bapna Family-Historical Record and References - Independent Sources - Used to authenticate information in this book 371

Table of Figures

Osian Sachiya Mata Temple - Osian	60
Jaisalmer Camel Trail Through the Desert	100
Jaisalmer Fort at Night	101
Indian Wedding Dress with Gold Brocade	113
Maharawal Mulraj of Jaisalmer (1762-1819)	114
Rajasthani Banjara Dancer	130
Rajasthani Banjara Dancers	131
Patwon Ki Haveli Built by Guman Chand	155
Patwon Ki Haveli Balcony Carving Detail	156
Patwon Ki Haveli - Interior Frescas	157
Seth Bahadur Mal Bapna - Kota	167
Seth Mangni Ram Bapna - Ratlam	168
Seth Zorawar Mal Bapna - Indore, Udaipur	169
Tatya Jog Kibe	171
Tatya Jog Kibe - Cenotaph - Chhatri	172
Col James Tod	177
Citi Palace Udaipur - Maharana Bhim Singh	180
Udaipur Mewar - A Panoramic View	181
Tod in Udaipur - Unknown Artist	181
Mehta Sher Singh - Right with Mewar Rana	182
Maharana Bhim Singh Mewar	183
Kuldhara Village Jaisalmer Ghost Town	187
Salim Singh Haveli in Jaisalmer	187
Prime Minister Salim Singh of Jaisalmer	188
Bapna Jain Temple Amarsagar Jaisalmer	195
Rishabdeo Aangi - Kesariyaji Jain Temple	196
Udaipur Sethji Ri Haveli - Bapna Residence	197
Seth Chhogmal Bapna Udaipur Mewar	212
Maharana Fateh Singh of Mewar 1884-1930	213
Rai Mehta Pannalal Prime Minister Mewar	214
Bapna's Sethji Ri Haveli-Udaipur Mural	215
Bankers of Udaipur Mewar Closing a Deal	216
Times Square New York - 1898 - Perspective	217
Sir Siremal Bapna	222
HH Maharana Bhupal Singh of Mewar	223
HH Mahraja Indore Tukoji Rao Holkar III	223

Mumtaz Begum - Courtesan to HH Tukoji Rao 224
HH Mahraja Bhupinder Singh of Patiala 226
David Lloyd George - British Prime Minister 227
HH Maharaj Yeshwant Rao Holkar of Indore 233
Bakshi Baugh Palace Indore 234
Sir Siremal Receiving Viceroy Lord Irvin 234
Sir Siremal Bapna with Mahatama Gandhi 235
Sir Siremal Bapna at League of Nations 235
Siremal Bapna Official State Portrait 247
HH Maharaja Ganga Singh of Bikaner 248
PS Bapna SB, IAS-Younger son of Siremal 248
PS Bapna SB, Age 70 326
Current Bapna House Indore 2014 340

Bapna Family Tree

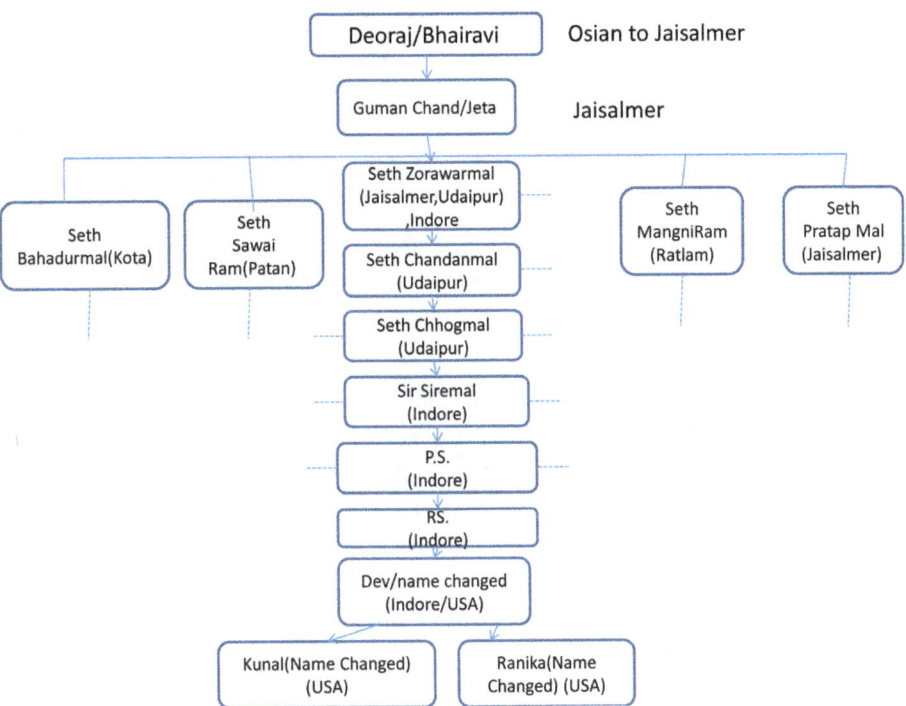

Introduction

According to economic historian Angus Maddison in his book *The World Economy: A Millennial Perspective*, India had the world's largest economy from the first to the eleventh century, and in the eighteenth century, with a 32.9% share of world GDP in the first century to 28.9% in 1000 AD, and in 1700 AD with 24.4%. There are other credible studies that confirm this and no one seriously disputes these figures.

Contrary to the general impression of India as an impoverished nation of half-naked *fakirs* for most of known history, India was one of the wealthiest civilizations on earth. The length of time that India had been a leading economic power, too, is unprecedented in history. It was only in the past couple of hundred years that India economically slipped badly, not being able to deal with the rise of European expansion and not able to fully participate in the industrial revolution. A major reason for the decline was that years of amoral institution building eventually caught up with the Indians in practical terms, where the existing institutions could not adequately deal with the problems at hand and became dysfunctional, weak, and irrelevant.

India was one of the greatest mercantile powers in history. The Indians achieved this despite the fact that India was never a unified political entity. As a unified single entity, India today covers a larger territory than at any time in the past with the exception of perhaps the Mogul Empire, the British Indian Empire (which really was never an Indian empire in the cultural sense), or possibly the Mauryan empire of the third century BC. India has always been more a collection of abstract ideas than a physical entity with defined boundaries. This collection of ideas was derived from its native religions such as Hinduism, Jainism, Buddhism, Sikhism, and even certain forms of animism practiced by a large section of the aborigine populations of India.

Even within Hinduism there were many influences and streams, some of them even contradictory. The beauty of Hinduism lay in harmoniously blending these diverse and sometimes contradictory ideas into one coherent and distinct culture. From the beginning of recorded history until approximately the fifteenth century AD the collection of ideas called "India" was a dominant force from modern-day Afghanistan to the Indian subcontinent—from Malaysia to Indonesia, from Thailand to Indo-China, and even parts of China, including Tibet.

The unraveling of the idea of India outside the Indian subcontinent started around 1100 AD, with the onslaught of Islamic expansion, and was pretty much complete by the sixteenth century with complete Islamization of the Malay people and most of Indonesia. Large parts of the Indian subcontinent ranging from Afghanistan to Pakistan and Bangladesh and the modern day India itself has been Islamized. The Islamic population of the Indian subcontinent as of 2010 stood at roughly 35%, some say, even 40% of the total. Therefore, the Indian cultural sphere (defined by the abstract idea of India where Hinduism or Buddhism or Jainism or Sikhism holds sway) over the centuries has shrunk to modern day India, Nepal, Thailand, Indo-China, Burma, Bali in Indonesia, Bhutan and Sri Lanka, while Tibet is hanging in the balance.

Despite the lack of geographical contiguity and continuity of India over time, as well as suffering massive invasions, wars and internecine warfare, Indians managed to excel at commerce and economics. The reason was that despite all of the religions that originated in India displaying a distinct bias towards spiritualism over materialism, Indians of all variety had one thing in common: they were always a commercially minded people. With the exception of a small number of saints, holy men, philosophers, warriors and a few common people, an overwhelming number of Indians did not feel much connection with spirituality, nor did they wish to ever establish such a connection. Indians were always a very hard-nosed, commercially-minded, materialistic and status-conscious people who were quite uninhibited in how far they would actually go in pursuit of monetary gains.

Therefore, in an almost continuous state of external and civil war right through their entire history, sometimes multiple external and multiple civil wars at the same time, Indians were successfully able to organize themselves in a way which ensured maximum economic output and financial gain. The caste system was one principle around which Indians organized their society. Contrary to popular belief that it is a religious concept, it actually was an economic system Indians invented, which could ensure steady and cheap labor while providing a certain amount of market stability amidst all the chaos. In fact, there is not a great deal of emphasis in Hindu texts on enforcing the kind of caste system that Hindus came to practice. It was a case of the tail wagging the dog, where organized religion had to accommodate some of the practices prevalent on the ground in order to retain its appeal. It is equally true, though, that Hindu texts allude to a form of the division of labor and they say nothing against the caste system as practiced in India on the ground. To be fair, it is also important to mention that there have been several movements within Hinduism throughout its history to reform and even exorcise the caste system. Therefore, the caste system was one of the means used to optimize economic performance. It worked. It was grossly immoral in the way it was practiced, but it worked.

Morality was never a consideration in the general and larger Indian society, and therefore the organizations and institutions that Indians developed over the years were practical and amoral. They worked just fine as long as people whose interests were served by these institutions could get away with it. Trouble started when the enforcement power of these institutions such as the caste system weakened.

Since 1947, though, there has been a sea of change in this area and the caste system has weakened a great deal and its days in India are numbered, at least in the way it has been practiced over the years. The danger now is whether the newly empowered erstwhile lower castes will use their sheer numbers to perpetuate their own brand of caste system or if they will be able to envision a truly open and just society based on equality for all.

A careful study of Indian history reveals a country and its people more preoccupied with a perpetual and sometimes brutal struggle with each other over economic resources than the stereotypical country of lions and tigers, superstition and holy men, mysterious and enigmatic. Right through history, Indians always put their individual economic and social interests above all else. All the mysticism and superstition and strange rituals were mostly oppressive and deceptive means to promote the economic interests of one section of the population or the other and creating barriers of entry for other sections, generally under the guise of religion and tradition.

16 INTRODUCTION

Indian history, particularly Northern Indian history, is replete with instances of invasions from the East (China and Mongolia), Central Asia (including Persia and even the Caucasus). Some of these invasions are believed to have occurred in pre-historic period. The most famous invasion around pre-historic times is known as the "Aryan Invasion," where supposedly fairer skinned people from the Caucuses arrived in India, with their bronze weapons and chariots, to supplant the darker skinned locals, bringing with them the Vedas and Hinduism. This theory is being increasingly challenged and new studies suggest that this "Aryan invasion" never occurred. However, dispelling of the Aryan invasion theory in no way negates the truth about scores of other invasions into India that did take place during that period of recorded history, with ample historical records. One such invasion was the invasion of the Scythians, and there is generally a consensus among scholars of all shades and opinion that this invasion actually occurred. This is further confirmed by the generational memories of certain families in India.

According to various historians, eastern and western — the author wishes to mention two Indian historians in particular, S Chatopadhyay and HC RayChoudhary, around 200 BC nomads of South Russian-Central Asian origins, called the "Scythians," were displaced from their habitat by some tribes from the East, presumably China. This displacement caused a domino effect to where some Scythian groups started to migrate south into the northern areas of the Indian subcontinent, mainly Afghanistan and Sindh. They later moved further south and established major empires all across North India under the name of "*Sakas*" around the first century AD. These Scythian groups that migrated into India were known as the "Indo-Scythians." In Indian languages, these people were called the "*Sakas*." The first empire was called the "*Saka* Empire" in what is now known as Gujarat, Central Indian provinces and Rajasthan. This empire lasted from about 10 AD until about 400 AD, when they were conquered by the Guptas. Some historians suggest that even the Kushans, who also were migrants into India, were of Saka origin.

The Hindu culture of India, perhaps partly out of necessity to accommodate various migrations and partly out of its relative inherent openness, had become very adept and hospitable to absorbing and accepting newer peoples into its fold. Hinduism became this large ocean which absorbed all these various streams, while each stream contributed some of its own philosophy, customs and traditions. The

Indo-Scythians, who were migrants and foreigners, were no exception and also quickly blended into the Hindu society and became Hindus, although they maintained their distinct ethnic identity right down to this day. Large populations of these Indo-Scythians continued to inhabit Northern and Central India, despite their loss of political power when their *Saka* Empire fell to the Guptas, around 400 AD. Even though they had lost political power, there was no ethnic cleansing or genocide attempted on them by their victors. In fact, it was amazing how a nation, constantly in state of civil war and war with outside invaders, managed to avoid ethnic cleansing and pogroms of the kind that were prevalent in other parts of the world. Not until the Islamic invasions (between the ninth and fifteenth centuries AD), when mass slaughter was undertaken by some invaders in the name of Islam, did this calamity hit India.

The migration patterns into India from approximately 1500 BC to 800 AD, an era before the first Islamic invasions occurred, were complex. Normally, when one major tribe or people migrated into or invaded India, there were several other related tribes, and sometimes unrelated tribes, that piggybacked and migrated together. Therefore, when Indo-Scythians migrated into India, there were several other peoples such as Georgians (yes, people from what is now the Republic of Georgia), Khazars, White Huns and other Turkish-Persians who came. These people were absorbed into the Hindu fold and continued to be closely associated with the Indo-Scythians and later completely merged their identities with them.

After the fall of the *Saka* empire, branches of the Indo-Scythians, who by 400 AD had become somewhat racially mixed after having been in India for hundreds of years, scattered over North and Central India, establishing their small kingdoms in obscure places wherever they could protect themselves from the might of the Gupta Empire. Most of the places where these chieftains established their kingdoms were in Rajasthan, although there were some in neighboring areas. Indo-Scythians not only survived, but thrived in Rajasthan, as it was considered infertile, and a desert, and was generally below the radar screen of the Gupta Empire. There are several theories on the origin of Rajputs, but the author's family tends to believe the one proposed by Col Tod and the legendary indologist A L Basham, that these small Indo-Scythian (Saka) chiefs became the ancestors of a warrior class, collectively and broadly known as the "Rajputs." Several of these chieftains later became prominent and ruled over large kingdoms within India, but the first of these to attain prominence were the Pratiharas, who ruled the longest and over the largest Rajput Empire in India.

Even after their first empires fell to the Guptas in 400 AD, the Indo-Scythians persevered. The Guptas themselves fell following a glorious 200-year rule, around 600 AD, and one branch of the Indo-Scythians (Sakas) called the "Gurjar-Pratiharas" re-established control over large areas of Western and Central India, including Gujarat and Rajasthan. Rajasthan was then called "Gurjaratra" (not to be confused with the neighboring state of Gujarat). It was not until the British arrived in India in the seventeenth century and coined the phrase "Rajputana," after the Rajputs, which by then the Indo-Scythians (Sakas) had morphed into, that Gurjaratra came to be known as Rajasthan. The word "Rajasthan" is a derivative of "Rajputana." Pratiharas held sway from 600 AD until around 1200 AD over most of North Western India, when a protracted internecine war of attrition between them and the Kingdom of Rashtrakutas which was ruled mostly by Jain rulers, resulted in the destruction of both and enabled the Islamic invaders to establish their empire in India.

Until about 700 AD, the Indo-Scythians (Sakas) were not exposed to any other Indian religion than Hinduism and most of them had become Hindus. However, there were two other major religions that had also originated in India, and at least one of them had antecedents going back to pre-historic times, thereby being far older than Hinduism. They were Jainism and Buddhism. Both stressed extreme non-violence and neither believed in the caste system. Buddhism was founded by a scion of a princely family in the East Indian state of Bihar, called "Gautam Siddhartha," who later came to be known as "Gautam Buddha." Siddhartha was a historical figure and lived around the sixth century BC. Because of its emphasis on simplicity as opposed to complex rituals of Hinduism, non-violence and opposition to the caste system, Buddhism grew popular in India as well as many other countries around the world.

Several ruling kings and dynasties in India over the centuries adopted Buddhism and patronized it with great vigor, generously financing Buddhist monks to travel across the globe to promote Buddhism. Emperor Asoka was a prime example of it in the second century BC. He famously sent Buddhist emissaries to places as far away as Japan, China, Malaysia, Indonesia and Indo-China. In contrast, Hinduism, which dates itself back to the Vedas, originated around 1500 BC, when the oldest Veda, the Riga Veda, was written. Hinduism also spread widely and until the Middle Ages it was the dominant religion of countries which are now known as Afghanistan, Pakistan, Thailand, Burma, Malaysia, Indonesia, Cambodia, Vietnam, Laos and Sri Lanka. Over the years, travelling Buddhist monks managed to establish almost equal status for Buddhism in all of these places.

Jainism, on the other hand, traces its antecedents to pre-historic times. It also stressed extreme non-violence, perhaps even more extreme than Buddhism. It was basically an atheistic religion in the sense that there was no intelligent God who observes or directs every minor action of a human being. According to Jainism, one attains Nirvana through not hurting anybody, not even an insect, through conquering ones emotions and weaknesses, and through complete detachment from the material world. Jainism recognizes twenty-four *Tirthankaras* (Gurus or Guides) who had attained the ultimate Nirvana and whose life examples can be followed by other Jains to achieve Nirvana. Twenty-two of them existed in pre-historic times and the last two, Parasvanath and Mahavira, were historical figures, living around 700 BC and 600 BC respectively. The last Jain, *Tirthankara*, Mahavira, also a Prince of the Royal House of Vaishali, was a contemporary of Buddha, but Jainism is universally accepted to be older than both Buddhism and Hinduism.

The first Jain, *Tirthankara* Adinath, lived before recorded history. Unlike Hindu and Buddhist monks, Jainism prohibits its monks from using any mechanized form of transport, even bicycles or bullock carts, as they could cause harm to small living organisms. Therefore, throughout history down to this day, Jain monks, barring very few exceptions, could not travel outside India to promote Jainism. In addition, they are also prohibited from aggressively seeking to convert people into Jainism. This has kept the total number of Jains very small (about twelve million worldwide by last count in 2009) and most of them are in India. There were many historical figures who were Jains—the great Emperor Chandragupta Maurya being one of them.

Jainism has influenced both Hinduism and Buddhism, and elements of Jainism have been incorporated in both. One can still see glimpses of Jainism in the practice of Hinduism and Buddhism in Thailand, Burma and Indo-China etc. By the time the Pratiharas established their empire in India, around 600 AD, Hinduism, Buddhism, and to a lesser extent Jainism were the main religions, not only in India but in the entire belt from Afghanistan down to Indonesia and everywhere in between. Jainism, Hinduism, Buddhism, and later Sikhism constitute one single cultural stream, diverse, no doubt, but unified at a central core from which emerged the idea of India as unique and distinct from any other culture.

While Pratiharas established a dominant empire in North Western India, around the same period (600 AD), another dynasty called the "Rashtrakutas," most of whose rulers were Jains, had established an equally powerful empire in the Deccan peninsula of South India and the Palas did the same in East India; the three empires competed with each other for influence and domination. For almost six hundred years, the Gurjar-Pratihara and Rashtrakuta empires fought almost annual wars which ultimately led to the demise of both around 1200 AD and gave an opening to the Islamic invaders to establish themselves in India. While the Pratiharas were fending off attacks from the Rashtrakuta to their south, they were also thwarting Islamic incursions by Arabs from the northwest and had managed to significantly slow the advance and establishment of an Islamic empire in India. While the Islamists ultimately did break through, it wasn't until 1200 AD, some four hundred years after the first Islamic incursions, that they were able to carve out their first major Indian empire, with Delhi as its capital. Some historians credit the Pratiharas for blunting and slowing the Islamic momentum enough to where unlike Malaysia, Indonesia, Afghanistan and other places, India has not become totally Islamic yet, even in the 21st century.

In addition to the Pratiharas, several other Indo-Scythian city-states were established all over Rajasthan between 600 AD and 1200 AD, a period that coincided completely with the dominant Pratihara's Pan-Indian empire. Some of those major city-states included Mewar (Guhilot and Sisodia Rajputs), Jaipur (Kachwaha Rajputs), Jodhpur (Rathore Rajputs), Bikaner (Rathore Rajputs) and Jaisalmer (Bhatti Rajputs). This was also a time during which the term "Indo-Scythians" and "Sakas" disappeared from common usage and the word "Rajput" was commonly used to describe these dynasties and people. Each city-state has a story which deserves one or several books in their own right. This book will not focus on all those states, but only two of the above, i.e., Jaisalmer and Mewar, because the destinies of the Bapna family of the Bafna clan and the city-states of Jaisalmer and Mewar are closely intertwined.

After the fall of the Pratihara Empire, various Islamic dynasties established their own Pan-Indian empires. Many of the Rajput city-states resisted these Islamic dynasties with extreme courage, sometimes fighting onto death. This was the most glorious chapter in Rajput history. Over time, though, during the last Islamic dynasty to rule India, the famed Moguls, the Rajput resistance faded and most of the Rajputs accepted the Mogul overlordship in exchange for a certain degree of autonomy and retention of their kingdoms. The House of Mewar and the House of Bhatti of Jaisalmer, in particular, resisted the Islamic rule the longest and with the greatest ferocity, performing the greatest sacrifices.

One religious development did take place during the rule of Rashtrakutas and the Pratiharas, from approximately 700 AD to 1150 AD. Jain monks had started to make significant inroads into Rajasthan from their already established bases in Karnataka and Gujarat to the south and Bihar and Orissa to the east. Several Indo-Scythian (Rajput) chiefs had allowed the Jain monks to establish their religious monasteries and temples within their territories across Rajasthan.

The Pratihara rulers, or Parihar Rajputs, as they later were known, established many new cities and towns during their reign, two of which were located on the western end of Rajasthan. One was the kingdom of Marwar (Mandore, near modern day Jodhpur) founded in or around 780 AD. The other was the temple city of Osian, also founded around 780 AD, about 40 miles from Mandore.

It is this Osian city where the Bapna dynasty originated. Indore is an Indian city, located in Central India, about 650 miles from Osian. The people originating from Osian are known as Oswals. There are several historical theories on the origin of Oswals, but the author, through his research has found the story mentioned in Chapter 4 as the most compelling, having the most credible historical references to back it up. Some of these historical references are cited in the bibliography at the end of the book. The author, though, acknowledges that other historians may have other theories.

Almost all the consequential events in this book are taken from historically credible sources cited in the bibliography at the end of the book.

Chapter 1 - Indore City, Central India

October 22, 2010

He lay in a coma in the Intensive Care Unit of Cure Well Hospital. He was in his late 40s and his head and forehead were almost entirely covered in crisp white bandages. His eyes were closed and he looked like a man sleeping peacefully. An IV tube connected his right arm to an inverted bottle on a pole next to the bed. Wires ran from various parts of his body to machines on the left which had green and red waves running ominously across the display. It was a small, sparse setting, separated from other ICUs by a blue hospital curtain, a small end table that had a magazine and a flask containing water sitting on it, and a stool where sat a woman, also in her 40s. Her name was Selena; the man lying on the bed was her husband of twenty three years. Selena had light brown hair, brown eyes, a pale complexion, and beautiful clear glowing skin with no signs of any wrinkles. She was about 5ft. 5in. tall, a hundred and ten pounds, not an ounce of fat on her body, and in her younger days she had often been mistaken for a Bollywood actress. She was pouring herself a glass of water from the flask when she heard her husband move his legs. She turned towards the bed and saw his face in contortion, his fists clenched, and one of his legs twitching. He seemed to be in pain and was struggling to move out of his current state. Concerned, Selena hit the bell to summon a nurse. She put her hand on his face, running it down to his neck and then his chest, attempting to calm him down. The nurse arrived and checked all the vitals, informing Selena that everything seemed normal.

"Is he in pain?" asked Selena.

"Patients in comas don't feel pain," said the nurse.

"Could he just be having a bad dream or a nightmare then?" persisted Selena.

"No" replied the nurse. She was present when the doctor had told Selena and the rest of the Bapna family earlier that as far as medical science could determine, patients in comas don't dream; they are in deep sleep.

But dreaming he was—Dev, Selena's husband—even in a coma. Or were they nightmares? Maybe he was in a state that medical science didn't yet recognize, some in-between state, between a coma and unconsciousness.

He was being beaten mercilessly by men—many men—ten, perhaps twenty, maybe even twenty-five. He had fallen to the ground and was trying to protect himself with his arms while the men were stomping on him and kicking him. Most of them were striking him with batten-like sticks on his legs, some on the arms, and some were trying to aim for his head, which he was attempting to bury behind his arms. He was surrounded by a sea of people: men, women and even children, dressed in typical Indore slum clothing, brightly colored and gaudy, poorly fitting and ragged. There must have been three hundred of them, men, women and even children. They were all crowded around Dev while the twenty or twenty-five men, mostly young men in their 20s and 30s, took the lead in the horrific beating. A short man in his late 30s seemed to be the leader, egging the young men from the side, his eyes almost popping out of their sockets in rage. Dev caught glimpses of taunting grins, as the relentless assault continued. Their faces, while he was experiencing unbelievable pain, appeared to Dev at that moment as pure unadulterated evil. His mind started playing games with him. The images of the crowd surrounding him morphed into a band of demons. He heard their hissing, but those were accompanied by a horrible constant goat-like bleating that gave the already macabre scene a surreal feel.

Just then, a direct kick from the right caused Dev's face to swerve violently to his left as the corner of his eye caught the source of the bleating. His security guard, Sarwar, was suffering an even worst fate, if that was at all possible. Sarwar's face was covered in blood and another man was stomping all over him, a few others, assaulting him with cricket bats. It was a miracle that Sarwar was still conscious, or at least conscious enough to be able to emit the bleating wail, which assaulted Dev's ears just as much as the battens and the kicks were assaulting his body.

"Get his head," Dev heard someone shout. *No, not the head,* Dev thought. *Oh, not my head, please.*

Dev desperately tried to get away, and even in this coma, his body reacted to the dream and strained to get away from the horror, which Selena heard and witnessed.

Selena walked out of the ICU with the nurse, where members of the Bapna family had assembled, as had become the ritual every evening. There was Dev's father, Ram Singh Bapna, a good looking gentlemen who looked much younger than his 79 years; Dev's mom, Damayanti, also a handsome woman of 69; Dev's son Kunal, a lanky eighteen-year-old and Dev's daughter Ranika, a sprightly fourteen-year-old along with a few other members of the extended Bapna family and a couple of family friends.

The Bapnas are a good looking family, thought the nurse as she walked away.

Looks were one of the few things the Bapnas could still take a bit of pride in, not that they were a shallow family. They belonged to a group of old and mighty Indore families which were now being superseded in power and influence by the new rich, since the 1970s. In their heyday, if a member of the family had been in Intensive Care for any reason, hundreds, if not thousands of people would gather at the hospital every evening. Now there were just a couple from the extended family and a few friends from outside the family. The hospital was one of the best in Indore and was a stone's throw from the Bapna family mansion, located in the best part of town. It was at that mansion that Dev had been assaulted three days ago by scores of men, accompanied by a supporting mob of about three hundred men, women and children. By the time they were done with him, Dev's skull had cracked open down to his brain and cat scans and MRIs had shown injury to the brain. The doctors in Indore were still trying to ascertain the extent of the injury, but a day after he was admitted he went into a coma.

Sarwar, Dev's guard, was a little luckier. Even though he was subjected to a longer spell of beating, he escaped with about eight broken bones, some of them smashed into many pieces. He had no serious injury to the brain or other internal organs and he was still conscious in the hospital, although in serious shock.

Selena informed the rest of the family what had happened inside. "I think, we should not delay anymore, Mom," said Selena. "I have already spoken to Reema Bhabhi in Washington. She has spoken to the neurologist at Hopkins and they are ready to take us in. If it is okay with you and Papa, we would like to fly out tomorrow. Hopkins is the best in the world and besides, we would be home in Washington and feel a lot more comfortable."

Damayanti looked at her husband. Dev was their only child. Even though they had a stormy relationship, Damayanti now realized how much they had depended on Dev and how much they had taken his presence for granted. This incident had shaken them both to their core and they were still in a bit of shock.

"Whatever you think is best, Selena," said Damayanti after getting a feeble nod from Ram Singh. Damayanti would travel with them to the States, but Ram Singh could not; he had to stay back and handle the affairs in Indore, including the affairs that had culminated in the assault on Dev. He was sure he would not see his son again once he left Indore, but that wasn't a good enough reason to keep him in Indore. Even if there was a remote chance of recovery, it had to be taken, and for that he knew very well that Hopkins was the best place to be.

"Kunal, can you contact Ashish Uncle in Bombay and make the travel arrangements immediately? We would all like to fly home to Washington as soon as the tickets become available," said Selena.

Kunal reached for his phone, glancing at Ram Singh, who had slumped into a chair, his eyes staring blankly at the wall in front of him.

Air India Flight 674 from Delhi to Washington Dulles International
Oct 24, 2010   1:10 AM

It was not an easy task to transfer a comatose patient even short distances, let alone transporting him on a long-haul flight from India to the US. Apart from the usual releases that the doctors, hospital, and various other authorities required the family to sign, normally commercial airliners refused to make special arrangements to be able to transport such patients. It required pulling out several seats in order to accommodate the patient and all the medical equipment and paraphernalia that went with him. True to form, no commercial airline was willing to carry Dev. Chartering an airliner was the only other option and it was prohibitively expensive. Damayanti's brothers, Dev's uncles, were powerful politicians and businessmen in India. They stepped forward and used their connections to pressure the state-owned Air India to take Dev on their direct flight from Delhi to Washington Dulles. They also sent their personal physician to accompany Dev and the family to monitor the life support and attend to any emergency on board.

I wonder what Dev would think of this, thought Damayanti. She and Dev were at loggerheads all their lives, she insisting that connections and contacts must be used to get ahead, while Dev totally rejected the idea of taking any help from anybody, including his uncles, and considered it a form of corruption to use contacts to circumvent the law. Dev had a pathological aversion to corruption.

The family boarded the seventeen-hour flight from Delhi in the early morning hours of Oct 24th.

Air India Flight 674 from Delhi to Washington Dulles International
Oct 24, 2010   3:03 AM India Time

Paris - 1983

The Bapnas settled in comfortably in the business class section of Air India. The airlines had upgraded them to business class as the officer on duty had already been made aware that Samir Dada, an important man, was Damayanti's brother. The flight had taken off on time and the accompanying doctor checked the equipment. He made sure all the vitals were okay and then positioned his chair back.

Dev started dreaming again. He saw a young man in his early twenties walk into the Musee D'Orsay in Paris. Then the scene switched. This man was with an attractive young girl. She had auburn hair and Eastern European looks. They both were admiring a painting. Dev tried to focus on the painting and after a minute or so he was able to recognize it. It was a nude. He now remembered; it was "Grand Nu" by Renoir. The woman in the painting appeared to say something to the young man, which he could not quite hear. Then it dawned on Dev. The young man was Dev, years ago. He now recognized the girl. It was Anna. The scene switched again. The young Dev and Anna were together in a spacious and well-appointed hotel room. The view through the large window was gorgeous. A well-lighted Eiffel Tower was in full grandeur, complemented by Paris city lights. They were in bed, kissing passionately. Anna softly asked if they could have some more champagne. Dev turned to pick up the phone.

"Bonsoir, Monsieur. George the V room service," said the voice on the other end. Dev ordered a bottle of champagne and went back to Anna, picking up where they had left off. After a few minutes, there was a knock on the door. Dev got up, pulled the blanket around him and answered the door. He was stunned. He saw a tall blonde girl, no more than 23 or 24, with bluish green eyes staring at him. The girl's eyes momentarily took in the scene inside the room and then quickly turned, around starting to run. Dev called after her by name as he heard Anna in the background asking what was going on. Dev tried to follow the blonde, but he couldn't; his legs wouldn't move. Dev was fading out now. He tried to hang on, but couldn't. He drifted into a deep sleep again. As he drifted into sleep he could see the blonde's face close up and changing shape, first elongated and then shrinking back only to widen disproportionately this time. The last thing he saw were tear drops as big as golf balls, dropping from her green eyes and his own, each time making a *thud* as they hit the floor.

The doctor heard Dev moving again. He leaned forward to see Dev attempting to fold his legs. The doctor checked the life support and his pulse. Everything seemed normal, and after a minute or so Dev was as still as a log, sleeping peacefully again.

Air India Flight 674 from Delhi to Washington Dulles International
Oct 24, 2010   5:48 AM India Time

Jaisalmer, Rajasthan India—1800
Dev became conscious of the faint buzz in the background. It sounded like a jet airplane. Was he inside an airplane? He opened his

eyes and realized that he was flying above a desert at very high speed. No, he was not inside an airplane above the desert. He was flying like a bird. It was exhilarating. He could see the desert below him as far as the eye could see. He saw the sand dunes and at first he couldn't see a soul. The vast desert seemed to him as desolate as the landscape on Mars, except this was golden in color, not red, and there were no rocks dotting this desert, but sand dunes—endless sand dunes. He came upon a camel caravan travelling underneath. There must be at least sixty or seventy camels with men and women riding on them. There were other people walking alongside the camels. All the men were wearing white *kurtas*, white *dhotis*, with brightly colored turbans on their heads, each unique in design and bright colors, each distinguishing one individual from another. The women were attired in colorful *lehangas* and *ornees*—bright orange, lemon yellow, turquoise, scarlet red, lawn green, magenta pink, amber… It was a magnificent extravaganza of colors. Dev slowed down and descended to just a few feet above the caravan. He noticed that most of the men were tall and handsome, with long curly moustaches. The younger women were beautiful and the older ones looked stately. All in all, the bright colors of their garments, the camels, the endless desert and the people themselves looked like a scene from a movie Dev had seen several years ago on the Indian city of Jaisalmer.

Dev had done extensive research on Jaisalmer and its history. Jaisalmer was a border town in the western Indian state of Rajasthan, which was an exotic mix of magnificent gold-colored sandstone mansions interspersed with sand-colored homes right in the middle of the famous Thar Desert. There were sand dunes all around the city for miles. It was an old trading post town on one of the branches that connected to the Silk Road via the Punjab and the North West Frontier, in the middle ages. By the mid-nineteenth century, maritime trade had taken over. The old Silk Road towns had declined and become ghost towns, to be revived again only in the mid and late 20th century as international tourist destinations. From the 1700s through the 1800s though, Jaisalmer had been in full bloom. Traders from all over India, China and the Middle East visited and the economy thrived. Jaisalmer's cosmopolitan nature and riches had added even more dynamism, vibrancy, spice, and fun to an already colorful Rajasthani culture. The people of the area were from a migrant stock, tall, almost Persian in complexion and generally handsome. They loved their music, art, architecture and dance. They also loved their wars. They had a side to their character which was warlike and fiercely independent.

As Dev recalled all of this, he asked himself if he was really in or around Jaisalmer. If so, how did he get here, and why?

As he flew past the camel caravan, he realized that the sun was setting, giving the desert a golden-red glow. The sun itself looked orangish-red and was looming on the horizon, ready to set. The whole scene looked like a dream…wait a minute! *He was* dreaming. He saw some smoke arising from what looked like a town at a distance. He picked up speed and headed towards the smoke. As he flew over town at a low altitude, his suspicions were confirmed and he instantly recognized the late eighteenth century Jaisalmer from his readings and the paintings he had seen. Narrow streets, paved with rolled compacted sand mixed with clay, magnificent temples rising up from the desert, and bazaars displaying just about everything under the sun. Men and women walked around in rich colorful clothes and the sound of local musical instruments filled the air. The magnificent mansions of Jaisalmer, with intricately carved facades dotted by hundreds of ornate *jharokhas* looked mysteriously charming in the setting sun, partly shaded and partly lit by the sunlight.

Suddenly, Dev found himself above a mansion, perhaps the grandest in Jaisalmer. It was enormous in size and the carving was exquisite. It looked newer than any of the other mansions and his eyes fell upon a tall, imposing man standing on one of the *jharokhas*. He was richly adorned in an off- white silk tunic and a turquoise-colored *dhoti* that reached well below his ankle. He wore a necklace studded with large deep green round emeralds. Emerald necklaces were a symbol of the very top in Rajasthani merchant hierarchy. He had a large diamond ring on his left little finger which seemed to emit a blue florescence. He had smooth pale skin and looked like he was in his late 20s. He was not wearing any turban and his thick black hair was shoulder length and neatly brushed back from his forehead. Unlike most men Dev saw in town, the man in the balcony was clean shaven. He was talking to a middle-aged European-looking man. Dev was now convinced he was in some sort of a dream. A European in Jaisalmer in early nineteenth century? The young man in the balcony had the bearing and manner of a man with authority and he just stood there, staring at Dev. Dev remembered something and smiled as if he had just solved a mystery. He clearly recognized the mansion and the man. Excitedly, he flew closer. A slightly detached yet curious half smile of recognition flashed across the man's face as Dev neared. Dev tried to fly even closer, but he couldn't, no matter how hard he tried. Then he felt a tug that pulled away from the mansion. He tried to wave to the man, but to no avail. From a distance he saw the man in the mansion raise his right hand close to his chest, palm facing out, in a Buddha-like gesture which signified a blessing. Dev strained to reach out to him by extending his arm, but everything went dark and Dev was back in deep sleep.

The doctor was awakened by the pretty round-faced stewardess who alerted him to the sound of the IV bottle, which was rattling due to Dev's arm movements. The doctor checked Dev's vitals and steadied the IV pole, and when he looked down, Dev was again very still and sleeping peacefully.

Air India Flight 674 from Delhi to Washington Dulles International
Oct 24, 2010   7:01 AM India Time

Beta Sigma Psi House – Illinois State University: Normal, Illinois – Fall, 1980

Dev was startled into semi-consciousness again. Air turbulence had caused the plane to dive abruptly before it re-stabilized. Dev felt a soft hand on his cheek. He heard the same annoying buzz of aircraft engines. It was beginning to give him a headache. He saw a younger version of himself walking through the quad at Illinois State University in Normal, Illinois. It was about 10:00 PM in a late fall Saturday night. It was quite windy and cold, as all fall seasons in central Illinois tend to be. The ISU quad was pretty, surrounded by mostly red brick academic buildings, but there were some buildings with off-beat architecture, giving the quad an out-of-this-world feel. There was the gothic Cook Hall with tall narrow towers that housed offices, and the campus radio station. Next to it was Fell Hall, which was designated as the International House Dorm, where students from around the world lived, with an equal number of American students. At a distance one could see the more contemporary Student Union and Milner Library. The quad was lined at various places by concrete and brick walkways meandering across its length and breadth. Along the walkways were lamp posts that kept the quad well lighted, even on the darkest overcast Illinois winter nights. As usual, the lighted quad on that particular foggy fall night looked romantic and straight out of a fairy tale. The quad was bustling with activity any Friday or Saturday night when school was in session, but on this weekend night it seemed even busier than usual. Dev saw figures walking across the quad. He couldn't quite focus on their faces and could not recognize anyone, but he was able to figure out kids smiling and interacting with each other, some leaning against the lampposts, couples walking hand-in-hand, while others gathered in groups, laughing and joking.

Dev crossed the quad and turned right on Stevenson. He was dressed smartly in blue jeans and a bright plaid shirt made out of a mix of flannel and rayon that he had picked up at a clearance sale. He had on a dark red overcoat, which his father had purchased during his own student days in England and was now part of Dev's wardrobe, along with a tuxedo and some other winter clothing which had also belonged to his father. He had on a long off-white cashmere and silk scarf around his neck and tucked inside his overcoat. He was particularly proud of that scarf, as he had had to save two full weeks' wages from his part time job to buy it from Saks. He was wearing the classic orange Hush Puppies pig skin boots. He had also liberally doused himself with Aqua Velva after-shave. It smelled better than just about any expensive after-shave, but it cost only a dollar a bottle. Dev paid particular attention to how he dressed. Despite limited funds, he managed to dress well by smartly mixing and matching inexpensive clothes that suited his body shape and skin color. Dressing well was a Bapna family tradition that Dev had inherited. All in all, Dev was feeling quite cool and confident and was eagerly looking forward to getting lucky that night.

After walking a few blocks on Stevenson, he turned right on Vernon Avenue where there were about six or seven Greek houses in a row. This was ISU's version of Greek Row and most of the houses had a steady stream of young men and women walking in and out. Dev walked into a large frame house which had a hand painted sign in the front yard, proclaiming "ΒΣΨ", pronounced Beta Sigma Psi. This was a Lutheran Fraternity, where Dev had several friends and was a regular at their parties. ISU was still not totally out of the closet as far as its reputation as a party school was concerned. If one knew where to find 'em, one could always find a party on any Thursday, Friday or Saturday evening. On Fraternity Row, though, party nights were Tuesdays through Saturdays. They scrupulously avoided having parties on Monday in the interest of devoting a certain portion of their week to studies. After all, one shouldn't forget the real purpose of why one is here: to study. As good Lutherans, Sunday was a day of prayer and atonement for the Beta Sigs and thus off limits for partying as well. Just about every Friday night there were "exchanges," where an entire sorority would come and visit a fraternity, have a fiesta and pretty much spend the night.

On this particular night there happened to be an exchange at the Beta Sig house, and Dev found himself in the basement, which was the epicenter of the party. It was still early and the party had not yet gotten into full swing. The dance floor in the center of the room, which had a disco ball hanging from the ceiling, was empty. Groups of kids were sitting at side tables, playing quarters and other drinking games. Duran Duran was on, on the bulky sound system, which took up one entire corner, singing their latest, "Hungry like a Wolf," and in another corner was a large TV, tuned to MTV, the volume turned down low. An image popped up on TV of Tony Basil and her dancers performing their "Hey Mickey" song.

From the other side of the dance floor, Shawn Henry Andeberry, or "Berry" for short, the fraternity president who happened to also double as the backup quarterback of the ISU football team, stepped forward and greeted Dev. He invited Dev upstairs to his spacious room where a bunch of seniors and juniors were sitting with some sorority girls. There was a game of strip poker going on and already some of the kids were naked or half-naked. Several bottles of bourbon and beer sat on a corner table. A bong with a longish pipe was being passed around and the room reeked of pot.

"Join the game, Dev," said Ned Luedke, a John Belushi look-alike who had even adopted some of Belushi's mannerisms. Dev took his place between Ned and a dark-haired girl who was clad in just a sweater and her panties. She introduced herself as Carol and said she was from Arlington Heights.

"I lost my skirt," Carol said, pointing to a heap of clothes on the other side. Dev now noticed several other boys and girls that were sitting in various stages of undress, with one guy totally naked and a topless girl with her pants on. There was no sense whatsoever that anything out of the ordinary was taking place and everybody was pretty nonchalant about the whole thing. Dev was instantly attracted to Carol and her almond-shaped hazel eyes, which were accentuated by high cheekbones. *She must have had some Asian or Native American blood back in her ancestry somewhere,* thought Dev, and that turned him on even more. The bong came to Carol. She inhaled and then passed it on to Dev, who took a long drag.

The scene switched. Dev was in the back seat of a black sedan in the fraternity parking lot. It was dark and cold. The wind seldom stopped blowing in central Illinois, particularly in late fall, but it was unusually still that night. Dev could see several other couples in other cars in the lot and noticed that the car next to them had two guys and one girl. He recognized one of the guys in the car with the threesome as Nick "the Buzz" Lawson, the guy who had been sitting nude when Dev had first entered the strip poker room. Buzz looked pretty buzzed and seemed to be thoroughly enjoying himself with the activity at hand. *It must be very late,* thought Dev, *because it is typically after the party is over that the action starts in the parking lot.*

Carol was with him in the back seat. They were covered in a couple of velour blankets to keep warm. He could feel Carol move her face up the length of his body until she came face-to-face with Dev. Her hazel eyes had turned several shades darker. She smiled. The smile exposed her upper canines, which looked like they belonged to a vampire. Before Dev could react, Carol dug her canines into Dev's neck. A strange sensation of pleasure swept through Dev and he felt lightheaded and exuberant. Carol disengaged herself from Dev's neck and looked straight into his eyes. Her eyes were back to hazel, softer now, and Dev gazed into them in a hypnotic state. He could do anything she commanded at that moment—anything at all.

Then Dev saw her face transform into something doglike, snarling and baring her canines again. It shook Dev out of his hypnosis and he tried to escape through the car door, but the door would not open. Dev started kicking the door. Carol's transformation into a werewolf was now complete. Dev slipped into the darkness just as he felt the werewolf reaching for his neck…

Selena was checking on Dev when she noticed him kicking and gritting his teeth. The doctor was napping on the next seat, and before she could get his attention the kicking had stopped and calm had abruptly returned to Dev's face. Selena asked the doctor to check Dev out. The doctor checked and didn't think there was anything to worry about, and Dev was already back in deep sleep.

❧ ☙

Back in the aircraft, Ranika strolled up and down the aisle, trying to keep the circulation going in her feet, when she noticed one small teardrop appear in the corner of one of Dev's closed eyes. Maybe she was seeing things, but Dev's face appeared sad, almost grief stricken, although he was not moving and there really was no other visible change of expression. She bent down and wiped away the teardrop ever so gently with her index finger. She returned back to her seat and never told anyone about the teardrop.

❧ ☙

Air India Flight 674 from Delhi to Washington Dulles International
Oct 24, 2010   10:00 AM India Time

Washington DC 1986
Selena and the doctor carefully turned Dev onto his side. This was necessary every few hours to avoid bedsores. The doctor ensured that he was still connected to the life support. Dev woke up into semi-consciousness and he felt relief at being turned on his other side.

❧ ☙

He started dreaming again. A good-looking older man came into focus. He was making a speech inside a packed chamber, addressing a crowd of men in business suits sitting on classroom type chairs. Dev could only hear bits and pieces, straining to make sense of what the man was saying. The man was well groomed and not only exuded confidence, but seemed to be inspiring it in his audience. The man's words travelled in slow motion to Dev's ears. He heard something and then the words "welfare queen." Next he heard "shining city on the hill," and then he heard "government is the problem," followed by "the evil empire." Light bulbs went off in Dev's mind and he recognized the man. It was Reagan. As soon as he realized that, Dev was suddenly sitting on the steps of the Lincoln Memorial, watching the sun rise over the Capitol. The sky was cloudless and it promised to be a lovely day.

Its morning in America again, thought Dev, as he looked at the red button he was holding which said "Reagan/Bush 80." He had saved this one button from back in his college days when he volunteered for the Reagan/Bush campaign.

In a flash, Dev was driving a large black Cadillac through the streets of Washington. He was in the northwest section. The buildings all seemed to be shiny and located on top of a hill.

With no warning, Dev found himself in the southeast section of the city. Dilapidated buildings falling apart, trash everywhere, abandoned lots, boarded up shops, and young black kids soliciting drug sales attack the senses. Dev started looking for Welfare Queens. He didn't know what or who to look for, but he just started asking around—for Welfare Queens. One kid said he didn't have a Welfare Queen, but he just got a new shipment of some mind-blowing Hawaiian.

Dev shook his head. He didn't think Welfare Queens were Polynesian. The kid did promise to inform his supplier that street demand for Welfare Queen was heating up.

Dev was getting desperate now. He started frantically knocking on doors, one dilapidated building after another, looking for the Welfare Queen—just one Welfare Queen. No such luck.

Dev now saw himself in Camden, NJ. He had just arrived from downtown Philly, where he had spent the whole day searching for Welfare Queens. Why could he not find any Welfare Queens? *They must be very cagey, these Welfare Queens. They must be hiding. Hiding from whom, though? President Reagan? Why? Why would anybody want to hide from a kindly old grandfather who brought morning in America again and put all of America on a shiny hill? Or was it the shining America on a hill?* Whatever… Anyway, Dev was very confused.

He kept running from city to city, coast to coast, one inner city area to another city area. The entire time he just couldn't shake the lines from a song he had listened to a lot as a teenager:

> And in the master's chambers
> They gathered for the feast;
> They stab it with their steely knives,
> But they just can't kill the beast

No matter how hard he tried, he just couldn't locate the Welfare Queen. Just as he was about to give up he saw a black woman driving an old junker of a Cadillac. It stopped in front of a pathetic looking row house. The woman got out of the car, went around and started pulling at the passenger side door. After a few tries the passenger side door gave way and a young Asian man, probably Chinese got out. The woman was wearing fake fur and smelled of cheap perfume. There was a halo around her head. *There she is*, Dev thought. *Finally, I have found the Welfare Queen.* As he moved towards her, she disappeared inside the house, with the Asian man. Dev waited outside the row house. After a while, the Asian man came out. Dev started to go in, but he felt something hitting him at the back of his head with a heavy thud. He blacked out.

When he awoke, Dev was lying on a filthy bed. He saw a little black boy and a little black girl running around, laughing. They were wearing cheap t-shirts and shorts. The room had junk everywhere, and an old refrigerator in the corner of the room was open and almost empty. He looked to the other side, and lo and behold—there was the Welfare Queen! Shangri La! Her clothes were cheap, but her movements were elegant and catlike, and she had a natural elegance, which she wasn't even conscious of. She moved forward and offered Dev a cup of coffee.

"How do you feel now, Hon?" asked the Welfare Queen.

"All right, I guess," said Dev. "My head hurts, though."

"You will be fine. You are lucky it was not a hard blow. You should be careful in these parts, you know," said the Welfare Queen.

"You are the Welfare Queen, right?" asked Dev.

"I can be anything you want me to be," replied the Welfare Queen, "but you best rest right now and when you are all healed you come back, you hear. I will be your Queen and it will be on the house. Okay, Hon?"

"You lied to me," said Dev. "You are not the Welfare Queen. You are the Queen of Hearts."

She turned around and smiled the prettiest, warmest smile he had ever seen. He felt the warmth of that smile envelope his body as he slipped into a deep sleep.

The doctor glanced at his wristwatch, then at Dev, then at the machines, and then he dozed off again.

*Air India Flight 674 from Delhi to Washington Dulles International
Oct 24, 2010   14:10 PM India Time*

Indore Central India – 2007
Kunal lifted the window shade and looked out. It was still mostly dark, with some pre-dawn light giving the sky a deep orange shade at a distance, changing to light orange in the middle and blending into a grayish yellow closer in. *We must be somewhere over Greenland, right about now,* thought Kunal. In a half hour or so, right around dawn, he hoped to catch a view of the desolate glaciers below.

Images continued flashing through Dev's mind in quick succession. He was now at a modest residence in the working class area of Indore. The neighborhood was only one level above slum, but the house was nicely painted and neatly arranged. A couple of white Ambassador cars made with old technology, holdovers from the socialist times and still the standard government issue to politicians, were parked outside the house. The cars had large ominous red lights mounted on top, signifying rank in modern India. It was early morning, about 8.00 AM and scores of people crowded the front yard of the house, overflowing onto the street outside. This was a scene typical of Indian culture at just about every day at any house whose owner or occupant was deemed to be an "important person." An important person could be a political leader, a rich man, a bureaucrat, any other office holder or anyone else who had it in his or her power to bestow favors upon people, either legally, illegally or by circumventing the law. These people constantly had a crowd around them, some of them sycophants, others seeking favors, yet others seeking redress to an injustice, perceived or real.

Dev noticed a couple of screeners selecting people from the crowd to go in, one after another, as the previous fortunate supplicant filed out. After about an hour of people filing in and out of the house, presumably to have an audience with the "important person" inside, the screeners disappeared inside, closing the main door behind them. A collective groan emanated from the remaining crowd. No one from the crowd was ready to leave yet. It quickly became apparent to Dev why. Shortly, the door to the main house opened wide again and the screeners reappeared. The crowd dispersed a little to make room for one of the white Ambassador cars with the red light on top to pull into the driveway. Out came a few arrogant young ruffians. They boarded the white Ambassador in the driveway and the car pulled out. The other white Ambassador pulled into the driveway, with just the chauffer inside.

After a few minutes a man in whites, surrounded by a small group of people emerged from inside the house. The man was short, with a broad face, stocky build, dark hair drenched in oil, and a moustache. The man's face had scar lines going horizontally across his forehead and vertically from the corner of his lips down to his chin, almost to the upper part of his neck. He was wearing a long saffron scarf over his crisply starched white *kurta* (Indian tunic). At the sight of this man, Dev spontaneously burst out laughing. He knew the man well. He looked and behaved like a Mafia Don, but here in India he was a "legitimate important man" or the "godfather." The godfather stood in the driveway by the rear right door of the white Ambassador and looked at the crowd. Several people stepped forward and touched his feet, others prostrated themselves flat on the ground, face down, conveying total obeisance to the godfather. The godfather took this totally in stride and made no effort to acknowledge their acts of submission. Nonchalantly, he started picking individuals from the crowd and beckoned them over in a manner reminiscent of patrons calling their waiters over in a restaurant. His movements suggested crude arrogance. After beckoning a few people and talking to them, the godfather opened the back door of the white Ambassador so he could get inside, but all of a sudden the crowd surged and blocked the door. Some rough looking men, presumably body guards, stepped in and dispersed the crowd, while the godfather climbed into the back seat of the white Ambassador. Three other men climbed quickly into the front and the back of the car with him.

"We really shouldn't allow this riff-raff get this close to us anymore," Dev heard the man mutter to his companion inside the car. The red light started to flash and sirens wailed as they pulled out of the driveway and drove off.

Some of the crowd dispersed, but at least half of them stayed behind. Slowly, the remaining crowd settled into the front yard and the street outside, some of them now sitting on the ground and unpacking their lunch boxes, others smoking cheap cigarettes, women having animated conversations amongst themselves, children running helter-skelter, and the sun directly overhead and bearing down strong.

Dev noticed a number of young men standing out in the open, facing the outside walls of adjacent houses, their flies open and relieving themselves while at the same time maintaining a lively conversation with each other. He saw a couple of middle-aged women he had noticed over at the godfather's house walk up to the house across the street, turn their back to the crowd, lift their dresses up, squat right by the external house wall and relieve themselves in full view of everybody. No one in the crowd, with the exception of perhaps one or two perverts, paid any attention or even looked.

Several similar scenes flashed across Dev's eyes in quick succession. Only the houses and the godfathers were different. Dev knew them all well. He wished he did not.

Air India Flight 674 from Delhi to Washington Dulles International
Oct 24, 2010   17:02 PM India Time

USA - 1980s-2000s
There was a lot of commotion on the plane. He could hear a cacophony of voices and the aircraft buzzing with activity. There was an announcement, saying that the flight had just flown past Boston, and was heading south towards New York, and that they were expected to land in Washington on time at approximately 9:00 AM Eastern Time. Dev caught some of that and the words which triggered another dream.

A man in his forties appeared on a television screen. He was pacing angrily up and down the stage. There were four people sitting up on the stage as he paced. The auditorium was packed. The man said something and reached for his coffee cup as the words "Morton Downey Jr. show will be right back" appeared on the screen. When the show resumed, Downey was pacing furiously again. Dev heard him rail against the liberals, calling them "puking liberals." He was cursing one of the men sitting on the stage, a rather forlorn-looking older person, with crew cut hair and a navy blue suit. After lots of gesticulation, Downey walked right up to the man he was cursing and leaned forward, putting his nose right up against the man's nose. "The only good liberal is a dead liberal," he said menacingly. And on and on he went. A pathologically angry, almost sick man Dev thought, with an inner core of unlimited hate out of which sprung geysers of obscene rage and prejudice.

Dev watched as Pat Robertson appeared on the same TV screen, with the caption "The 700 Club." Pat Robertson launched straight into a diatribe against homosexuals, non-believers, feminists who supported abortion and who knows who else. Finally he said, "Those who don't believe in Jesus will rot in hell."

Dev, in his mind, couldn't decide if time was going forward or backward. The television was no longer an old-style television, but a flat screen TV. Rush Limbaugh appeared on the screen, sitting in his radio studio, wearing headphones and speaking into a microphone that was sitting on the table in front of him. He was a balding, older man, with reddish clear skin—fat and dumpy. Another man in perpetual rage, a classic bully, Limbaugh let loose on Obama, females, blacks, browns, Obama again, yellows, Hispanics, immigrants, poor welfare recipients and Obama once again—anyone who was not white, wealthy and male. He abused the callers who didn't agree with him and brooked no opposition whatsoever.

Dev noticed Limbaugh's face changing. He saw a black turban appear on Limbaugh's head. His pudgy face was elongated and his complexion darkened a bit, while the skin on his face got wrinkly and grayish. His eyes turned darker and miraculously, he had instantly grown a gray beard that almost extended to his chest. A gray moustache appeared above his lips. The new Limbaugh face was calmer, more serene, and the only thing that carried over from the previous face was pure unadulterated hate in the eyes.

Dev recognized the face. Limbaugh had transformed into Ayatollah Khomeini. Limbaugh Khomeini slowed down and became much less animated as he continued to talk in an ominously low tone. Notwithstanding the change in style and manner, the words coming out of Limbaugh Khomeini's mouth were as hateful and venomous as before, still vitriolic and pure evil.

Then Limbaugh Khomeini stood up. He was now wearing the black Ayatollah robe, and he started to bounce up and down, up and down, up and down, building a steady rhythm, as Dev heard a chorus of demonic sounds in the background and Limbaugh Khomeini was still bouncing—up and down, up and down, up and down.

~ ~

The channel on the flat screen TV changed and there appeared another face. This face was softer than Limbaugh's, and he had a smile which could only be described as belonging to someone who was not quite normal.

"This president, I think, has exposed himself over and over again as a guy who has a deep-seated hatred for white people or the white culture. I'm not saying he doesn't like white people; I'm saying he has a problem. This guy is, I believe, a racist," he said. The man was wearing a different suit. "I'm thinking about killing Michael Moore, and I'm wondering if I could kill him myself or if I would need to hire somebody to do it… No, I think I could do it myself. I think he could be looking me in the eye, you know, and I could just be choking the life out. Is this wrong? I stopped wearing my "What Would Jesus Do" band and I've lost all sense of right and wrong. I used to be able to say, 'Yeah, I'd kill Michael Moore,' and then I'd see the little band: "What Would Jesus Do?" And then I'd realize, 'Oh, you wouldn't kill Michael Moore. Or at least you wouldn't choke him to death.' And you know—well, I'm not sure," Dev heard him say.

The next frame on the TV showed up. Same man, different suit. Now he was saying, "I really just really wanted to thank you having me over here to Wine Country, you know. To be invited, I thought I had to be a major Democratic donor or a long-time friend of yours, which I'm not. By the way, I put poison in your—no…"

Dev wanted to get up and change the channel, but the man's face wouldn't disappear off the screen. No matter what channel Dev tuned to, the same face appeared. Dev tried to turn off the TV. Dev just couldn't get rid of this man. His image was like a virus that had taken over the TV. The screen started flickering, displaying snow, and then the screen went black, and Dev blacked out as well.

~ ~

Air India Flight 674 from Delhi carrying the Bapnas landed in Washington DC exactly at 9:00 AM on October, 24 2010. It was an unusually warm day in Washington, although a little windy, and Selena, Kunal and Ranika felt relief and comfort as the familiar Dulles International Airport main terminal building came into view.

"At least we are home, Mom," said Kunal, squeezing Selena's hand, his other arm around Damayanti. "I am sure Papa will be fine now, Grandma," he continued, more in an attempt to convince himself than to reassure his grandmother or his mother.

Chapter 2 - Dev in Convalescence

October, 2010 – Washington DC/Baltimore

Dev was transported from Dulles International Airport to John Hopkins University Hospital via air ambulance. After three days of extensive examinations and tests, Dr. Anton Williams, who was in charge of Dev's case, called the Bapna family into his office for a conference. He informed the family that Dev had severe brain injury. He told them it was going to be risky, but surgery was the only hope for relieving the pressure on the brain and that despite the fact that he would try his best, the family should expect no miracles. Selena signed the consent forms, submitted all the health insurance paper work and Dev was taken in for surgery the next day.

Thank God I have insurance, even though it has a high deductable, thought Selena. She worked in the front office of a prominent regional bank which took off a significant part of her salary for the health insurance premium. The deductable was very high, but in this particular case where it would certainly cost over a hundred thousand dollars to treat Dev, and potentially even several hundreds of thousands, having insurance was the only way Selena could afford this treatment in America.

Selena, Damayanti, Kunal, Ranika, Dr. Reema and her husband Rick, who were long-standing family friends, and Khondekar Imran, a good friend of Dev's since college days, were all assembled in the waiting area. The operation went on for what seemed like an eternity. After nearly eleven hours Dr. Williams emerged, looking drained. Addressing Dr. Reema he said that he was guardedly optimistic, but it was too early to tell. Dev was moved to the ICU and the family took turns keeping vigil for the next several days.

After a few days Dev emerged from his coma, although he was still going in and out of consciousness, and he was moved out of the ICU into a regular hospital room. Slowly, Dev started gaining strength, and he started physical therapy. Dev was advised to rest for at least a month, with some regular exercises and physical therapy. After seventeen days in the hospital, Dev was released and allowed to go home, with instructions to follow a strict regimen of medication, physical exercises, rest, diet and other prescriptions.

Since the family had only one car, a sedan, Selena purchased a second-hand SUV which was already wheelchair accessible. Thankfully, Selena's health insurance covered that as well. Dev was transported in that van to the Bapna family residence in Tyson's Corner area. It was a tiny rambler in a nice suburban neighborhood, roughly fifteen miles from downtown Washington DC. In happier times, a few years ago, Selena had personally redesigned and redecorated the house, simply but elegantly, making it very warm and comfortable.

Dev underwent radical mood swings. One day he would be happy and cheerful, while he would get sullen and depressed the next. Sometimes the depression continued for days, while there were other periods where he was nearly normal. Kunal was a sophomore at the University of Southern California and had taken a few days off to rush to India after hearing about his father's assault and hospitalization and had worked out a special arrangement with the university to allow him to complete his semester remotely while he helped out in Washington. Kunal's staying back had a positive effect on Dev, who for the first time in his life seemed to draw energy, hope and enthusiasm from his son's presence. Ranika, too, had started to take some time from her busy high school schedule and spent part of her evenings with Dev to keep his spirits high. She had always been the apple of Dev's eye and Dev felt that special connection with her, which typically fathers develop with their daughters. Every evening, when they would all get together in Dev's bedroom, they would have long conversations in an attempt to come to terms with what had happened to the Bapna family over the past couple of months.

Like millions of Americans, the Bapnas were leading perfectly normal middle-class suburban lives. Selena, 46, worked full time in a bank which was only a few minutes from their house. There was no commute and she enjoyed her work and her colleagues and was quite satisfied with her job. Dev, 49, was transitioning to a new career, after a long-standing career as a software engineer. He wanted to pursue a career in journalism or international relations or some other related area. "Humanities" was his passion, he had only studied and pursued a thirty-year career in software engineering as a compromise and a way to make a living. Kunal, eighteen, was their elder child and he was attending USC on a scholarship. Ranika, fourteen, was a sophomore in high school. Even though money was tight because of Dev's transitioning into a new career and he had yet to get any breaks, life was quite contented and uneventful. They were a typical middle class American family—typical American middle class, with perhaps one difference.

Dev was a first-generation immigrant from India, but he was not a typical immigrant. His family background was quite unusual. He was an only child and his parents, now elderly, lived in their hometown of Indore, India. They lived in a large family home located between a very exclusive residential enclave on one side and a ghettoized neighborhood on the other.

By 2010, India was an emerging economic power in the world. After decades of flirtation with socialism, India had opened up the economy, and while the Western economies were in general stagnant or declining, China, and to a lesser extent India were booming. Both had started from a low base and were maintaining around ten percent growth rates. However, what existed in India was the worst form of crony capitalism, almost mafia capitalism. Partly as a result of the recent history of socialist experimentation and partly due to long-standing proclivity towards disorder in Indian culture and history, law and order was practically non-existent and instead there existed a medieval ad-hoc patronage system. Even though India was known as a democracy and certainly had all the external appearances of a democracy, such as regular elections and a multi-party system, the patronage-based political culture had further degenerated into what can best be characterized as mafia culture. The culture rewarded breaking the law, and therefore, only the criminals could rise through the political process and become the leaders and the ruling elite. This had a ripple effect right through the society at large, and in all spheres of life. The system rewarded the worst forms of criminals, the less able and the immoral. Conversely, the meritorious, able and good instincts in the society were severely penalized. It was a total perversion of a merit-based system. Most people had a choice: either fit in somewhere within the mafia hierarchy and adapt, or live on the outside of the society, vulnerable to falling victim to the ruling mafia without any protection or recourse from the state.

Dev's parents had descended from a long line of distinguished and historical figures, but now had practically run out of money and influence, and to make matters worse, they did not or could not adapt to this mafia system. Their last remaining significant financial asset, their family home, was constantly under threat from politically connected squatters who made frequent attempts to illegally occupy it. There was no recourse through the police and the courts, as they were all corrupt to the hilt, and compromised. They acted more as an enforcement arm of the ruling mafia rather than an actual police force and judiciary as most people would recognize it. The elections were held to choose between one political mafia and another, and generally these rival political mafias had arrived at an understanding with each other that no matter who won the elections, the basic mafia-ization of the country would continue unabated and there would be no structural reforms. There were, therefore, frequent attempts, almost one a week, by someone to forcibly enter and encroach on the Bapna property.

It did not help that Dev didn't live in Indore and was far away in the States. However, Dev had developed a lifestyle and arranged his work in such a way that for years he was able to visit Indore for about three to four months every year. While there, he took whatever necessary steps that he could to protect the house.

For this and other reasons Dev had also permanently moved to India for a few years before moving back to the States again. Dev did all this at a considerable sacrifice to his career and finances in the US, largely out of sentimental attachment to the house. He felt that the house connected him to his ancestors and their good deeds. It was also Dev's way of defying the current trends in Indian society towards "mafia-ization." It was his way of making a statement that it is possible to survive even in the "mafia-ized" modern day India without compromising one's basic ideals and without adapting to the point of joining the mafia. The house, for Dev, was a symbol of defiance, almost a rebellion, even if it was only a small symbol. He felt compelled to keep this small candlelight of rebellion burning and not give up the fight. Therefore, he resisted all advice to sell the house and invest the proceeds someplace safe in the States.

It was during one such visit in October 2010 that one attempt to illegally occupy the Bapna house resulted in the brutal assault on Dev.

Kunal and Ranika discussed all of this with Dev and inevitably concluded after every discussion how fortunate they were to not be in India, but in the States. Dev kept cautioning them that as great as America was, it was far from perfect and someday he would relate his own American experience to them.

Kunal and Ranika were both born in the States and had no first-hand experience of what was involved in legally migrating to the United States.

"How did you come to the States, Papa?" asked Kunal. "I hear it was not easy."

"It must be tough on you," said Ranika.

Dev smiled slightly and then his eyes turned glassy, as if he was straining to remember, then he haltingly narrated the following story of how he first came to America.

Chapter 3 - Story of Dev – Part 1

Attn:
Illinois State University
Normal, Illinois USA

Highly Respected Admissions Officer Sir,

I humbly request that in view of my high school academic excellence, being in the top ten percentile in all of India, you consider my application for admission to your esteemed University as a foreign student. In addition, I will be highly obliged, Sir, if you can see your way clear to grant me a tennis scholarship, based on my excellent record of being ranked number 48 in All India under-eighteen category last year and ranked number 33 in All India under-eighteen category this year.

While I am well aware that you have most certainly received many applications from candidates far more worthy than I am, I would be eternally grateful to you if you bestow upon me your kind favor by granting me admission and scholarship.

I have attached herewith all the required forms and supporting documents, duly filled out and attested to. Please note that the documents have been additionally notarized by the American Embassy, for which I have personally paid a fee of Rs. 1200.

While I have your attention, allow me, at the risk of irritating you by pushing my luck, to also request you to keep at the back of your mind that in the event that you will extend me the great favor of admission,

I will also require a part-time job to fully meet my expenses over and beyond the scholarship, which I am also very hopeful of receiving, non-deserving as I am.

Very humbly yours,

DS Bapna
Indore, India
Dated: October 19, 1978

So said Dev Singh Bapna in his cover letter of his application for undergraduate admission to Illinois State University in the fall of 1978. If the letter seemed like it had a ring of desperation to it, it was because the author indeed was desperate.

"This is my only chance of getting out of this goddamn place," Dev kept saying to himself. In his mind, this was his only chance of making something of himself—by going to America. America: every middle-class Indian kid's dream in the 1960s and the 70s—the land of Levis and Wrangler, of Coca Cola and hamburgers, of Clint Eastwood and Paul Newman, of Sophia Lauren and Raquel Welch, of *Playboy* and *Penthouse*, of Broadway and Las Vegas, and most of all, of Rock and Roll. Yeah, and of soul music of James Brown and his "I am black and I am proud," of Jimmy Hendrix, of Jim Morrison, of Disco Donna Summer. Of Love to Love You Baby, of Harold Robbins and Arthur Hailey, of long hair, pretty girls, and most of all, of immense and unlimited possibilities.

Dev had been reading Ayn Rand and her philosophy of Objectivism based on individualism, self-help, and the image of a pure merit-based society had captured his imagination. He thought that America, in fact, was a society which Ayn Rand portrayed in her books—a pure meritocracy. Her larger-than-life characters—Roark, Gail Wynand, Francisco D'Anconia and John Galt—immediately found resonance deep within him. *I think I could be like them*, he thought. He was smart, intelligent and talented. Surely he could discover some talent within himself in America and America would see and value it too. He was certain of it. Not having television or the Internet in a way nudged Dev to read voluminously, play various sports over at the local country club, and catch a Hollywood movie every Sunday at the only local movie theater, called "Starlit," that exclusively showed "English" movies.

Everything he had read, heard or seen in the movies about America told him that it was the land where anything was possible. A land that welcomed even brown people and where people not only got to be self-sufficient simply through their own efforts and hard work, but they could actually get rich.

Contrast that with India. He was sure he had no chance here. *You have to be connected here*, he thought, *and corrupt to the core*. He was sick of this place. He was in his final year of high school at Sydenham, a respected institution in Bombay, where he had transferred only a year ago. He hailed from Indore; a medium-sized unremarkable industrial city in Central India located five hundred miles to the northeast of Bombay.

Indore was kind of a backwater place, a place where national trends arrived a few years late. It was the late 70s and television had not yet found its way to Indore. Dev came from a long line of illustrious ancestors of a prominent family in that part of the country. His family, though, had fallen on hard times by the time he reached his teenage years. Still, his grandfather tried to instill in him a sense of confidence befitting his ancestry by educating him in art, music, culture and other areas which were typical of upper-class kids in India. The difference was that in the case of Dev, his grandfather had to stretch and take shortcuts to educate him, considering the extreme financial constraints the family was under by then.

With a great difficulty Dev's grandfather was able to scrounge up enough money to put him in one of the original ten British-style public schools in India, Daly College, which was fortunately located conveniently in Indore itself. Daly College was one of the most prestigious private schools in India, and a Bapna family tradition. All of Dev's cousins attended Daly College. So did his father and his uncles and his grandfather and grand uncle. Indore had a small-town feel, and the elite in town consisted of about one hundred families in those days, of which the Bapna family was one. Almost all the kids from those families attended Daly College. Due to financial hardships, however, Dev was put in Daly College in middle school, much later than other kids from his social circle who started there in first grade.

At seventeen years of age, Dev was a lanky lad. A little less than six feet tall, he had a tennis player's body—very slim and V-shaped. Everyone said that he had classic Indian good looks, and he tended to wear his dark brown hair long, just like his idol, Ilie Nastase, the legendary tennis player from Romania. Dev loved Nastase because of his flowing strokes and his on-court antics, which gave tennis much needed character and style. He never tired of visiting the club library which had just recently started keeping video tapes of classic tennis matches, including Nastase's.

Dev was terrified of his mother, Damayanti, right through his childhood. She came from a wealthy new rich family and was caught in a miserable marriage with his father, whom she considered not only personally inadequate but also a colossal financial failure. Ram Singh proved to be profoundly unable to take care of her basic needs. As a consequence of her husband's shortcomings, she developed a stern and sullen personality, which Dev being a child could not even begin to understand. Cognizant of his son's weaknesses and their effects on his daughter-in-law, his grandfather, whom everyone called P.S. *Saheb*, tried his best to be a surrogate father to Dev. The resulting atmosphere, due to constant conflicts in the house, was heavy and one of constant stress, particularly for Dev.

The Bapna household was the quintessential definition of dysfunction. P.S. *Saheb*, a high ranking retired bureaucrat, watched this dysfunction with a heavy heart while helplessly and silently mourning the fall of a once mighty family. His experience and logic had him convinced that it was impossible for Dev; the only son of his eldest son Ram Sigh, ironically named after the epitome of success, Lord Rama, to amount to anything and thus this branch of his family was doomed. Despite this, while he now concentrated all hopes of family revival on his two younger sons, Suraj Singh and Tara Singh (Dev's uncles) and their families, he did his best for Dev.

Being a sensitive child, Dev became well aware of his relative poverty as early as middle school. His clothes, compared to those of his classmates, were not just simple, but downright pedestrian. While other kids came out dressed smartly in blue jeans and alligator t-shirts, Dev's wardrobe was not only sparse, but consisted mainly of badly fashioned clothes by the neighborhood tailor made out of cheap fabric from local discount stores. He biked to school, as opposed to being dropped off in a chauffeur-driven car. His family home, though spacious and large, was now only a shadow of its former glory. It was falling apart at the seams, with the grounds in complete disarray, paint chipping everywhere on the inside walls and ceilings, and dark water patches dotting the exterior paint. The facilities inside the house had not been upgraded in the last fifty years, or so it seemed and a fresh coat of paint had not been applied in years. The household staff had dwindled to one full-time helper and a couple of part-timers.

There was one family car, an Indian made Fiat, about fifteen years old, built at best with 1940s technology. There was no money to pay for a regular chauffeur, but since Dev's grandfather, a retired and scrupulously honest civil servant (something unheard of even in 1970s India), needed to maintain some minimal status, the current chauffeur, out of loyalty and the fact that his father and grandfather had also been chauffeurs for the Bapna family, agreed to work for less than half of what he could get elsewhere for the duration of grandfather Bapna's life. It used to be quite a sight when a Bapna family member would venture out in town in the 1959 model Indian-made Fiat, chauffeured by a middle-aged man wearing rags for clothes, as his salary was not enough for him to both put food on his family table and purchase decent clothes. There were no more than a couple of hundred cars in Indore in those days, a city of almost 800,000 inhabitants, and almost every car could instantly be identified on the streets in terms of which family it belonged to. The Bapna family car was famous and a source of a lot of jokes, merriment and amusement in Indore.

Unlike other families within the social circle, there were no family vacations to "hill stations" (mountain resorts with cool temperatures in the summer) in the Bapna family and no perfunctory trips to Bombay in the winter to shop, catch up on the latest fashion and other trends, which provided additional snob value.

The social life within the upper crust in Indore revolved around an exclusive club called the Yeshwant club, which could accurately be described as an equivalent to a country club in the US. Dev was taught to play tennis by his grandfather and the tennis coach at the club. The tennis coach had very reluctantly agreed to coach him for next to nothing out of respect for his grandfather. The coach was so reluctant that Dev had to literally beg him for a few lessons a week and it took all of Dev's patience and energy to coax those lessons out of him. Dev's tennis attire also stood out because it was rough and badly designed, and it was not uncommon to see him play tennis in cheap tennis shoes full of holes, and cracked tennis racquets (wooden in those days) that were patched up by wrapping natural gut around the crack. This caused the racquets to have practically no throw whatsoever. Despite this, Dev did well in state level tournaments and later played the national circuit as a junior, with halfway respectable rankings.

As if all this wasn't enough to make Dev realize his family's pathetic financial condition, the kids in his circle made Dev's financial inferiority obvious. Kids, being kids, act the same as kids everywhere. They were often extremely insensitive, cruel and competitive. These kids never tired of making fun of Dev's clothes, house, car, bike, possessions, style and just in general his station in life.

The adults in Indore were also very basic and very status-conscious, but at least they, by and large, refrained from showing up the Bapna family to their face, and instead they took vicarious pleasure in gossiping about their fall from grace behind their backs. The story of how the mighty Bapnas, the one-time first family of Indore had fallen from their lofty perch, was common knowledge in Indore. The kids heard all this and never missed an opportunity to rub it in Dev's face.

Dev's own persona, his straightforwardness, his seemingly simplistic sense of optimism, his apparent lack of realization of his own inferior status in life and the way he carried himself didn't do much to engender any sympathy from his peers, or even the adults in his circle. He turned out to be a brilliant student, an accomplished sportsman, a good debater, and excelled at various activities, in school and outside. This, coupled with a deep-seated conviction, rooted in his grandfather's influence, led him to believe that the decline in financial fortunes of the family was not a sign of inferiority, but a badge of honor.

All around him, Dev saw people almost being forced by the system to compromise to get ahead financially. They had to let go of their ideals, their honor, their sense of self, and indulge in all possible forms of corruption to be able to make some money. Dev was always told by his grandfather that these traits were to be looked down upon. Financial success at the expense of honor was no success, and he always advised Dev to keep his head up high because his family was willing to sacrifice financial success in favor of personal honor and in favor of upholding all the other values that the family held dear, such as integrity, straightforwardness, not succumbing to sycophancy, of hard work and honesty. The proud tradition of deep-rooted values passed down for generations, along with his personal successes in various fields, inevitably gave Dev a bit of a swagger. He used that swagger to subconsciously and sometimes consciously defy his many adversaries and the world around him in general. Others perceived this swagger as undeserved arrogance, totally out of place and not in keeping with his financial and social status, and the narrow minded 1970s Indore society highly resented this.

Dev was clearly out of sync with his surroundings. His chosen path and his very being, his lack of inherited wealth and his inherited value system put him in a direct collision course with the world in which he lived.

There was in addition, yet another consciousness that Dev had had to deal with since as far back as he could remember. One would think that in face of declining fortunes, the Bapna family itself would close ranks and act as the bedrock of support for its young, such as Dev. In fact, the opposite transpired. Even within the immediate and extended Bapna family some were doing a little better than others. Though no Bapna in Dev's father's generation had attained anywhere close to the high status enjoyed by previous generations, some of them had respectable jobs such as government professionals, middle management in private corporations, some were accountants, and there was even a doctor or two. Dev's father, however, due to some personal shortcomings, never succeeded in eking out even a small living, constantly starting and failing in businesses and losing whatever little money he had inherited. This gave him an additional stigma, within and without the family. Just like the kids outside the Bapna family never tired of reminding Dev of his station in life, the kids, and even the adults within the extended Bapna family itself, never refrained from pointing out to Dev his relative inferiority compared to others within the family. Often it took the form of relatives and cousins making fun of Dev's relative simplemindedness, his clothes, his style and all the rest.

One of the biggest reasons for the decline in Bapna family fortunes was the changing times in India and the decline in morals, which made the highly scrupulous Bapnas uncompetitive, but also made the one quality they possessed in abundance, i.e., integrity, redundant and superfluous. Modern India by the 1970s had not much use for honesty and integrity. Any means to attain wealth and power was the order of the day.

This was a world the Bapnas were totally unaccustomed to and the family was rather shell-shocked and perplexed by a world with no scruples and only money and power as the sole sources of respect within the society. Instead of digging in and coming together, many in

Dev's father's generation decided to come to terms with the new India by attempting to adopt the new ways in varying degrees. This weakened the family bond, as the one thing that united them started to be undervalued, even by them, and an unhealthy competition developed within the extended family itself.

The weakest link in this competitive environment was Dev's father. Past bonds between brothers and cousins prevented them from openly showing up Dev's father, but provided no such restraint when it came to Dev. Since childhood, not an opportunity was missed to remind Dev of his weaker station in life. There were constant jokes at Dev's expense and constant put-downs, which again had a traumatic effect on him. There was almost a sense within the family that Dev's father's branch of the family was doomed. Dev, in their minds, just like his father, would never amount to anything.

After all of this, if there was any small measure of morale or spirit or optimism about his prospects in India that was still alive within Dev, the general conditions that prevailed in India in the mid and late 1970s smoked them out completely. After World War II, India, which had been a British colony for almost 200 years, attained its independence from Britain in 1947, largely because of the near destruction of Britain in the war and the resulting non-appetite among the British public to retain colonies. This coincided with the rise of Communism, the Soviet Union and Maoist China, which resulted in a cold war between the Capitalist West and the Communist world led by the Soviets. The Indian political elite, led by Nehru, attempted to bridge this gap between the Capitalist and Communist systems by creating a hybrid economic system, something called "Democratic Socialism," which allowed for some private enterprise, while the government retained control over vast foundational areas of the economy.

In theory, this hybrid system would ostensibly provide the benefits of both systems, but in practice, not only did this hybrid system fail to do so, it in fact provided the disadvantages inherent in both systems. Therefore, after a couple of decades of this bizarre exercise, what came to prevail was a combination of crony capitalism and the lowest form of oppressive Soviet style "apparatchik" bureaucracy, the worst-of-both-worlds scenario. This further emboldened the system of patronage, which has always been one of the negative defining forces in Indian culture. A system of patronage, by definition, is diametrically opposed to the system of "merit." Therefore, to achieve anything in India one had to either be connected or be able to bribe someone, often requiring both. And most times, even when an individual was both connected and not averse to bribing, this person failed to get anywhere due to the sheer lack of opportunities.

Dev, whose family background and traditions had conditioned him into being averse to both seeking patronage and offering bribes, saw himself as having no chance whatsoever of getting anywhere in India.

Having gone through a nightmare right through his early teenage years, by 1978, at the age of seventeen, Dev had started to intensely dislike everything about India. His parents, his extended family's pettiness, his narrow-minded and closed social circle, the city of Indore in general, the sight of the dilapidated infra-structure, the rickshaws, rickety buses, Indian cars built with 1940s technology, bicycles, trucks and camel carts, pigs and cows roaming the streets, men spitting anywhere and everywhere, people urinating and defecating in public, the traffic horns, the loudspeakers blaring music anytime during the day or night, trash everywhere, and cow dung—cow dung which one could not escape—it was ubiquitous. And worst of all, the cow dung within people's hearts and souls. The new value system—everything that some in the West romanticized as exotic or eclectic—he hated it, hated it all with a passion.

Outwardly, Dev put up a brave face, but every incident of abuse, every incident of ridicule, every time he was made fun of, every put down, chipped away at Dev's soul on the inside. Sometimes when he went to bed at night he could literally feel his soul bleeding, and often he would break down and cry, wondering when this would ever end. Sometimes he wished he would never wake up again. His bed at night was his only refuge, and the only time there was silence all around him and the only time he felt some peace. It was just before he fell asleep that he would fantasize about London, Paris, New York—all those magical places he read about in the novels that he read voraciously during the day. But alas, London, Paris and New York would only be a dream for Dev-a distant dream. Oh, what he would not do to get out. He was willing to go to any lengths, take up any blue collar job, work as an unskilled laborer or do dishes in a restaurant in Manhattan, to just experience the world, anything to get out of this hell. And so on and on he would think as he drifted off to sleep.

All of this, coupled with his social situation both inside and outside his family, combined with his perception of America as the proverbial "land of opportunity and endless possibilities," created a sense of desperation within himself as his only way out, which manifested itself in the letter he wrote to Illinois State University and several other universities in the States that fateful day in the fall of 1978. He did this with great help and encouragement from his maternal uncles, particularly his maternal uncle, Ramesh Dada, who, having spent a few years in the US himself, was instrumental in Dev's efforts to get there, an act of kindness he would never forget for the rest of his life. He wanted to make a clean break from Indore. In his own mind, he wanted to "make it" in America and then come back to fix Indore. He wanted to bring back the Indore that his ancestors had built—a clean, simple, prosperous and cultured Indore, not the cesspool it had become today.

"Amazing! So you got away from India to escape corruption, and yet you went back and corruption got you anyway in the worst possible way," said Kunal, alluding to the assault Dev had suffered.

"Ironic, isn't it?" said Dev. "It seems I couldn't escape it".

"Why is that place so corrupt? Was it always like that?" asked Ranika.

"I have heard and read so much about so many of our ancestors who historically were highly successful in India. Were they corrupt too? How did they reach the top without being corrupt, or at least making some accommodation with the corrupt?" asked Kunal.

Selena entered the room and said, "Time for you to rest, Dev. You can continue tomorrow."

The next day, after several entreaties by Kunal and Ranika, Dev related the following story of the beginnings of the Bapna family.

Chapter 4 - Story of Osian

In the years immediately following its founding in the eighth century, the city of Osian thrived, due to its religious significance as a holy city which housed many Hindu temples. The population soon exploded to several thousands and was almost entirely composed of Pratiharas, or Parihar Rajputs, and another Indo-Scythian branch, the Naga Rajputs, who were fierce warriors and who worshipped the Snake Goddess. Pratiharas or Parihars claimed descent from the God of Fire, while the Naga Rajputs claimed descent from the Serpent God.

Osian had its own local chieftain who accepted the overlordship of the Pratiharas. Even though it was a religious community, Osian soon developed a reputation for being home to a quarrelsome people who did not shrink from a good fight, whether they were fights within the city or raiding neighboring communities to steal their cattle. Drunkenness was common, and generally a state of anarchy prevailed. Legend says that a renowned Jain monk and scholar, *Acharya* Ratnaprabhusuriji, was stranded in the city during the four monsoon months of 782. He witnessed the chaos and disorder and started holding discourses every evening on non-violence, simple living and other Jain principles that deeply affected even the most hardcore of the anarchists.

Before the four months were out, the entire city of Osian, along with its chieftain, had decided to embrace Jainism and swore to renounce violence and lead a simple life. This was how the Pratiharas and the Nagas of Osian (who were only a tiny percentage of the overall Pratihara population across India) became Jains and came to be known as "Oswals."

The *Acharya*, however, permitted the Oswals to continue to worship their previous deity, *Chamundi Mata*, the Goddess of War.

Chamundi Mata required a blood sacrifice from her followers in the form of an animal sacrifice. Her followers also offered her liquor on special occasions. The *Acharya*, while permitting the Oswals to continue to worship their previous deity, forbade the Jains to continue to offer her animals in blood sacrifice and also liquor. Again, legend has it that *Chamundi Mata*, the deity, got upset with the *Acharya* and started torturing him. The *Acharya* did not flinch from the pain and, impressed by his steadfastness, she eventually relented and agreed to not accept any blood sacrifice or liquor from the Oswals. Acharya then christened her "*Sachiya Mata*," literally meaning, "The true mother." To this day, in addition to following Jain practices, Oswals continue to worship *Chamundi* in the form of *Sachiya Mata* as their personal family deity, even though she is not a true Jain deity.

Right after their conversion to Jainism, the city of Osian erected a grand temple to the last Jain *Tirthankara*, Lord Mahavira, in 783. The *Acharya* (meaning "learned man" in Hindi), then gave each clan of Osian Nagas and Pratiharas a Jain name. One of the clans was given the name "Bafna," which later also got corrupted into "Bapna," and the Indore Bapnas, whose story this is, belong to the "Bafna" clan of the Oswals. The Bafna clan is particularly devoted to "*Sachiya Mata*," or Goddess *Chamundi*, and continues to follow various Hindu traditions from the time that they were Hindus.

A thousand years after its founding by the Pratiharas and the mass conversion of its residents to Jainism, one Osian resident, a member of the prominent Bafna clan by the name of Deoraj, was having trouble in town. The year was 1740. Politically, India was in turmoil. The great Mogul empire was in shambles, with the Mogul emperor's authority not existing much beyond the capital, Delhi. The Marathas, a Hindu kingdom, had conquered large parts of the Indian heartland. The rest of India had fractured into many independent kingdoms, small and big, some nominally still accepting the overlordship of the Moguls, while others did not. The last nail in the coffin of the Mogul Empire was hammered by Nadir Shah of Persia, who had invaded India the previous year and conducted a systematic slaughter-and-loot operation in Delhi and the Punjab.

Internationally, the Ottomans were tenuously holding on to their shrinking empire, while the English were mired in a war with Spain in the New World. The English, though, were strengthening their trade presence in the eastern state of Bengal. The Rajput Kingdoms of

Rajasthan, small states, were also virtually independent, only nominally holding allegiance to a Mogul Emperor who had no way to enforce anything.

Osian continued to thrive as a religious town, culturally almost totally under the influence of Jainism, while remnants of Hindu traditions still persisted among the Oswals. Many Oswals had migrated out of Osian by the early 1700s and established flourishing businesses in all corners of India. Many others had been retained as ministers and treasurers in the various independent kingdoms across India. By the early eighteenth century, Oswals had started exercising influence well beyond their numbers in India.

Osian Sachiya Mata Temple - Osian
Courtesy – Rajiv Singh , Osian

It was in this environment that Deoraj Singh Bafna found himself in an untenable situation in Osian. Although he came from the powerful Bafna clan, Deoraj's father had died early, which put him at a great social and financial disadvantage vis-à-vis his own clan, and certainly vis-à-vis other residents of Osian. The Bafna clan was one of the original converts to Jainism and had maintained a continued presence in Osian for a thousand years. They were prominent merchants and one of the main pillars of Osian community. Deoraj's father and his two brothers were the inheritors of the Bafna legacy and businesses. They enjoyed contented lives, until Deoraj's father pre-maturely passed away, leaving behind a young widow and the infant Deoraj. Widows were placed in a low status in India in general, and in Rajasthan in particular. They were forbidden to remarry and were basically considered a burden to the family, often times blamed for their husband's untimely demise.

Deoraj's mother, Chelana, endured terrible hardships. Deoraj, still an infant, not Chelena, inherited his father's share in the business, as women could not inherit and Chelana acted as the caretaker or a guardian. Deoraj's uncles promptly stopped paying Chalena Deoraj's share of the profits from the business, under the pretext that they were suffering losses. Losing the income, Chalena could not make ends meet and was forced to distress-sell her share of the business to Deoraj's uncles, receiving only a small amount in settlement, which was barely enough for subsistence for herself and Deoraj. The powers-that-be in Osian saw all this, knew what was going on, and either stayed as silent spectators or allied themselves with the uncles. The principle of allying with the strong won out, as in a contest between the widow and two able men from a prominent dynasty the widow had no chance. Deoraj grew up impoverished, despite his glorious antecedents and his mother grew bitter, and they both got poorer and less empowered by the day.

Deoraj was considered a weakling, a simpleton because he was fatherless and particularly because he had no money. Even in those days the class and status-conscious Indians treated their weak abominably, to be avoided like a communicable disease. Compassion was reserved for those who humbled themselves often and ostensibly before the more wealthy or powerful, or humiliated themselves often, as was the more correct term. The greatest sin in India, historically, was to be a person with no means or power and yet retain some self-respect. Self-respect among the poor and the powerless was considered arrogance, haughtiness, impudence, obstinacy—a sign of profound dysfunction, and in some cases, madness.

Self-respect was a luxury even the mighty in India could scarcely afford. In those rare instances when a person with means aspired to self-respect, it was grudgingly tolerated as a quirk or a freakish idiosyncrasy of a rich eccentric, an anomaly, which unfortunately no one could do anything about because of the owner's significant means. On the other hand, how could a lowly person aspire for self-respect? That was considered to be against nature, something not natural, even perverted. It was somewhat akin to a cotton picker on the plantations in the US, aspiring for an estate of his own. That self-respect is highly overrated and particularly not desirable among the less powerful or the poor continues to be one of defining characteristics of a typical Indian today, regardless of what class, region, or religion he comes from. It is a common human trait, buried somewhere inside each human being, but nowhere is it accepted and practiced more blatantly and brazenly than in India, historically or modern. There is a saying in certain parts of India which roughly translates into, "Even a mother is partial to her more able child."

The Bafna clan of Osian was no different and chose to treat Deoraj with disdain on bad days and with benign neglect on good days. Deoraj was a young man, ambitious, but rebellious. Had he lived in modern times, he would undoubtedly be diagnosed as a genetic mutant. His DNA had somehow mutated to where a couple of his genes had become dormant. The first was the gene that permitted a person to be "pragmatic" and "expedient." When active, this gene permits a person to "strategically" compromise his or her self-respect for some real or perceived gain. In most people, this gene is overactive to where the individual need not have to gain anything strategic to compromise their self-respect. Deoraj's DNA had somehow been altered to render this gene totally inactive. The other gene that had gotten mutated out or altered into dormancy in Deoraj was the one that caused a person to realize that a poor and powerless person is not entitled to self-respect.

Deoraj's ambition far exceeded his means, yet he refused to accept his station in life, and he did not humble himself before the powers-that-be in Osian. He also refused to accept a lowly occupation or be subservient to the more powerful citizens of Osian. It was, and is still, uncommon in India to challenge the hierarchy directly in that manner, thus Deoraj was ostracized socially for being an uppity rebel. There was even a whispering campaign that made the rounds in Osian to brand him as "insane." Most were sure that at the very least, he had a loose nut or two, or as an American would put it, "he was missing a few marbles." He tried his hand at various occupations and failed. Unable to make ends meet, in 1740 Deoraj started thinking about leaving Osian and going elsewhere in search of a better life. He made a mental note to discuss this idea with his young wife, Bhairavi.

Bhairavi was the daughter of Jinendra, one of the *pujaris,* a person who assists in worship of the deity at the *Sachiya Mata* temple in Osian.

His was a middle-class family. The Bafna clan normally married within their class, but Deoraj, being exceptionally weak financially, the clan elders had allowed a middle-class match. Actually, they relished the prospects of saddling Deoraj with a girl who was not considered very pretty and whose father couldn't pay a large dowry. For the uncles, it wasn't enough that Deoraj was fatherless and poor; they would not rest until they could engineer his complete downfall.

"Bhairavi is a good-natured girl and will take good care of you in your old age," the elders had consoled Deoraj's mother, who as it turned out, did not wait around for "Bhairavi to take good care of her."

When she had turned twelve, Bhairavi's father started sending out feelers to prospective grooms. He got terribly concerned when there was no proposal for her that whole year. His worries were compounded as years went by and there were still no concrete proposals. When Bhairavi turned sixteen, Jinendra was losing hope of ever finding a match. *Who will marry an old maid?* he wondered, as the marriageable age for girls was twelve, maybe thirteen, fourteen at the most. The girl would customarily get married and then stay back at the parent's house until she turned sixteen. The groom would then arrive to take his bride home, with great fanfare. Marriage would then be consummated for the first time at the groom's house.

Bhairavi was attractive, but not considered conventionally pretty in Osian. She was tall, even for a Rajput woman. Her body was perfectly proportioned except for her hips, which were just a little rounder than ideal. Her eyes were almond-shaped, but too small, and were hazel colored instead of the preferred dark brown. She had sharp features, with a very well-proportioned nose, longish face and voluptuous lips. Her one fatal flaw, though, and what decisively took her out of the "beautiful" category was that she was a shade darker than most girls in the community. Indians were obsessed with their skin complexion. A fair complexion was given preference over sharp features any day.

The Indo-Scythians and the Rajputs were particularly obsessed with skin color. They were very conscious of their Central Asian heritage and fairer complexion and went to great lengths not to "darken" their stock. Acceptance of Jainism had not in any way tempered their notions of racial purity. It was one thing not eating meat or even not killing insects, but it was quite another to bring a *"sanvli"* – (Rajasthani term for a tanned girl) home. The darker shade, even if ever-so-slight, put Bhairavi firmly in the "less desired" category as a bride. As if this in itself was not bad enough, her father, being a man of limited means, further sealed Bhairavi's fate.

Deoraj's mother, Chelana, also held out for a better match until even Deoraj got past the conventional marriageable age for a man. She had the same problem as Bhairavi's father, only in the reverse. The girl's family also looks for an affluent match for their girl. Deoraj's lack of prospects stood in his way. Chelana started off in the hope that being a member of the Bafna clan would be enough to overcome Doeraj's personal lack of means. In order to improve her chances of finding at least an equal match for Deoraj, she appealed to her husband's brothers to offer Deoraj a small partnership in their thriving businesses on a sweat-equity basis. After all, Deoraj's father had been an equal partner in those businesses, and it was only after his death that Chelana was forced to sell out to her brothers-in-law at a ridiculously low price. Each appeal of this nature, however, was scoffed at. Finally, she lowered her expectations to where she would settle for a girl from any business family, even if they were small businessmen, so that Deoraj could get their support in starting his own business. None came forward. Everyone knew the antipathy the Bafna clan had towards Deoraj.

About Deoraj's eighteenth birthday, Chelana noticed a couple of drops of blood in her urine. She realized instantly that her days were numbered and she quickly accepted Jinendra's long-standing offer for Bhairavi's hand in marriage for Deoraj.

If there was one thing that rivaled a Rajput's obsession with skin color, it was his appetite for a dowry. Acceptance of Jainism had not tempered that appetite either. In fact, Jainism had liberated the Osian Rajputs from being only warriors, and opened the doors of commerce for them. Some of the Oswals had become phenomenally wealthy, both by staying back and in some cases by migrating to other areas of Rajasthan. Several Oswals had migrated out to the thriving city of Jaisalmer, one hundred and fifty miles to the northwest, strategically located on a major international trade route. These Oswals had started businesses and succeeded beyond their wildest expectations. The rise in wealth had increased the ability and willingness of the Oswals to pay sums in dowries, previously unheard of. This had correspondingly whetted the recipient's appetite to receive even more.

The dowry in the Oswal community went far beyond merely the sums to be paid to the daughter or the son-in-law at the wedding. The groom's immediate family had to be gifted with cash, lavish costumes brocaded with gold and silver, cattle, and sometimes even property. The extended family and distant relatives of the groom were also to be lavished with extravagant gifts. The wedding functions and receptions also had to be conducted in keeping with the status of the groom. Elaborate negotiations were conducted by the groom's family just prior to the wedding, normally represented by an uncle or the cousin of the groom with the bride's father. Every single gift, every single wedding arrangement, every single detail had to be meticulously worked out before the actual wedding.

While Deoraj's uncles took no interest in procuring him a bride, once the wedding was set they displayed considerable enthusiasm for negotiating a dowry with Jinendra. These negotiations dragged on late at night, and Jinendra was constantly reminded of how lucky he was that his daughter was being married into the Bafna clan and that it was the uncles who had finally persuaded Deoraj's mother Chelana to accept the match. Jinendra would do well never to forget that and take good care of them, as even after the marriage, Bhairavi would be living in the same house as the uncles, albeit in a different wing. This was a veiled warning that Bhairavi will be entirely at their mercy to do what they wished, if the uncles were not pleased by the gifts. Jinendra was put under considerable pressure and after a tense week of negotiations, he acceded to most of the demands, including some outrageous ones. *Fortunately*, he thought, *Bhairavi is my only child, and I could sell a part of my modest house to make everyone happy* if it becomes necessary.

Deoraj had seen Bhairavi many times, more often as a little boy when he visited the temple with his parents. She used to be a tiny girl running around like a doll, wearing colorful little *lehengas* and *cholis*. Even then, she stood out because of her duskier complexion, which made her hazel eyes even more striking. Eventually, she came out less and less and Deoraj had barely caught glimpses of her in recent years.

During the entire dance by his mother and the family to find him a suitable bride, Deoraj felt no pressure and no anxiety, despite not having much success. He frankly didn't understand the whole process and did not much care for it. Marriage was not a priority for him. He was too preoccupied with how he was going to make a decent living, or even a comfortable one. When his mother had finally settled on Bhairavi, he felt pleasantly surprised to discover that he actually liked the girl, with her striking features, her energy and aura, and even her darker complexion. They had barely exchanged a few words over all these years, but he still felt good. Now that they were going to get married, he felt an urge to see Bhairavi, to meet with her. But visiting alone before marriage was a big no-no.

During the engagement ceremony, Deoraj slipped a tiny piece of white fabric in Bhairavi's henna-painted hands. The cloth fragment had writing on it, asking her to meet him in an isolated corner of the temple compound where they would not be spotted. *This is scandalous*, she thought. After a great deal of thought, she decided to go.

Deoraj was already waiting, leaning against the boundary wall. Deoraj looked up as she approached, and for the first time, took a good look at her. She was wearing a violet-colored *lehanga*, with a matching *orni*. Her slightly rounded hips swayed a little as she approached him. She was wearing a round gold ornament right above her forehead, which she probably forgot to take off after the engagement ceremony. Her hair was no longer braided and was being blown gently by the wind.

She stopped a few feet away, looked at Deoraj and lowered her eyes in deference to her husband-to-be, as all Oswal and Rajput women were expected to do. Deoraj started to take a step forward, and reflexively, Bhairavi took a step back. Deoraj stopped. Bhairavi stood still again. Deoraj moved forward again, very deliberately. This time Bhairavi did not move. She kept her eyes lowered completely, facing the ground. Deoraj went and stood near Bhairavi. Her eyes were now closed tightly; her body stiffened and she had started to breathe a little hard. Deoraj extended his right hand and barely touched the fingertips of her left hand with the fingertips of his right hand. He let his fingertips linger for a second, enjoying the sensation, and then quickly pulled his hand back. He stepped back a little and just stood there, staring at Bhairavi. Bhairavi opened her eyes and looked visibly more relaxed. Her pouting lips lifted into a hint of a smile, but her striking hazel eyes were smiling more expansively, or so he thought. Deoraj smiled back. Bhairavi turned around to leave. She started to walk back, then, she stopped and turned around.

"I have brought a ring for you," said Bhairavi, as she slipped a golden-colored ring, a simple band, on Deoraj's left ring finger.

"Oh", said Deoraj, "I am sorry. I didn't bring anything for you. This looks expensive. You shouldn't have."

"You already gave me a ring at the engagement ceremony this

afternoon. It was real gold. The one I brought you is not expensive; it's only brass," said Bhairavi.

Deoraj looked at Bhairavi, not saying anything, but with an expression that said that this brass ring was more precious to him than gold.

"Don't worry, though, I will go to pick a gold chain for you tomorrow," Bhairavi said.

Deoraj looked at her, confused.

"Part of the dowry," Bhairavi explained. Her voice was clear and firm.

"Will there be a lot of dowry?" Deoraj asked

"Not much, by your family standards, but more than my father can afford," Bhairavi said.

"I didn't think he had a lot," said Deoraj.

"He doesn't, but we are selling the *pichwada* (the backside) of our house," Bhairavi said.

"What?" Deoraj replied, surprised.

"Yes, didn't you know that?" asked Bhairavi.

Deoraj just looked at her.

"Didn't your uncle tell you?" asked Bhairavi.

Deoraj kept looking at her.

"Didn't you know that your uncles were negotiating with my father all last week?" Bhairavi persisted.

Deoraj just kept staring blankly at her, as if lost in deep thought.

Bhairavi waited for a minute or two, and then turned around and walked away.

Deoraj stood there for who knows how long until he realized it was getting a little dark and sun was about to set. He looked around and found no sign of Bhairavi. *She must have left,* he thought. He started walking fast and soon found himself at the door of Jinendra's house, a little breathless. The main door was open and he could see Jinendra and his wife seated on a mat on the floor, in an animated conversation. He knocked on the door and stepped in. Jinendra and his wife were stunned to see Deoraj at that time of the evening.

"*Kunwar Saheb*! What a pleasant surprise," said Jinendra as he shot up on his feet. Any guest in India is to be highly honored, but the to-be son-in-law, and one so hard earned, would naturally be the most honored of guests. With folded hands, he invited Deoraj to take a seat. Deoraj sat down.

"Are you selling this house?" asked Deoraj.

"No, not the whole house. Just the *pichwada*, *Kunwar Saheb*," replied Jinendra.

"Why?" asked Deoraj.

"It will be our honor, *Kunwar Saheb*, to fulfill our responsibilities," replied Jinendra.

"What responsibilities?" asked Deoraj.

"You know…in our culture it is the most sacred responsibility of a father to get his daughter married off," said Jinendra.

"I will not accept it," said Deoraj, looking at Bhairavi now, who had tiptoed into the room and stood in a corner, listening intently.

"Bhairavi is our only child; she is all we have. Everything we have is hers," pleaded Jinendra.

"I will not have you sell your house," said Deoraj. He was surprised by the authority in his own voice.

"*Kunwar Saheb*, what will people say? I will not be able to show my face in Osian. Maybe people will force me to call off the wedding. You think your uncles will let the wedding go forward without the dowry? We finally found a son-in-law like you after years of praying to *Sachiya Mata*. Please don't put all this at risk. I am telling you, it is no hardship at all. It will be our pleasure. It really will be, will it not be? Will it not be?" he said, looking at his wife and Bhairavi, pleading with them to come to his aid.

"If you want me to marry Bhairavi you will not sell the house, and that is final," said Deoraj, as he stood up and glanced at Bhairavi, who for the first time stared him back straight into his eyes and kept her eyes locked with his until he turned around and walked out of the house.

Next day, all hell broke loose. Deoraj's irrational behavior was the talk of the town. The uncles and elders of the Bafna clan all descended like hyenas on poor Chelana, who had to face the brunt of everyone's anger. "Osian will not tolerate rebellion," she was told in no uncertain terms. The disease may spread, and pretty soon it would be the end of the dowry system. The elders cringed just at the thought of such a monstrosity. Chelana summoned Deoraj and tried to reason with him.

Deoraj wouldn't budge.

Chelana told him about her own hard life, how much she had had to endure, the financial hardships, the loss of a husband, the humiliations suffered at the hands of the Bafna clan, her high hopes from Deoraj. Why was he intent on destroying himself? Would he not listen to her even once? Had he no consideration for his mother's honor? What if the townsfolk called off the wedding? Deoraj still didn't budge. Chelana now played her final card. She revealed to Deoraj, for the first time, her health condition and that she did not expect to live long.

Tears welled up in Deoraj's eyes. He looked at her, this frail and disheveled woman who had raised him against all odds. He had seen her hurt for money. He had seen her save the best food portions for him, while she ate the leftovers. He had seen her suffer and die every day of indignities and humiliation. He knew she'd much rather be dead, but continued to live only for his sake, at least until he grew up. He also knew that now that he has grown up and about to get married, his mother had willingly surrendered her will to live. She had done everything in her power to raise him to adulthood. She had kept her part of the bargain. He had to keep his. He would honor his dying mother's last wishes, no matter how unpleasant it was for him.

Deoraj relented.

Jinendra sold the house. The wedding functions lasted almost a week. Deoraj was eighteen and Bhairavi was sixteen years of age. There were various parties thrown by friends and relatives. Deoraj couldn't help but feel that most of these parties were conducted more to discharge an obligation and to not look bad in front of the whole town rather than out of any real affection for him or his mother. Deoraj sensed a distinct lack of joy and excitement on the part of townsfolk and his own clan at the functions. It was all very formal. His mother, however, was overwhelmed, profusely thanking everyone for making this a memorable occasion. She even thanked the uncles for wholeheartedly participating in the dancing during the "*Sangeet*" function.

Jinendra was running around, trying to make everyone comfortable. As the father of the bride, he would lose face big time if any guest got displeased for any reason. Every guest raised his or her expectations to receive the highest level of pampering and Jinendra and his extended family spared no effort to cater to everyone's whims and fancies. Rajasthani weddings were known for their color and pageantry. But due to a palpable lack of genuine celebration and joy on the part of the towns people of Osian, Deoraj came away with a distinct impression that his wedding lacked color. It was as black and white a wedding as a Rajasthani was ever likely to see.

Finally, to Deoraj's relief, the wedding festivities were over and life returned back to normal. Bhairavi was immediately sent off to her husband's house without the traditional two-year waiting period, as she was already over sixteen years of age. Bhairavi wept at the *bidai* (send off) ceremony held at Jinendra's house and both Jinendra and his wife wept inconsolably, as they were sad to see their only child leave them. The last thing Jinendra did was to request Deoraj, with folded hands, to take good care of his daughter. He said that he had raised her with a lot of love and affection and that if she ever made a mistake, to forgive her and not take it to heart.

A few months later, Chelana's health worsened and she was near death. A Jain monk visited the house and chanted a few prayers for her. She requested permission from the monk to perform the ancient Jain ritual of *Santhara*. *Santhara* is a ritual performed when a person feels that their life has served its purpose and then they starve until death, no matter how long it takes for death to arrive. As per the Jain religion, the person performing this ritual is more likely to attain Nirvana. The monk gave his consent, as Deoraj and Bhairavi sobbed uncontrollably. Thankfully, Chelana died peacefully the next morning. She was cremated the same evening and Deoraj took her ashes to a nearby river and dispersed them. Just short of his nineteenth birthday, Deoraj was officially an adult, but he still felt like an orphan. The little boy in him now came out and he was scared of what lay ahead of him. He returned to his house and Bhairavi. After the few mourners who had been visiting Deoraj had left, they held each other tightly and sat there all night.

If life before his mother's death was difficult for Deoraj, life after her death, it became nearly impossible. He had not realized how much of a defense his mother had provided for him, his one shield, who deflected the fire directed at Deoraj from the townsfolk and the Bafna clan alike. She humbled herself, where Deoraj didn't. She visited people when Deoraj wouldn't. She maintained relations by behaving "appropriately," where Deoraj didn't. She accepted and assumed her lower place in the hierarchy, where Deoraj wouldn't, and this gave pause to the townsfolk from directing their full ire at Deoraj. With Chelana's death, Deoraj had no such protection left. The entire town of Osian now felt liberated to direct their full fury at Deoraj. They were no longer restrained, and their years of pent up resentment finally was all let out. Scorn and ridicule were heaped on him in abundance and everyone wished for Deoraj to be put in his place.

Fortune, too, had turned her back on Deoraj. Despite being

intelligent, presentable and hard-working, Deoraj just couldn't succeed in any business he undertook in Osian. Deoraj was quickly burning scarce and precious cash just to make ends meet, and everyone knew he was almost bankrupt. Jinendra was his only well-wisher in town, and he too watched in stunned disbelief at the intensity of the vitriol hurled at Deoraj. He silently suffered and prayed every day to *Sachiya Mata*, pleading with the Goddess he had served all his life, to look out for his daughter and son-in-law. It seemed, though, that *Sachiya Mata* was not convinced, and so it happened that one day Deoraj brought up the issue of leaving Osian in search of a better life with Bhairavi.

Bhairavi asked, "Where will we go? We have no money. We don't know anyone. We will be all alone." She was barely sixteen, trying to act like adult, well beyond her years.

"I was thinking about Jaisalmer. Jodhpur is closer and maybe a better option from your standpoint. Either way, we will never be as alone anywhere as we are here in Osian," said Deoraj.

Deoraj was fascinated by Jaisalmer, a desert city which lay in the extreme western corner of Rajasthan, about one hundred and fifty miles northwest of Osian. It was a relatively new city, founded by Bhatti Rajputs (another Indo-Scythian clan), around twelfth century AD. Coincidentally, Deoraj's namesake was the founder of the Bhatti Rajput dynasty. Some people said that there was a previous settlement founded around the tenth century AD by the Pratiharas, the same people who earlier founded Osian. In any event, by the fifteenth century Jaisalmer had become an important stop on one of the branches of the famous Silk Road. Caravans crossed Jaisalmer and the town became enormously wealthy by imposing levies on these caravans. Jaisalmer's bustling economy attracted traders and merchants from all over India, and even abroad, to set up businesses in town. This gave Jaisalmer a cosmopolitan hue, and Jaisalmer bazaars were overflowing with all kinds of goods.

Merchants and traders had built fortunes almost overnight, and it was the land of opportunity of its time, where any young man with any ambition wished to come to "make it." The city looked like a dream, located in the middle of the desert, and its streets were lined with magnificent sandstone mansions in Indo-Islamic architecture, built by expert builders from around the world. Many Oswals from Osian had migrated to Jaisalmer, made small fortunes and were the subject of envy amongst townsfolk in Osian. Whenever they returned to Osian for a visit, these rich Oswals from Jaisalmer were treated like royalty, as they dressed in style and carried themselves with the confidence of the city folk. Deoraj talked often about Jaisalmer and Bhairavi knew that Jaisalmer was where Deoraj wanted to be.

"Why not Jaisalmer?" asked Bhairavi.

"You sure?" said Deoraj.

"Yes," said Bhairavi.

"Will you be all right without knowing anyone in the big city?" asked Deoraj.

"I will be fine. Don't worry about me," said Bhairavi, her heart sinking at the thought of leaving her parents and all familiarity behind for the unknown of the big city.

Deoraj held Bhairavi's hand and embraced her, fully realizing the sacrifice this sixteen-year-old was making for him, to permanently leave her parents behind and trusting him, a man she barely knew, with her life. He was now falling in love with Bhairavi. *I will always take care of her*, he thought, *even with my life, if necessary*. He made this silent promise to Bhairavi. Although Deoraj had not made that promise aloud, almost as if by telepathy, right at that moment, a strange calm came over Bhairavi and all apprehensions left her as if by magic. Her body relaxed. She warmly embraced Deoraj, pulling him to her tightly, feeling protective of him now. They both were immersed in each other's deeply-felt emotions. Still in his arms, she started to think about what to pack to carry with them to Jaisalmer.

Deoraj had one last matter to settle before he left Osian. He visited his uncle at his grand establishment in the middle of Osian's commercial district. He folded his hands and bowed low, as was the custom in the Bafna clan.

"*Mujra Kaka Hukum*," said Deoraj, meaning, "Respectful greetings, exalted uncle."

"*Mujra, Deoraj*," responded the uncle. "*Aaj Kaka Hukum ki yaad kaise aye*," which translated to, "Why did you think of your exalted uncle today?"

"I am thinking of leaving Osian for good, *Kaka Hukum*," said Deoraj.

"Are you certain, Deoraj? You know there is always a job for you here. I can start you off as a stock boy. I owe it to your departed mother, my *Bhabhisa* and my late *Bhaisaheb Hukum*, your father," said the uncle.

"It is very kind of you, *Kaka Hukum*, but I would really like to leave," said Deoraj.

"So what can I do for you? You know I cannot lend you any money. The businesses are still suffering heavy losses," whispered the uncle, not even remotely conscious of the fact that his obscenely expensive Basra pearl and emerald-studded gold necklace was clearly visible through his transparent silk tunic.

"I have not come to borrow, *Kaka Hukum*. I have come to make you a business proposition," said Deoraj.

The uncle's ears perked up and his shrewd eyes narrowed under his bushy eyebrows and practically no eyelids, now directly peering at Deoraj.

"I would like to sell you my portion of the house. It is easily worth Rs. 1500. I can let you have it for Rs. 1000," said Deoraj.

"Who will pay Rs. 1000 for that house, Deoraj?" responded his exalted uncle calmly.

"800?" asked Deoraj.

"Who will pay Rs. 800 for that house, Deoraj? I can offer you Rs. 600. Take it or leave it," said his exalted uncle, haggling like he would with a fruit vendor at any open air bazaar.

"As you wish, *Kaka Hukum*," said Deoraj, smiling, amused by his exalted uncle's pettiness and greed.

"I will send the money with the *munim* (manager) after I close up this evening. You will hand him over the title?" asked the uncle.

"*Hukum, Kaka*, and one more thing. I will need some identification from the Osian town government to enter a new jurisdiction," said Deoraj.

"I will arrange that. The *munim* will bring it to you this evening, along with the money," said the exalted uncle.

"Thank you, *Kaka Hukum*," said Deoraj.

"Anything else?" asked the uncle.

"Yes, there is just this one last thing. Instead of the name 'Deoraj Singh Bafna' on the identification papers, can you please have them put the name 'Deoraj Singh Bapna'?" asked Deoraj.

His uncle stared deeply into Deoraj's eyes and after what seemed like an eternity, when Deoraj didn't blink, he lowered his gaze, maybe in shame or maybe in shamelessness, and reluctantly nodded.

On the morning Deoraj left Osian, he was dressed up in his father's silk tunic and white *dhoti*, made out of Daka muslin. He had wrapped his *dhoti* tightly, and he wore it in a long, ceremonial style. On his head he wore his best turban—bright yellow, with a long tail hanging out of it that extended down to his lower back. His wife was dressed in her best turquoise *lehenga* and a yellow *orni* to match her husband's turban. They laid a flat sheet of cloth on the ground and threw their belongings onto that sheet. Then they wrapped the sheet around their belongings, tying it into a knot. Deoraj lifted the garment bag, ran a stick through the top and balanced the stick over his right shoulder.

He and Bhairavi climbed into the back of a rental bullock cart. The driver was an acquaintance of Jinendra, who had agreed to drive them to Jaisalmer at a discount. They made a stop at the Sachiya Mata Temple along the way, where Bhairavi prayed for her husband's success and long life, embraced her parents, and boarded the bullock cart again. She felt strong and confident, and particularly connected to Deoraj at that moment. Perhaps it was because she was pregnant, even though she didn't know it yet.

While Deoraj and Bhairavi were getting ready to leave Osian, a place where he and his family had lived uninterrupted for a thousand years, none of the other townspeople, nor a single member of the Bafna clan was there to see them off. Eighteen-year old Deoraj Singh Bapna and sixteen-year-old Bhairavi Kumari Bapna were on their own, off into the great unknown to seek a better life. *A life of dignity*, thought Deoraj. As they crossed the town gates to exit Osian, and sped off on the dusty desert trail towards Jaisalmer, Deoraj never, not once, looked back at Osian.

Chapter 5 - Story of Deoraj – 1
1740 – 1750

Lal Singh, the cart driver, was a middle-aged man who had been back and forth from Osian to Jaisalmer countless times. They were to travel first to a major crossroads, where an assortment of bullock carts, horse-drawn carriages, camel carts, people on camel backs, people on horse backs and even in some cases, people on foot could rendezvous and form caravans to travel further. It was a small settlement called JaiSarai and it had a large roadside inn, called *Sarai*, in Rajasthani. As they pulled into JaiSarai in the late afternoon, they noticed scores of camels, bullock carts and hundreds of people sitting out in the open in groups. Lal Singh entered the inn and parked his bullock cart along with others, anchoring it with a rope to a tree. They were quickly approached by a man from the inn, who carried sacks of cattle feed which Lal Singh promptly laid in front of his hungry oxen.

Lal Singh ushered Deoraj and Bhairavi up the steps of the inn and entered a chamber to the left, asking the couple to wait. It was the owner's chamber and inside was a heavy-set man with a weathered face and a long, twirled moustache. The owner greeted Lal Singh with an amiable smile and Lal Singh asked him for a private room for the couple and a bed in the dormitory for himself. The owner told Lal Singh where to go and Lal Singh escorted Deoraj and Bhairavi to their private quarters.

"Make yourself comfortable and relax," said Lal Singh, "while I figure out which caravan we can join to go to Jaisalmer tomorrow morning."

Deoraj and Bhairavi entered the room and threw down their homemade garment bag in one corner. The room had a double cotton mattress in the middle of the room, covered with crisply starched clean white sheets. There were two pillows towards the head, and two folded sheets lay by the foot of the mattress. There was a mirror nailed to the wall on one side and a small bright green colored wooden door leading to the bathroom on the other. Next to the mattress on one side was a small clay pot filled with water covered by a flat brass plate and a spherical copper vessel on top. Both Deoraj's and Bharavi's bodies were sore from riding in the bullock cart all day. They took a cold bath and then slept for about an hour, until they were awakened by Lal Singh.

"It's past six and already dark," said Lal Singh. "Time to get something to eat."

The three of them walked down to the main level of the *Sarai*. The lobby area was lighted with oil-fueled lamps—a few large ones and several groupings of tiny earthen terracotta lamps. The lobby was crowded with people from all over. It was easy to figure out where a person was from and what their ethnicity was by the way they dressed. There were Sindhi women wearing loose, colorful clothes topped by a traditional *ajark*, which is a type of embroidered shawl made in Sindh. There were women from Gujarat and Kutch, wearing their own traditional dresses, also very colorful. There were, of course, Rajput and Rajasthani women, some Bhil women wearing their tribal clothes, even some Maratha women wearing their short *saris*, their borders lined with extravagant gold brocade. Then there were women from distant Baluchistan and Pakhtunistan, with their faces decorated by black dots on their chins and foreheads. The men, too, were in all different kinds of garbs. There were even a couple of Europeans, presumably English: two men and a woman.

Bhairavi had never heard of Europeans, let alone seen them. She kept staring at them in wonder—at their dress, their manner their demeanor and most of all, the woman's golden hair, until Deoraj, realizing that it was rude, gently pulled her away. Lal Singh explained that they were English merchants visiting Jaisalmer to sell their wares. Different languages, different outfits, different people, all gathered in the sarai lobby, and the uneven yellow light from the oil lamps left dark spots in certain areas of the room, creating a rather mysterious and heady atmosphere, the likes of which Deoraj and Bhairavi had never seen before.

JaiSarai was one of the many stops along the major travel routes in India, where caravans stopped to rest, refuel and regroup. These wayside stops inevitably became a melting pot of cultures and served as marker posts of safety along dangerous routes.

"Respite is temporary, sanctuary is for as long as you want it," said one writer to describe the sense one got at these Sarais. These Sarais also acted as consolidation points for solo travelers like Deoraj and his wife, and other smaller groupings who wished to become part of a larger caravan to head toward a common destination. Caravans naturally provided a much greater sense of security than solo travel, especially in India. Bandits, outlaws, robbers, rogue soldiers, and even perfectly affluent and respectable folks, not to mention a royal family or two, were always looking for an opportunity to victimize the defenseless. No point in leaving the low hanging fruit un-plucked.

As Deoraj, Bhairavi and Lal Singh walked out of the lobby, outside the sarai across the street was another spectacular sight. The large open area was lit by a thousand torches, which were attached at an angle on top of rows of thin wooden poles that were dug in the ground. The area closest to the street looked like an extended open-air barbecue, with all kinds of food being cooked—roasted, fried, charcoal-broiled or grilled. Deoraj and Bhairavi had not eaten all day and the different aromas that emanated from the open-air cook fest further whetted their appetites. Further down from the cookouts were several rows of fruit vendors who had stacked their products up high in large open baskets. Then there was one whole section where different carnival-style games were in progress, including rope-walking and knife-throwing.

Hundreds of people from all over were walking around, eating, drinking, playing or watching carnival games, and most of all interacting with each other, simply enjoying the novelty of meeting someone so unlike themselves. Most of these people would move on to different destinations the next morning, never to see each other again. It was almost like the wayside stop was also a place where time stood still for a while and people could temporarily forget all their worries and allow themselves a night of indulgence in good food, good wine, good company, good conversation—just simple fun. Bhairavi and Deoraj, along with Lal Singh, got into the spirit of the evening and allowed themselves this moment of childlike enjoyment.

Bhairavi looked around in amazement. Everything was new to her, laughing and animatedly admiring all she saw. She was acting her age, like a sixteen-year-old, for the first time since she got married. Deoraj kept looking at her, falling deeper and deeper in love with her.

During the course of the evening, Lal Singh introduced Deoraj and Bhairavi to a young man, dressed in black clothing. Even the color of his turban was black, although its shape was somewhat conical. He had a sword hanging off of his cummerbund, and he looked strong as a bull. His name was Alam Khan. He was a Muslim from Delhi who was also heading to Jaisalmer to begin a new life. His father was a commander in the Mogul army. During the Persian Nadir Shah's invasion of India the previous year, he had ordered an indiscriminate mass killing of the entire population of the Mogul capital of Delhi. Alam Khan's father, Dilawar Khan, had been killed by the Persians in an attempt to rescue and transport to safety an entire Hindu clan he happened to run into during the resulting mass exodus out of Delhi. Alam Khan had no other family left, and he wanted to run as far away from Delhi as possible, to as remote a corner of the world as possible.

After wandering aimlessly for several months, finally down to his last penny, he set his sights on Jaisalmer. He had heard that the *Rawal* (ruling prince) of Jaisalmer was always looking for brave young men to serve in his army. When introduced to Deoraj and Bhairavi, Alam Khan raised his right arm and touched his forehead with his fingers as he said, "*Adaab*" (polite greetings). Alam Khan was going to travel on horseback and he would join the same caravan to Jaisalmer that Deoraj and Bhairavi would be taking the next morning.

Lal Singh introduced them to another young couple, Tulsa and his wife Purvi. Tulsa was wearing a wide red turban, a white tunic and *dhoti*. He was clean shaven like Deoraj and had long thick jet black locks, curling and protruding out of his headgear from all sides. He was nineteen years old but far more mature and worldly than Deoraj. His wife, Purvi, was one of the prettiest young women Deoraj had ever seen. Petite and delicate, she had clear skin which glowed, and a lovely smile. Tulsa was a Paliwal.

Paliwals were a group of Brahmins (not Rajputs) that had migrated from their native Pali in Rajasthan, about fifty miles away, to Jaisalmer area around 1291. There they had established a cluster (83, as per legend) of villages. Kuldhara, about eighteen kilometers to the west of Jaislamer, was the largest village and also the main cultural center of the Paliwal community. Paliwal were particularly good looking people, with Paliwal women known and coveted for their beauty. However, the Paliwals held on tightly to their women and it was extremely rare for a Paliwal woman to marry outside her community. There were several incidents in which some regular people, high ranking officials, and even members of the royal family of Jaisalmer had gotten infatuated with Paliwal women and when rebuffed had resorted to kidnapping and abductions.

Rajput women were nice-looking, but in general their beauty was not of the delicate variety, while Paliwal women were generally petite and very feminine, with delicate features. Also in contrast with the Rajput women, Paliwal women were a little softer and more overtly kinder. Their beauty, however, was just one of Paliwal virtues. They were hard working and highly educated. The Paliwals made their fortune by the sheer brilliance of their business and agricultural acumen. They knew the art of growing a water- intensive crop like wheat in the Thar Desert; they could identify areas with gypsum rock layers running under the ground surface, to ensure water was retained for the crops. They had also become leading money lenders in Jaisalmer, a business dominated prior to their entry, by the Oswals. The Oswals continued to thrive as money lenders and bankers, despite Paliwal entry, as there was enough banking business to go around for everybody. Paliwals operated and competed fairly and magnanimously, thereby maintaining good relations with the otherwise prickly and competitive Oswals. The rulers of Jaisalmer depended on the Paliwals for much of their tax revenues.

Tulsa and his wife were migrating from Pali to Jaisalmer. Unlike Deoraj and Bhairavi, who had no clue what was in store for them in Jaisalmer, Tulsa and Purvi were migrating into a welcoming community. The Paliwals were known for their hospitality to all, but were famous for making new Paliwal migrants feel at home and welcomed each new migrant with a symbolic gift of a brick and a gold coin. The entire community would then assist the new comers build their first home and the elders got them started in some vocation so they could make a living and prosper. Tulsa and Purvi and Deoraj and Bhairavi greeted each other with folded hands and they developed an instant rapport. They spent the evening sampling different foods, playing games and having fun, and the more they got to know each other the more they liked each other.

Jaisalmer was founded in the eleventh century AD by a Rajput chief Deoraj Bhatti. The Bhatti clan had originally come from the northern province of the Punjab after they were defeated and displaced there by one of the first Muslim invasions. They were able to escape the attention of the Muslims until 1293, when the Islamic Khilji Dynasty that was ruling the Delhi Sultanate laid a long siege and captured Jaisalmer.

When the defeat was apparent and inevitable, the Rajput ladies of Jaisalmer, led by the ladies of the Royal House, performed the *Jauhar*, a Rajput ritual where the women would throw themselves into the fire to prevent their honor from being violated by the victorious Islamic armies. Despite guerilla resistance after their defeat, the Bhatti clan had to accept the overlordship of the Delhi Sultanate, and subsequently the Moguls. Both the Delhi Sultanate and the Moguls left the Bhatis alone, and for all practical purposes the Bhatis ruled Jaisalmer independently, while nominally sending tribute to the overlords.

Due to its strategic location on an international trade route, by the fifteenth century the city and its rulers were able to get phenomenally wealthy by imposing levies on the passing caravans. By 1740, when Deoraj and Bhairavi migrated into Jaisalmer, the Mogul empire was in its last throes and its writ no longer held sway beyond the Delhi city limits. Jaisalmer was now free from Delhi's yoke, but for the previous several years Jaisalmer had been facing a number of other existential issues, chief among them being an intractable dispute with the neighboring kingdoms of Bikaner and Jodhpur, both ruled by the Chauhan Rajputs, another Indo-Scythian derivative. This led to a relative decline in Jaisalmer's wealth and prestige and such was the case around 1740, when Deoraj and Bhairavi headed towards Jaisalmer.

Early the next morning, several large caravans formed outside JaiSarai. One of them was destined for Jaisalmer. Deoraj and Bhairavi gazed at the magnificent spectacle of pre-departure activities that was unfolding in front of them. The caravans included camels, horses, wagons, bullock carts, loose cattle, goats, and even some sheep. There was a flurry of activity, with some travelers loading their baggage and others bidding each other farewell. Several others offered prayers to their respective deities whose idols were installed side by side in one picturesque corner of the Sarai grounds. There was even a small mosque-like structure sitting right next to the idols of Hindu and Jain gods and goddesses. With all the advantages of mechanization and industrial revolution, the resultant death of the wayside stop culture, at least the Indian Sarai culture, was one of the more tragic losses to humanity. The diversity, the variety, the color, the food, the music, the aromas, the games, the human interaction of unlike people, the symbolism of all races and religions coming together briefly to simply play, became attached in the process and then dispersing forever the next day, all in a sarai or wayside stop setting, was one of the most touching rituals humanity has ever invented.

The journey to Jaisalmer, would take roughly ten days. The route was carefully planned to include a wayside stop at a sarai every evening, around dusk. Lal Singh had positioned his bullock cart towards the tail end of the caravan, as instructed by the caravan leader. Tulsa and Purvi's cart was right behind theirs. Alam Khan was on his horse, not far from the two carts. During the ten days, the five young people spent a lot of time getting to know each other. The desert seemed endless, with the same dreary sand day in and day out. By the afternoon of the tenth day, when they saw their first glimpse of a Jaisalmer fort at a distance, everybody was tired of the desert. The caravan was supposed to stop at a sarai outside of Jaisalmer town where the town officials would check the credentials of all who wanted to enter the city gates. The rest of the caravan would continue on beyond Jaisalmer. Those whose credentials didn't check out would have to stay over at the sarai and then decide what to do next.

Tulsa and Pruvi headed for the main Paliwal village of Kuldhara, another day's journey to the west. They broke off from the caravan, and along with a few other people on horseback, took off towards Kuldhara after bidding emotional farewells to Deoraj and Bhairavi.

"I am sure we will be meeting often, being so close to each other," said Purvi as she embraced Bhairavi, and Tulsa bid goodbye to Deoraj and with a heartfelt invitation to call on him anytime Deoraj needed anything. Tulsa was fully aware of the fact that unlike him, Deoraj had no social support system in Jaisalmer and would find things extremely difficult. He did not show it, but he was apprehensive and concerned about Deoraj's and Bhairavi's prospects in Jaisalmer, considering not only their lack of support, but also their innocence and childlike nature. Deoraj and Bhairavi watched Tulsa and Purvi's cart for a long time, until it finally disappeared from sight.

The police guards from the *kotwal's* (sheriff's) office were already checking the travelers' credentials. They went to all the horseback riders first and Deoraj saw them taking money from each rider before waving them towards the city gates. When Alam Khan was waved off, he stopped briefly by Deoraj's cart, told them where they could find him in Jaisalmer, then rode off. After an hour or so, the guards finally checked Deoraj's credentials. The guard who approached Deoraj was very young, dressed in a long white tunic which widened at the bottom and skin tight white pants with wrinkles, called a *churidar*. He looked at the Osian city identification paper Deoraj had produced for himself and Bhairavi and then asked, "Bapna, uh from Osian, why are you coming to Jaisalmer?"

"To find work," replied Deoraj.

"You need a guarantor in Jaisalmer. Do you have one?" asked the guard.

"No, we don't know anyone," said Deoraj.

"We cannot let you inside Jaisalmer. The law says you must have a guarantor," said the guard.

Lal Singh stepped forward and said, "Respected Guard, sir, is not there some other way? I am sure you would not want to leave this nice young couple stranded outside the city like this."

The guard looked Lal Singh over from top to bottom.

"Ok, one rupee each for a total of two rupees and I will act as their guarantor myself," said he.

Lal Singh looked at Deoraj, smiling triumphantly and fully expecting Deoraj to pull out two rupees to hand over to the guard. Deoraj didn't oblige.

"You expect me to pay a bribe, guard?" asked Deoraj, his voice rising. "I want to see your superior officer."

The guard was stunned. He had been checking credentials at the sarai for a couple of years now and he had seen all kinds—hardened criminals, ruffians, poor day laborers, rich farmers, millionaire merchants, even a few minor royals, but no one had refused to pay a bribe, and certainly no one had raised their voice to him. Since he had never experienced anything like this, for a moment he didn't know how to react. When he was able to gather his wits about him, the guard reached for his sword, pulled it out and grabbed Deoraj by the collar, muttering, "I can kill you for raising your voice to me like that, you lowlife."

Lal Singh and Bhairavi stood frozen in their position. Deoraj pushed the guard back and said, "I will have your head for this, guard. You don't know who I am. I am from the Bafna clan at Osian and my father used to be very close to the *rawal's* (ruler's) second cousin, Ratan Singh. You know of Ratan Singh, don't you, guard?"

"I know of no Ratan Singh and I have never heard of the Bafna clan," said the guard, still swinging at Deoraj with his sword.

Lal Singh came out of his shock and held the guard's arm, saying, "Don't take a chance at making a terrible mistake, guard. Allow them to stay here overnight and let the *kotwal* deal with them in the morning."

The guard stopped resisting and took a step back, letting Deoraj go. Bhairavi came running into Deoraj's arms, her face contorted in terror and shock.

The guard said, "You better hope that the *kotwal* lets you into the city, because if not, I will take your head off before the sun goes down tomorrow," and then he moved on to the next cart.

Lal Singh kept staring at Deoraj and Bhairavi, shaking his head in disbelief.

Early the next morning Lal Singh knocked on their room to wake Deoraj up. The *kotwal* was making his rounds and he demanded to see Deoraj. Apparently the guard had put in a report already. The *kotwal*, Hari Singh, was a middle-aged man, who was reputed to run his department with an iron fist in Jaisalmer. He had been a *kotwal* for ten years, and he had enriched himself by taking systematic bribes from criminals, and providing private security services to rich merchants and minor nobles. On the other hand, he didn't tolerate serious crime and was ruthless in punishing hardcore criminals. He was a highly intelligent, complex man who was able to assimilate this dichotomy with ease. People said he was a psychopath who was able to live with this contradiction without it pricking his conscience at all. There were whispers in Jaisalmer that the more amoral his conduct during the day, the better he slept at night.

On the positive side, he was loyal to the core and stopped at nothing to further the interests of the Kingdom of Jaislamer and its ruler. Therefore, normally, a minor altercation between a young man from Osian and a guard during credentials check, uncommon as it was, would be pretty low on the list of events demanding the *kotwal's* attention. However, one disturbing fact jumped out and grabbed Kotwal Harisingh's attention as he read the guard's report. The Ratan Singh, that Deoraj had mentioned was indeed a second cousin to the *Rawal*, but he had been exiled from Jaisalmer the previous year on charges of treason for attempting to overthrow the *Rawal*. *Kotwal* Hari Singh feared that Deoraj may be an insurgent, attempting to infiltrate into Jaisalmer to create trouble on behalf of the exiled Ratan Singh or his followers. If his fears turned out to be true, that would be a very serious matter indeed, so he immediately departed to check Deoraj out.

As Deoraj and Bhairavi walked down the steps of the sarai to present themselves to the waiting *kotwal*, Lal Singh and the Sarai owner nervously led the way. Lal Singh was breathlessly advising Deoraj to behave himself with the *kotwal*, otherwise something very inauspicious was sure to happen that morning. The *kotwal* was pacing back and forth when he noticed Deoraj and his entourage. Lal Singh pushed Deoraj forward towards the *kotwal*. Deoraj folded his hands and greeted him politely, while standing straight, his head held high.

"So this is the young man from the famous Bafna clan of Osian," said the *kotwal* mockingly.

"Yes, *Kotwal*," said Deoraj.

"I have never heard of this famous Bafna clan," said the *kotwal*. "Tell me about your connection with Ratan Singh."

"He was my father's friend," said Deoraj proudly.

"When is the last time your father met Ratan Singh?" asked the *kotwal*.

"Fifteen years ago," said Deoraj. "My father has been dead fifteen years."

The *kotwal* relaxed a little. "And you…when was the last time you met Ratan Singh?" he asked.

"I have never met him myself, but he will be happy to vouch for me. I am sure he will remember my father," replied Deoraj.

The *kotwal* looked visibly relieved now. His trained eye told him that Deoraj was no subversive. In fact, Deoraj seemed to be a simple boy, unschooled in the ways of the world. He glanced at Bhairavi and could immediately tell that she was another innocent child. An insurgent would not bring attention to himself by refusing to pay a small bribe. When he put all these observations together with the facts Lal Singh had given him about Deoraj's history in Osian, Hari Singh concluded that Deoraj was totally innocent. Something about Deoraj's simplicity penetrated and touched a small modicum of goodness that was buried deep inside Harisingh's soul. He decided to have some fun with the boy now.

"So you refused to pay my guard, boy," said the *kotwal*.

"Yes, my father taught me never to pay a bribe," responded Deoraj.

"What world was your father living in, boy?" asked the *Kotwal*. "In India we have been taking bribes since the beginning of time. Bimbisara's officials were corrupt, Nanda officials were corrupt, Maurya officials were corrupt, Gupta officials were corrupt, and today, Moghul officials are corrupt too. It is our birthright, our way of life. It is as natural as breathing. Corruption defines us. This is what makes us Indian," continued the Kotwal philosophically, as if giving a classroom lesson to a child. "What makes you think that a boy like you can challenge our way of life, our very Indianness?" asked the Kotwal mockingly.

Deoraj said nothing.

"What if I ask you for a bribe, you insolent twit? Will you refuse a *kotwal* too?" he asked, feigning anger.

"Yes, I most certainly will," said Deoraj.

Lal Singh covered his face with both his hands, now fearing the worst.

"Come over here, little girl, and stand beside your husband," said the *kotwal,* looking at Bhairavi.

The *kotwal* moved forward, his tall frame towering over both of them, his sword dangling menacingly by his side. He half extended his left palm and rested it gently, face down, on top of Deoraj's head. He half extended his right palm and rested it on top of Bhairavi's head. This was a Hindu symbol of an elder according protection to someone younger. Realizing what the *kotwal* had done, Deoraj and Bhairavi instinctively bowed down and offered a *mujra* in respect. The *kotwal* pulled out a large glistening gold coin from his pocket and laid it in Bhairavi's hand. He instructed his guard to escort the couple inside the city gates of Jaisalmer, then mounted his horse and sped away. The sarai owner and Lal Singh were looking at Deoraj and Bhairavi with a relieved smile and doting eyes, filled with paternal pride.

Deoraj and Bhairavi were chaperoned into the main market in Jaisalmer by the guard and left to their own devices.

The morning sun felt pleasant on this winter day. The market was still mostly closed, but sacks and stacks of merchandise were everywhere, even around the closed stalls or shops. People were moving goods around, with some shopkeepers stocking and re-stocking their merchandise. The market had a certain hum about it, a certain excitement, which filled Deoraj with hope, and he felt re-energized, shaking off the effects of the long journey. No one paid any attention to the young couple from Osian as they walked the market streets, looking for a temporary place to stay. They finally found an inn, which was very expensive. Having no choice, Deoraj and Bhairavi decided to pay, and they moved into a room. Having deposited their baggage in the room, they ventured out to look for a permanent place to live. Jaisalmer had very little rental housing and the few places available had very high rent or asked for some sort of a guarantee of payment from a high official or a rich merchant. They returned to the inn in the evening, exhausted and disappointed.

This became a routine for Deoraj and Bhairavi over the next several days. They would leave every morning, walk around in different neighborhoods, looking for a place to rent, and return in the evening, unsuccessful. The inn they were staying in was expensive and they were quickly exhausting their precious cash. They were advised by some to go and pay their respects to several rich Oswal merchants of Jaisalmer in the hopes that they might help the young couple out, due to kinship. Deoraj rejected the idea out of hand. He would not lower himself in that manner.

Finally, after a month, their luck changed. One morning they ran into Alam Khan near the spice market. He was on horseback in his usual black attire. He was happy to see Deoraj and Bhairavi and inquired about them. Alam Khan had been hired as a foot soldier in the Jaisalmer army and was granted a quarter to live in. He proposed that Deoraj and Bhairavi move into his quarter and he could rent the room next door from the family of another soldier in his regiment. Deoraj insisted on paying him rent. Exactly a month after they entered Jaisalmer, Deoraj and Bhairavi finally had a place of their own.

Deoraj's next agenda was to find work. He was ambitious and wished to start his own business. He had roughly Rs. 500 left from the sale of his house, and he started spending his days in various markets, observing the commerce on the streets and in the shops, trying to get ideas. All kinds of products were bought and sold in the markets, called *mandis*. One of the busiest markets was the precious metals market. Indians traditionally and to this day have a great appetite for gold and silver, both in jewelry or in bullion form. After several days Deoraj decided to enter the gold business.

One day, while in the gold market, Deoraj was approached by a man who said that he wanted to sell his gold shop, along with its inventory. His name was Jalchand and he wanted to move to the neighboring city state of Jodhpur to be closer to his family. Jalchand was a middle-aged Oswal and his manner, his dress and his language were all refined. Deoraj had seen Jalchand working deals in his shop many times and he felt comfortable negotiating with him. After some give and take, they agreed that Deoraj would buy forty ounces of gold at slightly below market price of Rs. 450, and Jalchand would throw in one month's rent for the shop free. Jalchand showed Deoraj the metal vault in the back of the shop where he had stored the gold. Deoraj took possession of the key to the vault, paid Jalchand almost his last penny, locked the shop and headed home to give the good news to his wife.

Bhairavi was ecstatic and she and Deoraj hurried to the shop to perform a *puja* to Lord *Ganesha* before Deoraj would commence his business. Alam Khan, who now lived next door, had just returned home and he accompanied them. Bhairavi performed the *puja* and Deoraj proudly gave Bhairavi and Alam Khan a tour of the shop. Deoraj then sat on a large square cushion, richly decorated with gold brocade on the floor of the shop. This was the customary seat of a merchant. Deoraj sold a couple of ounces of gold that day and took his first earnings home to Bhairavi and handed the money to her for safekeeping.

Bhairavi served dinner for her husband, smiling at him with great pride.

The next morning Deoraj headed out to his shop and assumed his position on the owner's cushion. About an hour later, a man dressed like a guard, riding on horseback, arrived at Deoraj's shop. Deoraj recognized him as the same young guard who had asked him for a bribe to let him enter Jaisalmer. The guard now had a winning smile on his face and told Deoraj that the *kotwal* wanted to see him immediately in his office.

Deoraj locked up the shop and headed out with the guard. When they reached the *kotwal's* office he saw two men having a conversation with the *kotwal*. Deoraj immediately recognized them as his customers from the previous day who had bought gold from him. As soon as they saw Deoraj they both pointed at him in unison and excitedly told the *kotwal*, "He is the one. He sold us brass pretending it was gold." The *kotwal* looked at Deoraj and his jaw dropped. His eyes filled with disappointment. He quickly composed himself and said, "I didn't expect this from you, boy. Did you come to Jaisalmer to cheat people?" Deoraj realized what was going on and his heart sank. He started to explain to the *kotwal*, but the two customers kept interrupting, animatedly asking the *kotwal* to accord Deoraj the strictest punishment in the book. The *kotwal* tried to calm them down and when they didn't, he motioned the guard to lead Deoraj to the back chamber with him.

In the back chamber Deoraj explained the whole story of how Jalchand had sold him fake gold and taken all his money. Being an experienced man, the *kotwal* immediately understood what had happened. He had heard that Jalchand was running heavy debts in the gold market and he left town owing a lot of people money. He had gotten an endless stream of complaints from people who were owed money by Jalchand since yesterday, when he apparently disappeared after scamming Deoraj.

The *kotwal* was beside himself with rage and pain. His heart ached for the innocent boy and his wife. He was particularly angered because he couldn't do anything to recompense Deoraj. Jalchand had skipped town, and who knew where he might be by then. Even if by some miracle Jalchand was apprehended, the *kotwal* was sure he would never recover any money from him. Out of concern and frustration, the *kotwal* gave Deoraj a good tongue-lashing for behaving in such a foolish manner.

"Never trust anyone in this town, Deoraj," said the *kotwal*, "and consider this an advice from an elder." He then went to the outer chamber and told the two complainants what had happened and that Deoraj was innocent. The two men kept insisting on pressing charges against Deoraj until the *kotwal* thundered, "If you keep this going, I will have the both of you arrested for filing a false complaint. There is no proof the boy sold you the fake gold. Trust me, once I have you thrown in jail, no one would be able to get you out." This silenced the two men, who quietly left. Deoraj too walked out, his dreams shattered.

What will I tell Bhairavi? he thought. *How could I have been so stupid?* he kept asking himself over and over. Many thoughts were going through his mind. All of a sudden he felt like a child. Barely twenty years of age, Deoraj felt like rushing into his mother's arms and crying, but his mother was no longer there to provide any solace. At one point he convinced himself that he should consume poison and kill himself rather than face Bhairavi. He had antagonized everyone in Osian, sold his house, brought Bhairavi to a strange and hostile city, and now they were penniless, all because of his doing. *Maybe the folks in Osian were right. Maybe I am a fool, a person of inferior intellect, an idiot who deserves nothing better. I don't deserve to live,* he thought. Then Bhairavi's face flashed in front of his eyes. Her lovely, innocent face, and she was pregnant too. He couldn't kill himself and leave her all alone, a widow, to be abused and mistreated by society. He had promised to take care of her. He was acutely aware of the miserable life his mother was forced to lead as a widow in Osian. Reluctantly, he decided to stay alive, and he slowly walked home to face Bhairavi.

Bhairavi's reaction surprised Deoraj. After the initial shock the young couple sat on the bed, leaning against the wall, Bhairavi warmly embraced Deoraj and held him tightly. Deoraj felt her warmth and it was as if a soothing balm was being applied to an excruciatingly painful wound.

"I will never trust anyone again," Deoraj kept repeating and Bhairavi kept hugging him tighter. Finally, when Deoraj went quiet, she started speaking.

"As far as I am concerned, you are still the smartest, most intelligent man in the world. Just because someone robbed us doesn't change that fact. We cannot let this experience change who we are. Not everyone is bad. We will be selective, but continue to trust people," she said.

"I will have to find a job now. I don't have any skills. It will be a lowly job at best. I will never be able to provide you the good things in life now—no gold ornaments, no jewelry, no fancy clothes, no house, no nothing. You will have to spend your whole life a poor man's wife, not to mention all the hardships that will come with that," lamented Deoraj.

Bhairavi responded. "I know one thing. With you, I will always live with dignity. I will take all the hardships and poverty in the world, as long as we live a life of dignity, and I will help you build that life. I will never complain, I promise you."

Deoraj detested the thought of working for anyone else, but now he had no other choice. He was never going to be able to save enough money to start another business, not in this lifetime. He dreaded the prospect of spending his whole life working in a lowly job, but Bhairavi's words gave him strength. *I have to do it for her. We will find a way to find some dignity and pleasure even while working for someone else,* he thought.

That wasn't all the bad news Deoraj was going to get that day. Bhairavi revealed that she had suffered a miscarriage that morning.

Deoraj woke up early every morning to look for a job. At the end of every day he would return, disappointed and exhausted. Bhairavi always kept a tub full of hot water ready for him to soak his tired feet and then served him flat hot bread with lentil and vegetables, all freshly cooked. Then the young couple would sit together, hand in hand, and tell each other about their day. Sometimes they would go for a late evening walk through the famed Jaisalmer markets and take in the vibrancy and get re-energized for the next day. Bhairavi was managing the household with the minimum possible expense, but they were down to their last few rupees and if Deoraj didn't find something soon they would be in big trouble.

One day, while looking for work, Deoraj saw several camel carts on the streets of Jaisalmer, carrying golden beige colored sandstone slabs. He watched the camel carts pull up near a site where a grand mansion was being constructed. The head of the camel cart caravan started asking people if anyone was interested in helping unload the sandstone. He promised good money. Deoraj volunteered and spent the next six hours unloading sandstone. It was grueling work and Deoraj was of a slender build and not very muscular. He thought about the last few pennies left in his copper cash box at home and egged himself on to finish the unloading. After six hours he got his first wages from the labor and rushed home to deposit them with Bhairavi.

Bhairavi went into the kitchen and mixed up some butter, hot water, broken wheat, almonds, sugar, raisins and cardamom powder in a pan and cooked it into a kind of sweet-smelling paste. It is called *lapsi* in Rajasthan and it is the traditional offering to *Sachiya Mata*. Bhairavi put some small pieces of coal inside a large spoon with a long handle. She poured some butter on the coal and lit it with a matchstick. She carried the smoking spoon in one hand and a small bowl of *lapsi* in the other and laid them both in front of the small idol of *Sachiya Mata* that she had brought with her from Osian and installed in their home. With folded hands, she thanked *Sachiya Maata* for Deoraj's wages. She then dug up the floor in one corner, pulled out the concealed cash box and deposited the money in it, burying it again for safekeeping.

The next ten years provided many life lessons for Deoraj and Bhairavi that they never forgot. Deoraj did what he could by odd jobs of manual labor. They survived, but barely. This was also an experience that shaped the emotions, thought processes and actions of their future generations. They realized that the worst part about poverty was not lack of money; it was the lack of respect. People tended to view the poor in a number of different ways, all of them demeaning. Deoraj and Bhairavi never complained about their situation to anybody. They never asked anyone for assistance or alms. They never begrudged anyone their better fortune. They never felt self-pity, and they were never bitter.

Deoraj didn't have any of these things in his nature and Bhairavi made sure that she would not be the cause of Deoraj ever succumbing to any weakness. She always maintained a cheerful disposition, ensuring that no matter how old her clothes got, she kept them clean and in good repair, and she always dressed smartly. She kept her home neat and tidy, putting her best foot forward and getting the most out of the few possessions they were able to have. She had also taken up sewing at home to supplement their income.

Despite this, not a week passed when Deoraj or Bhairavi did not have to endure some slight or another. When Bhairavi visited the Jain temple, for example, the priest would always make her wait while he preferentially took in the wealthier ladies for *puja* first. In the rare Oswal community gatherings that they did attend, men and women would not pull back from extending unsolicited advice on how Deoraj could advance himself. Wealthy Oswal families would give an example of Deoraj to their children as to what could happen to them if they didn't study or prepare themselves for some trade.

Deoraj and Bhairavi had become metaphors for failure all over Jaisalmer. It didn't help that almost all Oswal families in Jaisalmer owned their own businesses and were thriving, which further put the focus on Deoraj as a symbol of failure. Bhairavi was prone to frequent miscarriages, and not knowing this, some in Jaisalmer even suggested that Deoraj was not capable of producing a child. In the normal course of life people didn't feel like they had to abide by social niceties or follow rules of etiquette around Deoraj and Bhairavi, as someone of their status didn't deserve even basic politeness. The shopkeepers didn't flinch from taking petty advantage of them and overcharging them whenever an opportunity arose due to temporary shortage of some necessary commodity, something they would never do to the more affluent. The employers didn't hesitate to bargain Deoraj down to the absolute minimum wages.

No matter how much outward calm and dignity they tried to maintain, internally, the daily pinpricks and uncivilized behavior they were subjected to left an indelible impression on them. They didn't have much of a social life, as Deoraj and Bhairavi would not play second fiddle to anyone and not too many people wished to consider them their equal, with the exception of Alam Khan, Tulsa and Purvi.

Alam Khan was now a senior commander in the Jaisalmer army. He stood by Deoraj like a rock, providing moral support, but he felt helpless and frustrated that his friend would not accept any financial help from him. Over the years, Tulsa had established a good business in Kuldhara, and he was on his way to becoming one of the richest money lenders in Jaisalmer. Tulsa and Purvi had a son, Paras. They not only always stayed in touch, but were very careful not to hurt their friends' pride in any way.

Not once did either Deoraj or Bhairavi consider giving up their essential nature of self-reliance, self-respect, or kindness towards others and not thinking ill of others. They accepted their fate with no regrets, kept their faith in Sachiya Maata and in themselves, and trudged through life.

Deoraj had a curious mind and observed the political and social landscape of his immediate surroundings. Jaisalmer was a kingdom ruled in 1751 by Akhai Singh, who had ascended on the throne almost thirty years earlier. He was the descendant of the Bhatti Rajputs, the original founders of the Jaisalmer. The ruling Bhatti clan was always plagued by family rivalry and some of the clan members had either fled or were forced into exile on charges of treason. These exiles had taken refuge in neighboring states of Jodhpur and Bikaner, who laid claims on some part of the territory controlled by the kingdom of Jaisalmer. Over the last several years there had been many skirmishes between Jaisalmer and the other two states. Jaisalmer lately was on the receiving end and had been gradually losing territory.

Jaisalmer, like many other small kingdoms in India during the ancient and medieval times, started off as a refuge settlement. A refuge settlement typically had a ruling clan and a limited number of lesser noble families, constituting an elite group. Typically, this small band either conquered a limited area or settled in a previously unsettled area. Sometimes this group of elite carried with it a utilitarian population of peasants, workers, craftsmen and others. Other times, they co-opted the existing local population to perform the utility functions for the settlement. The kingdom was really organized along very simple principles. The entire activity of the population of the kingdom was mobilized to further the interests of the ruling elite. Therefore, it was a classic feudal system, where the social and political hierarchy was frozen and there was almost no social mobility. There was not even a pretense or an appearance made of promoting any social mobility and as all feudal systems, this too led to a stagnant, narrow and isolated culture, which was only shaken up sometimes by external aggression or internecine conflicts within the elite.

In this scheme of things, the concept of good governance was limited to providing basic law and order, a fair system of trial and punishment, collection of taxes and revenues and provision of national defense. Very *laissez-faire*, very free-market economically, while extremely conservative socially. There was no enduring set of formal laws which governed the state, but the ad-hoc dictates of the rulers. Therefore, the ruling clan could interfere in the free market anytime. It could, for example, impose any tax on anyone at any time. It could retroactively terminate contracts or confiscate any private property at will. There was almost no concept of a ruler's duties towards the non-elite in the areas of health care or education or any other common community endeavor. It was extremely rare for a ruler to organize or finance any kind of state-level relief effort for even natural calamities such as famines, earthquakes or floods. People were pretty much on their own. It was all about the ruling clan and the elite and that was the way it was.

The larger consolidated empires were a little different. They did undertake public works such as construction of public buildings and roads, also established universities and had in most cases a written set of laws, but the motivation for all of this was to glorify the rulers, not for the public good. A lot of the differences between a large empire and smaller kingdoms were simply due to the sheer size of the empire where centralized ad-hoc decisions by the emperor could not govern the lives of people in far-flung places. However, even in the case of larger empires, ultimately, it was all about the rulers, and people were pretty much left to their own devices. Since by definition the ruling elite held a special place in the society, they could make decisions relating to normal people and could be influenced to make certain decisions in return for payments in cash or kind. This system of payment in return for favors, now called corruption, was considered par for the course in India and accepted without challenge.

What this meant was that life was very unpredictable and difficult for the non-elites, including the men of commerce. They were constantly subjected to the whims of the elite, who missed no opportunity to extort money from the business people. The businessmen had to keep everyone in the elite happy by making regular payoffs in the form of gifts called *nazaranas* in Rajasthan, or in the form of offering a share of their profits or in the form of non-repayable loans, which really amounted to *nazarana*. In addition, the businessmen had to be very careful that they did not offend anyone within the power structure in any way. History is replete with countless examples of businessmen who inadvertently got on the wrong side of the rulers and were ruined as a result. Businessmen had to be entrepreneurs, diplomats, schmoozers, fixers, all at the same time. All in all, it was very difficult to do business in India during those times. Businessmen, therefore, developed a reputation in India which lasts to this day of being unprincipled and willing to do anything to succeed. They actually had to, given the socio-political situation.

Dev stopped, feeling tired after narrating this long story.

"So it was as difficult if not more to do business in India in the past as it is now," said Kunal.

"Yes, even more difficult, I think", said Dev.

"And India was as corrupt then too," said Ranika, his daughter.

"Yes, very much so, and the ruler's word was law. There was no rule of law as we know it," said Dev.

"At least in modern India there is some pretense of a modern state thinking about public good. When did that concept start creeping into Indian consciousness?" asked Kunal.

"Deoraj did not know this in 1750, but there was some change in mindset later, after the British took control of India in the nineteenth century. Despite their ulterior motives and systematic exploitation of the Indian colonies which resulted in reducing India from an economic super-power to unprecedented backwardness and poverty, some individual administrators made an attempt to introduce the idea of a modern state within Indian kingdoms. But, being primarily preoccupied with pursuing British interests and their perception of Indians as an alien and inferior race, the British Indian government at its level did not, with any seriousness, set about the grass roots institution building which is required for a democracy to thrive. Whenever and wherever British interests came into conflict with genuine reform within the Indian society, which was almost every day, reform and grass roots institution building naturally took the back seat.

Such was the nature of colonialism and racism. This, however, did not stop the British from imposing a western-style constitution on India before they left in 1947, with the assistance of the British educated Indians. It was bound to fail because this constitution did not have any legs to stand on, as there were no supporting grass roots institutions in place for it to succeed, nor was there any change in mindset on the part of Indians, which was also a pre-requisite of success for any such constitution. To this day, therefore, corruption—"ad-hoc-ism"—and the classic feudal mindset is well accepted and entrenched and despite all the outward trappings of a renaissance-style western constitution and democracy, Indian political and social landscape was fundamentally no different from what it had been since ancient times and right through medieval times.

In India today corruption is considered a part of life; it is not immoral. In India today it is considered perfectly acceptable for even the democratically elected leaders to brazenly pursue their own narrow interests at the expense of public good, along the same lines as absolute rulers of the past. In India today, governance is still by and large via ad-hoc, and "on-the-spot" decision made by the elite, as opposed to a strict following of a formal set of laws, despite the fact that such a formal set of laws does exist on the books. Such a system by definition is diagonally opposed to a merit-based system and promotes cronyism and perversion of the reward system," said Dev.

"No wonder that a man like Deoraj could never succeed and realize his dreams," said Kunal.

"He sounds like a man way ahead of his times—a twenty-first century man stuck in the eighteenth," said Ranika.

"I don't think fundamental human values ever change. I really think that people in any century instinctively know what is right and what is wrong. Some people chose to do the right things, while a vast majority didn't, choosing to do what was socially acceptable and convenient, regardless of the right or wrong. Deoraj was one of those rare persons, who had the strength of character to chart his own course and do the right things. Maybe he was just made that way; he couldn't be any other way. He was able to take massive blows and a tremendous amount of punishment for what he believed in. In effect he was capable of making great sacrifices for his beliefs, and these were not religious beliefs, per se. He was not an overtly religious man—quite the contrary. It was his wife, Bhairavi who was somewhat religious, even though only mildly. He had somehow arrived at his own code and he never deviated from it," said Dev.

"He was an amazing man and he paid a heavy price every time for doing the right things. Life never failed to knock him down every chance it got. Did he suffer a final knock out?"

"I really must get some rest now. Wait till tomorrow and I will tell you the rest of Deoraj's story," said Dev.

"Goodnight, Papa." said Kunal and Ranika.

Dev continued with the second part of Deoraj's story the next day.

Chapter 6 - Story of Deoraj – 2
1750 – 1772

One evening in 1750, a full ten years after their arrival in Jaisalmer, when Deoraj was twenty-nine and Bhairavi was twenty-six, a beautifully appointed horse-drawn carriage pulled outside their house. The carriage was drawn by four horses and had a canopy of smooth fabric of ornate design. Tulsa and Purvi stepped out of the carriage, along with another young man. His name was Vasu and he was also dressed in the traditional Paliwal style turban.

"We have come in uninvited today, without any advance notice," said Tulsa, as Purvi hugged Bhairavi.

"You know it is your house, Tulsa, you and *bhabhisa* are always welcome," responded Deoraj.

"Is our friend Alam Khan in his room next door? Shall I go and check?" asked Tulsa.

A little while later Tulsa appeared with Alam Khan and joked, "Commander Alam Khan here is becoming a very important man in Jaisalmer. We have to get him married now."

"Find me someone as pretty as *bhabhisa* (Purvi) and I will gladly do so," Alam Khan countered.

Tulsa introduced their guest, Vasu, to everybody.

After dinner, they all relaxed and started talking.

"Excellent dinner *Bhabhisa*," said Tulsa, looking at Bhairavi.

"Yes, delectable", added Vasu, who was clean shaven and looked very young for his age, locks of jet black hair curling out of his red Paliwal turban. He was impeccably dressed in clothing made of luxurious fabric and brocade.

Bhairavi couldn't help but notice the elegant gold brocade bordering Vasu's muslin dhoti.

"Thank you very much," said Deoraj in all sincerity, "but really this is nothing. Since we didn't know you were coming, we couldn't make adequate preparation".

Atithi Deo Bhava, was an important cultural tenet across India and Deoraj and Bhairavi practiced it with all their heart. It literally meant "guest is equivalent to God."

"Vasu arrived in Kuldhara from the neighboring Jodhpur, just a couple of days ago," said Tulsa, "he was running a successful brocade business there, which he wants to relocate to Jaisalmer."

"I don't know much about brocade, except that Bhairavi likes it," said Deoraj.

"THE golden brocade of India is known the world over as *kimkhab*, nothing less than a dream. The name itself conjures up a sense of pure luxury which, in ornamentation, is matched only by the splendor of jewelry. So what is brocade really? A textile woven, almost prayer like, by the nimble fingers of the *naqshband kaarigar,* the master craftsman, who lives in crowded and mystical lanes. It gets its opulence from gilded strands which are floated with pure silk threads to create a lush surface, textured with motifs that romanticized flora and fauna. The gold strand itself is made of pure gold, melted and pulled out of successive minute holes, each one smaller than the last, until it is stretched to the desired thinness. In Indian culture this border is used to design dresses, particularly festive dresses, and has always been in great demand." explained Vasu very patiently.

"Why Jaisalmer?" asked Deoraj.

"Well, there is great unfulfilled demand for brocade in Sind province, which borders Jaisalmer," said Vasu, "it will be much easier to cater to Sind from Jaisalmer than Jodhpur".

"Yes, that is true", said Deoraj.

"Vasu is opening up a brocade workshop here in the main Jaisalmer market," said Tulsa, "the Paliwal elders in Kuldhara have agreed to finance part of the enterprise".

"Congratulations, and welcome," said Deoraj.

Vasu bowed slightly to express his gratitude.

"Vasu is looking for an honest and hard working person to manage his workshop, since he will be constantly travelling to market the brocade in places far and wide," said Tulsa, "I cannot think of a better man than you, Deoraj".

Deoraj was surprised, but he managed to keep his excitement in check and looked at Bhairavi. Purvi noticed Deoraj looking at Bhairavi and gently touched Bhairavi on her arm, smiling, as if reassuring her. Bhairavi gave her assent to Deoraj with an eye signal.

"I am overwhelmed, Tulsa," said Deoraj.

Tulsa leaned over towards Deoraj and whispered something in Deoraj's ear.

"That is most generous, Tulsa. Are you sure the business can bear that salary for me," said Deoraj.

"You let me worry about that, Deoraj. I am so happy to have you join us in our enterprise," said Vasu with childlike glee.

Vasu and Deoraj stood up and sealed the deal with a warm embrace.

Within a month Vasu had established the shop, hired the master craftsmen and they were in business. Deoraj earnestly set about learning the business and soon his honesty, integrity and hard work, along with Vasu's energy and entrepreneurship, put the business on an even keel. Deoraj was now bringing in a decent salary and Bhairavi started saving and putting some money away, while using some of it to upgrade their living standard.

In the same year, 1750, Bhairavi got pregnant again. This time she told Purvi about her anxieties and Purvi insisted that Bhairavi move in with Tulsa and her until the first trimester was over so Bhairavi could be on complete bed rest to avoid any chances of a miscarriage. Once the pregnancy reached its second trimester she could go home, as the risk would have receded. Tulsa stopped by and had a word with Deoraj. Deoraj was concerned that it might be too much of an imposition on Tulsa and Purvi to take care of Bhairavi for three months, but Purvi was insistent. They had a house full of maids, and besides, Purvi wanted to take care of her friend. Alam Khan had finally gotten married and he assured Bhairavi that Deoraj could have his meals at his house, while Bhairavi was away. Deoraj reluctantly agreed and he waved after Bhairavi until Tulsa's carriage carrying Bhairavi disappeared from sight.

In early 1751 Bhairavi gave birth to a healthy baby boy. Deoraj was doing well enough financially to hire a midwife and Bhairavi quickly recovered. Soon after the birth, they all got together for dinner at Tulsa's house in Kuldhara. They all started brainstorming about baby names. Alam Khan and his wife Naaz suggested Khan Mal. Khan meant "chief" in Persian.

"Too grand," said Bhairavi. Tulsa suggested Daulat Mal. Daulat meant "wealth."

"What if he doesn't get rich?" asked Deoraj and everybody laughed.

"Rich or poor, all I wish for is that he grows up to be a confident boy, proud of who he is," said Deoraj.

Everyone thought for a while. "I got it," said Purvi. "Guman Chand," she said firmly. "Guman means pride." Everyone broke into applause.

"Guman Chand it is," said Bhairavi as she gently caressed the baby's soft scalp. Everyone around the table pulled out a gold coin and offered it as a gift to Guman Chand. Purvi had prepared a hamper full of gifts for Bhairavi and the baby. Naaz had brought a tiny gold ring and a gold bracelet made of little gold beads, a traditional gift for newborns in Rajasthan. She gently slipped the ring on Guman Chand's tiny index finger and wrapped the bracelet around his wrist.

The following week Bhairavi arranged a prayer service to *Sachiya Maata*, who was traditionally offered the baby's first hair. Only when this offering was made, *Sachiya Maata*, being the godmother to all Oswal families, gave her formal blessing and officially accepted the baby into her extended family. Purvi, Bhairavi and Naaz sang traditional Rajasthani songs to welcome a new baby into the family. Purvi pointed out to everyone that she had never seen Bhairavi so happy and filled with joy before, and she was right. Bhairavi had a special glow and she felt that her family was now complete.

Jaisalmer Camel trail through the Desert
Courtesy Jacob Linhar - Belgium

Jaisalmer Fort at Night
Courtesy – Angela Corrias – website – www.chasingtheunexpected.com

Later that year, Naaz also gave birth to a baby boy, who they named Akbar Khan, and Purvi gave birth to a baby girl, who was named Jeta.

Deoraj continued to work at the brocade shop for another ten years. Jaisalmer had a new ruler, Mulraj, who was crowned in 1762, at the death of his illustrious father, Rawal Akahi Singh, who had ruled for over forty years. Rawal Mulraj faced several challenges to his authority from within his own family and his hold on power was initially very shaky. To consolidate his power, he relied on his prime minister, Swaroop Singh, an Oswal. Swaroop Singh was a shrewd, ruthless individual who slowly usurped most of the state power in his own hands, leaving Mulraj as a mere figurehead. He placed his own loyalists in strategic positions within the kingdom, including in the army, and created his own parallel power base. In the name of protecting Mulraj he kept a strict check and vigilance over the members of the royal family. Even the heir apparent, Rae Singh, the eldest son of Rawal Mulraj, was kept on a very tight allowance. Swaroop Singh justified all this to Rawal Mulraj by explaining that curbing the powers of the members of the royal family was Mulraj's best security. During the reign of Mulraj and Swaroop Singh taxes on businesses were raised, arbitrary charges were imposed on rich merchants, both the Oswals and Paliwals, and levies on farmers were increased, causing mass dissatisfaction among those classes. More intrigues and conspiracies were hatched in the royal palace, both by Swaroop Singh and the merchants against each other.

In such an environment, at the end of 1762, when Deoraj was forty-one years old, his boss Vasu, along with Tulsa, paid him a visit one evening. Even though their brocade business was doing well, Vasu was ambitious and he had been able to locate even better opportunities in the neighboring province of Sindh. He wanted to sell his brocade business in Jaisalmer and move on. Tulsa had come with a proposition for Deoraj to buy this business from Vasu, pay him whatever he could and Tulsa would finance the rest of the purchase price on favorable terms. By now Deoraj had worked in this shop for a long time and knew the business inside out. He had saved a decent amount of money working at the shop for almost twelve years now, so he could afford to buy the business. He also knew that the price offered was a bargain. He was not sure, however, that, a man like him, who was not very "flexible," could succeed in business in the treacherous environment of Jaisalmer.

On the other hand, he now also had to think of Guman Chand's future. He observed that there were a couple of very slim lanes in this feudal setup of Jaisalmer for upward mobility. They both were long shots and chances of success weren't very good in either. Alam Khan was pursuing excellence as a fighter in the armed forces and could achieve high honor and success within the society and a certain place in the ruling elite.

Not being a fighting man himself, Deoraj looked at the only other remaining option that his friend Tulsa had taken and was now offering to Deoraj: the route of being a merchant in one's own right. He saw all around him Paliwals and Oswals breaking into the upper echelons by becoming major financiers of the ruling elites, and in due course becoming part of the ruling elite. There were any number of Oswals who were high level officials and very powerful ministers in Indian kingdoms, some of them even becoming more powerful than the ruler himself, but how they got there was a case study in human behavior. Since the rulers in these kingdoms were supreme and were not accountable to a specific set of laws, the Oswals had to depend entirely on the ruler's mercy or favor to climb up the social ladder. As a despot's moods swung violently from day to day, the Oswals had to calibrate their responses with the ruler's moods.

There were times when these Oswals had to go down on their knees for no fault of their own, while there were other times when they simply had to advance huge amounts of money to the ruler, either in the form of personal loans or increased taxes. A majority of the time they had to forgive these loans to the ruler, something extremely difficult to swallow, while still maintaining a cheerful disposition. There were even times when the Oswals indulged in petty intrigues, blackmail, and sometimes even murder to climb up the ladder or to maintain their position in court. To protect themselves, money lenders to the ruling classes started a practice of charging interest in advance and charging high interest rates to cover the high bad debts. It was a perfectly logical and financially sound response to the arbitrary non-payment of debt by the royals, but the practice later continued and was used to exploit poor peasants, which is what gave money lenders a bad name. The origins of the practice of high interest rates and advance payment of interest were in response to royal avarice.

Deoraj was now mature enough to observe that in order to attain a high level of financial success, a person typically had to enter and operate in a brutal no-holds-barred world, where scruples, self-respect and all that made a being human, had to be left behind. Violating treaties, breaching contracts, bribes, corruption, intrigues, black mail, extortion, the ability to prostitute oneself, lies and deception were the main features of such a world. Even if one was willing to play by these rules, the element of luck was always an important factor and there were no guarantees of success.

Deoraj shuddered at the possibility of playing this no-holds-barred game to attain financial success. That was what he disliked in the Oswals—the willingness to bend over backwards, to do anything at all, moral or immoral, for upward mobility.

How could he get ahead? It was a dilemma. He asked Vasu and Tulsa to wait in the outside chamber while he went inside to discuss this proposal with Bhairavi.

"No, I absolutely prefer to stay poor than to do those things. I thought you abhorred those things as well. Why are you even thinking about it?" asked Bhairavi.

"I can't help but think about this offer seriously, particularly now that we have Guman Chand. I don't want him to have the tough life you and I had, Bhairavi," said Deoraj.

"But you will not make it and you will be even more miserable. It is a fiercely competitive world and you know it," said Bhairavi.

"What kind of a world are we living in, Bhairavi? Will not hard work, intelligence, integrity, and entrepreneurship count for anything? You know, my dreams get shattered every day. How will I live out my life, Bhairavi? How will we all? What will happen to Guman Chand?" asked Deoraj, desperation creeping into his voice.

"We are fine the way we are. We really are. Please stop worrying. You have a good job. We are comfortable now. Besides, we have the greatest gift of them all—Guman Chand, a gift from *Sachiya Maataa* herself. We don't need anything else," said Bhairavi.

"But…but…sometimes I question myself. Is it really wise to make this tradeoff? Are all who play this game stupid and we the only smart ones out there? Most successful people I have met, no matter what else you say about them, they are not stupid. As a matter of fact, they are all highly intelligent. If they all, all of them, so easily give up human values in exchange for monetary success, what makes us so sure we are right and they are wrong? Maybe man is just another animal, meant to prey on each other," said Deoraj.

Bhairavi stood up and walked to the back veranda where Guman Chand was being tutored by his teacher. She whispered to Deoraj to take a good look at him, and then she walked over to the *Sachiya Maata* idol in the *puja* room.

"Look at *Sachiya Maataa*," said Bhairavi.

Deoraj looked.

"Take a good look. Are you still of two minds?" asked Bhairavi.

"What if I promise you, in front of *Sachiyaa Maataa*, that I will not change at all? I will operate my business with the highest ethical standards. We will stay true to the great sacrifices we have already made. I promise, we will not go corrupt now, at the age of forty-one. Please let me take this one last chance. You know I have always dreamt of running my own business. Don't you think that despite all odds, I have the inner power and strength to run this business honestly and yet succeed? Have you lost your abiding confidence in me, Bhairavi?" asked Deoraj.

Bhairavi looked at Deoraj. She smiled. The picture of the young Deoraj dressing up ceremoniously to leave Osian for Jaisalmer flashed through her mind. *How hopeful he was then to make a success of himself,* she thought. *I will not deny him his last chance to achieve his dream.*

"I think if any man can do it, you can. I told you once, and I am telling you again, you are the smartest, most intelligent and hardest working man I know. Go ahead with it," said Bhairavi.

Deoraj embraced Bhairavi and walked out to convey the news to

Vasu and Tulsa.

Vasu had done well in the brocade business due to two things. He was a very good salesman and had established lasting relationships with merchants and royalty alike. In addition, he didn't deviate from the existing business practices of the brocade merchants. They all used slightly lower purity gold and silver in their products, thereby making an extra profit. This would have been acceptable, except that they did not disclose this to the clients and sold the brocade claiming high purity. This had become an accepted practice in the brocade business. The first thing Deoraj did was to reverse it in his shop. He started purchasing high quality precious metals to use as input for his product and thereby cut his profit margins to dangerously low levels. On top of that, he was not as good a sales person as Vasu, and gradually his client list dwindled despite the higher quality product he produced.

Over the next several years, the Jaisalmer ruling establishment, led by Rawal Mulraj and his prime minister, Swaroop Singh, imposed crippling taxes on all merchants which hit Deoraj hard. He barely met his business expenses, such as salary for his master craftsmen, and he actually was financially worse off running his business than he had been when he was working in the same shop as an employee. He invested whatever little profits he made in better tools and innovative designs to come up with more luxurious looking brocade, with very little returns. He worked grueling sixteen-hour days and somehow managed to keep the family afloat. Bhairavi supported him all the way, lifting his often sagging spirits by reminding him that at least he was his own boss and that they had a business to pass on to their son.

"We are investing in our son's future," she would say, although she herself sometimes wondered whether they would actually be passing on an asset or a liability to their son by having him inherit this business.

One morning in 1770 a man showed up at Deoraj's brocade shop in the Central Market of Jaisalmer. He introduced himself as an Arab merchant and was attired in Arab robes. His name was Mustafa, and he pulled out a long brocade border with Deoraj's seal on it.

"Does this brocade come from your shop?" he asked.

"Yes," said Deoraj, recognizing his product immediately.

"This is the best, your designs are very popular in Arabia," said Mustafa.

"Thank you," said Deoraj.

"I would like to take some fresh design samples with me to Arabia and see if I can create a large market for them. The brocade from India generally has a bad reputation in Arabia because it uses low-purity precious metals, but your brocade is pure. I have tested it. That is what people like in my country," said Mustafa.

He went on to inform Deoraj that a merchant from Sindh had brought this brocade with him to Arabia and it had become quite popular there, so popular that Mustafa decided to travel himself to Jaisalmer to find more designs by Deoraj to take samples back to Arabia. Mustafa wanted to be the sole distributor of Deoraj's brocades for all of Arabia if he could get some success in the market with the samples he was carrying back.

Deoraj was ecstatic. Finally, he found someone who appreciated his artistic designs. He was on the verge of getting a big break and he was so close to success. He asked his master craftsmen to work extra hours, preparing exquisite brocade samples.

Deoraj had a new spring in his steps and felt currents of excitement travel through his fifty-year old body as he rushed home to inform Bhairavi of the good news. Bhairavi shared his happiness, but cautioned him that it was not a certainty yet and it was quite possible that the Arabians may not like the new samples. Deoraj did not want to think of that contingency and went about his business with renewed vigor.

One year passed, then two, and Deoraj never heard back from Mustafa. He kept struggling and one night he felt an acute pain in his chest, so acute that he cried out loud. Bhairavi found him clutching his chest and rolling from side to side in excruciating pain. She called out to Guman Chand, who upon seeing Deoraj in such pain, immediately rushed out to get the *vaid* (the doctor of Ayurveda, system of Indian medicine). The *vaid* arrived and prescribed some medication, which calmed Deoraj down, and he fell asleep.

"It is his heart," informed the *vaid*.

"How bad is it? He will be all right, won't he?" asked Bhairavi.

"His heart is weakened considerably. It is hard to tell how bad it is," said the *vaid*, "but people are known to survive for years, sometimes even decades, if they take care."

Bhairavi was overcome with emotions. As a teenager, Deoraj had set out to lead a life of dignity. He had by and large succeeded in doing that, except that he succeeded in very little else. *That is not exactly true,* she thought. Deoraj had managed to keep Bhairavi happy and raised an affectionate and capable son like Guman Chand. He had also created a business out of nothing, even if it was not terribly successful, but Deoraj had never compromised his principles and values, something that not too many people in India could boast of—not many merchants, not the high officials and not even many royals.

Deoraj is a true prince, she thought, *not just my prince, but a prince among men, and I am proud to be his wife.* Deoraj had once promised telepathically to always take care of Bhairavi, and he had. All through the years of struggle, of failures, of lows, of barely scraping by, he always shielded Bhairavi from the true unpleasantness of life. He took all the blows upon himself like a man, a real man, a true prince.

Now it was her turn. Bhairavi silently resolved to take good care of the ailing Deoraj and make his remaining years as pleasant and happy as possible. She went to *Sachiya Maataa* and prayed for a long life for Deoraj.

The *vaid* recommended that Deoraj not exert himself too much, cut down drastically on his work schedule and follow a strict diet and medicine. Deoraj was fifty-two years old and his business career was over, his business still fledgling and teetering on the edge, but all that was about to change dramatically soon, almost from the first day that his twenty one year old son Guman Chand would take over.

It was pretty late at night, by the time Dev finished the story.

"What a life and what a man! Deoraj's story puts to a lie the proposition that if you work hard, work smart, be a person of strong values and a person of principles, do everything right, that you will always succeed," remarked Kunal.

"One cannot deny that in addition to all the factors you have mentioned, Kunal, there is one very strong factor which can make or break a person. That factor is 'luck.' As long as Lady Luck doesn't smile on a person, he or she never makes it big. Fortune never smiled on Deoraj," responded Dev.

"I know you are tired and you should rest now anyway, but tomorrow you must tell us about Deoraj's son, Guman Chand Patwa," said Ranika.

The next day Dev narrated the story of Seth Guman Chand Patwa.

Chapter 7 - Story of Guman Chand - 1
1772 AD to 1775 AD

At the age of twenty-one, in 1772, Guman Chand took over the family brocade business. Purvi and Tulsa attended the official hand-off ceremony organized by Deoraj. They were accompanied by their children. Paras, 22, was a handsome young man who had taken after his father and had already started playing a significant role in Tulsa's now far-flung enterprise. Jeta, a couple of years younger, was striking like her mother and looked lovely in her colorful orange *lehanga* and sky blue chiffon *orni*.

Guman Chand had been visiting Tulsa and Purvi since childhood and over the last couple of years had started paying Jeta special attention. Jeta readily reciprocated. Their parents were only too happy to encourage the relationship, but there were societal complications.

Oswals and Paliwals, though on good terms, like most Indian groups, were very clannish when it came to marriage. Marrying out of their immediate caste or group was taboo and a marriage between Guman Chand and Jeta would cause serious problems for Deoraj and Bhairavi within the Oswal community and Tulsa and Purvi within the Paliwal community. Deoraj, being more independent and having been done no favors by the Oswal community, didn't much care about the consequences. In fact, in his heart he was eager to defy the Oswals and secretly enjoyed the prospects of watching the Oswal community's discomfort over this alliance, but Tulsa and Purvi owed a great deal to their Paliwal kin. It was the Kuldhara Paliwals that had welcomed Tulsa in their fold, helped him start his own business, and done everything that could be expected from a community. Therefore, Tulsa and Purvi were in a quandary over how to resolve this issue amicably. Their one hope was that if Deoraj's business flourished, they could then convince the Paliwals that an alliance with Deoraj's family was socially advantageous, but so far that had not occurred. If all else failed, Tulsa and Purvi had conveyed to Deoraj that they would go ahead with the marriage and face the wrath of their community if they had to, but they wanted to give Guman Chand some time to succeed.

Also in attendance at the hand off ceremony were Alam Khan and Naaz. Alam Khan had become the *kotwal* (sheriff) of Jaisalmer and was present in his full regalia. He was accompanied by his son, Akbar Khan, who at the age of twenty-one had just been made a captain in the Jaisalmer army. Deoraj and Bhairavi went through the ceremony of formally handing over the business to their young son, Guman Chand. At the end of the ceremony, Deoraj escorted Guman Chand to the *gaddi* in his shop and seated him. A *gaddi* would be akin to the CEO's chair in his office today.

Guman Chand had become a bright young man. He was educated by local tutors in the basics, but he was not much inclined towards academics. He was not very tall or imposing looking, but what he lacked in looks, he made up for in spirit. He was good natured, energetic, optimistic, and overall had a pleasant personality. He started apprenticing at the brocade shop with Deoraj at the age of fourteen and by the time he was eighteen he had acquired a total grasp of all aspects of the business. He was already traveling to neighboring kingdoms on selling trips and slowly was acquiring more clients. He was turning out to be a much more accomplished sales person than his father Deoraj.

Deoraj now visited the shop in late afternoons and returned in the evenings focusing mainly on designing, which was his passion. Guman Chand had very ably taken over the rest of the operations. Only a few days after Deoraj's semi-retirement from business, the Arabian merchant Mustafa showed up at the shop. He asked for Deoraj, but when told about what had happened, he sat down for a detailed conference with Guman Chand. It had taken him a couple of years to establish a dealer network all over Arabia, but now he had done it and he wanted to place a large multi-year order. Would Guman Chand be in a position to expand his operations to fulfill such an order? Guman Chand used his well-developed negotiating skill to convince Mustafa that all orders will be filled and delivered on time. Mustafa was very particular that only the high purity precious metals be used in the brocade, and Guman Chand made a solemn promise to do so. Mustafa wanted a formal meeting with Deoraj to finalize the contract. He had developed a great deal of respect for Deoraj's integrity and artistic abilities and it was mainly out of this respect that he had staked the business on his shop. Deoraj duly met with Mustafa and they made a solemn commitment to each other to be business partners for as long as they both lived. Mustafa made a last request of Deoraj to personally oversee the process of developing new brocade designs, which Deoraj readily agreed to.

Guman Chand immediately embarked upon setting up a large workshop, procuring the best craftsmen and the best equipment. The news of the contract spread quickly all over Jaisalmer and even in the surrounding kingdoms, becoming a hot topic of discussion among the merchant community. Several competing brocade merchants tried to intercept Mustafa on his way back home and offered all kinds of incentives and enticements to cancel his contract with Guman Chand and instead assign it to them. Mustafa was a man who valued integrity. He was disgusted by all the maneuverings and the intrigues, and he made it very clear that nothing on earth could make him terminate his contract with Guman Chand.

Guman Chand also received an invitation to visit the *Rawal* Mulraj in the Royal Fort of Jaisalmer, delivered to Guman Chand by Kotwal Alam Khan himself. Alam Khan cautioned Guman Chand that Prime Minister Swaroop Singh Mehta, the real power behind the throne, was responsible for this invitation. Swaroop Singh's grandfather, Mehta Fateh Singh, was a man with a noble soul who loyally served his master, Rawal Akhai Singh, the grandfather of current Rawal, Mulraj. Mehta Fateh Singh sacrificed his life to protect Rawal Akhai Singh in a battle. As a reward, his succeeding generations were offered the ancestral prime-ministership of Jaisalmer, the next most powerful position in the kingdom after the ruler himself. Fateh Singh's son and then his grandson, Swaroop Singh, took full advantage of this and gradually usurped most of the state power unto themselves. By the 1770s, Swaroop Singh was the real power behind the throne and the real ruler Mulraj had become a puppet in his hands.

The next morning, Guman Chand dressed himself in a beautifully brocaded light blue and gold *sherwani*, with a matching blue turban, with a sprinkling of glittering brocade on the edges. He had on white cotton tight pants, called *churidars*. Tulsa and Purvi had sent their son Paras to accompany Guman Chand to the Fort. Young Akbar Khan had also joined the party to the Fort, along with a couple of young presentable employees from the shop. They all mounted their horses and rode through the Central Market in formation on their way to the Fort. It was a tactical decision by Guman Chand to raise the profile of this visit to the Fort so that all of Jaisalmer would be aware of it. This would serve a dual purpose: Guman Chand's status would be enhanced in Jaisalmer mercantile community, which would help him in his future business dealings, but more importantly, Guman Chand was betting that if the whole town knew of their visit, Mehta Swaroop Singh would think twice before indulging in any kind of foul play, such as arresting him.

The five young men rode until they took the last turn out of town and started to climb up the road to enter the Fort. They were met at the gate by the commander of the Praetorian Guard, who escorted the young men to the Maharavali Palace, high up on the hill. The palace was grand and beautifully adorned by delicately carved sandstone. Guman Chand and his entourage were led along a long passage inside the palace to the back, outside a small chamber, where Maharawal Mulraj held his private audiences. The chamber had a large carved wooden door, which was closed, and two guards were posted, one on either side of the door. The commander asked the guard to announce to the Maharawal that Guman Chand had presented himself. The guard came out and said that only Guman Chand would be allowed in, and he waved him in.

Guman Chand entered the Rawal's chamber and was taken aback by its simplicity. He had expected richly carved balconies and walls studded with semi-precious stones. Instead, it was a largely barren room with ordinary walls and no balconies. Maharawal Mulraj was sitting upon a throne-like chair, which was upholstered in richly brocaded silk fabric. Guman Chand immediately recognized the brocade as being from one of Deoraj's premium design collections. Behind Mulraj stood a tall, stooping man, wearing expensive clothes but also wore a sneer befitting a thug. After Guman Chand had bowed, as per protocol, Mulraj introduced the foul-looking man as Prime Minister Swaroop Singh Mehta. Guman Chand greeted him appropriately and Swaroop Singh informed Guman Chand that in his infinite wisdom the Maharawal had decided to honor him by according Guman Chand the privilege of *baithak*, meaning to sit in the presence of the ruler. Without this formal privilege, non-royals could not be seated in the presence of the ruler and would have to stand through the entire audience or whenever the ruler was present. Guman Chand politely thanked them both and took a seat right across and below Maharawal Mulraj's throne. The royal also granted Guman Chand the title of *Patwa*, which meant "master brocade dealer."

"To what do I owe this high honor of your audience, my Lord?" asked Guman Chand confidently. He felt no nervousness or queasiness in the presence of the two highest personages in Jaisalmer.

"His Highness the Maharawal has heard good things about you, Guman Chand," spoke up Swaroop Singh. "He wishes to know if the news is true."

"What news, Your Excellency Prime Minister?" asked Guman Chand.

Swaroop Singh's foul expression turned into an even uglier sneer, thought Guman Chand.

"Don't trifle with the Maharawal, Guman. The news about your big contract with the Arabian merchant," said Swaroop Singh.

"Yes, with the Maharawal's blessings we have arrived at a very favorable agreement which will not only benefit the House of Deoraj, but the entire kingdom of Jaisalmer. Given the existing tax rates, it should yield thousands of rupees to the state treasury," explained Guman Chand.

"Be that as it may, Guman Chand, I am sure you are aware of the political situation facing us at the moment. All the neighboring states, particularly Bikaner and Jodhpur, have been eying Jaisalmer territory for quite some time now. The Maharawal's army has fought many battles and skirmishes over the last few months to protect our territory and citizens so that among other things, merchants can conduct business unhindered," said Swaroop Singh.

Guman Chand saw where this was heading and why he had been ordered to come. He had heard from others that whenever and wherever Swaroop Singh smelled money he would invite the merchant and put him through this shake-down routine. Many merchants were sick of this style of extortion and they blamed Rawal Mulraj, who had become terribly unpopular in Jaisalmer. Not everyone knew that he was totally under the thumb of his minister, Swaroop Singh, and even those who knew blamed Mulraj for allowing himself to be dominated by his minister in that fashion.

To be fair, the Bhattis and other Rajput rulers of Rajasthan had a tradition of shaking down the merchants. The Bhattis in particular started off by extorting money from the caravans that passed through

Jaisalmer, even before they had formally established their kingdom there. When it became a lucrative affair, the Bhattis decided to form the Kingdom of Jaisalmer with themselves as the ruling clan. Even without the pernicious influence of Swaroop Singh, over the centuries Bhattis and other Rajput rulers extorted money from whichever source they could find, usually merchant entrepreneurs, in the form of arbitrary taxes and levies well over and above regular taxes.

Indian Wedding Dress with Gold Brocade
Courtesy Wikipedia – Under GNU Free Copyright License

Maharawal Mulraj of Jaisalmer(1762-1819)
Courtesy Wikipedia - Under GNU Free Copyright License

In many cases, individual merchants were targeted either because they had run afoul of the ruling family or because they had reaped hefty profits on their business deals, and royal decrees were passed, naming individuals who had to pay those extra taxes. It was also quite common for the rulers to issue confiscation orders for all of a particular merchant's assets when the merchant had offended the ruling establishment in any way. There were also innumerable cases where a merchant was falsely implicated in some criminal case and their properties were attached to the state. There were even cases where through no fault or action of the merchant at all, a deliberate quarrel was picked up by the ruler with that merchant on trivial grounds with the sole intent to confiscate or impounding his entire property overnight via a simple royal decree.

It would be a very interesting historical debate: who was a bigger victimizer, the merchant or the ruler in Rajasthan? While most merchants were no saints, history will come down hard on the rulers for being the bigger victimizers and more money hungry—far more than the merchants. The final assumption was that the more scrupulous the merchant, the more he suffered at the hands of the rulers, because the shrewd and the unscrupulous always found ways to keep the rulers happy by victimizing other innocents.

True to form, the meeting between Mulraj, Swaroop Singh and Guman Chand was a classic exercise in extortion. Rawal Mulraj, the hereditary ruler of Jaisalmer, from the long line of the proud Bhatti Rajput Dynasty under the influence of Mehta Swaroop Singh, was reduced to shaking down merchants for cash in person. Swaroop Singh Mehta was an Oswal Jain like Guman Chand, but no two people could be more dissimilar. Mehta Swaroop Singh was a tyrant, a debauched man, an uncultured and petty man, who had few redeeming human qualities. His sole purpose in life was to consolidate more wealth and power in his own hands.

"The Maharwal thinks it is only fair that you contribute an extra Rs. 30,000 every year while your contract is in effect. You will agree with me that the Maharawal has extended extreme kindness towards you by demanding such a small percentage of your overall profits from this contract," said Swaroop Singh.

Guman Chand was tongue-tied. He had no experience in dealing with this kind of extortion before and he was at his wits end as to how he could negotiate them down to a reasonable amount. His contract could not bear an additional annual burden of Rs. 30,000.

Observing that they had Guman Chand totally flummoxed, Swaroop Singh attempted to put a quick closure on his demand.

"You may thank the Maharawal for his kindness, bow, and then leave, but before you go you must sign this special levy note, which essentially says that you agree to pay Rs. 30,000 annually to the treasury of Jaisalmer for the duration of the contract," said Swaroop Singh.

Guman Chand recovered quickly.

"With all due respect, I wish to inform Your Highness that the contract is not as generous as rumored. I can provide you figures which will clearly demonstrate that we will not be in a position to pay a penny more than Rs. 5,000 in extra levies to the treasury," countered Guman Chand.

After a couple of hours of negotiations, Guman Chand was forced to threaten to take his business out of Jaisalmer to neighboring Bikaner, and Swaroop Singh settled on an amount of Rs. 10,000 per year. Guman Chand walked out, feeling relieved that it was an amount he could afford. He went home and related this incident to Deoraj. Deoraj was beside himself in rage.

"How could you agree to such a thing, Guman?" yelled Deoraj. "and how can a Bapna submit to blackmail and extortion?"

"I had no choice, Baba. We now have a large establishment, with many people in our employ. They all depend on us. We have a contract with Mustafa. He depends on us. You yourself have given him your solemn word that you will fulfill the contract, no matter what. In our larger interest we have to make this payment, right or wrong," said Guman Chand.

This led to an argument which lasted several days, until Bhairavi's intervention caused both Deoraj and Guman Chand to agree to disagree and move on with the business at hand of delivering the best quality brocade to Mustafa. This argument symbolized the differences in personalities and approach between father and son. Where Deoraj was a purist who was willing to pay any price for standing up for what was right, Guman Chand was more pragmatic. He was more flexible, nimble and less confrontational. This difference in philosophy, personality and approach was a source of great heartbreaks for Deoraj going forward.

"We now have so much," Deoraj lamented, "and the more we have, the more we compromise. How ironic!"

Over the next year and a half, the brocades from the House of Deoraj became famous in places far and wide. Guman Chand was travelling like a man possessed, establishing branches and offices all over India and appointing agents and *munims* in some foreign countries. By 1774, less than three years after Guman Chand had taken over his family business, he boasted an operation with over 80 branches all over India, the Middle East, Iran and even Afghanistan. Guman Chand had become a business phenomenon, who was able to create an enterprise of great magnitude solely based on his business acumen, management and organizational skills. Deoraj continued to masterfully manage the artistic side of things back home in Jaisalmer, while Guman Chand focused on sales, distribution and contracts. Everywhere, he was now known as Guman Chand *Patwa* (*Patwa* being an honorific given in those days to a master in the brocade business).

What was even more amazing about Guman Chand's rise was that it occurred during a time of great chaos on the Indian political and social scene. The Mogul empire had practically collapsed and each independent state had their own rulers, set of laws, mercantile traditions, etc. To be able to reconcile with innumerable variations in business practices all over India and even internationally during the time of major transition and still attain the magnitude of success that Guman Chand did in a very short time was a rare and remarkable feat.

While Guman Chand was busy churning out brocade from his expanded workshop and increasing his revenues and profits at an amazing rate, dark clouds were gathering over Jaisalmer. Squeezing merchants and peasants for money and even looting caravans was a common practice among Rajput rulers in Rajasthan, including the Bhattis of Jaisalmer. Swaroop Singh, however, took it one step further. Swaroop Singh started doing something which was unprecedented in the history of the Rajputs. He was also a sexual deviant and went on a kidnapping spree, abducting young women and girls across Jaisalmer and the countryside. He had gotten together with some like-minded minor royals within the Bhatti clan, and recruited a few mercenaries from the Jaisalmer armed forces. These mercenaries were organized into a private army, controlled personally by Swaroop Singh, which was used to abduct women who would catch the fancy of Prime Minister Swaroop Singh and his coterie of minor royals.

Rajput women were out-of-bounds, since kidnapping them would have caused repercussions which even the powerful Swaroop Singh could not have withstood. Oswal women were difficult to get to as well because of the system of *purdah* among the Oswals, which meant that Oswal women in general did not go out in public without male escorts. This meant that Paliwal women were the primary victims of Swaroop Singh and his company's debauchery. It was a well-known fact that Paliwal women were in general very pretty. This was compounded by the fact that, unlike the Rajput and Oswal women, they walked around in public in relative freedom, as the Paliwals did not practice *purdah*. Their beauty and freedom of movement gave Swaroop Singh's mercenary army plenty of opportunities to kidnap some of these women. In many cases these women disappeared without a trace, never to be returned to their villages or their families. Even in cases where the women did come back to the villages, the stigma of being used and abused caused their lives to be ruined, as no man in those days would marry such a woman. This went on for quite some time and the Paliwal community was in an uproar. Rawal Mulraj and Swaroop Singh had already alienated the Oswal, Paliwal and the farming community of Jaisalmer (roughly 80% of the population) by imposing heavy and arbitrary taxes on them. The unprecedented abduction of their women was too much to bear for the Paliwals. They made several representations to Rawal Mulraj, sometimes even presenting credible evidence of Swaroop Singh and other royal's complicity in these crimes, but Mulraj was weak and remained a mute spectator. The emboldened mercenary army began breaking into homes and abducting some Rajput and Oswal women.

One day Swaroop Singh's debauchery directly struck the House of Deoraj. News arrived from Kuldhara that Tulsa's daughter Jeta was enjoying a morning walk in the center of the village when a group of horsemen rode into the village and abducted Jeta. No one could see the horsemen's faces as they were masked, and a badly organized Paliwal rescue party had failed to turn up any clues. Deoraj, Bhairavi, Guman Chand, Alam Khan, Naaz and Akbar Khan all rushed to Kuldhara to be with Tulsa and Purvi in their moment of grief. Guman Chand had also taken his senior *munims* (managers), along with a bodyguard force of eighteen fully-armed men.

Ever since he had expanded the business, Guman Chand had had to retain a private guard force to accompany him on his many travels. A shocking increase in lawlessness had given him due cause to increase the strength of his private force. The atmosphere in the traveling party was one of sadness and sorrow. Bhairavi could not stop crying, as she was the closest to Purvi. Besides, in her heart, Bhairavi had already accepted Jeta as a daughter-in-law. Guman Chand was strangely quiet, as he was not given to emotional displays, but internally he was seething. Alam Khan and Naaz were in a rage too, as Jeta had also been close to them since childhood. Alam Khan further blamed himself for not posting guards in Kuldhara to protect the Paliwal women, including Jeta, from this fate. As a *kowtal*, he felt he should have seen it coming. Akbar felt terrible for his friend Guman Chand.

When the party reached Tulsa's grand residence in Kuldhara, there was already a large crowd gathered there. The crowd consisted of

Paliwals from Kuldhara and neighboring Paliwal villages. When they noticed Alam Khan and Deoraj walk into the compound with their families, the crowd parted respectfully to give them way. Purvi stood up as soon as she saw Bhairavi and fell into her arms, sobbing hysterically. Deoraj noticed Tulsa standing in a corner in absolute shock. Deoraj had never seen Tulsa in such a weak state before. The normally spirited and flamboyant Tulsa simply stood there, helpless, staring out the window into nothingness. Deoraj and Alam Khan went and stood next to him, gently putting their arms around him. Tulsa simply looked at Deoraj, said nothing and went back to staring into nowhere.

Guman Chand approached Tulsa's son Paras and took him into the next room, along with Akbar, and they explored options on what could be done next. The first thing Guman Chand told Paras was that if and when Jeta was found, he would like to marry her without any delay, notwithstanding any objections from the Paliwal community. Akbar, who was now a captain in the Jaisalmer army, promised to have his troops discretely search the entire Jaisalmer fort, including its basements, dungeons, outhouses and underground chambers. Deoraj and Alam Khan convened in the front yard with the elders in the Paliwal community. Several other prominent Oswal businessmen and farmers had also reached Tulsa's residence. All the elders sat in a circle and discussed what their next steps ought to be.

First, a joint Oswal-Paliwal delegation went to meet with Rawal Mulraj and spoke to him bluntly about their concerns and the possible repercussions on Jaisalmer and Rawal Mulraj. "If things don't change drastically," they warned him, "the majority of the population of Jaisalmer will welcome an attack by the rebel nobles who are your brothers and nephews." "Undoubtedly this attack will be backed by the neighboring states of Jodhpur and Bikaner, and you will soon become ex-Rawal Mulraj."

The next thing they did was to suspend payments of all taxes until all the abducted women were returned. The Oswals told Mulraj in no uncertain terms that their community would socially boycott Mulraj. Whenever Mulraj would cross any Oswal business or residential establishment, everybody would move inside and shut all the doors and windows, thus indicating that they didn't even want Mulraj's shadow anywhere near them, symbolizing that even seeing his face was anathema for them.

Guman Chand, Akbar and Paras worked tirelessly, talking to

people, chasing down every lead and conducting their own searches with the small force in Guman Chand's employ. Alam Khan sprung into action like a man possessed, working like a one-man army, investigating every possible lead and shaking down criminals for information. He was approached by the crown prince, Rae Singh, who, unlike his father, possessed a character in keeping with the noble Rajput. Rae Singh was generous, educated, and genuinely concerned about the welfare of his subjects. He gave some concrete leads to the *kotwal* and asked Alam Khan to escort him to Tulsa's house. Deoraj, Guman Chand and Bhairavi were at Tulsa's house when Rae Singh arrived. Rae Singh expressed deep regrets on behalf of his family that such a thing could happen during Bhatti's rule. He informed everyone that Swaroop Singh had managed to appoint his own loyalists as commanders of the Jaisalmer army. Rawal Mulraj was a mere puppet now. If the *kotwal* could find the missing women, Rae Singh would personally lead a raid with some loyalist soldiers to release them. Even the puppet commanders would dare not oppose this raid, as the rank and file in the army would not want to be openly associated with these disgraceful kidnappings.

Over next few days the search continued. Finally, Alam Khan got a break. One of his guards had heard from one of Swaroop Singh's personal guards that some of the kidnapped women were hidden in the basement of Swaroop Singh's residence, about a mile outside of town. Alam Khan sent his spies to conduct a discrete surveillance of the prime minister's house. They came back and reported that indeed the women were in the basement. Crown Prince Rae Singh was informed. He gathered a small bunch of loyal Jaisalmer soldiers. Guman Chand and Paras volunteered, along with Guman Chand's personal guard force. They planned and executed a daring mid-day raid, when Swaroop Singh was on tour of a village half a day away. There was hardly any resistance and the women were freed. Jeta was one of them. The women were transported by camel carts to Kuldhara and from there to their respective homes.

Swaroop Singh was incensed by the raid. He had been caught by surprise. He did not expect Rae Singh to openly confront him and plan the raid in complete secrecy. Swaroop Singh's vast spy network had no inkling of the impending raid. He decided to seek vengeance. "I will not only get him removed as crown prince," he muttered under his breath, "but I will kill Rae Singh."

Fortunately, since Deoraj had insisted that neither Alam Khan nor his son Akbar participate in the raid, their role in this whole affair never came out and they both escaped the minister's wrath. As for Guman Chand, he had earned the eternal enmity of the foul man. Swaroop Singh swore to destroy Guman Chand and his entire family, even if it took him fifty years.

Jeta was received warmly by Purvi and Bhairavi at Tulsa's house. She was devastated mentally, but physically safe. It took a lot of caring and understanding on the part of Tulsa and Purvi to bring Jeta out of the shock of this ordeal. Finally, Purvi decided that it was time for the one event to take place which should completely heal Jeta.

Tulsa visited Deoraj's spacious new home in Jaisalmer. The year was 1774. It was late morning and he had timed the visit to ensure that Deoraj would be home. Tulsa greeted Deoraj with folded hands, as opposed to the normal warm embrace. Tulsa also addressed him formally as "*Seth*," a title reserved for the merchants who had achieved high status. Deoraj was surprised.

Tulsa kept his hands folded and then said solemnly, almost reverently, "Seth Deoraj, I am here in all humility to offer my daughter's hand in marriage to your son, Guman Chand. It will be my high honor if you accept her into your illustrious family."

Deoraj moved forward and covered Tulsa's folded hands in his own and said something to him, choking up in emotion. Tulsa soon left Deoraj's house, which was highly unusual, maybe even ominous, as whenever the two friends met they spent hours together.

Deoraj didn't go to work that afternoon. When Guman Chand came home that evening, both Deoraj and Bhairavi were sitting in the *baithak* (drawing room), with very serious faces. Guman Chand's heart skipped a beat. He wondered if Deoraj's health had taken another turn for the worse, since normally he didn't like to miss his afternoons at work. Besides, his parents' somber faces indicated something was amiss.

"Guman, come and sit over here," said Bhairavi.

Guman Chand walked over by her.

"We have picked a nice Oswal girl for you," said Bhairavi, as if the matter was final.

Guman Chand stared at his mother, stunned, then he looked at his father. *I am the one they say who has flexible morals. What has happened to them?* thought Guman Chand, pinching himself to see if he was having a bad dream.

"Pardon me?" was all Guman Chand could mutter.

"Yes," said Bhairavi. "We didn't think an ambitious boy like you, already a rich man in your own right at the age twenty-two, with ambitions to climb even further, would want to marry a girl who had been kidnapped and stigmatized for that. An alliance with Seth Mohan, on the other hand, could propel us to the stars, both socially and financially."

"I care about Jeta and she worships the both of you. Besides, what kind of people would desert someone when they are really down? What if I don't want this alliance with Seth Mohan?"

"Then you are free to leave this house—at once," said Bhairavi in apparent anger.

Guman Chand stood up. Looking straight at Deoraj he launched into a heartfelt diatribe.

"I never considered you as just my parents. I always looked up to you as *Devi* and *Devata* respectively (meaning God and Goddess). You have led an exemplary life, with no compromises, no matter how hard the times were. You raised me to always do the right thing. I know I have disappointed you sometimes, but I readily agree it was my weakness, not any shortcoming on your part. I may not have measured up to your expectations, but still, I am Seth Deoraj's son, not a complete charlatan, not an out and out opportunist. It may be hard for you to believe, but I have tried hard to model my character after you. I never thought my parents, whom I worship, would disown me for doing the right thing. If that's what you want, I will leave this house right now and never return." he turned towards the main door.

Deoraj stood up and intercepted Guman Chand. He embraced Guman Chand tightly and informed him that the whole thing was just a joke. Deoraj had never been this proud of his son before, not when his Guman was winning customers for the business at a young age, not when he was negotiating highly complex contracts which benefitted the House of Deoraj immensely, not even when he went to rescue Jeta.

They then told Guman Chand what had transpired that morning and how Tulsa had come with an offer of marriage and Deoraj had readily agreed, telling Tulsa that Deoraj had waited a long time for this moment. Since it was a formal ceremonial visit, Tulsa left immediately, as he couldn't wait to inform Purvi of the good news. All three of them burst out laughing. Deoraj asked Guman Chand to immediately summon the two senior *munims* (managers) to the house. He climbed into his beautifully appointed carriage, drawn by six famed Marwari horses. He asked the driver to take him to Kotwal Alam Khan's mansion.

Later that night there was a meeting at Seth Deoraj's house. Only a small group of friends and senior employees were present. In the meeting they discussed the wedding arrangements. The first task was for the *munims* to take Bhairavi and Naaz shopping that whole week so they could put together a fabulous dowry to be presented by the House of Deoraj to Tulsa and Purvi. In Paliwal tradition, it was the reverse. The father of the bridegroom offered a dowry to the father of the bride. In the meantime, Alam Khan and Akbar were supposed to acquire a wagon full of assorted flowers, dry fruits, fresh fruits and gold coins. As official representatives of the House of Deoraj, they were to personally escort the wagons over to Tulsa's house the next morning, signifying the formal acceptance by Deoraj of Jeta's hand in marriage for Guman Chand. In addition, Alam Khan was to take a formal message to Crown Prince Rae Singh, informing him of the impending alliance. In the message, Deoraj requested an appointment with Rae Singh to personally inform him of the marriage and to seek his blessing. It was customary to seek the blessing of the Ruler in Rajasthan when any significant event took place in an important family in his kingdom. Since the Oswal and Paliwal community were still boycotting Rawal Mulraj, Deoraj substituted Rae Singh for Mulraj.

Deoraj set out to the main Jaisalmer market to order large quantities of fireworks and illumination for the whole house. Deoraj loved bright lights and the child in him was excited at the thought of daily firework displays for the whole month of the wedding celebrations. While growing up, Deoraj coveted not gold, not diamonds, not land, not expensive things, but fireworks. Growing up, he had seen fabulous firework shows organized by his uncles in Osian during annual Diwali celebrations. He so wanted to have them in his own house. Diwali was the festival of lights in India which was traditionally celebrated with lights and fireworks. Fireworks were expensive in India. To his great disappointment, first his mother and then Bhairavi had denied him that extravagance during his years of struggle. *Bhairavi is not going to be able to deny me my fireworks now,* he thought with childlike delight. *There will be ample fireworks and bright lights at Seth Deoraj's house now for the whole month of my son's wedding celebrations.*

Guman Chand was given only one task, actually a negative task. He was jokingly asked by all not to go and see Jeta till the wedding.

Bhairavi organized a *puja* service at her house for *Sachiyaa Maataa*. She also organized a family visit to the nearby Jain temples to pay obeisance to Lord Adinath and Lord Mahavira. Her abiding faith in *Sachiyaa Maataa* and Jainism had given her solace during some very tough times of her life. She wanted to thank them for being so kind to her family now.

Deoraj was brimming with joy. This was more than Guman Chand's wedding; this was a celebration of Deoraj's own life and Bhairavi's. After years of struggle, Deoraj had finally climbed the ladder of success. Even though, technically, all the success really occurred after Deoraj stepped down and Guman Chand took over the business, the foundation that Deoraj had laid was largely the cause of the family's rise. It didn't even occur to him that he had accepted for his highly successful and sought-after son a girl who had the stigma of having been abducted or that he was doing Tulsa some kind of a favor. Deoraj was very clear in his mind that, contrary to what people generally thought in those days, Jeta was in no way responsible for her own abduction. As a matter of fact, she had gone through hell and he felt terrible for her.

Deoraj had known Jeta since her childhood. She was a headstrong girl, confident and non-compromising, when it came to her self-respect. Deoraj saw a lot of himself in Jeta, and in fact saw her as a validation of all of his own struggles. He loved her for that and looked to her to balance out the more materially ambitious, driven and sometimes compromising Guman Chand. She was smart, tough when necessary, sweet-tempered with Bhairavi and perfectly suited in every way to be part of Deoraj's family. She would be totally loyal and a great support for Guman, and they formed a perfect couple. She was also beautiful, compared to Guman Chand's rather rugged looks. He couldn't have wished for a better daughter-in-law. The Paliwal community had dropped their objections to this union in view of the kidnapping and the subsequent rescue. Deoraj was not sure how the Oswal community would react. On the one hand, he had received sympathetic messages from some elders, while others were still involved in a whisper campaign, branding the impending union as a scandal. However, Deoraj also knew that he was an affluent *Seth*, so most people would just accept it.

One of the few good uses of money, Deoraj thought, smiling mischievously to himself. At the age fifty-four and somewhat ailing, Deoraj still sometimes harbored thoughts of teenage rebellion and rattling the powers-that-be, although in the eyes of Jaisalmer, he now was one of the leaders of the establishment, a respected elder. He shared this gloating moment with Bhairavi, who gently chided him. "Your son is getting married shortly and you still behave like a little boy .When will you ever grow up?"

"Tomorrow," responded Deoraj. "Today I want to be a boy," he continued as he chased Bhairavi around and around in the bedroom.

The next day a woman came to see Bhairavi. She was dramatically, almost theatrically dressed, her *lehanga* tighter and shorter than usual and the *choli* more revealing of her ample bosom. Her face was heavily made up, with black *kajal* (eye paint) extending out from the corner of her eyes. She was ruggedly beautiful, which was characteristic of the *banjaras*, a tribe of desert nomads. Her body was as nimble as a snake and her movements were graceful like a dancer. She was wearing thick sliver anklets, which made a gentle rhythmic sound when she walked (not to be confused with the *ghunghroos* that Indian dancers wear on their ankles, which really are musical instruments in their own right). Both of her lower arms were totally covered by sliver bangles right up to her elbows. They echoed the rhythms of her anklets in perfect synchronicity. She was accompanied by a bevy of beautiful girls, one more elegantly shaped than the next, and a tall man with a totally weathered face and wrinkled skin. He wore a bright orange turban, again typical of the *banjara* tribe.

The woman introduced herself as Gulabo Bai and said that she was sent by the "Solanki Thakurian" (the wife of Crown Prince Rae Singh). Bhairavi had only heard of the famous Gulabo Bai, who was the unofficial dean of all *Dholnis* in the Jaisalmer area. *Dholnis* were known not only for their own physical beauty, but also for the beauty of their singing and dancing. While they performed all Rajasthani dances, they specialized in the famous *Kalbelia* dance, which was a kind of a sensuous snake dance, performed in Jaisalmer and its neighboring areas. Gulabo Bai was so much in demand that she now only performed for the first-line royals, but the Crown Princess Solanki Thakurian had told Gulabo so many nice things about the House of Deoraj that Gulabo could not resist visiting them. Gulabo, Naaz and Bhairavi charted out the musical program for every night of the month-long wedding celebration, including the special and never-before-presented items to be performed on the night of the *khas* reception (a reception that was restricted to only close family friends and the royal family). Gulabo quoted a price which Bhairavi thought exorbitant. After a moment of getting used to the figure, though, she laughed and gave her assent. Gulabo had totally charmed Bhairavi and Naaz.

Crown Prince Rae Singh's wife told Gulabo that the word around town was that the *Sethani* (Seth's wife, in this case, Bhairavi) did not haggle like other Oswal women and it turned out to be true. Gulabo, for her part, was very impressed with the regal bearing of both Bhairavi and Naaz and eagerly promised that the quality of music and dance at Guman Chand's wedding would be no less than any royal wedding. After promising thus, Gulabo and her entourage of graceful women were chaperoned out of Seth Deoraj's house by the man with the weathered face. Bhairavi and Naaz watched in serendipity and awe as the mysterious and enchanting *banajras* of the desert tiptoed out the main door in a single file, their anklets and bangles leaving behind a mild but refreshing fragrance of sweet chimes.

Deoraj and family continued the wedding preparations right through autumn of 1774. At the time, the Indian political landscape was marred with turmoil, internal strife and chaos. Several years ago by 1760, the Moghul emperor in Delhi was reduced to a mere puppet. The Marathas, a new Hindu power, originating from South Western India (around Bombay), had conquered most of the Mogul territories south of the Punjab. The Marathas had ambitions to expand further north in the Punjab, Kashmir and even to the borders of Afghanistan. Alarmed by the rise of this Hindu power, in 1771 the Mogul emperor Shah Alam II aligned himself with several other Islamic dispensations such as the Rohillas and the Nawab of Oudh and invited the Afghan king, Ahmed Shah Abdali, to attack the Marathas. Abdali's army and the Maratha army joined battle in the famed battlefield of Panipat and the Marathas were defeated.

The Marathas, though, continued to be a major power in all of Central and Western India. The British were ruling Bengal (Eastern India) through their proxies. In 1771, Warren Hastings arrived in India as the new Governor General of the East India Company. The Marathas had started making raids into various Rajasthani kingdoms, but Jaisalmer was spared, by virtue of its relative inaccessibility. Internationally, trouble was brewing for the British in the American colonies, as a group of native-born intellectuals were considering a revolt against the British overlords in order to become a new independent country. Osian, on the other hand, was a town in decline. Many Oswal families had moved out and a chronic water shortage caused the population to go down alarmingly, which in turn devastated local merchants. Deoraj's uncles were both dead and their families had moved to neighboring places such as Jodhpur and Bikaner, struggling to re-establish themselves. They were, however, sent proper invitations to attend the wedding functions at Jaisalmer.

Even in those prevailing conditions, Jaisalmer continued to prosper. Deoraj, Kotwal Alam Khan and Tulsa were busy passing out wedding invitations for Guman Chand and Jeta's marriage. They had visited all of their close family, friends, and the Royal family, with the exception of Rawal Mulraj himself, personally. Mulraj was still being boycotted by the Oswal community and practically all the population of Jaisalmer in opposition to the Rawal's over-reliance on Swaroop Singh, his imposition of draconian taxes on the Paliwal, Oswal and the farmer community, and lastly, for the disgraceful episodes of abduction of women for pleasure. Rawal Mulraj, on the other hand, was distraught. He had heard of the glorious celebrations going on at Seth Deoraj's house every evening, with sumptuous food and fabulous entertainment. Everyone who was anyone in Jaisalmer and the neighboring states was in attendance. The two rulers of the neighboring states of Jodhpur and Bikaner had been invited and were expected to arrive soon for a two-week-long stay in Jaisalmer to participate in this grand affair.

Rawal Mulraj felt embarrassed and slighted at being the only one left out of the grandest affair to be held in Jaisalmer for years. His prime minister, Swaroop Singh, was the only other notable not invited. He summoned his son, Rae Singh, to confer on how to make peace with the Oswals of Jaislamer. Rae Singh promptly suggested the obvious. Whenever a ruler wanted to make amends, he performed a symbolic ritual of visiting the aggrieved community, with a tunic spread out with both his hands. This ritual was called *palla failana* in Rajasthani, which literally meant that he had come like a beggar with an empty cloth, seeking forgiveness. Prime Minister Swaroop Singh vehemently opposed this idea, but Rawal Mulraj was personally very keen not to be embarrassed in front of his two rival rulers and the entire city of Jaisalmer by being so openly boycotted. He asked his son Rae Singh to start mediation efforts by offering to cut some of the most draconian taxes on the residents of Jaisalmer. Rae Singh promptly conducted these negotiations successfully and then Mulraj visited the merchants' establishments in the center of Jaisalmer, performing the *palla failana* ceremony. Such a ceremony was highly humiliating for any ruler and thus performed very rarely, and being such a public ceremony, it was an amazing spectacle for the citizens of Jaisalmer to witness. The Oswals,

Paliwals and the farmer communities formally forgave Rawal Mulraj, but hard feelings remained on both sides.

Deoraj still refused to invite Rawal Mulraj personally. However, Tulsa himself took the initiative and prevailed upon Deoraj to visit the royal palace. Rawal Mulraj graciously waived the Rs. 10,000 tax he had levied on Guman Chand as a wedding gift. All was now clear for a month-long unrestrained and joyous celebration in Jaisalmer.

There were actually two wedding celebrations going on. As per tradition in Rajasthan, the bride's side had its own celebrations and the bridegroom's side theirs, leading up to the marriage. Then a wedding party, consisting only of the men from the groom's side, departed from the groom's house and traveled to the bride's house. Sometimes the bride's residence was several days away. In Guman Chand's case, Kuldhara, Jeta's native village was only about a day away. The wedding party departed Jaisalmer three days before the wedding. It consisted of hundreds of people and a grand caravan, including Rawal Mulraj, Crown Prince Rae Singh, other rulers, important noblemen, wealthy merchants, Guman Chand's staff from many of his 80 branches, personal friends, relatives, associates and a contingent of *banjaras*, including dancers and musicians. The caravan was flanked not only by the personal guard of Guman Chand, which now numbered in scores, but also a large company of Jaisalmer army. They all traveled under the dual crests, one of the Royal House of Jaisalmer, and the other of the House of Deoraj. Tulsa had made arrangements for refreshments for the entire wedding party along the entire route to Kuldhara.

Upon reaching Kuldhara, each guest in the wedding party was greeted with a gold coin, flowers, and a fragrance, and escorted to guest houses specially constructed by Tulsa for the wedding. Numerous ceremonies in Hindu, Jain and Paliwal Brahamincal traditions took place over the next couple of days. Finally, on the wedding night, all the guests gathered in a large open area adorned with flowers and decorations. There was a flat, paved platform right in the middle of the open area. In the center of the platform was a pit, with some chopped wood. At the appointed time, a group of priests appeared and took their seats on one side of the platform, chanting hymns and lighting the fire. It was just about dusk, and the groom would be the first to arrive with his wedding party, which was welcomed heartily by the bride's side. Guman Chand walked up to the platform and took his seat on the platform, facing the priests.

Guman Chand looked dapper in his gold *sherwani* (long coat) and crisp white *churidar*. His turban was the ceremonial red, with a sprinkling of brocade. After about fifteen minutes of chanting by the priests, Jeta was chaperoned in by her bridesmaids. Guman Chand had known Jeta since childhood and was well aware of her beauty, but her stunning appearance and entrance that evening took his breath away. She was wearing a beautiful red chiffon *orni* and a red silk *lehanga*. Both of them were beautifully adorned by the best brocade that Deoraj could design, a task that took him many days. The bride's costume was also studded with semi-precious stones. She was wearing elegant gold jewelry, studded with diamonds, rubies and emeralds. She had an ornament on her forehead. She walked slowly and deliberately to the platform and took her place next to Guman Chand. They were joined by their respective parents. The priests had the couple take their vows and after taking each vow, he had the couple walk around the fire one time to formalize the vow. After seven walks around the fire, Guman Chand and Jeta were husband and wife. Tulsa and Deoraj and Purvi and Bhairavi hugged emotionally, tears in their eyes. The crowd showered the newlyweds with rice and flower petals. Fireworks lit up the sky and the festivities went on.

The descriptions of Guman Chand's wedding celebrations have passed on in family lore from generation to generation. The celebrations were colored with music, dance, drink, fireworks, light, beautiful men and women, costumes, camaraderie, lovely human interaction and joy.

Deoraj couldn't help but think wistfully that Guman Chand's wedding was as colorful as his own was colorless. After almost twenty years of a rough childhood and thirty years of hard labor, Deoraj Seth had finally arrived. And what a way he announced it!

Story of Guman Chand - 1

Rajasthani Banjara Dancer
GNU Open License

Rajasthani Banjara Dancers
Performing the Kalbelia Dance in a wedding – a sensuous snake dance, a
long standing tradition of Jaisalmer area in Rajasthan
Courtesy – Lake Nahargarh Palace Parsoli Rajasthan - Website

Chapter 8 - Story of Guman Chand – 2
1775 AD – 1777 AD

Deoraj and Bhairavi were in the prime of their lives. They had never been this happy before. They had a highly successful son, a lovely daughter-in-law, and a well-earned and well-deserved high status in Jaisalmer. It was almost as if there was nothing more they could ask for. Bhairavi continued to be a devotee of *Sachiyaa Maataa*, thanking her every day for her good fortune. She also made several pilgrimages to nearby Jain temples. Jeta accompanied her to these pilgrimages, despite the fact that she had not converted to Jainism. Neither Deoraj nor Bhairavi pressured her to change her religion, and they were just happy to have her in their house.

Guman Chand continued to make progress by leaps and bounds, but his nemesis Prime Minister Swaroop Singh continued to cause him trouble every opportunity he got. Swaroop Singh had sworn eternal enmity with Guman Chand and his entire family. He was further aggrieved when he was the only notable not invited to Guman Chand's wedding. He had not yet gotten a chance to physically harm Guman Chand, who was always well-known, well-respected and well-guarded in Jaisalmer and throughout all his travels, but he missed no opportunity to instigate Rawal Mulraj to impose unreasonable and unfair taxes and levies on Guman Chand. Despite the truce between Mulraj and the merchant community of Jaisalmer, mediated by Rae Singh, oppression and excessive taxation started creeping up again. Guman Chand would never think of leaving Jaisalmer, but he started seriously thinking of moving his commercial base elsewhere, where the climate would be friendlier.

The British East India Company had arrived in India at the dawn of the seventeenth century in hopes of generating windfall profits. Instead they found themselves mired in local politics and maintaining an army which was an extremely expensive proposition. To make matters worse, they encountered a great deal of difficulty identifying products to trade. The English in the mid and late eighteenth century did not manufacture products that had much demand in the Indian market and the spice trade did not reach the volumes the Company had hoped for. Therefore, the British East India Company after its arrival in India found itself suffering heavy losses, both on account of its trading operations and also on account of it having to spend a small fortune to maintain an armed force. They, therefore, were desperately seeking newer and better trading opportunities.

In 1773, the Company, operating out of the eastern Indian state of Bengal, which it had practically taken over by violently and treacherously overthrowing the *Nabob* of Bengal and placing a puppet as a ruler, finally discovered the lucrative business opportunity, they so desperately were seeking. There was big demand for opium in China, and India had several opium-growing areas, including in Bengal. The British created an opium-buying monopoly in Bengal, where opium growers could only sell opium to the East India Company. The Company then turned around and sold it to various agents in Calcutta on the condition that the opium be smuggled into China, as direct import of opium into China was illegal.

There were other opium-producing areas in India, in Rajasthan and the surrounding Malwa region which were not under the British yet, and therefore not under the British monopoly. Traders and merchants in these areas were free to buy opium from the growers and smuggle it themselves into China or sell to intermediaries, who would then in turn smuggle it into China. This was a lucrative trade and provided great opportunities for Indian merchants who knew the geography and had contacts, around Jaisalmer, as Jaisalmer was a stop on the land route to China. For Guman Chand, it was a golden opportunity to move his business base to an opium-growing area and then use his familiarity and contacts in Jaisalmer to transport opium into China. He was well capitalized and eager to get into this trade.

The other opportunity Guman Chand was looking at was the one his father- in-law-specialized in: the money lending business. There was always a shortage of capital in the peasantry and the upper classes alike. Capital was in great demand and interest rates in India were traditionally high. With the exception of the few first-line royals, lending was done against security and it was very easy to foreclose on the security in the event of non-repayment. This profession was infested with unscrupulous money lenders, and a fair and honest money lender, Tulsa being an example of the latter, could truly flourish. Tulsa encouraged Guman Chand to get into money-lending.

Guman Chand was leaning more towards the opium trade, as it was more lucrative. Besides, he was not terribly comfortable with foreclosing on peasant's property if they failed to repay a loan, which he would have to do if he got into money-lending. Deoraj and Guman Chand were on the opposite side of this issue. Deoraj considered opium trading immoral, as he was well aware of the ill effects of opium. Rajasthan was an opium-producing area and Deoraj had seen, firsthand, families ruined when the main breadwinner got addicted to opium. He considered money-lending to be the lesser of the two evils and had witnessed his friend Tulsa deal with people humanely and with compassion. Guman Chand, on his part, argued that buying and selling opium was legal in India and there were no ethical issues involved in trading a legal commodity. For almost two years after Guman Chand's wedding in early 1775, the argument continued while Guman Chand felt a lot of pressure from Swaroop Singh's policies and actions to find an alternate business to brocade.

This was not the first time Deoraj and Guman Chand's views had clashed over business ethics. Deoraj's health had also been steadily declining since Guman Chand's wedding, and he had lost a lot of weight. Finally, sensing Guman Chand's great enthusiasm for the opium business, Deoraj very reluctantly gave his consent. One day in 1777, Guman Chand announced that he was ready to embark on a journey to Kota, one of the prolific opium-producing regions. Deoraj was sitting in the outside veranda, observing the frantic preparations for Guman Chand's journey. Deoraj's face looked ashen and a little drawn. Bhairavi and Guman Chand attributed it partly to an unusually low temperature that day, partly to Deoraj's aversion to opium trading, and partly to Deoraj's sadness at Guman Chand being potentially away from Jaisalmer for the coming several months.

When the preparations were almost done, Guman Chand went inside the house to seek parting blessings from *Sachiya Maata* and to take leave of his mother and his wife. They both accompanied Guman

Chand to the outside of the house to see him off. Guman Chand then approached Deoraj and touched his feet, to take leave of him. Deoraj stared out into the distance. Guman Chand was surprised that Deoraj didn't rest his palm on his son's head like he normally did. He looked up and softly said, "Baba." Deoraj didn't react. Guman Chand touched Deoraj's shoulders gently and repeated, "Baba," with a little more emphasis. Deoraj still didn't react. Bhairavi and Jeta moved towards Deoraj. Bhairavi touched his face with her hands and found Deoraj totally cold. Guman Chand knew in his mind what had happened, but his heart refused to believe it. His whole being refused to believe it. He now stood up, swallowing his tears, and shook Deoraj's shoulders violently. Deoraj still didn't respond. "Please Baba, please…" sobbed Guman Chand. Bhairavi collapsed on the floor, with Jeta trying to fan her and attend to her, with tears streaming down her own face and sobbing uncontrollably.

"Baba, I will not go to Kota. Please, Baba," sobbed Guman Chand.

There was still no response from Deoraj.

"Baba, please. I will not get into the opium business at all," shouted Guman Chand.

Guman Chand's employees and guards who were preparing for Guman Chand's journey to Kota gathered around Deoraj upon hearing Guman Chand's loud entreaties. They too sensed immediately what had happened.

Deoraj was totally unresponsive, his eyes blankly staring into nowhere. Guman Chand was now sure what had happened.

"This family will never deal in opium as long as I live. I promise, Baba," shouted Guman Chand, as if a louder voice would somehow reach Deoraj. "Baba! Guman Chand Patwa, son of the Noble Seth Deoraj will never deal in opium. Never!"

Guman Chand, normally so stable and in control, broke down and sobbed like a child. It was as if all the emotions he had not shown in his entire life came bursting out like a broken dam. He cried and cried and cried inconsolably for days.

Deoraj Singh Bapna of the Bafna clan was fifty-seven years old when he passed away. Most first-generation success stories involve men who started with nothing and without the advantage of a good education or culture, were somewhat crude and almost uncouth. They didn't think twice about using any means at their disposal, legal or illegal, brutal or not so brutal, to climb up the ladder. Deoraj was the exception. Despite starting with nothing, he set the highest standards of honesty, integrity, culture and compassion, which some even in his future generations found difficult to uphold, despite having all the advantages of money, power and influence. The amazing thing, however, was that there were others among his succeeding generations who were able to meet his high standards, inspired by the values he inculcated in his son and which were passed on from generation to generation.

Deoraj had a certain innocence and child-like quality about him which led most people to consider him naïve or simple-minded. In reality, it took a high degree of intelligence and strength of character for any man to start at the bottom and achieve what Deoraj did, without hurting anybody along the way and without compromising his self respect. His greatest attribute was his ever-willingness to walk away from success if it was not on his terms, a tradeoff only the very best of us can make.

A thousand people attended Deoraj's funeral and they all agreed on one thing: in all of his thirty-eight years in Jaisalmer, Deoraj had never hurt a soul. The harsh hand that life dealt him over and over again had made him rebellious, but he was the gentlest rebel anyone had ever known.

Chapter 9 - Story of Guman Chand – 3
1777 AD – 1789 AD

Guman Chand Patwa at the age of twenty-six, was now the head of the house of Deoraj. He also inherited the brass ring that his mother had gifted to his father at the time of their betrothal, so many years ago in Osian. It was a humble ring, but Deoraj never took it off his ring finger and always treated it as his most precious possession. Guman Chand wore it as a revered family heirloom, a reminder of his father and a part of his identity. His fame and business operations had already spread, both nationally and internationally. The need to expand in the other businesses was as acute as ever in view of the ever increasing tax levies and extortion by Prime Minister Swaroop Singh on the populace of Jaisalmer, particularly the business community. Rawal Mulraj, the ruler, was complicit in implementing this oppressive economic regime. Swaroop Singh singled out Guman Chand for his worst atrocities, levying special cess on his operations and his exports and demanding huge sums of money as extortion on a regular basis. Guman Chand had lengthy, detailed conversations with his father-in-law, Tulsa, and planned to expand into banking and money-lending.

The demand for capital in India in the 1770s had increased. While the European economies had gone into a slump, the pan Indian economy was booming. The British East India Company had firmly established its foothold in large parts of India, particularly Bengal, and they were in constant need of debt financing. They had established an opium monopoly in Bengal and other areas where they were virtual rulers, and the opium trade further fuelled the demand for capital. Famines in various parts of the country, including a major famine in Bengal, also caused an increase in the demand for money.

Guman Chand had the good fortune of entering the money lending business when it was booming and on its way up. He also had the distinct advantage of already having branches and experienced staff in scores of locations across the country and even internationally through which he conducted his brocade trade. He could use the same infrastructure to quickly expand his banking operations. Guman Chand very quickly set up his new business and created a distribution network where his wealth was kept in various locations outside of Jaisalmer and started distributing his wealth across these locations to guard and act as insurance against draconian actions against him by the Jaisalmer ruler and the prime minister.

By 1785, Guman Chand Patwa was one of the leading bankers in Rajasthan and by far the richest man in Jaisalmer. This was no mean feat, as Jaisalmer was a rich mercantile town, full of established and rich merchants, both Oswal and Paliwals. For a young man not yet thirty-five years old to achieve this distinction despite the sworn enmity of the Jaisalmer ruling establishment was remarkable. His personal life was also strong, as within eight years of his marriage he had four sons and his wife Jeta was pregnant with a fifth child.

Bhairavi, Guman Chand's mother, never quite recovered from the death of her husband, Deoraj, who was truly her soul mate, and she had withdrawn deeply within herself for years. The birth of her grandsons seemed to have given her life a new meaning. She adored her grandchildren and wanted to ensure that the values of Deoraj and the standards he set were thoroughly passed down to the next generation of the House of Deoraj. She set about her task in earnest, combining her natural softness with a little tough love to raise her grandsons. She couldn't help but notice that each of the grandchildren was handsome, spirited and an individual in his own right. Physically, they had all taken after Jeta, as they were all striking in looks. Deoraj was pleasing to look at, but could by no means be called handsome. Guman Chand certainly fell in the rugged category. His sons, in contrast, all looked like little angels.

Life was going good for the House of Deoraj—until tragedy struck. During the birth of their fifth child, another son, Jeta died. Neither the midwife nor the *vaidya* could tell exactly what happened, but right after childbirth Jeta became unconscious and never recovered. The entire House of Deoraj went into deep mourning. Guman Chand was stunned and in deep shock. This was the second mortal blow for the normally stoic Guman Chand—the first one being the death of his father, Deoraj. Jeta was as much his soul mate as Bhairavi had been Deoraj's, and they had gone through a lot together. She was a huge motivation for Guman Chand to achieve greater and greater success, as in his heart he did it as much for Jeta as for himself. This was a great setback for Guman Chand personally, and after Jeta's death he was not quite the same man.

Bhairavi, too, was devastated at Jeta's sudden demise. Contrary to the normal Indian mother-in-law/daughter-in-law relationship, which was marked by distrust and rancor, Bhairavi and Jeta's relationship, was more like that of a mother and daughter. It may have been because Jeta was the daughter of Bhairavi's dearest friend, Purvi, and Jeta had known Bhairavi all of her life. It may also have been because both Bhairavi and Jeta were soft, gentle, caring and very good natured, or it just may have been because Bhairavi and Jeta really communicated well together. After Jeta's death, Bhairavi took even a firmer control over the upbringing of her grandchildren and became more protective towards them.

One evening in the winter of 1789, Kotwal Alam Khan, the lifelong friend of Seth Deoraj, stopped by Guman Chand's residence. He informed Guman Chand that Crown Prince Rae Singh had convened a conference of his trusted advisors that night in his wing of the royal palace to discuss the ever growing atrocities being perpetrated by Prime Minister Swaroop Singh on the population of Jaisalmer. Guman Chand's father in-law, Tulsa, though not in good health, was expected to attend the meeting. Alam Khan carried an invitation from Rae Singh to Guman Chand to attend this conference and not to tell anybody about it. Sensing something was afoot, Guman Chand dressed up in a black cloak, masked his face with a black cloth and rode a black horse up the slope into the back entrance of the royal palace, where he was met by a force commander who escorted Guman Chand to Crown Prince Rae Singh's living quarters. Guman Chand noticed several important merchants from Oswal and Paliwal communities, along with several members of the Jaisalmer royal family. Everyone stood up in respect as Seth Guman Chand Patwa entered the room. Crown Prince Rae Singh welcomed Seth Guman Chand into his house and gave him the pride of place around the table.

"We are all gathered here tonight, to plan a final decisive action against the usurper Swaroop Singh," started Rae Singh. "If anyone has any ideas, please put them forward."

Prithvi Singh, a minor royal, rose up and said, "Perhaps we should figure out a way to assassinate the tyrant."

Tulsa said, "It may be a better idea for a delegation of important people lead by Rae Singh to visit Rawal Mulraj and try to convince him to oust Swaroop Singh."

"Rawal Mulraj does not have the will or the persuasive power," said Rae Singh.

Guman Chand stood up and said, "The best approach might be to prepare a charge sheet against Swaroop Singh and present it in open court to Rawal Mulraj, with the entire Jaisalmer court in attendance. That way Mulraj may be forced to act."

Everybody gave their assent to prepare the charge sheet with details and evidence and it was left to Rae Singh to present the charge sheet. A long list of atrocities committed by Swaroop Singh was prepared, and Crown Prince Rae Singh stepped forward in open court to formally bring up charges against the prime minister. Sensing the general mood against him and feeling trapped, Swaroop Singh cleverly tried to divert attention by trying to provoke Rae Singh into exhibiting intemperate conduct, thereby undermining his credibility. Rae Singh, though very liberal and capable, was known for his quick temper.

"May I know by what authority Kumar Rae Singh is presenting this charge sheet against me?" asked Swaroop Singh in his usual haughty manner.

"In my capacity as the crown prince," replied Rae Singh.

"How can a man whose paternity is in doubt become the crown prince?" asked Swaroop Singh, challenging Rae Singh.

Rae Singh turned red. His teeth clenched, he pulled out his sword and rushed towards Swaroop Singh.

"You foul mouthed son of a swine! You filthy rotten bastard!" spat Rae Singh as he reached Swaroop Singh, held him by his collar and before anyone could intervene, cut off his head with one quick blow.

The entire Jaisalmer court was in disarray. People were screaming and running helter skelter. The royal guard moved in and tried to restore order, with only partial success. Rawal Mulraj stepped off the throne and approached Rae Singh, trying to say something, but almost no one could hear. Rawal Mulraj approached the commander of the guards and asked him to arrest Crown Prince Rae Singh. Several of Rae Singh's followers had crowded around him, creating a protective cordon. There was a minor scuffle between the palace guard and Rae Singh's followers, after which Rae Singh and his followers escaped. It was later rumored that the palace guard had allowed Rae Singh to escape, as they were sympathetic to him. Rae Singh and his band of rebels, which included some minor royals, a few merchants and a few loyalist soldiers slipped out of Jaisalmer and sought refuge in the neighboring kingdom of Jodhpur, the arch rival of Jaisalmer.

Practically all of Jaisalmer broke out in celebration at the news of Swaroop Singh's beheading. Spontaneous celebrations included fireworks and the exchange of sweets. The Oswals celebrated quietly behind closed doors, congratulating each other. A large party of prominent Oswal merchants gathered at Guman Chand's residence in a celebratory mood. However, both Bhairavi and Guman Chand had an uneasy feeling about the whole affair. Guman Chand was sure that this would not be the end of it and that there would be reprisals and recriminations which might spell bigger trouble for the merchant community in Jaisalmer.

"Be very careful, Guman. I feel in my heart that something dreadful is going to happen," said Bhairavi.

Guman Chand was his normal controlled self. He did not wish to alarm Bhairavi by expressing his own apprehensions, but he was not a man at peace with himself.

The greatest celebrations, however, were at the Paliwal villages, including Kuldhara. Paliwal women broke out in dance in the village squares as the news of their tormentor's death spread like wildfire. Tulsa and Purvi did not participate in the celebrations as they too sensed dark clouds ahead for their beloved son-in-law Guman Chand.

Chapter 10 - Story of Guman Chand – 4
1789 AD – 1805 AD

Since the position of the Prime Minister of Jaisalmer was a hereditary one, Swaroop Singh Mehta's eleven-year-old son, Salim Singh Mehta, was appointed prime minister in 1789. His uncle and Swaroop Singh's brother, Martand Singh, were to act on behalf of the minor child until he attained the age of eighteen. Martand Singh, though no angel, was a slightly milder version of Swaroop Singh, and therefore there were no wide-scale recriminations against the merchant community of Jaisalmer. Taxes and levies remained oppressive and both Rawal Mulraj and Martand Singh continued to target individual merchants for extortion. Guman Chand continued to be their main target, but they also focused their energies on several other Oswal and Paliwal merchants.

Famines continued to plague the Jaisalmer peasantry and instead of providing assistance, the rulers imposed further taxes. Guman Chand was able to sustain this onslaught as he carefully planned to distribute his wealth outside Jaisalmer in a manner not quite apparent to the rulers, but several other merchants were literally ruined. All this was compounded by the fact that the British were gradually gaining power and taking control of most of the international trade in and out of India. They were conducting this trade through the sea, thereby diminishing the importance of Jaisalmer as a major transit point on the land route. The declining revenue from the travelling caravans put even more pressure on the rulers of Jaisalmer to victimize the merchants to make up for the deficit. Jaislamer, until now a prosperous city, started on a path of steep decline around 1790 and there was a great deal of unrest in the general populace. Many Paliwal clans and families petitioned to leave Jaisalmer, but the rulers refused permission, ensuring that some family members were left behind as hostages whenever Paliwal merchants travelled outside Jaisalmer on business, to ensure their return. Paliwals provided much of the revenue for the Royal House of Jaisalmer and the rulers were unwilling to let go of this lucrative source of income.

Guman Chand's sons were growing up under the watchful eye of their grandmother Bhairavi, now in her sixty-fifth year and revered around Jaisalmer as *MaSaab* (dowager mother). Bhairavi seldom stepped out of the house, but whenever she appeared in public, people bowed with respect; the shopkeepers vied with each other to have her grace their shop; no one accepted any payment from her; women, children and even young men, known or unknown, stopped to touch her feet and wealthy merchants were ever eager to receive the grand old lady in their houses.

What a difference a few years and a few gold pieces make, thought Bhairavi, who could still distinctly remember all the indignities directed at her and Deoraj in Jaisalmer during their years of struggle.

Guman Chand's money-lending business was on the ascendency. The British continued their advance in India, and by 1795 it looked inevitable that the British would dislodge the Marathas and take over Delhi to become the pre-eminent power in India. Guman Chand's sons were growing up to be fine young men, one more outstanding than the other. Bahadur Mal, the eldest, was now eighteen and was already taking a keen interest in Guman Chand's business, almost singlehandedly handling all their operations in Rajasthan and Central India. Mangni Raam and Sawai Ram were sixteen and fourteen respectively and were being groomed as businessmen in their own right. It was Zorawar Mal, the fourth son, not quite twelve yet, a sort of a prodigy, who showed the most promise. He was extremely handsome, tall for his age, quick of mind and wit and even at this young age had varied interests in arts, music and politics, in addition to an avid interest in the family business. The last, Pratap Mal was still young, but spirited and precocious.

During one of his travels, Guman Chand happened to meet a British teacher by the name of Samuel Marshall in Calcutta. The British had established a school for the children of the employees of the British East India Company inside the Calcutta Fort, and Samuel Marshall was the Head Master. He gave Guman Chand a tour of the British school and explained to him in detail the British education system and the curriculum. Marshall was a renaissance man who believed in a well-rounded education, which included the liberal arts, humanities, philosophy, music and the performing arts, in addition to science, history, commerce and politics. He himself was an accomplished painter and a poet.

Guman Chand was impressed and was well aware by now of the British power and ambitions in India. He already was dealing extensively with English merchants and the East India Company and realized the tremendous advantage that could be gleaned by knowing their language and culture. His shrewd mind told him that the British would dominate India for times to come, and he quickly made an offer to Samuel Marshall to come and tutor his sons in Jaisalmer. Reluctant to leave the school he had founded, Marshall was finally persuaded by an extremely lucrative offer and he accompanied Guman Chand back to Jaisalmer.

Marshall quickly became enchanted with Jaisalmer and got particularly attached to the five motherless children of Guman Chand. He set about in earnest to impart to them an education befitting the highest aristocracy in Europe. He informed them about World History and European History, the new world, the renaissance artists, philosophers, political movements and thought and languages. Knowing full well that he was educating the scions of a famous mercantile dynasty, he laid particular emphasis on informing the children about the history of commerce, economics, mercantile and banking practices and trading practices, prevalent around the world. Marshall found all five of them to be quick studies and again, Zorawar Mal was particularly curious, debating with Marshall on various issues relating to philosophy and religion.

Marshall stayed in Jaisalmer until 1800, when the youngest of Guman Chand's son attained the age of eighteen. During his twelve years in Jaisalmer, he had ensured that each of Guman Chand's sons was as well read and educated as the best educated European prince. Fluent in English and the ways of the world now, Guman Chand's five sons were all set to take Jaisalmer and the world around them by storm.

The relationship between Samuel Marshall and the five Bapna brothers lasted till the end of Marshall's life. Even when Marshall retired back to the Midlands in England, they constantly exchanged letters, with Marshall sending the brothers recently published books in England and informing them of ongoing developments in Europe, while the brothers sent him lavish gifts and news from India. It was a relationship based on mutual respect and affection and the brothers never forgot and were forever grateful to Marshall for the education he had imparted to them.

Before he left India, however, Marshall told a young public servant, James Tod, about his experiences in Rajasthan, Jaisalmer in particular, and all about the five dashing Bapna brothers, the sons of Guman Chand Patwa. This same James Tod soon became the British political agent for Rajputana and would play a pivotal role in the lives of the Bapna brothers, as they were to play in his life. To this day, James Tod's three volume Annals and Antiquities of Rajputana, written in the mid 1800s, is considered the authoritative treatise on Rajasthan in the 1700s and 1800s.

By 1800, Bahadur Mal, twenty-five, Mangni Ram twenty-three, Sawai Ram, twenty-one, Zorawar Mal, nineteen, and Pratap Mal, eighteen, were already heading up their own sub-operations within their father's extensive business empire. All five Bapna brothers had a certain amount of glamour associated with them, wherever they travelled, due to their good looks, regal bearing, business acumen, controlled aggressiveness and the fact that they were Seth Guman Chand's sons. However, Bahadur Mal, the eldest, with his chiseled good looks and a tall, lean frame was particularly striking and glamorous. Bahadur Mal, Mangni Ram and Sawai Ram were already married to girls from prominent Oswal merchants from Jaisalmer. One night in 1800, when Guman Chand was away travelling, Bhairavi fell seriously ill. Zorawar Mal and Pratap Mal were the only men in the house; the rest of the males were travelling. The grandchildren's three wives did their best to comfort Bhairavi, but Bhairavi knew that the end was near. She asked for the idol of her beloved *Sacchiyaa Maataa*, asked her permission to perform the ritual of *santhara* (fasting unto death), and passed away the next afternoon. At the age of seventy-five, the grand old mistress of the House of Deoraj was no more. She had seen the peaks and the valleys and was as much responsible as Deoraj for the family's success. Her strength of character, her steadfastness, her loyalty, her generosity of spirit and her love for Deoraj and the entire family was exemplary. The word of her demise quickly spread all across Jaisalmer and Kuldhara. Since Guman Chand and the elder three sons were far away, they could not make it back in time for the funeral. Zorawar Mal took charge and several thousand people attended Bhairavi's funeral. A mourning period of one month was declared in the Oswal and the Paliwal communities around Jaisalmer.

In 1795 another development had serious consequences for the people of Jaisalmer and was a turning point in the history of the city. Salim Singh, who had been appointed the Prime Minister of Jaisalmer at the age of eleven upon his father Swaroop Singh's beheading, had turned eighteen. He was an adult now and he took full charge of the office. He was short, effeminate, soft-spoken, but extremely cunning and shrewd. He was a pathological liar who would say anything to anybody to serve his evil designs. As soon as he took over, he resumed his father's atrocities with renewed vigor. More taxes were levied on all, merchants were put through more and more elaborate extortion routines. Rawal Mulraj, the Bhatti ruler of Jaisalmer, was indifferent to the plight of his subjects, or even complicit in some of the actions of Salim Singh.

Salim Singh was a small minded, vengeful man, and he had not forgotten the beheading of his father. He particularly held a coterie of royals headed by Crown Prince Rae Singh, who was responsible for his father's murder. He also continued to harbor his father's deep hatred for Guman Chand and spared no effort to make life more difficult for him, via extortion, oppressive levies, etc.

By 1800, Guman Chand's business suffered a decline across India, as British were on the ascendency and a new political order was replacing the old. Radical economic policies were promulgated by the British, and a different set of officials were put in place. All this led to the rise of a new business class with political patronage from the British, which started edging out old business families such as Guman Chand's. The changing of the guard, along with Salim Singh's targeting, put Guman Chand under considerable financial pressure. He conferred with his young sons on the family's direction in the future and the conversation inevitably turned to opium. The five young sons of Guman Chand saw opium trade as the only way out of their predicament. The British had expanded the opium exports to China, and since Jaisalmer and the Central Indian opium-producing regions were not yet under the British, the brothers saw this as a window of opportunity to start their own opium exports to China, without British interference and at lower prices than British companies such as Jardine could sell at. Guman Chand knew in his heart that his sons were right, but bound by his pledge to the dying Deoraj he would never give his consent.

"I have just returned from North India. Our entire operation in Punjab, Delhi, Multan and Afghanistan is in shambles. Our *munims* (managers) are all corrupt and mixed up with the local bandits, and our couriers, branches and staff are routinely robbed of large amounts of cash and gold. In this age of chaos and disorder I see no point in continuing our money-lending business," said Bahadur Mal, the eldest.

"I have the same experiences in Malwa and Central India operations that I run," said Mangani Raam.

"Our overseas operations are also running at huge losses as the political situation in China and the middle-east is very volatile," said Sawai Raam, the second son.

"And with Salim Singh breathing down our neck here in Jaisalmer, things don't look very good for us here at home," rejoined Zorawar Mal.

Guman Chand looked pensive. He could not argue with his sons, as they were right. Grimly, he asked, "So what's next? What do you suggest?"

"You know what the solution is, *Kaka Saheb* (in families belonging to the upper crust, all the sons called their fathers *Kaka Saheb*, meaning "uncle," but in Rajasthan, "uncle" was a formal way of addressing the father). We have discussed it many times," said Bahadur Mal.

"*Kaka Saheb*, the only way out is opium," said Mangni Raam.

"I have told you many times before, and I will tell you now, as long as I am alive this family will not enter the opium trade. Why do you keep coming back to opium? Can't we get into any other line of business? How about precious metals? Gold is always in demand," said Guman Chand firmly.

"Too much competition in gold," said Sawai Raam, "and besides, the gold business involves transportation, which in these chaotic times is extremely dangerous."

"Why not opium, *Kaka Saheb*? Opium is legal, and even the British are expanding their opium trade," added Zorawar Mal.

"'Cause opium is immoral. *Baba* believed that selling addictive products is not only against our religion, but an inhuman act. To profit from such an enterprise is unthinkable," thundered Guman Chand.

"Is transacting in liquor as immoral then? People have been consuming liquor for ages," asked Bahadur Mal.

"Opium is more addictive than liquor," declared Guman Chand. "I say again, we are wasting time. As long as I am alive, the family of the Bapnas will never enter the opium business."

"Then let us be prepared to go to the poor house, and mark my words, *Kaka Saheb*, once we lose our economic clout, Salim Singh will have all our heads. That is a guarantee." warned Mangni Raam.

"Your grandfather, the noble Seth Deoraj, went through much

more trying periods than this throughout his life and he didn't feel the need to resort to immoral acts. We will also persevere, and this time too shall pass," reassured Guman Chand, ending the conversation.

All five brothers sat there in disbelief, all of their collective brilliance unable to come up with an alternative.

The brothers consolidated their business branches across India and then turned their attention to Central India, where they had extensive contacts with the ruling princes of several kingdoms. They were able to squeeze out reasonable profits to keep the family afloat during this difficult period. The brothers grew impatient to expand, but were frustrated by the strong headwinds they encountered and their father's steadfast refusal to resort to the obvious choice of opium trade, which could catapult them into a much higher plane of success.

In the meantime, Zorawarl Mal's personal life was beginning to flower. In the Oswal community, women followed *purdah*. This tradition had been adopted by several communities, including the Rajputs and Oswals in Rajasthan, from the Muslims in order to protect their women from kidnappers and the powers-that-be. The Paliwals were one of the few communities which did not practice *purdah*. This made it very difficult for young men and women within the Oswal community to have much interaction before marriage, and therefore most marriages were arranged.

In the case of Guman Chand's five sons, they were all handsome and imposing, and they became well known among young Oswal women. The brothers had several secret liaisons with young women, and meetings were held with great caution and in complete secrecy. By 1800 the eldest three brothers were married to girls from prominent Oswal merchant families and had settled down. Nineteen-year old Zorawar Mal, probably the most imposing and handsome of the brothers, was yet unmarried and was enamored with the daughter of his neighbor, a prominent Oswal merchant involved in the grain trade. The merchant's name was Inder Mal, and his daughter Aarya was only sixteen. Aarya was pretty, spirited and independent. Zorawar Mal had known her since childhood when he would go to his terrace to play and would sometimes find Aarya and her sisters playing on the neighboring terrace.

As they got older, they stopped playing on the terrace and instead met each other on the facing *jharokhas* (balconies) of their respective *havelis* (mansions). Aarya had a pretty voice and was often heard humming a Rajasthani song as she walked about in the many balconies of her house.

Zorawar Mal, a strong-willed, intelligent and well-educated young man, was quite taken by Aarya's beauty and spirit and the sentiments were more than returned. They first started meeting, Zorawar Mal in his balcony and Aarya on hers, which only had a foot or two's distance between them, as even mansions in Jaisalmer were situated right next to each other in close quarters. As their affection grew, they started having long conversations, with Zorawar Mal telling Aarya about all that he had learnt about the world from Sam Marshall—descriptions of places in faraway places such as Arabia, Europe, and even the New World. She was particularly enthralled by Amerigo Vaspucci's account of the New World, which he called America. Zorawar Mal had read Vaspucci's letters about his voyages to America, which were published and gifted to him by his tutor, Sam Marshall. Zorawar Mal told Aarya that he would one day travel to the New World and take Aarya with him.

As they grew closer, Aarya and Zorawar Mal started planning secret meetings on the terraces, or even inside Guman Chand's spacious mansion. The wives of Zorawar Mal's elder brothers were only too happy to arrange such liaisons inside their private quarters, where the young lovers would not be disturbed and not found out. Since Bhairavi's death, Bahadur Mal, the eldest's wife, Chatura, had taken charge of Guman Chand's household. The other sisters-in-law, Jiwan and Pratapan, treated her with the respect due a mother-in-law, and she too looked out for them like a mother. Chatura, in particular, encouraged the relationship between Aarya and Zorawar Mal, as she knew how much Zorawar Mal liked Aarya and she was sure Aarya would be an excellent addition to their family, so they met mostly in Chatura and Bahadur Mal's quarters.

Zorawar Mal never tired of telling Aarya stories and interesting facts that he had learned from Sam Marshall and from reading the many books he and his brothers had accumulated over the years. Aarya, on her part, would often sing Zorawar Mal a romantic song or two, all in Rajasthani, sometimes dancing to the songs. On many occasions, Zorawar Mal would join Aarya, and the young couple would dance with an abundance of passion and joy. One would think that the romance between Zorawar Mal, who was the most eligible bachelor in Jaisalmer, and Aarya, the beautiful daughter of a prominent merchant, was destined for a happy ending, particularly considering that they were from the same community and had the blessings of their respective families.

In 1801, Chatura finally informed Bahadur Mal of her intention to get Zorawar Mal married to Aarya. Bahadur Mal, in turn, informed Guman Chand, when he returned from his business travels to Jaisalmer and was planning to spend the winter at home. Guman Chand sent Bahadur Mal to Aarya's father, Inder Mal, with the proposition of marriage between Zorawar Mal and Aarya, and Inder Mal, not believing his luck, immediately agreed. A grand engagement ceremony was arranged and the reception that followed was the talk of the town in Jaisalmer. However, when Prime Minister Salim Singh found out about this engagement, he was consumed with envy and hate—envy of Zorawar Mal, whom he had known since his childhood and felt inferior to in all respects, and hatred of Guman Chand, whom he considered complicit in his father's beheading.

Salim Singh swore to never let the wedding between Zorawar Mal and Aarya go forward. To that end, he imposed arbitrary and exorbitant taxation on Aarya's father, Inder Mal. Inder Mal, first, could not fathom why he was visited upon by this curse and tried his best to keep up with the payments in order to keep Salim Singh happy. However, his business suffered greatly as a result and Inder Mal was at his wits' end as to how to rescue his business from this calamity. One day a palace guard arrived at Inder Mal's residence and informed him that he was to have an audience with Prime Minister Salim Singh and he was commanded to appear before the prime minister within the hour.

Inder Mal was politely received and asked to stay standing, while Salim Singh paced up and down the room.

"I understand Seth Inder Mal is having some difficulties paying his tax dues to the Royal House of Jaisalmer," said Salim Singh in his normal soft, almost effeminate voice.

"Yes, Your Excellency, I am sure the prime minister is aware, I am not one of the bigger businesses in Jaisalmer, and for years I have paid more than my fair share of taxes with no complaints. The recent increase is so steep that it has broken my back," replied Inder Mal, nearly choking with emotion.

"It is I who decides what is fair in Jaisalmer and what is not," said Salim Singh, "and I have decided to impose an additional tax on you today, Seth Inder Mal. You will now pay an additional Rs. 1000 every month for an indefinite period. Dark clouds are gathering over Jaisalmer, Inder Mal, and your ruler, Rawal Mulraj, needs your help in combating forces inimical to our motherland."

Salim Singh's pronouncement stabbed through Inder Mal's heart like a dagger. It sounded more like a death sentence rather than a tax levy. He would be ruined now, and what would happen to his daughters? He had done everything right—worked hard, labored through several decades to finally attain some small status in Jaisalmer—and all that would disappear if he had to make such payments. Inder Mal kneeled down and started to cry, begging Salim Singh to have mercy on him, asking what he had done to deserve such a fate.

"What have you done, you ask, Inder Mal?" said Salim Singh, shrewdly watching Inder Mal collapse right in front of him. "You have done nothing. It's your daughter. She has chosen to marry into a house which is responsible for my fathers' death. Guman Chand Patwa is guilty. Guman Chand Patwa is the enemy. My father had sworn to destroy his entire family and all its future generations. Guman Chand's sons are therefore equally guilty and every bit an enemy as Guman Chand. By marrying into the House of Deoraj you have brought upon yourself my eternal enmity. I will destroy Guman Chand Patwa and his sons, and I will destroy you, Inder Mal, if you allow your daughter to marry into that house."

Inder Mal now understood what had happened to him. He stopped crying and stayed down on his knees, his eyes lowered. He was speechless, and he did not know how to respond.

Salim Singh circled around the kneeling Inder Mal, with a cane in his hands. When Inder Mal still didn't say anything, he gently touched his cane on Inder Mal's shoulders and said in a soft voice, "There is only one way out for you, Inder Mal, if you want to avoid complete ruin. Cancel Aarya's engagement with Zorawar Mal."

"Please, my Lord, I beg you. Please, in the name of Lord Adishwar, please don't do this to me. My daughters are all motherless; their mother died in their childhood. I have raised them with great affection. They will hate me if I come between Zorawar Mal and Aarya. Please don't make me do this," wailed Inder Mal.

"Then pay an additional thousand every month, and maybe, in due course, Jaisalmer will call upon you to make even greater sacrifices," said Salim Singh calmly. "What will it be, Inder Mal?"

Inder Mal was speechless still, his face dejected, his eyes staring at the ground below him.

"More taxes?" asked Salim Singh, teasing and mocking.

"No, please," cried Inder Mal, taking off his turban and putting it at Salim Singh's feet, a sign of complete submission in Rajasthan.

"Fine, then," said Salim Singh. "I will expect the engagement cancellation announcement before sundown today."

Inder Mal got up slowly, as if in a trance. Picking up his turban, he walked slowly towards the door. Before he could reach the door he heard Salim Singh say, "One more thing, Seth Inder Mal."

Inder Mal looked back in a daze and Salim Singh continued. "I want to make it up to you, Seth. I will arrange for Aarya to go to an even more exalted house than the House of Deoraj. I myself will do you the honor of marrying Aarya, Inder Mal. I told you, I am a generous man and I will perform this sacrifice for you and your daughter."

Tears streaming down his cheeks, Indermal managed to drag himself out of Salim Singh's chamber. The palace guards helped him down the steps and onto his saddle. Inder Mal rode slowly down the road which led from the palace to the central district of Jaisalmer, where both Guman Chand and he lived. He felt like a dead man, helpless to preserve his daughter's happiness.

Guman Chand was equally devastated when he was informed about this. He and his able sons were all highly successful and accomplished. They were not accustomed to setbacks and defeats, and this was not easy for them to accept. Besides their ego, they bristled at the injustice of it all. The entire family felt terrible for Zorawar Mal, who had his heart set on marrying Aarya. They hastily convened a family meeting and tried to explore their options. They discussed the idea of Aarya eloping with Zorawar Mal and Guman Chand and their family would accept whatever repercussions Salim Singh might cause them to endure in the form of more draconian taxation. The family also talked about leaving Jaisalmer for one of many other locations where they would be more welcome. However, all options left Aarya's father, Inder Mal, in a lurch. Inder Mal was a small businessman who did not have the vast business empire and network that Guman Chand had, and he could not flee Jaisalmer without being financially ruined. After a whole night of deliberations, Guman Chand and his five sons finally accepted the inevitable and sent a message to Inder Mal that under the circumstances they would be amenable to cancel the engagement between Zorawar Mal and Aarya.

Aarya was quickly betrothed to Salim Singh. Chatura and the other sisters-in-law saw fit to quickly find a suitable girl for the heartbroken Zorawar Mal. They picked a well-bred, pretty girl from another prominent Oswal merchant family, called Chautha. Salim

Singh married Aarya in a highly ostentatious wedding. Zorawar Mal, in contrast, married Chautha in a fairly low-key wedding by the standards of his family. The year 1801 ended for the House of Deoraj on a rather disquieted note.

The period between 1801 and 1805 was a period of great turmoil for Jaisalmer. Salm Singh was at the height of his powers and his atrocities continued unabated. This, coupled with the fact that Jaisalmer's importance as a wayside stop on the land route to the Silk Road was diminishing fast in view of the increasing importance of maritime trade, preferred by the British, resulted in a mass exodus of people out of Jaisalmer. Business and commercial activity greatly declined, leaving both the Oswal and Paliwal communities greatly diminished. An enduring drought had equally devastated the peasant and the farming communities. Instead of stepping up to implementing progressive and far reaching policies to reverse this decline, Rawal Mulraj and his prime minister, Salim Singh, resorted to more extortion, more oppressive taxation, and more repression, further accelerating the decline.

A group of progressive merchants, both Paliwal and Oswal, who were emotionally attached to Jaisalmer, took it upon themselves to stem this decline in the absence of any measures by the rulers. This group was headed by Guman Chand, who convened a meeting where it was agreed that despite the precarious financial health of all merchants, they would sponsor public works projects. They raised enough money to finance these projects for the next twenty-five years. The idea was to curtail outward migration by providing local employment for the people of Jaisalmer. Each merchant agreed to sponsor his own project, and Guman Chand Patwa and his five sons undertook sponsoring the construction of five grand mansions (*havelis*), one for each brother, which would be constructed by local and foreign artisans.

Guman Chand and his sons intended these *havelis* to be one of a kind, without parallel anywhere in the world. The façade would be exquisite carved sandstone. The walls inside would be studded with precious and semi-precious stones, while the ceiling would be coated with thin layers of gold and silver. The walls would be adorned with mural Rajput and Mogul paintings, while each mansion would have scores of *jharokhas* (balconies). Guman Chand promised that whether he would be alive or not, his sons would finance the construction of these gorgeous mansions for the next twenty-five years. All five brothers took up this challenge, despite the fact that their financial situation at the time could be described as precarious at best. Other merchants sponsored their own projects, big or small, depending on each's financial capacity. For a while it seemed that the rot was stemmed in Jaisalmer, and Jaisalmer's markets were again humming with energy.

In 1803, the battle of Delhi put the British firmly in control of vast areas of the Indian subcontinent. Central India and Rajasthan was still not under the British, as the Marathas (a Hindu power) held sway in Central India, while kingdoms in Rajasthan such as Jaisalmer were now officially independent. The Marathas took advantage of the situation and launched semi-yearly raids into these small hapless kingdoms, extracting tributes from them well beyond their abilities to pay. Jaisalmer was spared the worst of these raids due to its remote location.

At fifty four, Guman Chand Patwa was a grandfather of six grandchildren, two of them Zorawar Mal's named Sultan Mal and Chandan Mal. Even though he was the head of a wealthy business house, the last few years had been a struggle. His early years which marked a miraculous rise due to his business acumen, strong character, steely resolve, buttressed by phenomenal good luck and a strong foundation laid by his father Deoraj, had now given way to some personal and business misfortunes. His money-lending business had stalled and he now acutely felt the loss of his parents, Deoraj and Bhairavi, who had been his pillars all along. The most devastating for him was the early loss of his beloved wife Jeta, whose memories he tried to drown out earlier by immersing himself in his business and travelling extensively. Now, his body could no longer endure extended travel on horseback, and now his sons were doing the bulk of the travel and managing his business. As a result, he spent more time in Jaisalmer than at any time since his childhood.

With Jaisalmer as his base and more time in hand, he was nostalgic for his parents, his wife, and even his friends, Akbar Khan and Paras, who had both recently passed away. He was fatigued, and at the same time quite worried about the future of his sons. He was caught in a dilemma, as deep in his heart he knew that opium trade could be the salvation of his family going forward, but he still was bound by the oath to his father to not enter the opium business.

The year 1805 ended on a gloomy note for Guman Chand, despite the grand wedding of his youngest son, Pratap Chand, who married a lovely girl called Mana.

Patwon Ki Haveli built by Guman Chand
Under GNU Free Document License

Started by Seth Guman Chand Bapna, as a public works project for providing employment in an economically declining Jaisalmer, finished by his son Seth Zorawarmal Bapna. This mansion is one of five started by Guman Chand, one for each of his sons. The construction took fifty years to complete (1795 – 1845) and skilled craftsmen from all over India worked on this mansion and was designated as a National Monument by Prime Minister of India, Indira Gandhi during her visit in 1965 and nationalized. Currently this mansion is owned by Ministry of Archeology of the Government of India.

Patwon ki Haveli Balcony Carving Detail
Photograph by Ralf Heynen of the Netherlands

Patwon ki Haveli - Interior Frescas
Courtesy – Kothari Patwon Ki Haveli Website

Guman Chand's story was a long one and it was almost 1:00 AM when Dev finished it. As usual, Kunal and Ranika listened in rapt attention and fascination. It was Saturday night and Ranika didn't have to worry about school the next day.

"Seth Guman Chand certainly led a very full and eventful life. He was less awe-inspiring than his father, Deoraj, who had a larger-than-life personality. Despite that, Guman Chand was a much more consequential figure than Deoraj. No question, he was very lucky all his life, but what also comes across is that he was a highly understated man, a man of no drama, few words and lots of action. He was highly driven and goal-oriented, but he knew not to flaunt either his ambition or wealth. All in all, he was an extremely intelligent man who had tremendous foresight. His ambition led him to be flexible sometimes, but he also showed that he could be as firm as Deoraj when he wanted to be. No matter how much sense it made for the family to get into the opium business, once he made that promise to his dead father about not getting into opium, he stuck by it, no matter what," said Ranika.

"While I feel a great deal of reverence and admiration for Deoraj, I find Guman Chand to be very enigmatic. He certainly kept a lot of his deepest feelings and emotions hidden from everybody. I wish I could have a conversation with him. There is so much more I want to know about him and would like to ask him," said Kunal.

"Quite true. He was the most mysterious of all our ancestors, but had it not been for Seth Guman Chand Patwa there would have been no Bapna Dynasty and no *Seth* Zorawarmal," said Dev.

"Oh, the famous and multi-faceted *Seth* Zorawarmal," said Kunal. "Who became one of the richest and most powerful men in India in his time and about whom history books talk a great deal."

"Yes, the very same Zorawarmal about whom I will tell you tomorrow," said Dev.

Chapter 11 – Story of Zorawar Mal – 1
1805 AD – 1810 AD

The years between 1805 and 1807 were years of struggle for Seth Guman Chand Patwa and his five sons. Despite their best efforts, profits from their national and international operations had dwindled, although sufficient to keep them in prominence in Jaisalmer. The construction of the "Patwon ki Havelis," the five grand mansions, one for each one of Guman Chand's sons undertaken as public works projects to provide employment to people of Jaisalmer, was in full flow. Expert craftsmen had gathered from all over India and were performing specialized work, while thousands of local people were employed in the construction. The young Bapna brothers continued to slog and toil, travelling all over India, trying to get better control of their business.

Salim Singh was following in his father's footsteps by perpetrating the same depravities that his father was infamous for. He became a debauch, recklessly kidnapping any woman who caught his fancy. As usual, the Paliwals were the ones who faced the brunt of these atrocities. The Paliwal villages were up in arms and were seriously considering leaving en-masse, except that Salim Singh was preventing this mass exodus by literally holding people hostage.

Salim Singh's atrocities reached their climax in 1808. *Rawal* Mulraj had permitted the exiled Rae Singh, who used to be the crown prince and the slayer of Salim Singh's father Swaroop Singh, back into Jaisalmer. However, he and his wife and children were kept under house arrest a few miles from Jaisalmer. Salim Singh conspired with a few loyalist soldiers to light Rae Singh's house on fire in the middle of the night, burning alive Rae Singh, his wife and all his children. Thus ended the saga of the gallant and noble Rae Singh, who was beloved by all in

Jaisalmer. The residents of Jaisalmer went into mourning and this event spurred a further exodus of people who had the opportunity to leave.

Later in the same year (1808), Salim Singh finally accomplished the one thing he most wanted to accomplish. There was an Oswal merchant by the name of Bardhaman, who was close to Guman Chand and family. Bardhaman was about the same age as Guman Chand's eldest son, Bahadurmal and he had practically grown up with the Bapna brothers. He was a prominent merchant in his own right and caught Salim Singh's attention. Salim Singh extorted money from him and Bardhaman made the mistake of initially defying Salim Singh and refused to make some payments. Salim Singh had Bardhaman's property confiscated and a settlement was reached, with the help of the ruler *Rawal* Mulraj.

Unbeknownst to Rawal Mulraj, Salim Singh altered the terms of the settlement and imposed stiffer taxes on Bardhaman. Guman Chand picked up cudgels on behalf of Bardhaman and personally went and complained to *Rawal* Mulraj. It was decided that a meeting would be held at a neutral place with *Rawal* Mulraj, Salim Singh, Bardhaman and Guman Chand to sort out the matter. The meeting was held at the *Rawal's* lakeside mansion, called Amar Sagar. When Guman Chand returned from the meeting, he felt sick to his stomach. He turned pale and then blue. He kept going in and out of consciousness. The ladies of the house, his daughters-in-law, tried their best to look after him. Only the youngest son, Pratap Mal, was in Jaisalmer. He immediately summoned all the best *vaids* (doctors of Indian system of medicine) and even a European doctor who was visiting Jaisalmer. They all confirmed that Guman Chand had been poisoned and there was no hope for his survival. Guman Chand suffered great agony all night long and died in the morning. He was fifty-seven years old.

All of the brothers were less than two days journey away from Jaisalmer. They all arrived the third day, but the funeral had already taken place. Guman Chand Patwa's death and the manner of his death brought forth a genuine outpouring of grief, sorrow, anger and rage in all of Jaisalmer and the Paliwal villages. The golden boy of the golden city in the desert, Guman Chand Patwa was admired for his business acumen and intelligence, while loved for all the philanthropic activities he was involved in. He upheld the high ideals of his father, Deoraj, and was famous as a compassionate and fair merchant. Even Rawal Mulraj, who attended the various funeral services, was genuinely grief stricken and delivered a touching eulogy to Seth Guman Chand Patwa in a gathering in the main market of Jaisalmer, where Guman Chand had his *pedi* (main office). Rawal Mulraj also profusely apologized to the five sons of Guman Chand that the alleged poisoning occurred in the *rawal's* own house. However, beyond words, *Rawal* Mulraj found himself incapable of taking any action against the powerful Salim Singh. Salim Singh also came to attend Guman Chand's funeral, but he was turned away at the gates by an angry crowd that had gathered at the open air crematorium.

The Bapna brothers were understandably stunned by the sudden death of their father. They alternated between shock, grief and anger. Guman Chand was not only their father, but their idol. All their life they strived to prove to Guman Chand that they were his worthy sons. Now their rock was gone. Despite having differences with their father on the issue of opium trade, they adored him, and his death left a deep void in their lives. At the same time, the manner of his death and their difficult experiences in Jaisalmer over the past decade made them somewhat cynical and more prone to taking liberties with the high moral and strict ethical standards set by their grandfather Seth Deoraj and continued by their father, Guman Chand. They believed that the rulers and their coterie did not play by any ethical rules and the concept of morals and ethics was simply a tool in the hands of the ruling classes to keep the rest of the populace in line. Now that they were no longer bound by the oath of their father to their grandfather, the five Bapna brothers set about in earnest to plan their entry into the opium business.

After a year of planning, the brothers could not come up with a plan which would keep all five of them together in one place, whether in Jaisalmer or another town. The entire Bapna family was very close. They were loath to part, but there seemed to be no other way. The plan called for leveraging their existing contacts with the rulers of several Central Indian states, which at this juncture were independent states, out of the Moghul sphere and not yet under the British. The eldest four brothers took up residences in the four top opium producing areas of Central India.

Bahadur Mal was to move to Kota, a town on the edge of Rajasthan where the reigning ruler had invited him to be the "*Nagar Seth*," the pre-eminent merchant in town. "*Nagar Seth*" was a title of great honor and brought with it many commercial and political privileges, such as concessional tax rates, monopolies in certain trades and certain political powers. This title had certain responsibilities, the main ones being the responsibility to lend to the ruler personally and to the state treasury when needed. Sawai Ram was to assume the position of *"Nagar Seth"* in the opium- producing state of Patan, also in Rajasthan. Mangani Ram became the *"Nagar Seth"* of Ratlam state, a site of a major regional opium exchange, which lay in the Central Provinces (not Rajasthan). Finally, Zorawar Mal was named the *"Nagar Seth"* of the opium market city of Indore in Malwa. Each of the brothers planned to purchase opium in large quantities in their respective areas and then ship it, using their traditional contacts to Jaisalmer. The youngest brother, Pratap Mal, would stay based in Jaisalmer and coordinate exporting this opium to China via the land route, which the Bapnas uniquely had a great deal of familiarity with.

After the plan and all the details were finalized, it was decided that the brothers would move on Feb 1, 1810. There were many farewell events and banquets leading up to that fateful day, when after seventy years of a continuous, eventful and by and large highly successful stay in Jaisalmer, the bulk of the Bapna family was finally moving out of Jaisalmer. They were well known in Jaisalmer and had created a lot of good will. Barring Salim Singh, they scarcely had an enemy in town, and the Oswals and the Paliwals were deeply saddened by their imminent departure. There were tearful farewells after each private banquet and the brothers assured everybody that Jaisalmer would always be their hometown and they would visit often. The public works project of "Patwon ki Haveli" mansions was to continue over the next several years. To say that they were impressive was to understate their grandeur, and the brothers arranged for sufficient funds to be expended via Pratap Mal and their managers to last another forty years.

Thus having sealed their permanent association with Jaisalmer, the brothers' wives set about packing their belongings and household for another new beginning in the family's lives. A nineteen-year-old Deoraj had arrived with a sixteen-year-old Bhairavi in Jaisalmer some seventy years ago, penniless and full of hope. His four grandsons were now leaving Jaisalmer, millionaires, but still full of hope of an even greater future. When Deoraj left his native Osian for Jaisalmer, he was an innocent lad, ignorant of the ways of the world, while his four grandsons were far from innocent, highly educated, seasoned and experienced in business, highly intelligent and wise to the ways of the world.

On Feb 1, 1810, all was packed into four different caravans, one for each brother. Each caravan consisted of countless horses, wagons, bullock carts, scores of servants and staff, and many armed guards, and was ready to roll out of Jaisalmer. In contrast, their grandfather Deoraj had left Osian in one rickety old hired bullock cart. Thousands of residents of Jaisalmer—Rajputs, Pailwals, Oswals, peasants and others—thronged at the gates of the city to see the brothers off, in stark contrast to their grandfather Deoraj, whom not a single resident of Osian came to see off. As was the custom, the *Maharawal* of Jaisalmer, Mulraj, sent an emissary, dressed in full military regalia, to formally ask the brothers to reconsider leaving Jaisalmer. Not that the *Maharawal* had any intentions or expectations to change their mind, but it was a customary mark of respect and an honor granted to the brothers, a formal way of expressing that they would be missed.

At exactly six o'clock in the morning the standard bearer for each brother's caravan, in reverse order of their ages, started blowing their conches one by one to announce their departure out of Jaisalmer. First it was Zorawar Mal's standard bearer, with a blue and white colored standard, that sounded his conch, and his caravan rolled out. Then it was Mangani Raam's caravan, led by his orange-colored standard, followed by Sawai Raam's deep green-colored standard. Finally, the eldest Bahadur Mal's caravan, led by his gold-colored standard, rolled out, with Bahadur Mal and his wife Chatura in a standing position inside their magnificent black carriage, appointed with fine drapery embroidered in gold and drawn by twelve tall Marwari horses, standing with folded hands, bidding farewell to the residents of their beloved city. Not an eye was dry as the last of the horsemen and bullock carts finally exited the city gates of Jaisalmer, and even *Rawal* Mulraj wiped a tear, watching from afar, standing at the top of his palace tower within the famed Jaisalmer fort. In contrast, Prime Minister Salim Singh, standing right next to the *Maharawal,* had a winning smile on his face, his lips curled, eyebrows raised and eyes open wide.

It was a victory of sorts, but a hollow one for Salim Singh, and it came at a very high price. Jaisalmer was in shambles, an almost dying town. Its population had dwindled to half of what it was a decade ago. The diminishment of the land route in favor of maritime trade had wreaked havoc, further devastated by the cruel, stupid and idiotic policies of Swaroop Singh and Salim Singh. The enduring droughts put the finishing touches on the ultimate decline of Jaisalmer. What was worse was that indiscriminate taxation, extortion and kidnappings of women had eroded the moral base of the city and its rulers. Parts of Jaisalmer already looked like a ghost town.

As Zorawar Mal's carriage travelled out of Jaisalmer, he turned around to take a last look at Jaisalmer fort, which still looked magnificent from a distance under the morning sun. Even though he couldn't see *Rawal* Mulraj and Salim Singh standing on top of the tower, he knew they were there. Unlike his grandfather, Deoraj, who never looked back as he was leaving Osian and never ever visited Osian again, Zorawar Mal took a good look back at the Jaisalmer fort and swore an oath to return to avenge his father's death.

Chapter 12 - Brothers Parting
Feb 2, 1810 AD

    Growing up virtually without a mother, the five Bapna brothers had drawn much closer to each other than most normal brothers. Under the maternal influence of their grandmother Bhairavi, who had drilled into them the values of family first, loyalty to family, and family before wealth, they had come to strongly believe in the tremendous strength of a united family. Even in the day and age and place where extended families were the norm, Guman Chand's sons were particularly attached. Since each of the brothers had towering and powerful personalities, it was not difficult for them to impart these values to their respective wives, most of who were selected very carefully by Bhairavi. Bhairavi made sure that the girls she selected for her grandsons were already predisposed towards a strong united family. After Bhairavi's death, Chatura, the eldest son's wife, took over and continued a lifestyle and regimen within the family that promoted that unity. There was genuine love and affection, in fact very deep emotional bonds, between the brothers, but also surprisingly between the brother's wives. After years of living together, therefore, the hardest thing for the brothers and their wives to do was to part ways with each other.

    The brother's caravans, as they left Jaisalmer, were supposed to travel together for a day to a wayside stop near Jodhpur. There they would rest together for the night and in the morning embark on their separate routes to their respective destinations. As the caravans approached the wayside stop called "Gajsarai," the ruler of Jodhpur having been informed of their arrival had a welcoming party with a guard of honor waiting for them. They had set up special arrangements for the Bapna brothers, including tents and food. The youngest brother,

Pratap Mal, and his wife had also accompanied the caravans until this point to see the brothers off at "Gajsarai." All five brothers decided to spend the final evening together in one tent, while their wives spent the evening and night together in another. No one got any sleep that night, as they chatted away, reminiscing and making proclamations of eternal unity and attachment.

Bahadurmal, being the eldest and a father figure, gave a parting gift to each of his brothers. The three brothers graciously accepted what Bahadurmal had chosen for them. When it came Zorawarmal's turn, he declined his fabulously expensive gift and asked for "Deoraj's ring" instead, which Bahadurmal was wearing on his ring finger. After Guman Chand's death, Bahadurmal, being the eldest, had inherited that ring, the simple brass ring which their grandmother Bhairavi had gifted to Deoraj on the day of their engagement. As much as Bahadurmal loved his brothers, even he hesitated to part with that ring, but after a moment's hesitation he smiled and slipped "Deoraj's ring" on Zorawarmal's ring finger. Zorawarmal bowed down and touched Bahadurmal's feet, after which the two brothers embraced warmly. Zorawarmal swore to obey Bahadurlmal all his life, like a son does to his father.

Finally, as dawn approached and along with it the inevitable final parting, the scene was something to behold. The younger brothers and wives touched the feet of the elders, seeking their blessings. The entire family marched up to the idol of *Sachiyaa Maata*, which was installed on one end of "Gajsarai," and performed the *puja* ceremony, seeking her blessings. There were hugs and tears and sometimes literal wailing. Emotions took over at the last moment and the departure was delayed by a couple of hours as the brothers just could not bring themselves to part. Finally, reason prevailed and each caravan pulled out in separate directions amidst the cries of "Hail to Seth Deoraj" and "Hail to Seth Guman Chand" from the staff, caravan members, and the welcoming party.

The five Bapna brothers finally parted ways, never to reunite as a complete family again, but they always stayed in contact, collaborating with each other in business, helping each other in business, and establishing a model for future generations of a strong, united family and its virtues. The eldest brother, Bahadurmal, and his wife acted as surrogate parents for the rest of the family and it was largely due to their devotion to family that the brothers and their descendants stayed unusually close.

Seth Bahadur Mal Bapna - Kota
Courtesy – Budh Singh Saheb Bapna Family, Kota

Seth Mangni Ram Bapna - Ratlam
Courtesy – Budh Singh Saheb Bapna Family, Kota

Seth Zorawar Mal Bapna - Indore, Udaipur
Seen here with his two infant sons Sultan Mal and Chandan Mal
(Courtesy – Bapna House Family Collection)

Chapter 13 - Story of Zorawar Mal – 2
1810 AD – 1820 AD

The period between 1810 and 1820 was a time of rebirth and rebuilding of the Bapna clan. India was still one of the richest countries in the world. Its economic decline had not yet begun. Each branch of the Bapna family prospered and the end of this era marked the ascendency of the Bapna family collectively into one of the richest families in all of India. They collectively were known as the "Rothschild's of India." Despite being well-educated, cultured and groomed well to succeed in big business, for years the collective ambitions of the brothers were hemmed in by the difficult business conditions they had faced in Jaisalmer and the rest of India, not to mention their inability to enter the opium trade due to their father's oath to their grandfather. Now the brothers were liberated to pursue their own dreams in their own way. They had many businesses, but they primarily used opium as the means to climb the ladder to amazing success.

Bahadur Mal soon ensconced himself in Kota by making liberal advances to the ruler and the treasury, which was always starved for cash. He obtained a virtual monopoly on all opium buying in the region and was able to procure opium at concessional rates. He became fabulously wealthy and held the levers to exercise tremendous political influence in Kota.

Sawaii Raam settled very nicely in Patan, which was a friendly environment, as Sawaii Raam was personally very close to the ruler. He too established an opium-buying monopoly in his region.

Mangani Raam became a dominant player in the Ratlam opium exchange and gained favor of the ruler by making significant advances to him. His wealth and status were also legendary.

Tatya Jog Kibe
Prime Minister of Holkar State – 1815 to 1815, A legend, a hero, a political genius and a Holkar Family confidante, also a business magnate in his own right

Friend of Seth Bahadur Mal Bapna of Kota and business partner of Seth Zorawar Mal Bapna of Indore. Together the three dominated the Malwa, Ujjain and Kota Opium Exchanges in the first part of the 19th century before the British East India Company clamped down on independent Opium traders in this region, in order to create and perpetuate its own opium monopoly. Both the Bapna Family and Kibe Family had become two of the wealthiest and politically most powerful families in India by 1825.
Courtesy – Ahilya Library – Indore MP India

Tatya Jog Kibe - Cenotaph - Chhatri
Chhatri Bag Area Indore, where Seth Zorawar Mal's Cenotaph was also built, but has been dismantled since due to its dilapidated condition
Courtesy – Bapna House family collection

Pratap Mal, the youngest, became fabulously wealthy, transporting all the opium purchased by his brothers to China via the land route that he was intimately familiar with and where he had wide ranging contacts. His great wealth insulated him from some of the most vicious attacks against him by the tyrant, Prime Minister Salim Singh Mehta.

Zorawar Mal, however, became even more of a risk taker than his formidable and hugely prosperous brothers. When Zorawar Mal Bapna arrived in Indore, the ruling prince was Malhar Rao Holkar III, still a minor, and therefore, the State was run by a powerful minister called Tantia Jog Kibe, who also was a very rich businessman, a fellow dealer in the opium market. Zorawar Mal struck an alliance with Jog with the help of his elder brother Bahadurmal, who was a personal friend of Jog's. Together, they cleverly manipulated the Indore opium market, the largest in the region, to become dominant players and were able to procure opium at a highly concessional rate.

Zorawar Mal was able to procure transporters at cheap rates to send his opium to Jaisalmer, again under the protection of his elder brother, Seth Bahadur Mal, now based out of Kota. Besides, he had volunteered to take over his father's old money lending branches, which the other brothers wanted to shut down, and he was able to revive those businesses by establishing good relations with the British who ruled most of those territories. He was able to do so because of his knowledge of the English language and his diplomatic skills. During one of his visits to China he came across fine silk fabric, which he started importing from China in exchange for opium, thus creating a highly profitable barter system with his counterpart merchants in China. His China office became his greatest profit center by 1820.

Zorawar Mal travelled constantly, always taking his two sons, Sultan Mal and Chandan Mal, with him. This was also a period when Zorawar Mal's fame spread all over India, particularly in Rajputana (Rajasthan), and he established enduring friendships with various rulers of the independent kingdoms within Rajasthan. He also was a trusted advisor to the Maratha king Holkar in his adopted city of Indore. Zorawar Mal's striking good looks, his refined manner, his regal bearing and his high intelligence won him many friends in high places, which further cemented his position as one of the premier merchants of his time in India. All this acted as a foundation for his even greater successes in the following three decades.

Zorawar Mal was a great patron of art, architecture and religion. He built several mansions for himself, the most notable of which is of course the "Patwon ki Haveli" in Jaisalmer, which was considered an architectural and artistic marvel. However, this mansion never became his primary residence, as he never returned to Jaisalmer as a full-time resident. He did spend a great deal of time in his famed mansion in Ajmer, which was described by some historians as a fabulous example of Mogul and Rajput architecture. He was also a great philanthropist, donating large sums of money to various temples, charitable causes and trusts all over Rajasthan and Gujarat.

By 1818, the independent kingdoms of Rajasthan were in complete disarray. Yearly raids of the Marathas extracted stiff tributes. Zorawar Mal, intimate with many of the rulers in Rajasthan, was sympathetic to their plight. He established direct communications with the British East India Company headquarters in Calcutta and Delhi via his existing British contacts to petition the British to come to the aid of these hapless Rajasthan kingdoms. The British were already facing problems on many fronts, and they resisted intervention for fear of over-extending themselves.

The British were very methodical in how they advanced into a territory and they felt that they did not have enough firsthand knowledge of the political situation in Rajasthan to intervene. Upon repeated entreaties by Zorawar Mal, the British finally decided to send Col. James Tod, the same gentlemen whom Sam Marshall informed about the Bapna brothers that he tutored in Jaisalmer, as a political agent to Rajasthan, or "Rajputana," as the British called it. Col. Tod arrived in Rajasthan in 1818 and his mission was to gather as much political information about Rajputana as possible in order to lay the ground work for British expansion there in the near future. He was also empowered to suggest and recommend any possible treaties with any of the independent states to the Governor General. Col. Tod was an extremely able British officer who turned out to be a legendary information-gatherer and a diplomat. His experiences and travels through Rajputana were well documented in his famous "Annals and Antiquities of Rajputana," a three-volume collection published after his retirement and return to England in 1829.

One of the first persons Col. Tod sought out once he got to Rajputana was Zorawar Mal, as he remembered being told about him by Sam Marshall. Tod found Zorawar Mal interesting, well-rounded, well-read and extremely well-informed about the inner power circles in

Rajputana. Zorawar Mal's command over the English language made it very easy to communicate with him, and Tod and Zorawar Mal became great friends. Zorawar Mal also introduced Tod to Jainism and a Jain guru, Yati Gyanchandra, who Tod accepted as his own guru. Zorawar Mal's friendship with Tod yielded a major windfall for Zorawar Mal in the coming years. Tod relied heavily on Zorawar Mal's analysis of the fast-changing political landscape of Rajputana. Zorawar Mal informed Col. Tod that almost all of the independent states of Rajputana were ready to accept the overlordship of the British via a treaty. These states saw this as their only salvation and the only way to protect themselves from the yearly onslaughts of the Marathas. The annual Maratha raids had virtually brought Rajputana to its knees.

From 1818 to 1819, Col. Tod orchestrated treaties with almost all the major Rajputana kingdoms. Zorawar Mal was instrumental behind the scenes in facilitating these treaties by acting in an intermediary role, friend to both the rulers and the British, but partial to none. Most of these independent kingdoms had border issues and other squabbles with each other. Now that most of these Rajputana kingdoms were British allies, Zorawar Mal assisted Col. Tod in acting as an honest broker to resolve many of these squabbles. Zorawar Mal's status and influence was at its zenith among the rulers and princes of Rajputana.

There was one treaty between the British and one Rajputana kingdom which was of personal and particular interest to Zorawar Mal. That was the kingdom of Jaisalmer. By 1818, Jaisalmer was close to complete collapse. The economy had shrunk to disastrous levels. Sensing its weakness, the neighboring kingdoms of Jodhpur and Bikaner were slowly seizing territories from Jaisalmer. Salim Singh was highly unpopular and was the virtual ruler of Jaisalmer. Rawal Mulraj was very old and a puppet. Zorawar Mal desperately pleaded with Tod for British intervention in Jaisalmer to remove Salim Singh. The British did not yet have a treaty with Jaisalmer which would give them a legal basis to remove Salim Singh. Salim Singh, however, was now desperate for British protection, as he faced difficulties from all sides. He thought that as part of the treaty with the British he could codify and secure his and his successors' position in Jaisalmer as hereditary prime ministers.

Tod started negotiating the treaty with Jaisalmer and the negotiations got stuck on the point of Salim Singh and his successors being appointed hereditary prime ministers for posterity. In one of his few decisive actions, Rawal Mulraj signed the treaty with the

British in 1818, making Jaisalmer a British protectorate, without any provision made for Salim Singh and his successors. Salim Singh, to great disappointment of Zorawar Mal, was able to get a verbal assurance by the British that they would do nothing to dislodge him personally from the prime ministership. Zorawar Mal continued to plead with the Governor General via Col. Tod to intervene and remove Salim Singh in the interest of the kingdom of Jaisalmer. Col. Tod supported such intervention, but the Governor General was reluctant to intervene. Rawal Mulraj died a year after the treaty was signed in the year 1819. Mulraj's grandson, Gaj Singh, was installed Rawal by Salim Singh as his puppet.

Salim Singh continued to hold the increasingly desperate Paliwals hostage, not allowing them to leave their villages and migrate elsewhere. He continued to oppress them with heavy taxation and kidnap their women for his pleasure. Col. Tod's entreaties to the Governor General for intervention in removing Salim Singh continued to fall on deaf ears.

Col James Tod
British Agent to Rajputana – 1817 - 1823
Legendary Historian of Rajputana, Responsible for bringing Rajputana States under the British Dominion, Friend and ally of Seth Zorawar Mal Bapna
Picture part of Public Domain

COLONEL JAMES TOD.

Chapter 14 - Story of Zorawar Mal – 3
1820 AD – 1824 AD

In 1820, Zorawar Mal's life crossed paths with another great kingdom in Rajputana, the kingdom of Mewar, with its capital at Udaipur. The ruling family of Mewar, the Sisodias, were considered the most distinguished Rajput family in all of India. The Sisodias acquired this claim by providing to Mewar a series of rulers who were noted for their gallantry and service to their people. Bappa Rawal, Rana Hamir, Rana Kumbha, Rana Sangha and Rana Pratap were the most prominent of the great Sisodia rulers who ruled Mewar from the 8th century AD until 1947. The Sisodias claimed to be one of, if not the oldest ruling families in the world.

Indeed, the Sisodia rulers of Mewar were a distinguished lot. Unfazed by adversity, gallant to a fault, warriors of great courage, and patriotic to their core, they resisted the Islamic dynasties in India with great vigor and with more success than any other dynasty in India, with the possible exception of the Marathas. Much later, the Maratha chieftain, Shivaji broke the back of the Mogul empire. Sisodias were known to fight unto death in the battlefield and history is replete with tales of their battles and their high sense of honor. Since they resisted the Islamic dynasties the longest, while others made treaties with them, they remained relatively less wealthy compared to their other Rajput counterpart ruling families of Jaipur and Marwar. Even the Sisodias ultimately accepted the overlordship of the Moguls during the reign of Emperor Jehangir, but they were the last Rajput ruling family to do so.

After the downfall of the Moguls, the kingdom of Mewar became independent for the first time in about two hundred years, around 1800.

This independence lasted until the 1818. This period of independence coincided with arguably the greatest suffering the people of Mewar had ever had to endure in their history, far more than even the worst hardships they had suffered at the hands of the ruling Muslim dynasties in India. The Hindu Marathas had superseded the Muslim Moghuls as the pre-eminent power in India by 1750. The Marathas started conducting annual raids on the small, nominally independent kingdoms of Rajputana, including Mewar, in the late 1700s until 1818. The Marathas inflicted severe damage to the property and the morale of the people of these kingdoms by extracting exorbitant tributes annually.

By 1818 these Rajput kingdoms, especially Mewar, were impoverished, their populations dwindling to very low numbers, and the ruling family itself straining to make ends meet. The conditions in Mewar were pathetic with the ruler in great debt, the capital city Udaipur's population being down by half from its peak, the commerce at a complete standstill, and the Royal house of Sisodias not even having the financial wherewithal to feed their elephants and horses. This was the condition that Col. Tod found in Mewar when he visited it in 1818. When he extended to Rana Bhim Singh, the then ruler of Mewar, an offer of treaty with the British under the terms of which Mewar would become a subordinate state of the British, Bhim Singh readily accepted, as this was his only protection against the marauding Marathas. The treaty allowed the Sisodias to continue administering the state, with almost full autonomy but under the overlordship of the British.

Once Mewar was a British subordinate, Col. Tod, as the British Political Agent, turned his attention to reviving the finances of Mewar. He wanted to appoint capable trustees in charge of the state treasury so tax collection could be streamlined and accounted for, and he also wanted to instill confidence in potential investors so merchants and businessmen would move into Mewar to start businesses and thereby invest their money. Col. Tod solved both of these problems by recommending that the ruler Bhim Singh invite Seth Zorawar Mal Bapna from Indore and appoint him the state treasurer. Zorawar Mal's presence would signal to the business community all over India, of Mewar's business- friendly climate, which could pull in massive investments. A delegation of high nobles and senior military commanders was dispatched by Bhim Singh to Indore to formally invite *Seth* Zorawar Mal to Mewar.

Seth Zorawar Mal arrived in Udaipur, the capital of Mewar, with his entourage on Sept. 18, 1820. He was accompanied by his wife, Chautha, nineteen-year-old son Sultan Mal, and sixteen-year-old son Chandan Mal. His four brothers with their wives accompanied Zorawar Mal into Udaipur to express their support and to celebrate with Zorawar Mal this great honor bestowed upon him by the scion of the great Sisodia Dynasty. *Seth* Bahadur Mal had also used his contacts in the British Governor General's office to get Zorawar Mal's appointment in Udaipur ratified quickly after the recommendation was made by Col. Tod and Rana Bhim Singh. Zorawar Mal's party of roughly five hundred relatives, employees, security detail and attendants was warmly received at the gates of Udaipur by a large crowd, led by Maharana Bhim Singh himself with his entire family. Col. Tod was also in the receiving party and warmly shook hands with Seth Zorawar Mal and his brothers as they entered the almost deserted town of Udaipur. It was a typical Rajput reception, with the guests being sprinkled with perfume, offered flowers and their foreheads adorned with red *tika*, signifying that they were honored guests. Seth Zorawar Mal was also accorded the status of *"Nagar Seth"* by Rana Bhim Singh and presented with a beautiful mansion right in the heart of Udaipur, known as *"Nagar Seth's Haveli."*

Zorawar Mal had visited Udaipur a few times earlier during his business travels. As he rode in the welcoming procession through the city, he could not help but marvel at the natural beauty of the hills that nestled the city. There were several small natural lakes that added to its charm and the pure Rajput architecture of the city palace and other buildings made the overall effect breathtaking. While Jaisalmer was an enchanting place right in the middle of the desert, with its golden sandstone buildings, Udaipur was a lush lake city, surrounded by hills, dotted by white limestone buildings.

Citi Palace Udaipur-Maharana Bhim Singh
Under GNU Free Document License

Udaipur Mewar - A Panoramic View
Picture taken in 2012 - Under GNU Free Document License

Tod in Udaipur - Unknown Artist
Dated 1880s – Also riding is Tod's Jain Guru Yati GyanchandraJi, introduced to him by Seth Zorawarmal Bapna

Mehta Sher Singh - Right with Mewar Rana
Prime Minister Udaipur State, from Bachhawat Oswal Family in mid and late 1820s, while Seth Zorawarmal was reviving the Udaipur Finances. Seth Zorawar had good relations with the Mehta, as the Prime Minister was an upright person of good moral character and loyal to Mewar
Picture courtesy Peter Blohm and his website- http://www.indianminiaturepaintings.co.uk/

Maharana Bhim Singh Mewar - 1778-1828
Portrait from a Wall Painting at Seth Ji Ri Haveli (the erstwhile residence of the Bapna Family in Udaipur)

The esteemed *Seth* Zorawar Mal quickly acclimatized himself with the state of affairs in Udaipur and re-organized the entire tax collection system. He made large advances to the ruler, Bhim Singh, so he could run his household with the dignity befitting the House of Sisodia. It was reported that he advanced in 1820, a sum of Rs. two million, out of which he forgave the sum of Rs. one million, a staggering sum. He spent his own money, created an agency, and placed trusted employees of the agency as tax collectors all over the state and collected taxes through his agency. His presence inspired confidence and within a couple of years, hundreds of merchants had either moved back or made a first-time move into Udaipur, setting up businesses and providing employment, resulting in the return of most of the population that had fled. By 1823, Udaipur finances were on solid footing and it was again a thriving commercial city that it had been a few decades prior. British protection provided security and Marathas no longer could raid Mewar at will. *Seth* Zorawar Mal got his two sons, Sultan Mal and Chandan Mal, involved in the business-at-hand in Udaipur.

While staying busy in Mewar and handling his business which extended well beyond India's borders, Zorwar Mal never lost touch with nor forgot about Jaisalmer. He visited there often, providing moral and material support for Pratap Mal, to keep Salim Singh at bay, thus preventing him from harming his brother. His almost continuous entreaties to the Governor General to intervene to remove Salim Singh were getting more serious attention, considering Zorawar Mal's enhanced status as a top businessman of his time and further bolstered by his apparent miraculous successes in Udaipur in single-handedly restoring the city's fortunes.

By the beginning of 1824, in Jaisalmer, the entire Paliwal community—men, women and children—had picked up and left overnight, leaving their villages abandoned. No one knew where they went and now Jaisalmer's pride and biggest revenue generators, the Paliwals, were gone suddenly, as if mysteriously disappearing into thin air.

The Governor General finally gave his approval to empower the local British agent to remove Salim Singh. However, the orders were stalled before they could be sent out from the Governor General's office amidst bureaucratic wrangling on the matter. Earlier, in 1823, Zorawar Mal's trusted friend and confidante Col. Tod was called back to Delhi and sent back to England. Seth Zorawar Mal decided to take matters into his own hands. In February of 1824, Zorawar Mal arrived in Jaisalmer, leaving the responsibility of Udaipur affairs with his young sons, Sultan Mal and Chandan Mal. Sultan Mal showed great promise as a businessman as he had learned well from his father.

In Jaisalmer, Zorawar Mal parked himself in the largely completed "Patwon ki Haveli," which was shaping up beautifully. There he established clandestine communications with a group of Bhatti nobles led by the ruling prince, *Rawal* Gaj Singh, who all had been sidelined by Salim Singh. A plan was hatched by which a minor Rajput royal would accost Salim Singh within the royal palace and stab him to death. The *Rawal* would then claim that Salim Singh was murdered by a palace intruder who escaped. True to plan, Salim Singh was ambushed in the palace by the Bhatti nobleman, but he was able to avoid serious injury by taking evasive action and quickly escaping to his magnificent mansion, called *Zalim Singh ki Haveli*. He had constructed it to outdo the Bapna's *Patwon Ki Haveli*. There he started recovering under the care of his wife, Aarya, the same Aarya who was to first marry Zorawar Mal, the same Aarya whom Salim Singh married by threatening to ruin her father if he refused. Consistent with his character, even after his marriage to

Aarya, Salim Singh inflicted all kinds of physical abuse on Aarya, who was condemned to live the life of a physically and emotionally battered wife. Salim Singh had married another woman and kept two wives, not to mention many concubines.

Zorawar Mal and the entire royal household of Bhatis were confused. They knew that once Salim Singh recovered and emerged from his chambers, he would take revenge and possibly massacre all responsible for this conspiracy, including Rawal Gaj Singh and Seth Zorawar Mal. In desperation, Zorawar Mal asked *Rawal* Gaj Singh to arrange to send a secret message to Aarya, asking her to meet with him, even if she could slip out only briefly.

Aarya met Zorawar Mal on the terrace of the Royal Palace of Jaisalmer. It was a moonlit February night, with clear skies and stars filling the heavens. Aarya stepped forward onto the terrace uncertainly to meet Zorawar Mal. Zorawar Mal had changed a lot from the slender, clean-shaven, boyish looking nineteen-year old that Aarya had known. He was now a man in his prime, his body and face filled out, his posture straighter and his manner befitting one of the most powerful men in India. His beard had a touch of grey, making him look very distinguished and a man of authority, while his clothing was luxurious and richly adorned. He was wearing two necklaces, one studded with large sparkling round emeralds, while the other studded with large round *basra* pearls.

Zorawar Mal stepped forward and intercepted Aarya's advance. They both stood there for a while, looking at each other, as moonlight illuminated both their faces. Aarya looked a little haggard and disheveled, but she still had the same glowing skin and lovely lips that Zorawar remembered. Looking at Aarya, Zorawar Mal was transported back in time to when he was nineteen, and he was overcome by emotions and feelings. At that moment, on the terrace of the Royal Palace of Jaisalmer, Zorawar Mal was standing not as one of the most powerful men in India, but as a simple human being, capable of love, affection, tenderness and melancholy. The emotions Zorawar Mal felt must have shown in his eyes, as Aarya sensing his vulnerability, extended her hand and held Zorawar's hand. It was a complete contrast—Zorawar's hand being ice cold, while Aarya's was warm. Aarya instinctively started warming Zorawar's hand by clasping it with her own on this cold Jaisalmer winter night. After a couple of minutes of intimacy, both Zorawar Mal and Aarya came back to reality and pulled away from each other.

"*Pranam* Seth Zorawar Mal Ji," said Aarya, greeting Zorawar Mal very formally.

"*Pranam*," responded Zorawar Mal, equally formal.

All the sense of intimacy disappeared between the two. They both knew why they were there. It was not a happy situation for either, and neither wanted to do what both knew must be done for the sake of everybody—the population of Jaisalmer, the House of Bhatti, Seth Zorawar Mal, and Aarya herself.

"I know what is worrying *Seth Ji* and why he wants to see me," said Aarya.

Zorawar Mal said nothing.

"By this time tomorrow *Seth Ji* will not have to worry any more. The problem will be solved," said Aarya firmly, staring at Zorawar Mal full in the eye.

Aarya turned around quickly, and without waiting for an answer from Zorawar Mal, walked away from the terrace.

Zorawar Mal stood there a long time, staring after Aarya. He was completely lost in the memories of his early years—of Bhairavi, of Guman Chand, of Aarya, of his five brothers growing up, of his Paliwal maternal grandfather Tulsa and his uncle Paras, of his father's close friend Akbar Khan… They were all gone, with the exception of his brothers and Aarya.

Fate has made me one of the richest men in India, but in return it also took Jaisalmer and Aarya away from me, thought Zorawar Mal, filled with nostalgia. "What I would not give today for my grandmother and father to witness my great success," said Zorawar Mal to himself. *Even I am not rich enough to buy that,* thought Zorawar Mal, suddenly feeling very small, as a very fuzzy image of a beautiful lady flashed inside his mind. It was the image of his mother, Jeta, whom he vaguely remembered holding him in her arms when he was two years old, shortly before she died.

Zorawar Mal took in the panoramic view of Jaisalmer at night, glittering with the lights of oil lamps, from the terrace of the palace. He gave a silent salute to his ancestors, the noble Seth Deoraj and Bhairavi, the famous Seth Guman Chand Patwa, and finally his beautiful mother, Jeta. Then slowly and very deliberately, Zorawar Mal climbed down from the terrace through the staircase, into the hallway, down the long corridor to his waiting carriage, and rode out of the palace complex.

The next morning the news spread across Jaisalmer like wildfire.

Prime Minister Salim Singh of Jaisalmer, the virtual ruler, had died of poisoning in the early morning hours. Who poisoned him and how was never definitively known.

Kuldhara Village Jaisalmer Ghost Town –
After Paliwals fled in 1824 due to Salim Singh's atrocities
Courtesy – Bapna House Family Collection

Salim Singh Haveli in Jaisalmer –
Famous for its carving, built by Jaisalmer Prime Minister Salim Singh, also called Zalim Singh because of his cruelty, to compete with his rivals the Bapna's Patwon Ki Haveli
Courtesy – Bapna House Family Collection

Prime Minister Salim Singh of Jaisalmer
Also known as Zalim Singh because of his atrocities and cruelty to Citizens of Jaisalmer
His father, Saroop Singh, also Prime Minister of Jaisalmer before him had a bloody rivalry with Seth Guman Chand Patwa which continued with rivalries between their sons, Salim Singh and Seth Zorawar Mal respectively.
Picture Courtesy – 1) Nanda Kishore Sharma, Founder Desert Museum Jaisalmer and renowned historian
2) Bhanwarlal Sutar - Jodhpur

Chapter 15 – Story of Zorawar Mal – 4
1824 AD – 1851 AD

Different parts of Jaisalmer broke out in spontaneous celebrations at the news of Salim Singh's death. People had long stopped calling him "Salim Singh" and started calling him a similar sounding "Zalim Singh" (Zalim meaning "cruel" in Urdu). There were random fireworks and some people even danced in the streets. Crowds of people thronged outside the royal palace and Patwon Ki Haveli, chanting "Long Live Rawal Gaj Singh" and "Long Live Seth Zorawar Mal."

Rawal Gaj Singh quickly summoned Seth Zorawar Mal to the palace and he immediately assumed full powers. On the advice of Zorawar Mal, Rawal Gaj Singh decided to abolish the position of the prime minister for a while, until Gaj Singh could take full stock of the situation. He then went ahead and officially appointed Seth Pratap Mal, the younger brother of Seth Zorawar Mal, who had stayed back in Jaisalmer, as the "*Nagar Seth*" of Jaisalmer. Seth Pratap Mal advanced a significant amount of money to the Rawal to facilitate his assuming of full powers in Jaisalmer, thus clearing his debts.

A few days after Salim Singh's death, Zorawarl Mal went to Salim Singh's *haveli* to visit Aarya and was surprised to find scores of Jain monks sitting inside *the haveli*. After Zorawar Mal was announced, a lady wearing a simple white garment appeared before him. It took Zorawar Mal a few seconds to recognize the lady in Jain nun's garb. It was Aarya. Zorawar Mal realized that Aarya had renounced the world and had become a nun.

"Why, Aarya?" asked Zorawar Mal in complete shock.

"I have to make amends for all my sins, *Seth Ji*," responded Aarya.

Zorawar's eyed teared up as Aarya turned around and joined the Jain monks and nuns sitting on the floor of the haveli, singing hymns.

Zorawar Mal, for the second time in his life, felt very small. All his power and wealth could not make Aarya's life a happy one. This incident reminded Zorawar Mal once again of the limitations of all his wealth and might.

Returning to Udaipur, Seth Zorawar Mal used his good offices with the ruling family of Mewar to arrange a matrimonial match between Bhim Singh's daughter and Rawal Gaj Singh of Jaisalmer, thus cementing an eternal friendship between the two most illustrious dynasties in Rajputana. Bhim Singh appointed Seth Zorawar Mal to oversee the arrangements of this grand marriage celebration, which he did with his usual diligence.

The House of Deoraj now had the confidence and the ear of two prominent kingdoms in Rajputana. It also had the ear of the British East India Company, who was by 1824 the overlord of practically the entire Indian Subcontinent. The House, through its five scions, was close to practically all the major ruling families in Rajputana. This, along with their knowledge of English and diplomatic skills, made them, particularly Seth Zorawar Mal, an obvious intermediary to any internecine dispute that might arise among the ruling establishments of Rajputana. Zorawar Mal was known for his fairness and impartiality and he settled scores of disputes among various Rajput ruling houses with equanimity and grace. Arguably, the House of Deoraj was by 1824, one of the richest and most powerful business houses in all of India. Lt. Boileau, the British officer, called them "the Rothschild's of India" in his book on his travels across Rajputana in 1834.

In 1824, Zorawar Mal's elder son Sultan Mal married the daughter of a prominent Oswal merchant family of Jaisalmer. The wedding ceremony took place in Jaisalmer and the completed portion of Patwon Ki Haveli was the site of this grand wedding celebration. Rawal Gaj Singh and his entire circle of nobles were in attendance, along with the neighboring princes and rulers.

In 1825 it was the turn of the younger son, twenty-year-old Chandan Mal. He was married to the daughter of a certain Sethia family of Mewar, whose patriarch was one of the important merchants of Rajputana. Since this was going to be the last wedding in Zorawar Mal's direct line during his lifetime and the first since arriving in Udaipur, Zorawar Mal decided to have a fabulous wedding, the likes of which

Udaipur had never seen. All the Rajputana ruling princes and noblemen were invited, and most attended. Several senior British officers of the East India Company, including the resident agents from Rajputana and neighboring agencies, attended. Several ruling Maratha and Muslim princes also attended. Scores of the richest businessmen and merchants of India attended, while thousands of minor merchants came. Hundreds of horses, scores of elephants and countless carriages were arranged for the transportation of VIPs. Public squares and roads were decorated with *rangoli*, a traditional Indian coloring pattern. The sound of musical instruments filled the air and could be heard everywhere in Udaipur. Thousands of terra cotta and other oil lamps illuminated the whole city at night during the celebrations. Mewar's famous dancing girls performed traditional Mewari dances including the famous *Ghoomer*, while food and drink was aplenty. It was estimated that one million rupees was spent on this wedding in 1825.

After years of turmoil and chaos, peace had prevailed in Udaipur for the last few years, its exchequer revived by clever handling of Zorawar Mal Bapna, and this wedding was a celebration of sorts of the return of Udaipur to peace and prosperity. Chandan Mal's wedding was a major social event in recorded history of Udaipur.

In 1828, *Rana* Bhim Singh of Mewar died in Udaipur. He was succeeded by *Rana* Jawan Singh. The Udaipur finances were now very sound, and the taxes of Mewar continued to be collected by Zorawar Mal's agency, on behalf of the treasury. His task now completed, Zorawar Mal requested the new ruler, Jawan Singh, to permit him to leave Udaipur and attend to his other business interests all over India. Jawan Singh reluctantly agreed on the condition that his sons, Sultan Mal and Chandan Mal, stay back in Udaipur to continue the good work started by Zorawar Mal. Zorawar Mal left Udaipur and spent most of his time in Indore, Ajmer and Jaisalmer, where he continued to finance and oversee the construction of Patwon ki Haveli until his death in 1851. He returned to Udaipur often, to provide valuable guidance to his two sons, and much valued counsel to the ruler.

Unlike Zorawar Mal and his brothers, Sultan Mal and his brother Chandan Mal were not educated in the classical sense. They had had no British tutors, or any consistent tutors for that matter. Zorawar Mal took both of them with him on all his travels and thought it fit to educate them practically through observation of how he himself managed his business affairs. In addition, they were the first generation since Deoraj to have grown up primarily outside of Jaisalmer, having no deep emotional attachment to it. They were also transplants of sorts in Udaipur and they still found Udaipur culture and mentality alien and rather narrow. As soon as Zorawar Mal left Udaipur, they were subjected to all kinds of petty intrigues and conspiracies on the part of the older establishment of Mewar State. These interests could not touch Zorawar Mal because of his high status and the fact that he was so far above the fray that he was practically out of reach of these petty peccadilloes. However, now they found Sultan Mal and Chandan Mal to be easy targets.

Both Sultan Mal and Chandan Mal had been born with a silver spoon in their mouths, and despite all the travelling with Zorawar Mal, they were not used to the rough and tumble or rolling in mud. The brothers were a contrast in personality. While Sultan Mal was a little tougher and more quick-witted, Chandan Mal was gentle and deliberate. Sultan Mal, with guidance from Zorawar Mal, was ultimately able to stamp his own personality on the family business in Udaipur and started ably managing the business affairs. Chandan Mal ably assisted him and took on the role of a supporting brother. After about ten years of this joint arrangement, Zorwar Mal, in 1838, decided to establish two separate firms, one for each brother, and he divided certain business assets among these two firms. The two firms were called Sultan Mal Zorawar Mal and Chandan Mal Zorawar Mal. While the two brothers continued to live in "Nagar Seth ki Haveli" in a display of family unity, their businesses were now distinct. Sultan Mal's firm prospered far more and the matters continued in this manner for the next forty-two years, until 1870. Both Sultan Mal and Chandan Mal had children when they were well in their forties, a curious coincidence. Sultan Mal had two sons, Gambhir Mal and Inder Mal, and Chandan Mal had two sons, Juharmal and Chhog Mal.

In 1851, when Zorawar Mal was in his seventy-fifth year, he returned to Udaipur to spend some time with his sons. On his way back to Indore he decided to take his four grandsons with him to spend the winter. By this time, Zorawar Mal had consolidated his business empire into fewer large branches so his sons would find it easier to manage the affairs. He had practically taken retirement and now mainly Sultan Mal was looking after the business enterprises. He spent more time now in Indore, which he liked because of the moderate climate and the genuine friendships he had established with the Holkar rulers. His grandsons ranged in age from thirteen to six. Chhogmal, the youngest, was the younger son of Chandan Mal and showed the most promise early on. Zorawar Mal was particularly fond of him, as he was a curious child who asked all kinds of questions.

In his later years, Zorawar Mal was getting disillusioned with the British. He noticed that the British were big proponents of law and order and liberal thinking as long as it did not get in the way of the commercial goals of the East India Company. When it came to protecting the core interests of the company, the British could be as or more brutal than any Indian tyrant. He also noticed that the British sometimes spoke in forked tongue and thought nothing of violating treaties and agreements if it served their ends. In the final analysis, they believed in the principle of "might is right" and liberalism was merely a veneer they put on when it was convenient for them.

Since he had been intimately familiar with the high British officers of the company over many decades and had extensive dealings with them, he was often on the receiving end of failed promises and breach-of-contracts on the part of the British East India Company. During the time he spent with his grandchildren, he told them about his experiences with the company and the nature of their business dealings.

One day in late 1851, little Chhogmal was awakened very early in the morning by his cousin, Inder Mal. It was still dark and Chhogmal wondered what was going on. Inder Mal chaperoned Chhogmal to Zorawar Mal's chambers. All the staff and grandchildren had already assembled there, along with their grandmother Chautha. Zorawar Mal was lying on his back in his bed, his eyes closed and his breathing heavy. As soon as Chhogmal entered the chamber, Chautha whispered something in Zorawar Mal's ears. Zorawar Mal opened his eyes with a great deal of difficulty and beckoned Chhogmal to him. Chhogmal walked close to his grandfather's bedside and heard Zorawar Mal say in a very weak voice, almost a whisper, "Beware of the company (the British East India Company), my boy," while he very unsteadily slipped an ordinary looking brass ring onto the ring finger of little Chhogmal. Chhogmal didn't know it yet, but it was "Deoraj's ring," the most revered heirloom for all Bapnas. Zorawar Mal then closed his eyes and after a while stopped breathing.

Zorawar Mal Bapna, one of the richest and most powerful men in India for almost half a century, was no more. Son of Seth Guman Chand, grandson of Seth Deoraj, confidante of kings and princes, friend of the British and a shaper of the destiny of Rajputana had passed away.

The ruling Holkar prince of Indore announced a state funeral for Seth Zorawar Mal and declared that a memorial be built in his memory in the Chatribag area of Indore, which housed all royal memorials.

"A large man, indeed in all senses," said Kunal.

"And highly educated and cultured too," said Ranika.

"Highly educated and cultured, but also extremely competitive and ruthless when he wanted to be," said Dev.

"Definitely a man of many contradictions. It is amazing that each of the five brothers were phenomenally successful. They were all educated and cultured. But were the others as ruthless as Zorawarmal?" asked Kunal.

"Yeah, they all were equally competitive and combative. Seth Bahadurmal, the eldest brother, was known to inflict severe punishment on clients who did not repay him his loans, loans on which he famously charged "swinging interest." But they all were known philanthropists too," said Dev.

"Amazing contradiction," said Ranika.

"Will you tell us about Zorawarmal's son, *Seth* Chandanmal, next?" asked Ranika.

"Well, not much is known about him, even in family folklore, except that he was a transitional figure and held together the business under very trying circumstances. Tomorrow I will tell you about Zorawarmal's favorite grandson, and *Seth* Chandanmal's son Chhogmal. His is another remarkable story-a great man," said Dev.

Bapna Jain Temple Amarsagar Jaisalmer –
Adeshwar Temple of Lord Parshwnath Built by Seth Himmat Ram
Bapna son of Guman Chand's youngest son, Seth Pratap Mal of
Jaisalmer - An architectural masterpiece, some say that the carving of
this temple is even better than Patwon Ki Haveli
Courtesy – Bapna House Family Collection

Rishabdeo Aangi - Kesariyaji Jain Temple
Said to be donated by Seth Sultan Mal Bapna and Seth Chandanmal Bapna, sons of Seth Zorawarmal Bapna, about the same time that another Aangi was presented to Kesariyaji temple near Udaipur by the Maharana of Mewar. The aangi in the picture was said to cost about $ 100,000 in 1870s and is worth several millions today. It is made of gold and studded with precious stones.
Courtesy – Jain.Com Website

Udaipur Sethji Ri Haveli-Bapna Residence –
Home of five generations of Bapnas (1820 - 1960) - Seth Zorawarmal,
Seth Chandanmal, Seth Chhogmal and then Seth Chhaganmal and
Seth Dhanrupmal- with a gap from 1894 through 1930 when it was
under acquisition of Mewar Royal Family as part of the bankruptcy of
Seth Chhogmal
Courtesy – Bapna House Family Collection

Chapter 16 – Story of Chhogmal
1851 AD – 1893 AD

The news of Zorawar Mal's death quickly travelled to Udaipur. After his funeral, his wife Chautha and the grandchildren went back to Udaipur to be near her sons, Sultan Mal and Chandan Mal. The entire extended family of Zorawar Mal, the remaining brothers and their families, gathered at *"Nagar Seth ki Haveli"* in Udaipur to mourn his death. The reigning prince of Udaipur, *Rana* Swaroop Singh (not to be confused with the long dead Prime Minister of Jaisalmer), along with his nobles, visited *"Nagar Seth ki Haveli"* to pay their respects.

Due to Zorawar Mal's advancing age, the last few years had been filled with neglect of the larger enterprise. While Sultan Mal and Chandan Mal were ably handling affairs at Udaipur, their Udaipur component of business was only a small fraction of the overall national and international operations of Zorawar Mal Bapna. During the last few years, because Zorawar Mal had to curtail his travel drastically, many of his operations nationwide started losing money due to mismanagement and even in some cases, embezzlement on the part of his managers. Many of his senior staff had struck up alliances with local strongmen and rulers and had declared themselves the owners of Zorawar Mal's businesses.

Sultan Mal and Chandan Mal travelled through the country, trying to ascertain what assets remained. They found that there was very little left that they could actually inherit. Still, even a very small portion of a massive fortune Zorawar Mal had built was significant and the brothers decided to consolidate all their assets in Udaipur. Being burnt by their remote managers, they saw it fit to locate all their assets in the vicinity of where they lived so they could manage those assets personally. They were on excellent terms with *Rana* Swaroop Singh of Udaipur, and with all that they and Zorawar Mal had done for the House of Sisodias, they saw no reason why they should hesitate in moving all their assets to Mewar.

Over the next ten years, Sultan Mal and Chandan Mal meticulously moved all of Zorawar Mal's remaining assets to Udaipur. They invested mostly in gold, silver, precious stones, real estate and a myriad of businesses that they had come to own in Udaipur. In 1857, there was a major rebellion against the British rule in North India. The rebellion almost succeeded in dislodging the East India Company from power, but with good fortune and the loyalty of some British allies such as the kingdoms of Rajputana, the British were able to put down the rebellion. After the rebellion, the British brutally cracked down on any dissent and the British Parliament passed a law, transferring India from the control of the East India Company directly to the British Crown (meaning the British Government). Sultan Mal and Chandan Mal further lost the businesses and assets that were located in North India due to the chaos during and following the rebellion of 1857.

Unfortunately, in 1861, Sultan Mal died, quickly followed by the premature deaths of his two sons, Indermal and Gambhir Mal. Since both Indermal and Gambhir Mal had no children, Chandan Mal inherited all of their estate. In 1869 Chandan Mal died too, soon followed by his older son, Juharmal, who also died childless, leaving the younger son of Chandan Mal, Chhogmal, the inheritor of all what was left of Zorawar Mal's empire. Almost all of those assets were invested in Udaipur by 1870.

Chhogmal, the only remaining descendant and heir of Zorawar Mal, was a favorite of his grandfather's. Zorawar Mal had realized the mistake he had made by not formally educating both his sons. He had therefore, left special instructions with his sons that all his grandchildren should be educated by tutors and scholars in Calcutta. Chhogmal excelled in studies, made several important contacts in Calcutta and developed a love for music, philosophy and the arts.

Chhogmal came of age in Udaipur as an idealistic and enlightened young man, full of ideas and dreams for the future. When he took over the reins of his business after the death of his brother in 1870, he was twenty-five years old, just married, and full of energy. *Seth* Chhogmal, as he was now called, consolidated all his holdings under the name of a firm that he called Chhogmal Zorawarmal. Being highly educated and having a modern outlook, he had a deep aversion to opium trading and money lending. He wanted to modernize his lending operations by converting them into modern banking and completely shut down his opium trading desk.

Chhogmal ran into trouble when he tried to convert his money-lending operations into banking. No one in Udaipur understood the concept of taking loans by signing legal contracts which were enforceable in the court of law. Also, the idea of making regular and timely interest payments was anathema to the ruling elite, which wanted the flexibility of making payments whenever their whims dictated.

He soon ran into trouble shutting down his opium operations, as his managers and employees went on strike. Some of his managers and senior employees were making illicit overriding commissions on the sale and purchase of opium. They made these without the knowledge of Chhogmal, and were reluctant to let go of that income. He also ran into trouble when he wanted to diversify some of his investments outside of Udaipur by purchasing newly constructed modern shopping complexes that were coming up in cities such as Bombay and Calcutta. He was successful in making some of these investments, and at one time the firm of Chhogmal Zorawarmal owned several blocks of the famed Crawford Market in Bombay. Finally, it was not easy to find other lucrative businesses to invest in Udaipur and Chhogmal, as hard as he tried, could not make a significant transition from his traditional businesses into the modern business world.

While Zorawar Mal and his sons, Sultan Mal and Chandan Mal, were highly ethical by the standards of their day, they did have a streak of pragmatism. Even Guman Chand had a bit of that pragmatism, while his father Deoraj never did. Chhogmal was a stickler for business ethics and was more in the mould of Seth Deoraj. He was very conscious of his illustrious heritage and his own capabilities, and therefore, was naturally more aristocratic than any of his ancestors, with the possible exception of Seth Deoraj. He was soft-spoken but very direct. He did not mince his words, and he submitted to no man, no matter how high his status, if Chhogmal felt he was in the right. He had contempt for the hypocrisy of the Udaipur royal family, who on the one hand claimed divine ancestry and illustrious heritage, while on the other, thought nothing of accepting gifts and extorting money from merchants. The royal family of Mewar was notorious for not repaying their debts and seeking frequent debt forgiveness. Chhogmal also despised the idea of frequently visiting the royal court and pandering to the whims of the ruler by dispensing the latest gossip to him or by participating in petty court intrigues against certain individuals. All in all, Chhogmal wanted to challenge the existing order and thought processes in Udaipur in much the same way that Deoraj wanted to rebel against the powers-that-be in Osian.

Unlike Deoraj, who realized that staying in Osian would yield no results, Chhogmal took the establishment in Mewar head on. Seth Chhogmal's aristocratic bearing, his modern outlook and his sense of self-respect rubbed the Udaipur establishment, including the rulers, the wrong way. Mostly out of envy, but also out of ignorance, the ruling elite now trained their fire on Seth Chhogmal. The rulers started demanding more and more advances from Chhogmal, while other merchants started taking shots at Chhogmal for continuing to hold the monopoly on collecting taxes through the agency that had been set up by Seth Zorawar Mal.

This agency continued collecting the taxes of Mewar on behalf of the treasury. The revenue first went to Seth Chhogmal's "*Nagar Seth ki Haveli*." The monies were then weighed, as counting of such large sums was impractical. Then the agency fee, interest payment on loans to the treasury and some principal repayment was deducted from these monies before the balance was transferred to the state treasury. Both the rulers and rival merchants resented the state revenue going to Seth Chhogmal's establishment first, as this signified his first rights over the collection. Out of deep respect for Seth Zorawar Mal's rescue of the state of Mewar, no one raised their voices during his lifetime and that of his sons, but now there was sufficient distance in time between Zorawar Mal's benevolence towards Mewar and Chhogmal to allow people to question Chhogmal's monopoly over the tax collection.

The tax collection agency was the only operation that was making any money for Seth Chhogmal, as he was in the process of transitioning his other businesses, and he could not afford to lose the agency, which he guarded zealously. Chhogmal had inherited good contacts with the British from his father and grandfather and developed some of his own while he was in Calcutta. He used these contacts to counter any attempt by the rulers of Udaipur to take away his tax collection agency.

Until 1884, things were not terribly bad for Chhogmal, despite the fact that he was not fully able to modernize and professionalize his business the way he wanted to. However, in 1884, a new ruler ascended the throne of Mewar. His name was Fateh Singh. He was adopted, as the previous ruler Sajan Singh had no son. Fateh Singh was thirty-five years of age, had an inflated view of his own importance and was old-fashioned and traditional. Fateh Singh fancied himself in the mold of his famous ancestor, Rana Pratap, who in resisting the Moguls right to the end was a man of legendary courage and one of the most illustrious heroes in Indian history. Fateh Singh considered it his mission to get out from under the "thumb of the British," as he called it. However, although many historians and writers wrote glowingly about him, he was ill equipped educationally, financially, militarily, organizationally, intellectually and temperamentally to challenge the British in any meaningful way. He quickly realized his limitations in seriously hurting British interests and started resorting to mere symbolism to demonstrate his independence from the British.

Soon this symbolism deteriorated into childish tantrums and defiance and targeting officials and merchants whom he considered close to the British. In actuality, he couldn't hurt merchants and officials close to the British as the British zealously protected their own, but he was able to hurt certain people who merely had peripheral relations with the British or whom Fateh Singh mistakenly thought had relations with the British, or people he could deliberately brand or defame as having relations with the British. To make matters worse, he had gathered around him a coterie that pumped up his already over-inflated ego, resulting in Fateh Singh suffering from Caligula-style delusions of grandeur.

Fateh Singh was a regressive man who was highly suspicious of any new technology. For example, for years he resisted the idea of establishing a railway line to Udaipur. Another example of his prejudiced and regressive mindset was illustrated in the following dialogue, which occurred much later in his term when Fateh Singh went to the airstrip in Udaipur to receive the Viceroy and Vicerine during their state visit. Fateh Singh was waiting at the bottom of the steps, along with his interpreter (Fateh Singh did not speak any English), while the Viceroy and Vicerine alighted from the plane.

"It is a pleasure to meet you, Your Highness," said the Viceroy.

Fateh Singh, turning to his interpreter, asks, *"Yeh lal muh ro bander kai keve hai?"* (What is this red faced monkey saying?)

The interpreter responded, "He is saying that it is his great pleasure to meet Your Highness."

"*Eene keh de, aur iske saath jo raand hai, une bhi keh de, ki mane bhi inse milne bahut khushi whi* (Tell him and tell the whore who is with him too that I am also very pleased to meet them as well)," said Fateh Singh.

Fateh Singh quickly learned of Seth Chhogmal, as his agency was collecting all the tax revenues of Mewar. Besides, Seth Chhogmal still held the title of "Nagar Seth," meaning the dean of all merchants in Mewar. Chhogmal, being educated and intelligent, was as progressive as Fateh Singh was regressive. While Seth Chhogmal had good contacts with the British, he was far from being a part of the British inner circle. Unlike most businessmen, he was straightforward and meant what he said, and neither participated in gossip nor palace intrigues. In fact, he had nothing but contempt for the archaic palace procedures and avoided as much as possible visiting the court and paying his obeisance to Fateh Singh. He also had an air of confidence, almost a bit of a swagger, which rubbed the coterie around Fateh Singh, comprising of all "yes men," the wrong way.

The coterie, led by one Bhandari Baldeo Raj, out of envy, pettiness and angered by Chhogmal's refusal to submit himself fully to Fateh Singh, embarked upon a campaign to malign Chhogmal to Fateh Singh. Every chance they got, they would point out to Fateh Singh any real or imagined defect in Chhogmal's conduct towards the ruler. Sometimes the allegations would border on the absurd, as illustrated by a conversation below.

"What a glorious day it has been, Your Highness," said Bhandari Baldeo Raj. "Your Highness's thirty-fifth birthday, a truly auspicious day for all your subjects."

"Yes, it was quite a celebration you arranged, Bhandari," said Fateh Singh, quite pleased with how the day had gone.

"The only thing that marred the celebration was the odd behavior of *Nagar Seth* Chhogmal," said Bhandari Baldeo Raj. "Did you notice the way he was dressed, trying to compete with Your Highness himself, and the way he bowed to you, how stiff he was, as if it was a huge effort to bow before one's sovereign."

"I guess he did appear a little stiff," responded Fateh Singh. "Are you sure he is not suffering from a bad back or something? He did not stay too long at the celebrations either, left rather early. Was he not well?" continued Fateh Singh with a straight face, camouflaging his sarcasm.

"Did Your Highness also notice the ostentatious emerald necklace he always wears, the one belonging to his grandfather, Seth Zorawar Mal? What a show-off!" said Bhandari Baldeo Raj.

"I really like that necklace. Can you get me one like that, Bhandari?" asked Fateh Singh.

This question alarmed Bhandari Baldeo Raj. He did not want to be put in a position to gift something so valuable to the ruler. Cleverly changing the subject, he said, "Everyone in Udaipur is saying that Seth Chhogmal is the real ruler, as the entire tax revenue first goes to his mansion, before it arrives in the state treasury. They say that Your Highness is only a titular head, with no real power."

"Is that so?" said Fateh Singh, turning red in anger. "I think he behaves in this manner because he has some secret understanding with the British. Don't you think, Bhandari? Otherwise, how can a man defy his own sovereign? *Seth* Chhogmal might even conspire against the royal house of Mewar if he is not checked. He needs to be abased."

And on and on it went. Day in and day out, Bhandari Baldeo Raj and the coterie around Fateh Singh kept poisoning his mind against Seth Chhogmal. Fateh Singh, not being terribly well educated and narrow of mind, was primed to be manipulated, already predisposed towards tyranny. He did not appreciate the fact that Chhogmal had already gotten out of the opium business. He did not appreciate the fact that Chhogmal was desperately in the midst of transitioning his money lending and tax collection operations to modern banking and taking huge losses as a result. He did not establish enough of a communication with Chhogmal to understand his point of view and his take on the various issues of the state. He simply believed what he wanted to believe and the coterie very cleverly knew how to bring out the worst in Fateh Singh.

Fateh Singh now started leading a campaign to brand Seth Chhogmal as a British ally, an enemy of the House of Mewar, the same House of Mewar that Chhogmal's grandfather, Zorawar Mal, had rescued upon being invited by the then-ruler Bhim Singh. At the time of Seth Zorawar Mal's arrival in Udaipur, the then ruler could not even meet his household expenses-such was the state of Mewar. Chhogmal's family had time and again bailed out the Royal House of Mewar through crisis after crisis, forgiving staggering amounts in loans. That was conveniently forgotten and a defamation campaign was launched against Chhogmal. When the pro-British label against Chhogmal did not stick with the populace of Mewar, Fateh Singh came up with a new ploy. He produced some phony corruption charges against the highly ethical and straightforward Chhogmal. It was alleged that Chhogmal had taken large and inappropriate advances from the state of Mewar while operating a mail cart from Udaipur to the nearest railway station, about fifty miles away. Overnight, the public sentiment turned against the most morally upright Bapna since *Seth* Deoraj.

Pouncing upon this opportunity in 1891, Rana Fateh Singh, the ruler of Udaipur, the descendant of the great Rana Pratap, the scion of the great Sisodia Rajputs who claimed their descent from the Sun itself, issued a royal decree, confiscating and impounding all assets of Seth Chhogmal and stripping him of the title of "*Nagar Seth.*"

At the time, when the royal decree of confiscation was issued, Chhogmal had three sons. Chhagan Mal was twenty years old, Siremal was seventeen, and Sangram Singh a mere infant. A fourth son, Devi Lal had died while still very young. Chhagan Mal and Siremal were married, Siremal to the daughter of a minister of Udaipur state, Mehta Bhopal Singh. The news of the confiscation order quickly spread all over Udaipur. The same day, there was a run on Seth Chhogmal's bank and by that evening his bank did not have enough cash left to cover the withdrawals. No one would honor Chhogmal's promissory notes and commercial paper called *hundis* was rendered worthless. Chhogmal tried to raise cash advances through his personal contacts, but the British banks refused to loan him any money. On the brink of bankruptcy, Chhogmal finally asked for intervention by the British Viceroy, who was the overlord of Rana Fateh Singh.

Chhogmal's case was vigorously supported by the local British resident agent, Samuel Barrett Miles, Udaipur Prime Minister, Sir Mehta Rai Pannalal, and Commander of the British Garrison, Wingate, who were intimately familiar with what had occurred. They all knew very well that Seth Chhogmal was a person of high moral character and that Fateh Singh had orchestrated a vicious and malicious campaign to destroy an honorable man. The Viceroy was reluctant to intervene because the corruption charges had turned public opinion against Seth Chhogmal. In addition, Fateh Singh's clever use of anti-British symbolism had made him popular among the gullible populace. Fateh Singh had shrewdly tapped into a deep desire among the populace for independence and the return of Mewar's former glory and while Fateh Singh had no chance of either, he used demagoguery and provocative rhetoric to portray himself as the potential restorer of past glories. The

Viceroy did not want to stoke further anti-British feelings by intervening on behalf of Seth Chhogmal, no matter how honorable a man he was.

Miles and Wingate undertook a trip to Delhi to personally make the case for Seth Chhogmal to Viceroy Lord Lansdowne. Lansdowne had only recently become the Viceroy in 1891 and was not yet as familiar with India and the nature of its intrigues and treachery. He was not a bold man and he was uncertain as to what to do in this case. A series of meetings were held in Delhi on *Seth* Chhogmal's request for intervention in 1893.

"I have decided not to intervene in the case of *Seth* Chhogmal and *Rana* Fateh Singh of Mewar," said Lord Lansdowne, the Viceroy.

"I once more request the Viceroy to reconsider," said Resident Agent Samuel Barrett Miles. "We have looked at the facts over and over again. We know that *Seth* Chhogmal is being framed."

"Not only framed, but viciously framed. It is out and out character assassination of an honorable man. *Seth* Chhogmal is a proud man who takes a great deal of pride in his heritage and pride in his integrity and honesty. For *Rana* Fateh Singh to destroy such a man, not only by depriving him of his finances, but by depriving him of his good name, is the ultimate travesty. British justice cannot allow that," said Col. Wingate.

"Be that as it may, we cannot allow this one case to come in the way of the larger British interests of not antagonizing any of the friendly states of Rajputana," said the Viceroy. "There is again rebellion in the air in India. The Indians want to be free of the British. We will need all the friends we can get, and Mewar is a friendly state."

"Mewar, under Fateh Singh, is not a friendly state. Fateh Singh has delusions of grandeur and consistently espouses anti-British views to his population. He is the ultimate demagogue," said Col. Wingate again.

"Then we must attempt to win over Fateh Singh on our side," said the Viceroy "All the more reason not to offend him."

"And what about *Seth* Chhogmal, My Lord? Is he disposable? I know Fateh Singh very well and I know the situation on the ground very well. Even if we allow *Seth* Chhogmal to go down, my considered opinion is that Fateh Singh cannot be won over. He is hostile," said Resident Agent Miles.

"I want us to take a chance on bringing around Fateh Singh. And yes, in the interest of larger British policy, *Seth* Chhogmal is dispensable, as honorable as he is," said the Viceroy.

"But My Lord..." started Col. Wingate before he was interrupted by the Viceroy.

"My mind is made up. The decision is final. Please ask *Seth* Chhogmal to submit himself to the mercy of Fateh Singh and rely on his benevolence. Col. Miles, please see to it that *Seth* Chhogmal be given an opportunity for one last personal audience with *Rana* Fateh Singh, where he can humbly plead his case," said the Viceroy Lord Lansdowne dismissively, indicating that the meeting was over.

And that was the final meeting on the matter.

Wingate and Miles walked out of the viceroy's office, disappointment written on their faces.

"I need a drink," said Col. Wingate.

"A stiff one," said Col. Miles.

In Udaipur, both Col. Miles and Col. Wingate put as much pressure on Fateh Singh as they could in their personal capacity to be reasonable with *Seth* Chhogmal. They also conveyed to Fateh Singh the Viceroy's wish to grant a personal audience to *Seth* Chhogmal. Fateh Singh agreed, relishing the idea of finally seeing Chhogmal on his knees, begging him to spare him and his family from financial ruin.

On the day of the meeting, both Wingate and Miles went to visit *Seth* Chhogmal in his mansion. Chhogmal was dressed formally, wearing white tight pants and a long black Rajasthani coat. He had on an orange turban (orange in Rajasthan signifies a determination to fight to the end and attain martyrdom), clearly indicating that he was going to fight the last battle of his life, and his beard was neatly trimmed. He had with him his two sons, Chhaganmal and Siremal, also dressed formally. They each had a sword dangling at their side from their *kamarband*.

"*Nagar Seth* Chhogmal, we are here to wish you the very best in your meeting with His Highness Fateh Singh this morning," said Col. Wingate.

"Yes, it is a very important meeting. May we take the liberty of advising you to be very humble and submit yourself upon His Highness's mercy? I am sure Fateh Singh, being a proud Rajput, will not disappoint a supplicant," Miles added.

"I am truly grateful to both of you. I assure you, regardless of the results, that I, Chhogmal, descendant of *Seth* Deoraj, will not do anything that my ancestors, my family and my friends will not be proud of," said Chhogmal. His face was drawn and it clearly showed a lot of stress. "I have deliberated with my wife and my two adult sons. We are all of one mind and we have decided on a course of action."

The two officers sensed what was in *Seth* Chhogmal's mind. Their worst fears were coming true. *Seth* Chhogmal would not humble himself. *It is so ironic,* thought Col. Miles, *that it would be Seth Chhogmal and not the Rajput Fateh Singh, who would go down fighting like a true Rajput.*

"You know, *Seth* Chhogmal, we have always held you in very high esteem. We want you to know that we consider it a distinct honor to have known you. We respect what you are going to do and we expected nothing less from you. Good luck and I hope, regardless of our respective stations in life, you will find it in your heart to always consider us friends," said Col. Miles with great emotion.

Seth Chhogmal and his two sons arrived at City Palace of Udaipur in his black carriage. He confidently walked past the palace guards to the chambers of *Rana* Fateh Singh. He was quickly admitted into the chamber where he found Fateh Singh sitting on a high chair. The long standing and legendary Prime Minister of Udaipur State, Sir Mehta Rai Pannalal, a family friend of Chhogmal's, was standing besides the ruler. Chhogmal and his sons made a formal courtesy bow to the ruler and an appropriate bow to the Prime Minister, and then they all were asked to be seated.

"I was given to understand by the British Resident Agent that *Seth* Chhogmal is here to make a plea," said Fateh Singh.

"You were misinformed, Your Highness. There will be no plea," said Chhogmal in a clear firm voice.

"Oh…" said Fateh Singh, his face in shock, eyebrows raised.

The Prime Minister now guessed what was to come next.

"I, Chhogmal Bapna, grandson of *Seth* Zorawar Mal Bapna who was the savior of the House of Sisodias and benefactor of the State of Mewar, am here with my sons, Chhaganmal and Siremal, to make one final gift to the descendant of *Rana* Bhim Singh, who my family came to Udaipur to rescue. I, Chhogmal, relieve you, *Maharana* Fateh Singh, of any obligation you and your House may feel towards the House of Bapnas. You are free, *Maharana* Fateh Singh, to pass any decree that may please your heart, without any consideration to anything my family has ever done for you or the House of Sisodias in the past," said Chhgomal. Then he stood up, took each son by his hands, bowed slightly, turned around, and walked out.

Mehta Rai Pannalal had a barely visible smile on his lips, while Fateh Singh looked stunned.

Fateh Singh looked at his prime minister and said, "Mehta, I want that man destroyed and I want his family destroyed. Make sure that the decree against *Seth* Chhogmal is so punitive that even future generations don't have a chance to rise again. And after you have issued that decree, Mehta Pannalal, please draft up your own resignation letter and submit it to me at the earliest. I do not want any supporters of Chhogmal Bapna in positions of power in Mewar."

The confiscation decree was never reversed. In fact, it was so stringent that *Seth* Chhogmal declared bankruptcy in 1893. He sold every last personal belonging he and his family had with the exception of the clothes on their backs, his wife's wedding dress, which was adorned with heavy 24-carat gold brocade and studded with precious stones, and the emerald necklace of Seth Zorawar Mal that was so dear to Chhogmal and as much a part of his identity as his arms or his face. As he and his family stepped out for the last time from the confiscated "*Nagar Seth ki Haveli*," his family home since Seth Zorawarl Mal first came to Udaipur, some seventy-five years earlier, a few of his remaining creditors had gathered outside, demanding what was owed to them. Seth Chhogmal pulled out the last two items of value he had, his emerald necklace and his wife's wedding dress. He called upon one creditor to act as an auctioneer and auction the items off right there and pay off whatever he could. First went the emerald necklace. It was purchased by Bhandari Baldeo Raj on behalf of Rana Fateh Singh. Then the wedding dress. As the family started to walk away after the auction, one of the creditors stopped them and pointed to the solitary ring on Chhogmal's finger.

"What about this? There is this gold ring left." It was Deoraj's ring, and before anyone could explain that it was merely a brass ring which had no commercial value, the creditor took it upon himself to extract the ring off Chhogmal's finger by force. The moment Deoraj's ring left his finger, *Seth* Chhogmal suffered a massive heart attack and passed away in the front courtyard of his beloved home. The last image that flashed through his mind was that of his dying grandfather, Zorawar Mal, saying, "Beware of the Company (British), my boy."

As Chhogmal collapsed, Siremal, known as the pacifist of the family, grabbed the ring from the creditor and hid it in his inside pocket.

After a sparsely attended funeral, *Seth* Chhogmal's sons,

Chhaganmal and Siremal, and his widow, holding the infant Sangram Singh in her arms, left Udaipur forever and headed to the city of Ajmer, some two hundred miles away, to make a new beginning. Just like Seth Deoraj, when he and his wife, Bhairavi left Osian, no one in Udaipur was there to see off the disgraced Bapna family as they left Udaipur, after a seventy year stay. One of the greatest fortunes in the history of India, made first by Seth Guman Chand Bapna and then by Seth Zorawar Mal Bapna, a fortune that took four generations to make, disappeared overnight. In no time, Chhaganmal and Siremal went from being heirs of great wealth to being on the streets—a riches to rags story.

As for Fateh Singh, he thought he had achieved what the tyrants Swaroop Singh and Zalim Singh of Jaisalmer could not achieve—the destruction of the famed Bapna Dynasty of Jaisalmer. In actuality, he did succeed in destroying their wealth. The day of *Seth* Chhogmal's death should have been a day of celebration for Fateh Singh, but somehow, as hard as he tried, Fateh Singh could not feel any happiness that day. He did not admit that to anybody, but his heart that day was filled with great sadness. Somewhere, the noble Sisodia blood in him would not let him celebrate the destruction of the noblest Bapna of them all.

Dev's eyes filled up as he came to the end of Chhogmal's story.

"Of all our ancestors, it was *Seth* Chhogmal who was most proud and regal. Truly a man who all of us Bapnas can take inspiration from," said Kunal.

"Chhogmal's experience changed the course of Bapna family and shaped the lives of his son, Siremal, and his grandson, PS," said Dev. "Chhogmal transitioned the family from being noble merchants to being actual noblemen, from men of great wealth to men of great humanity, from commoners to aristocrats. The family never chased wealth again, but sought dignity through civilizing influences of art, music, culture and a quest for a just and humane society."

"So what happened to *Seth* Chhogmal's sons? Did they suffer countless indignities?" asked Ranika.

"Papa has fallen asleep now. We will ask him about Chhogmal's sons tomorrow," said Kunal.

The next day, Dev told them the story of the Bapna family in the aftermath of Seth Chhogmal.

Story of Chhogmal

Seth Chhogmal Bapna Udaipur Mewar 1
Grandson of Seth Zorawarmal Bapna
Estimated Birth – 1849, Estimated Death – 1898
Courtesy – Bapna House Family Collection

Maharana Fateh Singh of Mewar 1884-1930
A Portrait by Raja Ravi Verma , Sri Chitra Art Gallery, Thiruvananthapuram
Issued confiscation decree against Seth Chhogmal causing his bankruptcy and ultimately, death

Rai Mehta Pannalal Prime Minister Mewar
From 1978 – 1894, A portrait by Raja Ravi Verma ,Sri Chitra Art Gallery, Thiruvananthapuram

A friend and well wisher of Seth Chhogmal and the Bapna Family, was also disliked and ultimately retired by Rana Fateh Singh. Also of the Bachhawat Oswal clan, a highly capable, upstanding and loyal patriot of Mewar.

Bapna's Sethji Ri Haveli-Udaipur Mural

One of many beautiful mural paintings inside the Haveli, whose interior is an extravaganza of colors, wall paintings, cut tiffany glass, intricate mosaics, high quality marble, exquisite jharokhas. Is currently open to public as a heritage hotel called Jagdish Mahal Hotel, run by a family that respects and is a worthy custodian of the Bapna Heritage, legacy and history
Courtesy – Bapna House Family Collection

Bankers of Udaipur Mewar closing a deal
Typically, the bankers used to meet in the courtyard of a Haveli and sit on the floor, as they haggled and closed deals, while a recorder transcribes the minutes which was the evidence of an agreement between parties. The person accepting the loan would then issue "IOU's" in the form of commercial paper called Hundis in India.
Courtesy – Bapna House Family Collection

Times Square New York - 1898-perspective
The picture is provided here to provide a historical perspective on where the world was about the time of the story of Chhogmal
Courtesy Website - ephemeralnewyork.wordpress.com
Under GNU Free License

Chapter 17 - Story of Siremal
1894 AD – 1939 AD

When Siremal arrived in Ajmer with his mother, elder brother, sister-in-law and infant brother, the family had nothing. Their legendary mansion in Ajmer, built by his great grandfather Zorawar Mal, had been sold to pay off Seth Chhogmal's debts. Their sprawling commercial properties in Bombay and Calcutta were also sold. The only property the family had remaining was "Patwon ki Haveli" in Jaisalmer, which was started as a public works project by Guman Chand and finished a year before the death of Zorawar Mal. Jaisalmer by now was almost a ghost town.

All the public works projects could not make up for the loss of revenues from the declining importance of the land route and nor to keep the city of Jaisalmer alive. Therefore, it made no sense for the family to move to Jaisalmer. Siremal's father-in-law, Mehta Bhopal Singh, helped the family find a modest rental house. His daughter and Siremal's wife, Anandi Kumari, joined them in Ajmer a few months later. Siremal was a brilliant student and soon graduated from high school with high honors. He then entered law school and graduated four years later ranked first in his class and earned a much coveted gold medal for his efforts.

Siremal was deeply affected by the great trauma his father and the whole family had undergone in Udaipur. A sudden catastrophe that rendered the scion of a great dynasty homeless and poor at the impressionable age of seventeen can easily destroy a person psychologically and leave him scarred and damaged for life. Siremal, on the other hand, showed remarkable courage and strength of character and set about rebuilding his life from scratch. He did not permit the tragedies that had befallen him to harden him or coarsen him or embitter him. He stayed very open to new people, new ideas, and therefore very open to learning.

His generosity from a young age was legendary. As a child, when the family was still extremely wealthy, he would pick up handfuls of money from his father's cash box and give it away to poor people who thronged the gates of their mansion. His father, Chhogmal, never chastised him for it. While Siremal was just an average student when his father was still alive, after the family's downfall he started working much harder and focused a lot more on his education, resulting in him excelling right through college. In 1903, he graduated, first in his class from law school, and also became a father for the first time to a son called Kalyan, nicknamed KB. Siremal opened up a law office in Ajmer, practicing general law for two years, and established a fine reputation for himself as a brilliant attorney.

In 1905, he was offered a position of a session's judge in Holkar State. He was posted in Indore, the same city where his great grandfather, Zorawar Mal, spent a great deal of his later life and where he died. It was a distinct honor for someone so young and Siremal embarked for Indore with his wife and young son. After serving with distinction and honor as a session's judge for four years he was selected by the reigning Prince Tukoji Rao Holkar to be his law tutor. The young prince was so impressed by Siremal's intelligence, knowledge, temperament and character that he appointed Siremal his home minister in 1912. By that time, in addition to his eldest son, KB, Siremal had had two daughters and another son, called Pratap, nicknamed PS.

Siremal gradually became a star in the Holkar State cabinet. As home minister, he instituted many reforms in the administration, particularly in the field of primary and secondary education. Literacy greatly increased and Siremal, buoyed by this success, went on to initiate other major social reforms. His pioneering initiatives resulted in his fame spreading across India and he came to the attention of not only the Viceroy of India (a Viceroy was the representative who ruled India in the name of the British Crown), but also of the British ministers including the British Prime Minister David Lloyd George, who led Britain in World War I and established the foundation of a welfare state in Britain. He later also developed good relations with Prime Minister Ramsay MacDonald, Antony Eden and Winston Churchill. It was at Churchill's request that Siremal met with Hitler and Mussolini before the start of World War II in an attempt to gauge their true intentions.

While Siremal rapidly climbed the ladder of success, Fateh Singh, the ruler of Udaipur, was having major confrontations with the British, and the British government wanted him out. This was the same *Maharana* Fateh Singh who had sworn to destroy Siremal's father, *Seth* Chhogmal, and his entire succeeding generations. By 1920, things had come to a head between the British and Fateh Singh to the point of the Viceroy seeking to remove him and merging his state into British India. Fateh Singh was desperate. All of his friends and courtiers had jumped ship, leaving him isolated. They all were fair-weather friends who did not want to incur the wrath of the almighty British by being seen too close to Fateh Singh. Fateh Singh had been kept informed of Siremal's meteoric rise in Holkar state. Initially, he resented Siremal's rise, but he was powerless to do anything about it, as his writ didn't extend beyond Udaipur, and certainly not to Holkar State. Being now cornered, Fateh Singh sent an important member of his family to Siremal, cordially inviting him to visit Udaipur.

When Siremal reached Udaipur he was accorded a royal welcome and invited to a dinner at the City Palace of Udaipur. Siremal was astonished as to why Fateh Singh, who had sworn to destroy the Bapna family for posterity, would show such hospitality to him. When Siremal reached the City Palace he was accorded many honors, starting with *baithak*, which permitted a person to be seated in the presence of the royal. He was also lavished with several gifts and titles. During dinner, Fateh Singh addressed Siremal and reminded him of the unbreakable and old connections that the House of Sisodia (Fateh Singh's family) had with the Bapnas and how ties that strong were a rarity and to be cherished. He said in chaste Mewari language, "*Mharo aadmi itni tarak-ki kari, mein bahut khush huun,*" meaning, "I am so pleased, my own man has risen to such great heights." He didn't even mention how he had confiscated all of Siremal's father's property, causing his death, and an almost complete destruction of an old and illustrious family, not to mention subjecting Siremal and his family to financial ruin. It was only through tremendous perseverance, intelligence and good luck that Siremal was able to rise again so quickly, which eased somewhat the pain that Fateh Singh was personally responsible for inflicting on the Bapna family. But there was no talk of any of that now from Fateh Singh. He acted as if nothing unpleasant had ever transpired between them.

After dinner, Fateh Singh came to the point.

"Could you possibly intervene on my behalf with Prime Minister Lloyd George in London, considering the excellent relationship you enjoy with him, and arrive at some kind of settlement that would save me from being removed?"

Now it dawned on Siremal why Fateh Singh had arranged this dog-and-pony show. *So now I am his own man*, thought Siremal.

"I must decline to intervene on your behalf. I fear that it would be a futile exercise," Siremal said. "I am certain that your fate is sealed. The prime minister will assuredly not pay any heed to me on that issue." But Siremal, being Siremal and the gentleman that he was, agreed to put his weight behind a settlement with the British government, whereby they would not take over Udaipur State under their direct control, but settle for Fateh Singh abdicating and allowing his son Bhupal Singh to be the new ruler.

Fateh Singh was disappointed, but he politely requested that Siremal at least try to work out a way to save the State from being taken away from his family. Siremal communicated with the British Prime Minister Lloyd George, who had great regard for him, and added his considerable weight to the already ongoing efforts by others on Fateh Singh's behalf.

The State was rescued, with Bhupal Singh ascending to the throne, and Fateh Singh was removed. Siremal, however, also arranged for a face-saving for Fateh Singh, allowing him to continue as the titular head of state, with no actual powers, while Bhupal Singh assumed all his powers. Bhupal Singh, unlike his father, developed a genuine regard for Siremal. Siremal, too, did not dwell on the past and reciprocated by being a mentor of sorts for Bhupal Singh, who frequently took Siremal's advice on State matters. Many years later, when Siremal was forced out of Indore by the Holkars, Bhupal Singh strongly insisted that Siremal become the Prime Minister of Udaipur State, but as forgiving as Siremal was, he could not bring himself to go back to Udaipur where his father had died and his family had suffered such ignominy. Instead, he arranged for an equally capable man, his good friend R. Acharya, to take over as Prime Minister to Bhupal Singh, and Acharya went on to do wonderful things for Udaipur.

Bhupal Singh was grateful to Siremal. While the damage done in the past couldn't be undone and the entire Bapna family fortune could not be restored, as a token of his gratitude, Rana Bhupal Singh returned the grand Bapna Haveli in Udaipur, which his father had confiscated from *Seth* Chhogmal, back to Siremal. Siremal's elder brother, Seth Chhaganmal, was respectfully moved into the mansion and lived out his life there before it was sold by Chhaganmal's son, Seth Dhanrupmal.

Siremal was glad that some kind of closure was put to a very ugly episode in the relations between the Bapnas and the most exalted house in India, the Sisodias of Udaipur. The House that had been destroyed by the Sisodias, had again come to its rescue.

The British were at the peak of their power in India around 1912. They were firmly in control of the entire subcontinent. They had divided India primarily into two categories: British India and the Princely States. British India was that territory within the subcontinent that was not part of any erstwhile established kingdoms in India when the British arrived. The British ruled this territory directly under its laws and jurisdiction. The Princely States were comprised of those territories that were part of small and large kingdoms, with whom the British had signed treaties. These states accepted the overlordship of the British and in return the British, via a treaty, allowed these states to retain their hereditary rulers and gave these rulers a great deal of autonomy.

Sir Siremal Bapna
As a young Home Minister Holkar State 1914
Courtesy Bapna House Family Collection

HH Maharana Bhupal Singh of Mewar
(Reign - 1921 – 1955)
A man in keeping with true Sisodia Tradition, noble and generous, a great admirer of Sir Siremal Bapna
(Courtesy Bapna House Family Collection)

HH Maharaja Indore Tukoji Rao Holkar III
Great Personality, Decisive, Large Hearted, Proud Maratha, a Great Nationalist and Patriot, known till the end of his life as "Bade Maharaj", despite being forced to abdicate by the British, early in his life
(Courtesy - Deshraj Holkar)

Mumtaz Begum - Courtesan To HH Tukoji Rao
Fled to be a concubine to Abdul Kader Bawla whose murder in 1925 scandalized India and resulted in the abdication of HH Maharaja Tukoji Rao Holkar III of Indore. Sir Siremal Bapna used his contacts at the highest level of the British Government in London to ensure that the state was not taken over by the British but was passed on to Tukoji Rao's son, Yeshwant Rao Holkar in 1926
Photo – Courtesy Bapna House Family Collection

The British established various oversight offices across the Indian subcontinent to keep an eye on these Princely States, called "Residencies." Each Residency oversaw a number of Princely States within the Indian subcontinent. One of the outcomes of such a governing structure was that it secured for the princes their rule within their territories without fear of invasion from others, as the British ensured that no Princely State could attack the other. Having thus freed themselves of any defense-type considerations, these princes ruled their states as complete autocrats. Each Princely State had its own set of laws, its own ministers, its own judiciary, its own taxation, etc. Some of the states were large, such as the Holkar State, while others were merely as big as a village. Some princes were benevolent rulers, while others were tyrants. The British, by and large, did not interfere in the internal affairs except in cases where these princes acted against British interests or the mismanagement and tyranny reached extreme proportions so as to threaten British interests.

Holkar State was one state that had mostly benevolent rulers, largely due to the precedence established by Ahilya Bai Holkar, one of the earlier rulers of the dynasty. She was famous in history as being an able, just and highly effective ruler.

There was yet another state in India, far from Holkar State, called Patiala. It was in North India and was governed by a Sikh-ruling family. The rulers of Patiala were known for their hearty appetites in food, drink and women. In India, whisky in bars was served in three sizes. In addition to a single and a double, there was what was called a "Patiala peg," which was roughly double the size of a double. The Patiala prince most famous for his appetites was the ruler from 1900 to 1938. His name was Bhupinder Singh. He had ten wives and eighty-eight children, not to mention scores of concubines in his harem. He travelled in a motorcade of twenty Rolls Royces. He was also famous for having extravagant and decadent parties in the Royal Palace, with scores of party women. Bhupinder Singh was a complicated man who, quite in contrast to his personal lifestyle, conducted the matters of the state with prudence and magnanimity.

In 1923, while still home minister of Holkar State in Indore, Siremal received an offer to be the Home Minister of Patiala State from HH Bhupinder Singh. It was an attractive offer and gave Siremal the opportunity to experience another administration, another people, and another culture. Being young and ambitious, he was inclined to accept, but the Holkar Prince Tukoji Rao was reluctant to let him go. After many deliberations with the Holkar Prince, including a personal request from Bhupinder Singh to Tukoji Rao, Siremal was reluctantly allowed to take over the home ministership of Patiala. Siremal had heard stories of Bhupinder Singh's famous appetites, and since he himself maintained a very simple lifestyle, in his acceptance letter to Bhupinder Singh he famously requested to be excused from all after-hours activities and parties in the Royal Palace of Patiala.

Siremal very ably served in Patiala for three years, until in 1926 he received a frantic visitor from Indore. The visitor was a personal envoy of Prince Tukoji Rao Holkar of Indore. He conveyed Tukoji Rao's invitation to Siremal, more a demand, to return back to Indore to get the Holkar ruler out of a messy situation. Upon further inquiry by Siremal, the envoy told him the facts.

It all happened within a matter of minutes on the evening of the twelfth of January 1925, in a favorite and frequented promenade, at a beauty spot of Bombay, viz., the Hanging Gardens on Malabar Hill. It was at the tranquil and peaceful hour of the evening, about 7:30 PM when there was still twilight, and many people were walking along the road, enjoying the fresh air. There was a good amount of vehicular traffic on the road. A motorcar, containing, besides the driver and his assistant, two men and a woman, drove up Gibbs Road from Kemp's Corner, towards the Hanging Gardens at the top of Malabar Hill. Almost immediately thereafter another car, a red Maxwell with Holkar State number plates, containing six or seven men drove up, and deliberately bumped into the first car. Both cars came to a stop. The passengers of the red Maxwell jumped out, shouting abuses at one of the men and the woman in the other car. They surrounded the first car on both sides, two or three men mounting the foot-boards on either side.

HH Maharaja Bhupinder Singh of Patiala
Reign, 1900-1938
Courtesy Bapna House Family Collection

David Lloyd George-British Prime Minister
Reign – 1916 – 1922
Great Statesman, creator of the modern welfare state, arguably one of the three greatest Prime Ministers of Britain
Had regard for Sir Siremal and Sir Siremal sent a personal representation to him to retain HRH Fateh Singh of Mewar as a titular head, despite being deposed in favor of his son in 1921, which he accepted

Courtesy – Bapna House Family Collection, picture of a portrait by Sir James Guthrie in 1928

The first car belonged to Abdul Kadar Bawla, a wealthy businessman of Bombay. The other man was his manager, named Mathew. The woman in Bawla's car was Mumtaz Begum, a beautiful Muslim dancing girl, who had been in the keeping of the Maharaja of Indore, Tukoji Rao, for about ten years, until sometime before the incident of the twelfth of January 1925. According to her story, she was fed up with her life in the princely harem at Indore and had managed a few months back to get away from her gilded cage. After sundry stays at Delhi, Nagpur, and other places, she ultimately found a harbor, a home, and an unofficial husband in Abdul Kadar Bawla. At the time of the murder she had been living with Bawla as his mistress. This escapade of the girl had apparently caused fierce resentment in the court at Indore as an affront to the dignity of her quondam princely patron. The British claimed that the evidence in the case suggested that a conspiracy had been formed to avenge this slur on the dignity of the Durbar and to reclaim, if possible, or at least punish the runaway Helen of Indore.

Her whereabouts and movements in Bombay were traced, and a gang of ten hirelings and hangers-on of the Durbar proceeded to Bombay to teach an unforgettable lesson to the fair but fickle fugitive and her present protector for meddling with the private affairs of a princely house. The red Maxwell contained this gang, determined to kidnap the girl by force. On the evening of the twelfth of January this gang apparently tracked down their intended victims, pursued them on their journey up Malabar Hill, and overtook the car near the Hanging Gardens. Several members of the gang were armed with pistols, knives, and a *kukri*. As soon as the cars had come to a standstill, the men jumped out of the red Maxwell and surrounded Bawla's car. They tried to drag Mumtaz from the side of Bawla. On her resisting this attempt and crying out for help, with Bawla trying to shield her and prevent her from being carried away, one of the gang slashed at the girl's face with a knife, inflicting four slashes on her face which partially disfigured her. Simultaneously, more than one shot was fired at Bawla. Bawla was seriously wounded and died shortly after the incident. In fact, according to the evidence of Mumtaz, one of the men who had boarded Bawla's car aimed and fired a pistol at him almost immediately after mounting the footboard.

As luck would have it, another car drove up from behind and its inmates, hearing the shots and the woman's cries for help, stopped their car, jumped out, and rushed to their rescue. This car was occupied by three Englishmen, all military officers: Lt. Saegert, who was driving the car, and accompanied by two of his military comrades, Lt. Batley and Lt. Stephen. Saegert immediately threw himself into the thick of the fight, grappled with the miscreants, and succeeded in rescuing the girl from the clutches of her assailants, and although more than one shot was fired at him and he was wounded in three or four places on his body, he managed to carry Mumtaz to his own car. With the assistance of his comrades, Lts. Batley and Stephen, Saegert overpowered several of the assailants and snatched the murderous weapons out of their hands. With the assistance of another English military officer, Col. Vickery, who also drove up shortly after, these men succeeded in securing some of the assailants and handed them over to the police, who soon arrived on the scene. Lt. Saegert, besides being struck with bullets, was also attacked during the scuffle with a knife, which inflicted a deep wound on his shoulder. Some of the assailants had also sustained injuries, mainly from a golf stick which Lt. Saegert had used both for attack and defense.

The Bombay press ran amuck over the case with its tinge of romance and gallantry, with the shadow of a ruling prince in the background. For days after the incidents of the twelfth of January 1925, the morning and evening papers of Bombay were full of the Bawla case, recounting all sorts of stories, exploring and raking up the past history and speculation on the future prospects of the tragic heroine of this bloody drama. The Viceroy of India claimed that HH Tukoji Rao Holkar, the ruling prince whose harem had once housed Mumtaz, was part of the conspiracy and was threatening to try Tukoji Rao and annex his state. Tukoji Rao urgently wanted Siremal Bapna Sahib to immediately return to Indore to plan his defense and future strategy in view of this most unfortunate situation.

Bhupinder Singh had so come to depend on Siremal that he refused to give permission to Siremal to leave Patiala. For almost fifteen days there was an impasse, when ultimately on Siremal's representation that it was a matter of life and death for the Holkar prince, he was allowed to depart. Siremal arrived back in Indore in February of 1926 and immediately met the British Agent for Central India who was the Viceroy's agent and overseer of the Princely States in Central India, which included the Holkar State. The agent informed Siremal that the British had decided to annex the state and merge it into British India. Holkar was a huge state. It would have been a catastrophic loss for the ruling family if the British would have annexed the state. Besides, the agent informed Siremal that the Viceroy was incensed with the brutality of the crime and was intent on trying Tukoji Rao Holkar in court for murder.

Siremal started negotiating with the British on behalf of the prince. Tukoji Rao, who was Siremal's former law student and who still respectfully addressed him as *MarSaheb*, meaning "respected teacher," swore to Siremal that he was not part of this conspiracy. The British had a great deal of respect for Siremal for two reasons. They knew that Siremal was a person of high moral character and impeccable record as a public servant. It also did not go unnoticed that he was a great administrator who had distinguished himself as a minister in both

Holkar and Patiala state. They also knew Siremal's antecedents as Chhogmal's son, as well as the entire history of the family. Siremal was able to leverage this respect, and he gradually managed to get the British to agree to a settlement in the case whereby Tukoji Rao Holkar would abdicate and his twelve-year-old son, Yeshwant Rao, would take over as the ruler. The British also agreed not to annex the state. Since Yeshwant Rao was a minor, it was necessary to find a regent who would rule in his name until he turned eighteen. Both the British and Tukoji Rao could only agree on one name: Siremal.

In 1926, Yeshwant Rao Holkar was crowned the Ruler of Holkar State in Indore, while Siremal was appointed the prime minister and regent. At the age of forty-four, Siremal was for the next six years the virtual ruler of one of the largest kingdoms in the Indian subcontinent. In half a lifetime, while he could not restore to himself and his family the great wealth that his ancestors enjoyed, Siremal had overcome his family's great misfortune and became one of the most powerful men in all of India. To top it all, he was highly respected and trusted by all sides—the British, the ruling Holkar family and the common people of Holkar State. He took up residence in a palace allocated to him by the state in Indore city, called Baxi Baug, which while small in size was adorned with the most beautiful gardens and grounds in Indore.

Siremal turned out to be a just and brilliant ruler. Honest to the core, a deep sense of fairness imbedded within him inspired by his own experiences, that of his father Chhogmal and his ancestors, mainly Seth Deoraj, Siremal set about instituting reforms in policies and the administration of Holkar State. He was a great modernist and a renaissance man, very much in keeping with his father, Chhogmal, and very keen on women's rights and the rights of the so-called "untouchables." As a ruler and without any voting bank pressure, he piloted the Women's Education Act and the Untouchability Abolition Act through the Holkar State cabinet. These were landmark pieces of legislation for their day. In addition, he fundamentally reformed and modernized the administrative structure and judiciary of the state to be more responsive to people's needs.

Siremal had a vision of what a "state" should be. He believed that at the foundation of every state, there were two pillars. The first was the defense of its territory, and the second, financial affluence. Since the defense of the state was guaranteed by the British, Siremal went about the task of establishing the foundation of a great economy in Holkar

State. Cotton was one of the chief cash crops grown in the black soil of Holkar State. Siremal recognized textile mills as the logical step forward towards economic growth. He leveraged his deep family connections with the mercantile class in Rajasthan and invited rich merchants to set up textile mills in Indore. He instituted friendly economic policies and offered incentives to these merchants to locate their enterprises in Indore.

Between 1926 and 1939, the time Siremal was Prime Minister, several mills were set up in Indore, making it one of the biggest textile manufacturing and trading centers in India. Hundreds and thousands of workers migrated from the countryside and other states to work in these mills, and Indore became known all over India as an affluent boom town, a place with business-friendly policies to set up an enterprise.

Siremal, by 1928, had laid a solid economic foundation for Indore, but Siremal believed that mere money was not enough to build a healthy society. While money provided the fuel and the energy for the society, it did not by itself provide for the soul of the society. To develop a soul, the society needed educational institutions, art, architecture, music and culture, so he provided further patronage to the existing Holkar College and established many state-owned schools. He was instrumental in re-energizing the state Art School in Indore, which later produced legendary and world famous artists such as MF Hussain and Bendre. He invited the famed young maestro of Indian classical music, Ustad Amir Khan, to revive the Indore *gharana* of music (gharana is a unique and original style of Indian classical music).

Indore already had a great architectural and town planning tradition with exceptional buildings such as King Edward's Hall, which was the Prime Minister's Office, and Daly College, the exclusive school for princes and nobles. In 1918, Tukoji Rao Holkar, the reigning prince, had invited the legendary Irish town planner, Patrick Geddes, a friend of Siremal's, to develop a plan for the new city of Indore. Siremal also continued, with all of his vigor the Holkar ruler's passion for sports such as cricket and Indian-style wrestling. Several great cricketers were patronized by the Holkar state during Siremal's tenure as a regent and prime minister, chief of them being Col. CK Naydu, Mushtaq Ali and others. The Holkar cricket team became one of the best in India, and Indore also became a leading center for Indian-style wrestling in India.

Affluent, artistic, musical, sports-oriented, well-planned and well-governed Indore by the early 1930s had become the envy of all of

India. Writers, intellectuals and entrepreneurs moved to Indore, along with its share of shysters, scam artists, criminals and the low life. This combination made Indore an eclectic and vibrant city, but still a city where law and order was maintained and people felt safe. Indore also went on to develop its own hospitable culture and its own cuisine.

Siremal Bapna served as the Prime Minister and Regent of Holkar state from 1926 until 1932, when Prince Yeshwantrao Holkar attained majority status (adulthood) and took over full powers of the government. While Siremal was no longer regent and an absolute ruler, he still retained the powerful position of prime minister. Siremal's rule during his regency was legendary and known as one of the golden periods in Holkar State history. After assuming full powers, Yeshwant Rao Holkar, on behalf of the city of Indore, honored him with numerous titles and decorations, such as Rai Bahadur and Wazir-ud-aulah. To provide an efficient and just government, while at the same time building a city as per his vision, required that the regressive elements and vested interests within the state be kept in check. Holkar State had its share of powerful vested interests that saw Siremal as an impediment to the advancement of their narrow personal goals. There were also several extreme traditionalists who resented Siremal's modern outlook and modernization of the city of Indore. Because from 1926 through 1932 Siremal held absolute power, these interests did not have much room to maneuver and basically were forced to go into hibernation.

After the assumption of full powers by Yeswhant Rao, these vested interests started stirring again. Yeshwant Rao was an enlightened and educated man. However, one of his few flaws was that he was gullible by nature. He was also given to frivolous partying, liquor and hunting. He also suffered from slight insecurity, causing him to not be able to deal with strong, confident personalities and preferring sycophants and the hangers on types. Therefore, an opportunist coterie of national and international set developed around Yeshwant Rao, dominated by a few families who had migrated to Indore from Punjab. This coterie wanted access to state resources to enrich themselves, and therefore saw Siremal as an obstacle in their way. Yeshwant Rao, therefore, was bombarded by criticisms of and intrigues against Siremal. Yeshwant Rao was a little intimidated by the popularity and strength of Siremal's personality. All these things combined for a clash between Siremal and Yeshwant Rao.

Siremal, having experienced uninhibited freedom to build Indore as per his vision, found it difficult to adjust to the lightweight intellectual environment that surrounded Yeshwant Rao. He was intensely loyal to the state and loved the city of Indore and its people. However, he managed, just through the strength of his personality, to develop a certain personal loyalty to Yeshwant Rao.

Siremal, being the older and more experienced of the two, was initially able to shrug off some of the slights that Yeshwant Rao directed at him. Siremal had developed a tremendous amount of mass popularity in Indore because of his sense of fairness, vision, administration, and most of all his love for the people of Indore. This popularity made Yeshwant Rao enormously insecure. The slights by Yeshwant Rao to Siremal increased in frequency, to the point where Yeshwant Rao condoned disrespect exhibited to Siremal by the coterie that surrounded him. Siremal struggled through this relationship to continue building up the city of Indore as prime minister for six years after Yeshwant Rao assumed full powers, but those years were difficult for him. Things, however, took a turn for the worse in the year 1939, and in the fall of that year Yeshwant Rao made his move.

Siremal, unlike most successful people, liked to share his success with his friends and family. His generosity was legendary. He would give the shirt off his back to the needy, and it was said that he never turned away a person who came to ask him for help.

HH Maharaj Yeshwant Rao Holkar of Indore
Reign, 1926 - 1959
Courtesy Bapna House Family Collection

Bakshi Baugh Palace Indore
Official Residence of Sir Siremal Bapna and the Bapna family during his Prime Ministership in Indore (1926 – 1939)
Courtesy Bapna House Family Collection

Sir Siremal receiving Viceroy Lord Irvin
At Bakshi Baug Palace during a State Visit to Indore in 1928
Courtesy Bapna House Family Collection

Sir Siremal Bapna with Mahatama Gandhi
During the Mahatama's visit to Indore in 1929
Courtesy Bapna House Family Collection

Sir Siremal Bapna at League of Nations
In Geneva in 1935, as one of three Indian Delegate, seen here with other delegates
Courtesy – Ek Yug Ek Purush – Biography of Sir Siremal Bapna

In India there was a tradition that a successful person in a position of power or authority over public resources helps his family and friends by dispensing some of the public resources to them. In other words, it was common practice to engage in corruption by allowing not only themselves, but their relatives and friends to dip into the public exchequer. Siremal abhorred corruption. He had brought up his immediate family by inculcating into them a value system which excoriated corruption. Therefore, the immediate family could never indulge in it. However, his extended family and friends from Rajasthan expected Siremal to help them out, whether to finance their children's education or to get their children married off. Siremal never refused, but instead of using the state treasury, he used his own personal resources to help everyone out.

Siremal had a large immediate family, with sons, daughters, daughters-in-law, grandchildren, but an even larger extended family. Slowly, all of these became part of Siremal's household, and he met all their expenses. Even his princely monthly salary would be exhausted before the month was out, as he supported a household of almost two hundred people. These included his companions, his friends, their families, a large household staff, and of course his own family. He paid for everyone's education and all other expenses.

One day in early 1939, a well-dressed man in a smart three-piece woolen suit arrived at Baxi Baug Palace to meet with Siremal. It was in the early morning hours and Indore was bitterly cold that particular winter day. The man was in his early forties and wore his jet black hair neatly cut and brushed back. His sideburns betrayed some shades of grey and he had an angular face. He had the small beady eyes of a shrewd and intelligent man while his lips wore a permanent scowl. His name was Col. Dinanath and he had become the de-facto leader of the coterie around Prince Yeshwant Rao Holkar. Ironically, he was brought to Indore from Patiala by Siremal himself, where as a young junior officer he had impressed Siremal with his intelligence and efficiency.

Siremal was a simple and trusting man and he was initially fooled by Col. Dinanath's professional manner and conduct. After coming to Indore, however, Col. Dinanath found the court of the more gullible Yeshwant Rao to be fertile ground to sow seeds for fulfillment of his high ambitions. Col. Dinanath desired both money and power and he quickly realized that he could use Yeshwant Rao and the Holkar state to attain both. The man that stood in his way was his mentor and benefactor, Siremal.

Col. Dinanath surveyed the fabulous roses of the famed Baxi Baug Garden from the outer veranda as he smoked a cigarette and waited for Siremal. He turned around as he heard familiar footsteps. "Dinanathji, you are up bright and early," said Siremal, as Dinanath stepped forward and touched Siremal's feet.

"Bapna *Saheb*, I thought I would catch you early, and considering that you are my mentor, I took the liberty of setting up an early morning appointment," said Col. Dinanath.

"It is very kind of you Dinanathji, but the pupil today commands the confidence of the prince far more than the master," said Siremal, smiling.

"This is what I have come to talk to you about," said Col. Dinanath as Siremal motioned for Col. Dinanath to take a seat in the sitting room inside the veranda.

"What can I do for you, Dinanathji?" asked Siremal.

Col. Dinanath leaned forward, folded his hands and lowered his eyes as he spoke. "Bapna *Saheb*, it is well known how popular you are in Indore. But there are people in the court—important people, powerful people. They are saying that Bapna *Saheb* is a fool. They are saying it, not me. You did not make any money while you were regent, and Lord knows you could have amassed a huge fortune. Not only that, you did not allow anyone else in the government to make any money either. Now that Yeshwant Rao has assumed full powers, you continue to come in the way of people close to His Highness from benefitting. Your foolish behavior, if I may be so impertinent in saying so, is causing great consternation to many powerful people, and naturally, if people around His Highness are distressed, so will be the Prince," said Col. Dinanath.

"And how may I do away with this consternation, Dinanathji?" asked Siremal, smiling, fully understanding the significance of Dinanath's words.

"Bapna *Saheb*, you know of all the people in the court, I continue to openly espouse my loyalty to you. I get mocked and ridiculed for it every time, yet I cannot bring myself to detach from you. Trust me. I have only your best interests at heart. Please withdraw your objections to my appointment to head the Department of Treasury with full powers over all finances. I know better than anybody else the huge personal financial obligations you carry, with your large household, and how you could use some much needed financial security. I will ensure that only the very close circle around His Highness and you yourself will be financially secure for the rest of your life, and perhaps the lifetime of your children and grandchildren, if you simply step out of the way. I assure you, Bapna *Saheb*, I have His Highness's full blessings on this offer and I will act so discreetly that no one in Indore but the very inner circle would come to know about it and we all will become enormously wealthy. After all, that is how it is meant to be. The elite and the rulers have always personally benefitted from their positions in India. They will continue to do so as long as India exists. You and your ideas from the rationalist philosophers in Europe are alien to our culture. If you continue to get in the way of what comes naturally to us as Indians, you will be the one who will be swept away. The powerful men around Yeshwant Rao will most assuredly get rich. It is inevitable. The question is, will you choose to commit hara-kiri in a futile attempt to stop the inevitable, or will you be pragmatic and join them? As your loyal servant, my ardent hope is that you will not be a fool, Bapna *Saheb*. Please join us," implored Col. Dinanath.

Siremal listened with great patience. He leaned forward and said in his characteristically soft and dignified voice, "Don't you think the idea of becoming wealthy has occurred to me as well, without the need for anybody to point it out? Don't you think that I have been approached with these kinds of offers almost monthly since joining the service, almost three decades ago? When I have chosen not to go for it so far, what makes you think, Dinanathji that I will change my mind now? Wait! You think it is your engaging personality and charm that can do the trick this time, right?"

"Earlier, you were a rising star, Bapna *Saheb*. Today you must know that the winds are blowing against you. You are fifty some years of age, with a large family and huge commitments. You are not getting any younger and the window of opportunity is shrinking. The word in the court is that His Highness may remove you any day. Perhaps reality will trump idealism for you this one time. Not many men get an opportunity like you have. Not many men in history reach the pinnacle of power like you have. Not many powerful men in India use their power for general good, as you have done. They do it for personal gain. Would you ignore an opportunity like that, Bapna *Saheb*? Please don't be a fool," said Dinanath, now literally pleading.

Siremal stood, and Dinanath shot up in response.

"Since you are so loyal to me, Dinanathji, I forgive you for this conversation. Please convey my regards to your wife and family," said

Siremal calmly, while gesturing with his hands, indicating that the meeting was over.

Col. Dinanath walked out of the room in a huff, and realizing that he had forgotten something, reappeared a minute later, touched Siremal's feet and stomped out again. His normally shrewd eyes were lost in thought, his face in weird contortion and his body all bent out of shape in contrast to the picture of poise he normally presented. "I have never seen a bigger fool," he kept repeating to himself as his car pulled out of the long driveway of Baxi Baug Palace.

A few years earlier, in 1936, Siremal Bapna had been awarded the title of "Knight Commander of the British Empire." He was now addressed as "Sir Siremal." The people of Indore broke into spontaneous celebrations. Yeshwant Rao watched this development with mixed feelings. On the one hand, his nobler instincts caused him to be proud of the fact that his prime minister was selected for this unique and distinct honor. On the other hand, this award increased his insecurity vis-à-vis Siremal. He became even more susceptible to intrigues by Siremal's critics, and finally in the fall of 1939 he constructed a hand-written letter to Siremal.

Dear Sir Siremal,

For a long time now, I have been thinking. I would like for you to take retirement, from your position as my prime minister, effective immediately. I would offer you a pension which would amount to one-third of your salary and the use of a car, with certain conditions attached.

Sincerely,
Yeshwant Rao Holkar.

Siremal was caught in a bind. He had worked tirelessly for the state and the city of Indore for almost three decades. He had practically built modern Indore by using his own vision and with tremendous effort. He had come to love the people of Indore and they loved him back equally. All of a sudden, in the prime of his life, at the age of fifty-four, he was out of a job. His elation at being knighted earlier that year dissipated. He was particularly concerned about how he would support the two hundred people in his household. Most of them depended on him and while his two sons, KB and PS, were in good government positions in Holkar State, they were far from wealthy. The pension offered was quite generous, but at one-third his former income he would have to drastically cut back on his support to his household. Besides, he didn't own a house to live in, and there was a tradition that retired prime ministers would be granted the government house that they had lived in while they were in service. However, no such offer was forthcoming in the letter by Yeshwant Rao and there was widespread speculation as to whether such an offer would be forthcoming in follow-up correspondence. Siremal sent a letter back to Yeshwant Rao which said something like the following.

Your Highness,

I have received your letter and noted its contents. I hereby tender my resignation as your prime minister. I wish to say that despite our differences, I have always remained and will continue to remain loyal to our beloved Holkar State and to you personally.

I am grateful to you for your offer of a generous pension and the use of the car. Kindly elucidate the conditions attached. In addition, please indicate by what time I should vacate Baxi Baug (the official prime minister's residence) so I can make alternate living arrangements elsewhere in Indore.

Your most humble servant,
Siremal Bapna

Yeshwant Rao Holkar II, fourteenth ruler of the famed Holkar dynasty, the descendant of pious and legendary Ruler Ahilya Bai, wrote back the following:

Dear Bapna Saheb,

I received your letter of resignation and noted its friendly tone. It is a pity that differences arose between us, but I am glad that there are no hard feelings. Please take your time in leaving Baxi Baug. However, finding other living accommodations in Indore I am afraid, is impossible. As a condition of your pension, I am stipulating that you not live in Indore or anywhere near Indore. It would not be appropriate for a former prime minister and regent to live within or near the borders of the state.

I wish you all the best for the future and good health.

Sincerely,
YRH

Siremal could not believe his eyes. Not only was he to lose his job, he was also to be banished from Indore if he were to avail his pension. Siremal knew well that Yeshwant Rao's intelligence had informed him of the size of Siremal's household and the extent of their dependence on him. Siremal had been resolutely honest to the point that his bank account had an overdraft. He owned no personal property, not even a small house he could call his own. All of his life he had only done for others, seeking no favors. An example of such absolute honesty and generosity in such a high position would be next to impossible to find in all of Indian history. Where would he go? What would happen to his household if he had to move someplace far away? Some of the members of his household had minor jobs in Indore, while others were mere children studying in Indore. Their entire lives would be disrupted and turned upside down. On the other hand, if he didn't move out of Indore he would have no income. How would he support his household anyway? He was being punished for being honest, being an able administrator, for building a city, for being loyal, for being Siremal Bapna.

Siremal, reluctantly accepted the pension in the interest of his household, and decided to move back to Ajmer, where he had found shelter at the age of seventeen, when his father was forced to declare bankruptcy in Udaipur and had perished. He rented a modest house, and since his wife had already passed away and his sons couldn't move with him due to their jobs, his eldest grand daughter-in-law was to become the lady of the house.

Siremal took about a week to pack up and settle his matters in Indore. Most of his household would now be dispersed. Some would find other relatives or places to stay in Indore. Others were taken in by Siremal's younger son, PS, who from all accounts took after him in character and generosity. However, about fifty people were to move to Ajmer with Sir Siremal. Every day that passed was another day closer to his departure from Indore, and Siremal became sadder and sadder. Almost every day of the week there was a parade of visitors—regular people and VIPs—from morning to evening at Baxi Baug palace, paying their respects and wishing Sir Siremal well in his future life.

The British officers, led by the British Agent, arrived on the penultimate day with their full pageantry and in full uniform to pay respects to Sir Siremal. His Highness Tukoji Rao Holkar, the deposed prince and the erstwhile law student of Sir Siremal, arrived with his new American wife to bid farewell to his beloved *Mar-Saheb*. Tukoji Rao had retired to his Versailles-style palace, called "Lalbaug" in the outskirts of the city and was leading a quiet life. Countless citizens of Indore from all walks of life came to bid farewell to their beloved leader. On the last day, just before Siremal was to leave Baxi Baug for the train station, HRH Yeshwant Rao Holkar arrived with Her Highness to bid Siremal farewell. Both men met in the outer veranda of Baxi Baug and were most gracious with each other, albeit a little formal.

A large crowd of thousands of people had gathered outside Baxi Baug Palace to accompany Sir Siremal to the train station. The procession left Baxi Baug several hours before the departure time of the train to cover the two kilometers to the train station. Every couple of minutes the procession was stopped by temporary wayside stations, where Sir Siremal was presented a bouquet of fresh flowers and his forehead anointed by the holy red *tilak*.

The procession reached the train station after a couple of hours, where another several thousand people were waiting. Several traditional send-off ceremonies were performed. Finally, Siremal's family that was to accompany him boarded the train. Siremal was the last to climb up into his railway car. Hundreds of people kneeled on the station platform in a gesture of touching Siremal's feet as the train slowly pulled off the platform, bound for Ajmer. As the train picked up speed, so did Siremal's tears, which people said did not stop for the entire journey until he reached Ajmer.

A very old woman, all haggard and bent over, had walked all the way to the train station to see Siremal off. She must have been more than a hundred years old. Lord knows what good deed Siremal had done for her or what connection she had with him, but as Siremal's train disappeared from her sight she looked up at the sky and in a voice that came from deep within her declared, "Indore will never again have a leader as good as Siremal. Never ever." And true to her prophecy,

Indore, to its misfortune, no longer had Siremal and it was doubtful they ever would have a leader like Sir Siremal—never—with the possible exception of his son, PS.

⊰⊱

"Siremal was known as the saintly ruler. His people loved him," said Dev.

"I know. Even today, his memory lives on in Indore. Whenever people in Indore found out that I was a descendant of Sir Siremal, they would immediately start treating me with a certain reverence," said Kunal.

"Can you imagine a ruler of a vast state not having his own house to live in when he retired? Something absolutely unheard of in India! But his son, PS, your grandfather, was equally honest and saintly, correct, Papa?" said Ranika.

"Yeah, I will tell you about him, tomorrow", said Dev looking a little ill.

Chapter 18 - Story of PS
1916 AD – 1992 AD

Siremal left a huge legacy in Indore which became a boom town during his reign. The booming economy caused a population explosion, mostly due to inward migration from other areas, which in turn caused severe water shortages. One of Siremal's enduring legacies was an artificial reservoir that was created by damming the Gambhir River near Indore. The reservoir was called Yeshwant Sagar, and it was an engineering marvel of its time. Siremal took personal interest in supervising the construction of this dam and he invited engineers from as far away as England to assist. The project was completed on budget and on time in the 1930s, to the chagrin of many naysayers and detractors of Siremal, who had predicted that this project would be a great failure. Upon the completion of this dam the water shortages were alleviated, further stimulating the already strong economy. This reservoir was to be the sole source of drinking water for the city of Indore from 1930s right up to 1978, when Siremal's equally noble son, PS under his supervision got another water supply project of much greater scale completed.

Another legacy that Siremal left was his vision and its realization of what an ideal community and a city should be like. His conceptualization of a community as not just a predominantly economic and muscle-driven entity, but also having a soul composed of music, art, culture, architecture, education and healthcare was unprecedented and unique, at least in the Indian context. He was successfully able to realize this vision in Indore during his reign. His son PS continued to not only subscribe to and protect, but also advance this vision.

Siremal also left a great legacy in the national and international spheres. He later served as prime minister of several other Princely States such as Bikaner and Alwar with great distinction. He was a great promoter of the Hindi language and counted many famous Hindi writers such as Makhan Lal Chaturvedi as his friends. He had contacts, sometimes close, with most British and Indian political figures of prominence such as Winston Churchill, Lloyd George, Ramsey Macdonald, Clement Atlee, Mr. Jinnah, Prince Aga Khan and Mahatama Gandhi. Many business leaders of their day in India such as Seth Hukum Chand, Seth Govind Ram Seksaria, GD Birla, JL Bajaj and others were his friends. He toured Europe several times, once at the behest of the British government, to hold discussions with Hitler and Mussolini to gauge their intentions just prior to World War II. He was part of the Indian delegation to the 1931 round-table conference in London. Most importantly, he was chosen to be one of the three delegates to represent India in the League of Nations, along with his dear friend, His Highness Prince Aga Khan, in 1935.

Sir Siremal indeed was a world statesman and a major historical figure of his time. After 1947, India became independent and all the Princely States were basically abolished. They were absorbed into modern India. Siremal retired at the age of 65 and returned to Indore to live with his two sons, on the express invitation of his former pupil, the ex-Holkar prince Tukoji Rao, who wrote a touching letter to his former law tutor, respectfully asking him to return. Since the Princely States had been abolished, Prince Yeshwant Rao, like all other princes, went into retirement with generous pensions from the new government of India. He could no longer prevent Siremal from returning to Indore and with his state now gone, he had no reason to either. Yeshwant Rao later realized that the coterie around him had used him and enriched itself, only to desert him, once his state was gone. In his later years, Yeshwant Rao and Sir Siremal were able to reconcile themselves and settle into a cordial relationship. Siremal lived to the ripe old age of eighty-two and died in Indore in 1964, mourned by the grateful citizens of Indore, who shortly thereafter raised a statue of Sir Siremal in a prominent intersection in Indore.

Most people thought that Siremal was the culmination of a great dynasty and imbibed all the collective goodness and abilities of his ancestors. All of his direct ancestors, going back to Deoraj, were outstanding individuals in their own right, but each also had their flaws.

Zorawar Mal and Guman Chand, the most successful money makers, for example, were somewhat flexible on their morality, while Chhogmal and Deoraj were perhaps too rigid. Siremal too had flaws. He was simple and too trusting, but he was less flawed than any of his ancestors. People attributed it to generations of good breeding and culture. People referred to him as a "saintly administrator," someone who did not have the great appetites and desires of a Zorawar Mal or the seething ambition of a Guman Chand. If people wondered if any of Siremal's descendants would be able to replicate his "saintliness," they didn't have to look far. It was Siremal's younger son, PS who was in fact the culmination of the many illustrious generations of Bapnas, representing all the very best of his ancestors with only minimal flaws.

Pratap Singh Bapna, or PS, as he was popularly known, was born in 1908 and grew up during the time when his father's career was at its ascendency. He grew up in Indore, son of a popular home minister who later became the prime minister. He excelled in academics and sports and was a brilliant student right through his career, much like his father. Growing up a son of one of the most powerful men in the country, he could easily have acquired the trappings of a prince, but instead he developed elegant yet simple tastes. To his credit and that of the upbringing of Siremal, PS had a noble bearing and carried himself like an aristocrat. While his tastes were simple and he was not a conventionally handsome man, he projected natural aristocracy and authority. Even at an early age, people couldn't help but be a little awed by PS.

It had become a fashion in India in those days that young men from good families get educated in Britain and then travel the world to round off their education. PS too travelled to England in 1928, at the age of twenty, to pursue a master's degree in the prestigious London School of Economics. He had recently gotten married to a lady from an aristocratic Bachhawat Mehta family in Udaipur, called Ratan. In 1929, PS earned his master's degree in economics, with distinction. He went on to acquire his law degree in India.

Siremal Bapna Official State Portrait
Courtesy Bapna House Family Collection

HRH Maharaja Ganga Singh of Bikaner
Reign – 1888- 1943
Great Statesman, Soldier, Patriot, Reformer, a Legend
Persuaded Sir Siremal to serve as his Prime Minister from 1939 to 1944 (HRH Ganga Singh died in 1943). Sir Siremal greatly admired HRH. Courtesy – Bapna House Family Collection, picture of a portrait by Sir James Guthrie in 1930

PS Bapna Sb, IAS-younger son of Siremal
Upon joining the Holkar State Administrative Service in 1933
Courtesy Bapna House Family Collection

London, and in particular the London School of Economics in the 1920s was, a hot bed of left-wing activism. Russia had recently had a Bolshevik revolution and young Brits were taken in by ideas of Marx and Engels, Lenin and Trotsky. PS did not remain unaffected by this and developed a lifelong affinity with some mild form of socialism. He looked at some socialist ideas as possible solutions to the backward and fragmented Indian society. However, even then, he never subscribed to the most extreme form of socialism nor the tyrannical regimes that came to be associated with socialism. After completing his education in London, PS and a group of friends travelled all over Europe in 1929 and 1930. He wanted to visit Russia and see firsthand how the Bolsheviks ran their economy of collective farms and built their industrial infrastructure. He was particularly taken by the railways that the Russians were building to connect even remote areas, and he travelled from Moscow to Vladivostok via the Trans-Siberian Railroad.

PS returned to India in 1931, and at the age of twenty-three he joined the Holkar State Administrative Service as a collector, a starting position on a fast track for the highest Civil Service positions. PS's elder brother KB, too, was in the Holkar State Service in the Revenue Department. Both PS and KB were in transferrable jobs and they worked in various small towns and villages in Holkar State. This experience gave PS a particular insight into rural India and its social problems. He became empathetic to the plight of the villagers. This empathy stayed with him all of his life and he spent his life working to alleviate the problems of the rural poor, albeit in high Civil Service positions within the provincial government of the State of MP.

Between the years 1931 and 1947, PS worked as a Senior Civil Service officer in Holkar State. In 1947 two things happened. After two hundred years of British rule, India attained its independence. The British, devastated by the two World Wars and in face of growing rebellions, started relinquishing their colonies. The other was that PS was "adopted" by a distant relative, an old lady with no children, and inherited a reasonable amount of money, which if properly handled could make him comfortable for life. PS never actually received his inheritance until 1955, after going through protracted court procedures such as probate, which took a long time to resolve in the Indian judicial system. His father, Siremal, despite being a ruler, lived under severe financial constraints all his life, but PS was to be financially comfortable. To top it all, he, through sheer merit, was appointed to a powerful

Civil Service position within the new independent Indian provincial structure.

PS was the worthy son of a worthy father. He was generous with his money, along the same lines as Siremal. In fact, he had taken over Siremal's mantle as the financial support for many of his relatives and friends. In addition, he also supported, for a while some of Siremal's companions. His wife, Ratan, supported him fully in this generosity, without which PS would not have been able to assist all these people.

Housing in India in those days was rather scarce and expensive, so culturally, Indians were accustomed to a joint-family system. Normally, a joint family system consisted of several brothers and their families who all pooled their resources to run a common household. In case of Siremal and PS, however, it was a different version of a joint-family system. Unlike normal joint-family systems, PS and Siremal supported scores of distant relatives and even friends and friends' families. Also, unlike normal joint-family systems, Siremal and PS provided their sole financial support, as opposed to a pooling of resources among family members. Therefore, the burden of managing the household also naturally fell on the wife of the sole provider, as only the sole provider had a stake in running the household economically. PS's wife Ratan very ably ran the household, looking after everyone's comfort and needs.

Again, PS and his wife financed several weddings of close and distant relatives (weddings in India in general are very expensive compared to weddings in the West). They also financed the education of many relatives and friends. Again, true to their father's creed and their own upbringing, it was out of the question for PS to make money through corruption, and gradually PS's wealth started eroding. It was said at the time that someone in PS's position within the government acquired one house a year through corruption, while PS kept liquidating roughly one property a year which he had inherited from his adopted mother.

Professionally, however, PS was brilliant. He oversaw projects for the development of rural India. He kept his projects simple, worked on pre-defined timelines, and progress was easily measurable. Year after year as Secretary Planning or Development Commissioner, as the position was popularly called, PS toured remote villages and oversaw their development. Gradually, he was recognized as an outstanding Civil Servant and in Indore in particular, he was regarded as the spiritual and intellectual heir of Sir Siremal.

PS also shared his father's deep attachment to Indore and its people.

Having been born, brought up and practically spending his entire working career in and around Indore, he was a "son of the soil," or a native son. The people of Indore until the 1980s returned his affections, and even though there were no absolute rulers in independent India, PS's direction was voluntarily followed by the people of Indore on all important issues, and therefore carried his weight well beyond his pay grade.

PS retired in 1970 and by then had given away most of his inheritance. His most significant accomplishments came in the decade right after his retirement. The population of Indore had grown by leaps and bounds, and by 1970, it had well outgrown the water reservoir built by Siremal. Indore was again experiencing acute water shortages. There was no other river or stream nearby which could be dammed. There was the mighty River Narmada that flowed almost fifty miles away, but to carry water from there would be a technical challenge as the water had to be transported upslope.

PS, after his retirement, worked with a group of engineers to assess the feasibility and cost of bringing Narmada water to Indore. He came up with a technical plan and a financial plan. He set about trying to sell the idea to the government. The government at the time was unable to meet the financial requirements for such a plan as there was a lot of competition for government funds. Besides, detractors and opponents started criticizing the technical plan by labeling it "not sound," further weakening PS's argument. PS was able to rally various civic groups and the press in Indore around this cause. Finally, using his credentials as a Bapna, a Civil Servant par excellence and connections within the government, not to mention the support of all of Indore, PS was able to get his plan approved by the Prime Minister of India, Indira Gandhi herself.

The project started in 1975, amidst grave doubts about its success. By 1978, the first phase of the project was successfully completed on time and within budget, under strict supervision of PS, who was appointed the Chairman of the Advisory Committee by the government, without even an allegation or hint of corruption. The naysayers were proven wrong again and Indore was relieved of its water shortages.

The phrase "epitome of unparalleled grace, class and dignity" has so been so overused and beaten to death that it has lost some of its beauty and impact. It almost seems like the software to churn out canned obituaries has this phrase hard coded in it. However, no other phrase described PS as well. It was as if God had coined this phrase just for people like PS. He was such a natural person, so comfortable in his own skin, and a man of such unshakeable confidence and limitless compassion that he seldom got rattled or excited. Yet he was a human being, not God, and when he woke up on that morning of 1978, the day when Narmada water first arrived in Indore, PS could not contain his joy.

Dev had just arrived in Indore the previous day from Bombay, where he was finishing up his high school. Dev distinctly remembered that his grandfather had a great spring in his steps. He was brimming with excitement when reporters came to interview him about the inauguration ceremony scheduled for later that day. The phone didn't stop ringing off the hook. People from all over the country were calling with their congratulations. All of PS's hard work and almost a decade of struggle to bring water to his beloved Indore had finally paid off. PS, a man of innumerable accomplishments during his five-decade record of public service, considered this his crowning achievement. His beloved Indore would no longer go thirsty and now nothing could come in the way of Indore transforming itself from a medium-sized town into a large modern metropolis. *If the politicians play their cards right and not mess it up, that is,* he thought.

But there was an even more compelling reason for PS's elation—a personal reason. His father, Siremal, had been instrumental in building the reservoir that had supplied water to Indore for the past forty years. Siremal too had struggled against a lot of opposition to build that dam. PS, likewise, was a man far ahead of his times and had to overcome a lot of narrow-minded opposition to accomplish this. PS had followed in his father's footsteps. He had done his father proud. He was almost childlike that day. Dev had never seen his grandfather this happy. PS was a modern, forward-looking man and Dev had never seen him look back, despite a great heritage to look back to. On that day, however, he saw PS standing in front of the large portrait of his father, Siremal, with an expression that said, "I did all right, father, didn't I?" There were not many truly and deeply joyous days in Dev's young life of seventeen years, but Dev felt a tremendous high that day, watching his grandfather prancing around so joyously.

PS's happiness and joy that day said something profound about him and his father Siremal. PS was terribly excited because a community project which he had been working on for a long time finally ended in success. If PS had won the lottery, or even found a billion dollars someplace, he would not have been this excited. In fact, he would not have been excited at all. That was because he valued community building and city building. He didn't value having a billion dollars in the bank as much.

It was a simply a question of the value system. PS's value system, which he had inherited from his father, Siremal, put a lot of premium on building and promoting healthy societies, a model which is not a zero sum game, but a win-win for everyone. He believed that all individuals would be much better off in a society that was fundamentally just, had law and order, had civilizing influences of education, art, music and sports and where the economy was strong and everyone had a level playing field. On the other hand, if some people had huge amounts of money, but the system was corrupt and dysfunctional, then even the billionaires would not have a good quality of life. This value system, followed by PS and his father Siremal, was somewhat of a departure from the value system followed by the early patriarchs of the Bapna family. Guman Chand, Zorawarmal and Chandanmal put a high premium on building personal fortunes. They were very enlightened and also strongly believed in community building, but they placed making money above all else.

With Siremal and PS it was different. Making money for them was way down on the priority list. While certain values remained constant in the Bapna family, from Deoraj to Dev, in other areas the value system diverged from Zorawar Mal to Siremal, with Chhogmal acting as a transitional figure and even an active catalyst to bring about that final change.

Why did this value system diverge? Perhaps, for a variety of reasons. The foundation that Deoraj had laid down made it inevitable that at some point a more evolved value system would become dominant in his family. Also, Chhogmal's personal example of preferring to retain his honor rather than compromising his dignity to salvage his fortune left an indelible impression on Siremal that money was not the be-all and end-all of everything. Honor was more important. It was to Siremal's and PS's credit that they expanded the definition of honor from merely meaning "not personally submitting to anyone" to "respect and justice for all of humanity."

Therefore, Siremal and PS consciously fought an inner battle to not let a deep rooted history of building huge personal fortunes come in the way of living in relative poverty, focusing instead on making the world around them a better place. The family, thus, evolved to a much better value system and this evolution was complete with PS. Both PS and Siremal may have been financially broke most of their lives, but they were more enlightened in relative terms than either Guman Chand or Zorawar Mal, who in the whole scheme of things were not exactly unenlightened. It would have been unthinkable for a Siremal or PS, for example, to even consider getting into the opium business or plotting assassinations of even the worst kind of tyrants, as Guman Chand and Zorawar Mal did against Swaroop Singh and Salim Singh respectively.

India had very old cultural traditions, all which supported a form of government that glorified, almost deified, the ruler. It was a culture that did not have a strong set of codified laws. Laws were made by the ruler and the small ruling elite surrounding him and were meant to keep the rest of the population in line. The laws did not necessarily apply to the ruler or the ruling elite and they could change the laws at their whim. The greatest achievement of Siremal and PS was not even the well-rounded and culturally rich town they built; it was not the water supply projects they oversaw and succeeded in executing; it was their success in providing India, particularly the people of Indore, a glimpse of how things could be different from the Indian cultural norms. Their rule saw a fair and consistent legal system, a rule of law. Law and order was maintained, while all- round development of the city took place.

There was no personality cult around either Sir Siremal or PS and they both performed as humble public servants. Most of all, during their reign, neither enriched themselves. In fact, when both died, their bank accounts were drained to the point of overdrafts. They were counter culture revolutionaries who attempted to and succeeded in going against the grain of their culture, a culture of corruption and exploitation. They were visionaries who understood that human beings could best live in healthy and harmonious communities and they never allowed themselves or their families to feel a sense of entitlement to power and riches, despite their glorious heritage and illustrious family backgrounds. In their personal lives they were able to blend simplicity with elegance, which only years of refinement can instill in a person. They couldn't help but be aristocrats, and no matter how simply they were dressed or how sparse their surroundings or environment, Siremal and PS always exuded easy confidence and authority.

By 1980, PS, at age seventy-two, was losing his grip on power in Indore. The Bapna "rule" in Indore which had started in 1910, when Siremal was first appointed home minister in Holkar State, was at an end. Almost seventy years of uninterrupted and benevolent rule by two saintly individuals who saw Indore become one of the largest and major urban and cultural centers in India was now over.

By the 1980s Indore and modern India were taken over by a number of mafia-type organizations. Under the guise of democracy, each political party had started organizing themselves as crime syndicates whose sole purpose, once voted in, was to loot the public exchequer, grab public lands and steal public resources. Siremal and PS's style of administration and governance was anathema to these types of organizations. Laws were gradually diluted and their implementation was completely compromised. Unruly mobs, loosely organized along caste or occupational lines, provided the only check or balance to the powers of the political parties which were nothing but mafia organizations. An uneasy alliance between mobs and these political parties started to rule India and Indore in which the middle class or the honest and ethical classes were severely squeezed. Gradually, members of the middle classes also started participating in memberships in either the mob or the political parties, leaving a further vacuum among the voices for sanity, rule of law, meritocracy and good governance.

In such an environment, the society had no use for people like PS. While his father Siremal was revered and honored by people of Indore for providing good governance, PS was ignored in his later life for doing the exact same thing. There had been a massive shift in the value system in the 1970s and 1980s and slowly, PS started feeling marginalized in Indore as he grew older. He never regretted his life and the values he lived by and continued his life, living simply, playing tennis and still doing what he could for the people of Indore.

PS died in his sleep, a king's death, at the ripe old age of eighty-four in 1992. His funeral was modestly attended by only a few hundred people, while newspapers delivered touching eulogies on their front pages.

But soon, PS was forgotten. While streets in Indore were now being named after mafia figures and criminals and statues of political figures were going up, not a stone in Indore was named after PS, in spite of all he had done for the city of Indore.

While PS was alive he was able to keep Indore a civilized city.

After his death, Indore went completely downhill. The music died very quickly and so did art, civic sense, law and order, and Indore descended into chaos, with brutal mafias ruling the streets and ordinary people being beaten down and cowering into submission to exploitation by the varied criminal interests that ruled.

Dev realized in 1992 that with the passing of PS, another glorious chapter in the family saga had come to an end and the Bapna family of Indore was in total disarray and staring into an abyss. Personally, PS's life was a model of how a person should view, adopt and internalize change. Often times they were sudden changes, and sometimes even destructive changes. In PS's lifetime, he transitioned from a colonial India with a feudal-type setup, with no electricity, no cars, no airplanes, no radio, no television, and no telephones to a modern India which was democratic, industrialized, had most modern amenities and was a unified country. While it was difficult for him, he also saw in his lifetime Indian society going from a somewhat orderly and rule-of-law based society to a chaotic, lawless and mafia-ized society. He saw a transition from a less materialistic to a highly materialistic mindset. Finally, he was successfully able to transition his thought process, work style and life style from being a powerful prince to a more common status under the new independent India.

These were all cataclysmic changes, not always for the better, but PS did it without complaints, with unusual grace and calm, and always with a hint of a smile and a glint in his eyes. Till the end of his life he retained the childlike qualities of being very trusting of people to the point of being taken advantage of, of always looking for and focusing on the good in people, while ignoring their shortcomings. Till the end of his life he stayed generous to a fault, while wearing repeatedly mended and aged clothing, but never turning back a needy person from his doorstep. Till the end of his life, he stayed dignified, graceful and a true aristocrat, no matter how hard things became for him.

Dev couldn't remember a single time since PS's death when he would think of him and not choke up or have tears streaming down his cheeks.

"I am 49 years old, have travelled the world many times over, met thousands of people, but I have never met a man like my grandfather—relative or not," said Dev to Kunal and Ranika.

"No matter how good or bad life has treated me or will treat me, I will always feel blessed for having known and been raised by a man like PS," continued Dev with great feelings, as he turned on his side and fell asleep, again looking positively sick.

Over the next couple of days Dev told his children about his own life and experiences.

Chapter 19 - Story of Dev – Part 2

Many centuries have passed since we first saw Dev in the story of the Bapna family. Now, however, the story cannot continue without returning to him.

※

Dev landed at O'Hare Airport in Chicago in August 1979, just a couple of days after his eighteenth birthday. He was admitted to Illinois State University on a tuition scholarship. He was astounded by the size of the airport, the number of terminals, the gates, and the planes parked and taxiing along the many runways. O'Hare, in those days, was the largest and busiest airport in the world. Dev had a four-year student visa, called F-1 by the US Immigration Service, but he was still a little apprehensive as he stood in line, waiting to clear immigration. This was well before the terrorism scare days, and the atmosphere at the airport was far more relaxed than it is these days.

It was not the security-type interrogation that Dev was worried about. He had heard from people that immigration officials at airports did occasionally turn back people, even with valid visas, if they suspected that the passenger intended to stay permanently in the US. Dev kept rehearsing answers to anticipated questions from the immigration officials while he waited in line. When it was his turn, he walked up to the officer and handed him his passport. The immigration officer was a balding, middle-aged man, smartly dressed in his blue uniform, with a no-nonsense attitude and a severe face.

"Good Evening," said Dev, as it was closing in on about 9.30 PM.

"How are you doing today, sir?" said the immigration officer, politely but very formally, giving Dev a thorough looking over.

"The visa is on page eleven," said Dev.

"What is the purpose of your visit to the United States, sir?" asked the officer.

"Only to go to the university and then certainly to go back home after that, sir," replied Dev.

"Where will you be going to university?" asked the immigration official.

"ISU in Normal, Illinois," replied Dev.

"Welcome to the US, sir", said the official in a more relaxed tone as he stamped Dev's passport firmly.

"Thank you, sir," said Dev.

Dev felt a little lost as he picked up his baggage from the belt and looked for the exit where he could pick up a cab. A pretty Air France staffer directed Dev to the right exit. Dev stepped into a cab and told the taxi driver to take him to the Greyhound station in downtown Chicago. The taxi driver was a friendly, young-looking black man who immediately realized that Dev was innocent and naïve and away from home for the first time. He tried to be friendly and put Dev at ease, as he gave Dev a night-time tour of Chicago on that beautiful warm August night. Dev was tired from the long twenty-hour flight, but he found the nighttime view of Chicago's skyline breathtaking. The driver kept pointing out different landmarks such as the Sears Tower, at the time the tallest building in the world, the John Hancock building and the Lake Point Tower. Lake Shore Drive looked beautiful, with the lake dark and vast like an ocean. After this condensed "drive by Chicago at night" the taxi arrived at the Greyhound station at the intersection of Clark and Randolph, very close to the loop. Dev paid the driver his twenty dollar fare and a two dollar tip, which the driver accepted graciously, wishing Dev all the best.

Dev was a little apprehensive when he had first boarded the cab and noticed that the driver was black. It was 1979, and a lot of the American books he had read and movies he had seen until then had not painted a terribly flattering picture of blacks in America and Dev had no other frame of reference when it came to judging black people.

This guy is like everybody else, thought Dev after his tour and after he was dropped off at the bus station, *He didn't seem to have a violent bone in his body.*

Dev's education had already begun.

Dev climbed down one level from Clark and Randolph, where he found the ticket counter. The next bus for Bloomington, Illinois was at 5:30 AM and it was a two-and-a-half-hour trip. The bus would also make a stop at Bloomington's twin city, Normal, where ISU was located. Since it was about midnight, Dev was directed to the waiting room at the same level to wait several hours until bus time. Dev had never seen a bus station like this before—multi level with buses actually departing from the lowest level.

The Greyhound station provided another bit of education for Dev. Eighteen- year-old Dev somehow had formed the impression that America was a rich country, with no poverty whatsoever. The Greyhound station in Chicago opened his eyes to poverty in America. When his taxi cab had pulled outside the Greyhound station, he saw a big McDonald sign on one side of the building. He saw several people dressed in run-down clothes and even some bag ladies hanging out around the station. These people clearly looked homeless and several of these homeless people were scattered inside the bus station lobby and some were even in the waiting room. Most of these people were black, although not all.

The McDonalds in the building was also mainly patronized by black patrons, mostly young men and women who did not look terribly affluent. The outside of the bus station and the lobbies and hallways inside were littered with a fair amount of trash. Most of the passengers in the waiting lounge and in the lobby looked like typical minimum-wage travelers. Dev realized for the first time in his life that there were people in America who were less than rich, in fact, even poor. Dev realized something else for the first time too.

People's reactions to Dev since he landed were also an education for him. He was either treated with indifference, very formally, or ignored entirely. He noticed that some people at the airport and the bus station, such as the ticket agents, even looked at Dev with a bit of contempt, although they behaved quite correctly. As much as Dev felt not adequately respected in India due to his relative poverty, he had never experienced the total nonchalance and indifference in India that he experienced as soon as he arrived in America. Dev's looks, clothing, bearing and manner had always stood him out in India, and while he was not even conscious of it, the man on the street in India immediately sensed and was fully conscious of Dev's higher social status and treated him with a certain respect. Only a few hours on American soil and he was already learning a new vision of himself. The reality of life was grabbing him by the collar fast.

Dev left his baggage in the waiting room, requesting a fellow passenger to keep an eye on his baggage while he climbed up the steps and decided to visit the McDonalds. He ordered a Coke and small fries and walked back down, where he snacked on the fast food he had just purchased. Being very tired from the long journey, and feeling a little intimidated by a new country at the age of eighteen, Dev drifted in and out of a fitful sleep for the next few hours as he waited to board his bus. It was kind of surreal—Dev sitting in this strange place with a strange collection of homeless, low-end travelers, tourists, and a few students in the lower level of a large terminal building in downtown Chicago right through the night. He thought about the send-off he had been given when he had left India to come here. His grandfather, PS *Sab*, and his grandmother, Ratan, had come to Bombay from Indore to see him off. PS *Sab* had taken him to the inside room and had a private conversation with him.

"Western society is very permissive," he told Dev. "One of the concerns your grandmother and I have is that you will become a part of that permissive culture, since you are going there at such a young and impressionable age. We hope you will take all the good things from that culture without losing the good in our own Indian culture. We hope you will not imbibe the relativism and permissiveness of the West."

Dev felt a lump in his throat, thinking how naïve his grandfather was, even after having lived a full life to the age of seventy-one. *He still thinks that Indians are not relativists and are not permissive,* thought Dev. Dev didn't know a lot of details about Indian history then, but he was sure that in the year 1979 India was a far more morally permissive and relativist society than most others. After all that Dev had gone through in India, he was convinced of that. He didn't want to argue with his grandfather, whom he adored, just before leaving, therefore he promised him that he would hold the basic values of their family dear to his heart and never forgo them. His grandparents and his parents had cried at the airport. International phone calls were prohibitively expensive. Also, frequent trips to India were not going to be possible for Dev, considering his financial situation. Letters took two to three weeks by regular first-class mail to get back and forth between India and the US. America appeared really far away to everyone, and Dev's family was saddened by the fact that there would be very little communication between Dev and them. Lastly, there was no telling when they would get to see Dev again.

Dev boarded the Air France flight, bound for Paris where he would have a few hours layover, before taking another flight to Chicago. Now here he was, sitting at the Chicago Greyhound station in the middle of the night with all these strangers.

Dev took a good look around the waiting room and suddenly his mood changed from melancholy to curious. A smile appeared on his face as he noticed the humor in his situation. *Each one of these people must have a story*, thought Dev. *I wonder what their story is*. Around 4:30 AM, while it was still dark, a pleasant voice in a flat accent announced Dev's bus to Bloomington Illinois over the public address system. He dragged his two heavy bags to the boarding platform, where he saw a long sliver and blue bus parked, with a long sleek silver hound painted on the side. A uniformed man, whom Dev presumed must be the driver, accepted the baggage from Dev and handed him the baggage checks.

Dev climbed inside the bus and a faint odor hit him. Dev realized later that this odor was present in all Greyhound buses everywhere in America and he could never figure out what it was, except that cigarette smoke certainly was a component of that odor. About seven other people boarded the bus, including a couple of other students also bound for ISU. At precisely 5:30 AM, as the first morning light appeared on the sky, the bus pulled out and headed for Bloomington-Normal, Illinois.

The bus drove through the loop in Chicago, out to Lake Shore Drive, then onto Kennedy Expressway, out to some other freeway, and ultimately Interstate 55. Once the bus was on I-55 it didn't take long for all urbanization to disappear. The bus now entered a flat highway, with farmland all around. It seemed like a never-ending sequence of cornfields and Dev again was taken aback. His impression, false as it was, was that all of America was basically urbanized or subarbunanized, full of shiny glass skyscrapers. Intellectually, he had read about America and the Midwest being a farming area, but emotionally he wasn't prepared for all these cornfields.

Dev tried to have a conversation with the girl student sitting across the aisle from him. Her name was Cindy and she said that she was from Moline, Illinois, and that she had grown up on her parent's farm there. She was a junior at ISU, majoring in agriculture. She was nice, but had little knowledge of where India was or what a foreign student was. She had no interest in learning about where Dev was from or what he was doing here.

Iran was in the news, as the Shah had been recently overthrown and Ayatollah Khomeini had taken over. Cindy kept confusing India with Iran or "Ai-ran" as she pronounced it and kept asking Dev what his countrymen had against America to have such an anti-American government. When Dev tried to explain that India and Iran were two entirely different countries, she laughed, said sorry and started talking about her life on the farm, farm animals and detussling corn. Cindy was a striking girl with blonde hair, and in Dev's mind a pretty blonde and a conversation about cattle and detussling corn somehow did not go together. He wondered what his friends would think if they knew where he was heading was located right in the middle of rural America. All of his friends and Dev himself had this impression of all of America as being this highly cosmopolitan, almost an avant gard place.

Dev wondered what ISU would be like, being in the middle of cornfields and all. He had seen pictures in the catalogue that had been sent to him by the International Student's Office, and the campus looked pretty, at least in pictures. Dev felt a little strange riding the bus through the flat landscape of Central Illinois. His mind wandered back to his family, whom he already missed. He particularly started thinking about the time he had spent with his grandfather, PS, who had practically raised him since he was a child.

Dev's earliest memories were of PS returning home from work, getting dressed in his casual clothes and sitting outside on the front lawn with Dev. It would be about dusk and the stars would already be visible in the sky. Dev would point to the stars and ask PS about what they were. PS would patiently explain what stars were, what the moon was and what the other heavenly bodies were. He would then go on to explain the vastness of the universe and how mysterious it was. Dev would listen, fascinated, and then ask how old the universe was. PS would reply that the universe had existed since the beginning of time and would continue to exist till the end of time. Dev would listen with rapt attention, in awe. Then there were the evenings when Dev was a little older and PS would explain to him the geo-political situation in the world.

"The world is divided into two major spheres of influence," he would say in late 1960s, "The Russian sphere and the American sphere."

PS would then go on to explain how the world came to be divided between the Capitalist and the Communist world. Evening after evening they would spend time together and PS would talk about politics, astronomy, geography, geo-politics, authors, books, music, paintings, artists, history and a myriad of other topics. His evenings with PS stimulated in Dev a thirst for knowledge of all kinds, an interest in travelling the world, and exploring many different avenues. This led Dev to become a voracious reader, and here he was in a new strange land, riding a Greyhound bus to a regional mid-western university, a logical end to what started as just innocent evening conversations between a child and his grandfather all those years back in Rosslyn Bhopal.

My grandfather always talked about the world around us, always imparting knowledge, but never, ever did he speak to me about how I was going to make money or what profession I would choose, thought Dev.

PS never talked about money or materialistic things with Dev. Even though PS taught Dev about the value of antiques and various other fine items which PS had owned at one time or experienced. Unlike most parents or grandparents, PS never indulged in a conversation with Dev about what he was going to do in the future. That was just how PS was. Money and materialistic pursuits, or even talking about them, was not in his mental makeup.

After two hours, the bus pulled into Normal, and Dev, Cindy and one other student who had simply slept all the way alighted from the bus. Dev and Cindy shared a cab to campus, and as they entered into campus, Dev was pleasantly surprised. The campus was beautiful, with traditional red brick academic buildings, high rise dorms, some modernist architecture buildings and even a gothic architecture building. It was a thousand-acre campus with its own physical plant, heating plant, its own symphony, dance company, radio station, TV station, newspaper, movie theater, theater company, computer center, science labs, world class library, International house dorm, cafeterias, Greek row, and much more. There was a beautiful quadrangle, which is a rectangular lawn around which were located the main administrative and other buildings, were closely packed. It was lined with shady trees and benches and scores of old-fashioned light poles. The campus, however, looked almost deserted as the move-in day for the dorms was not until the next day and the fall session was supposed to start the following Monday.

All of Dev's apprehensions about being in the middle of the cornfields disappeared as soon as he saw the campus. He immediately fell in love with it and felt proud to be here and felt gratitude towards the University for granting him admission and a scholarship. He had a room waiting for him at the International House Dorm, located on the quad right in the heart of the campus. International House was a co-ed dorm where most International students lived, along with an equal number of American students. Dev said goodbye to Cindy, who was heading to another dorm, an all girls dorm, and he dragged his heavy bags to International House. He walked into the small lobby and went to the reception area.

It was quite early in the morning, about 8:15 AM, and the lobby was totally deserted. Even the reception desk was closed. Dev waited around for a bit and then he saw a tall, thin woman walk down the steps into the lobby. She introduced herself as Lindy Nicks and said that she was the house manager of International House. She was expecting Dev and she opened the reception area and pulled out a list, found Dev's name, and put a mark around it. Then she opened the key cabinet, found a key and handed it to Dev, telling him that his room was number was 314. Dev dragged his baggage to the elevator and went up to the third floor, where he found his room in a corner. It was a spacious, comfortable room—a triple, with a bunk bed and a single. His two roommates where already there, sleeping, when Dev entered the room, but both woke up and introduced themselves. One was Nasser Stoubadi, a second-year undergraduate student from Iran, and the other was Alex Leung, a graduate student from Hong Kong. They were both pleasant enough and soon after the introductions Dev lay on his bed and went to sleep.

Dev was awakened by the sound of music emanating from a distance. It was 1979 and disco music was at the peak of its popularity, at least in Central Illinois. Dev recognized the unmistakable beat of disco in the music. He looked at the clock in the room; it showed 4:05 PM. Dev had slept through the morning and most of the afternoon. He got out of bed, went to the common bathroom on the floor and took a shower. Feeling refreshed, he headed down to the cafeteria and found Nasser and a few other people sitting at a round table. Nasser waved to Dev and Dev went and joined his table. Dev was introduced to others at the table. In addition to Nasser, there was Farideh the Iranian girl, Abdulai from East Africa, Ziggy, a diminutive German girl from Munich, Godfrey Mendes from India, Shahed and his sister Hasina from Bangladesh. It was apparent that Farideh and Abdulai were together, and Hasina was the "head honcho."

Hasina dominated the conversation. She was a junior, and having spent three years in ISU already, she seemed to know everybody and everything. She started interrogating Dev about where he was from, why he had come to ISU and what he was going to study. Hasina proceeded with a list of do's and don'ts for Dev and cautioned him against not following her advice. Dev asked why there weren't any American students there. Ziggy said that official move in-day for local students was the next day and only the foreign students had moved in already. During dinner, Ziggy kept talking about going out to a "speak easy" later that night, while Godfrey kept asking Dev questions which indirectly related to his finances and how much money he had.

Towards the end of dinner they all decided to visit Bill Bailey's Speak Easy, a college disco located in Bloomington, a few miles away. Since Dev didn't have a car, Ziggy offered to give him a ride. Godfrey bummed a ride from Abdulai and it was agreed that they would all meet there around 9 PM.

Dev and Ziggy reached the disco at 9:30 PM. Bill Baily's Speak Easy, or "Speak Easy" for short, was a typical 1970s disco, though the name came from illicit booze joints of the 1930s—the prohibition era. It had a wooden floor with a raised, round red glass dance floor in the center, above which hung a disco ball. The walls were all black and the ceiling had rows of blinking disco lights. There were two bars, one on each end of the lounge, and it was already packed with young men dressed in polyester shirts and sports coats and young women in shiny polyester tops. Most young men had a shag hairstyle and the women were wearing feathered hairdos, Farah Fawcett style. The scene was straight out of Saturday Night Fever, which Dev had seen in a Bombay movie theater a year ago and which was a huge worldwide hit, spawning the international disco phenomenon.

Young couples were dancing, many of them close and intimate. The whole place reeked of romance and sex, making it very exciting for eighteen-year- old Dev. He and Ziggy caught up with the rest of their crowd. Dev ordered a beer, while Zigi ordered a whisky sour. After a while the kids, including Dev, hit the dance floor. They danced to Vicky Sue Robinson, The Silver Convention, The Tramps, The Manhattans, Michael Jackson, and of course Donna Summer. Dev felt a little insecure and conscious on the dance floor, as he was not a good dancer, but he managed to stay with the music and tried his best to synchronize with his partner for the night, which was mostly Ziggy. Ziggy sensed Dev's lack of dancing skills and did her best to make Dev look good and feel comfortable. After a couple of beers and a while on the dance floor Dev relaxed and started to enjoy himself.

At 2:00 AM, the main lights in the lounge came on, indicating that it was about closing time. There was a last call for drinks and the kids decided to leave. Dev drove back to campus with Ziggy in her 1976 Datsun and there was an awkward silence between the two. As Dev said goodbye to Ziggy in the hallway of International House, Ziggy gave Dev a hug and a big kiss. Dev grabbed Ziggy by the back of her head and kissed her hard. They walked to the side, behind the old fashioned stairwell and made out for a while before they finally split and said goodnight. Dev's first day at ISU had ended and he felt elated and high on the great evening he had just had, great folks he had met and made friends with, and the beautiful ISU campus.

Dev woke up the next morning to a cacophony of sounds. He looked at his watch and it was close to 10 AM. The sun was streaming in from the large windows of his dorm room which overlooked the quad. Unlike the previous day, when the campus had a deserted look, the quad this morning was teeming with students. There were literally thousands of kids walking across the meandering pathways of the quad. Dev looked out of the side window and he could see the street lined with cars and a literal traffic-jam type situation. Dev jumped out of bed, took a shower and went downstairs from his third floor room to the lobby of International House. The dorm was much livelier, with many more kids than the previous day, and kids were moving their stuff in from outside. Dev could hear the Patrick Hernandez song, called "Born to be Alive," blaring at a distance in some room. When he reached the lobby he saw Hasina talking animatedly with a bunch of kids. They were mostly American kids. It was move-in day for them and Hasina clearly knew most of these as they were returning students.

Hasina beckoned Dev over and introduced him to some of them, and then looking at Dev's lost expression, urged him to go out and see for himself what "move-in" day was like. Dev stepped out. It was a warm August day, but he could hear music everywhere, coming from inside the dorms, inside the parked cars, inside the cars that were lined up on the campus streets inching forward slowly, and even from some boom boxes in the quad. Kids, mostly in shorts and t-shirts, were walking around, moving their stuff in or catching up with old friends, or in some cases making new friends. To Dev it looked like the entire one-thousand-acre campus had come alive, and he found it exciting and exhilarating.

Dev spent the next couple of days familiarizing himself with the campus and his surroundings. Kids in the International House dorms visited each other's rooms, introducing themselves to the newcomers and catching up with people they already knew. Most of the American kids in International House were from rural Illinois, a few from Chicago, and a handful from the rest of the country. On the weekend before the classes were supposed to start there was a big party in International House and people danced till the early hours of the morning.

Dev had an undeclared major when he arrived at ISU. He was already convinced that he wanted to stay in America and not return to India, and therefore was looking for a major which would not only easily get him a job, but would get him a job with a "sponsorship." A job with sponsorship meant that the company that would offer a job would also sponsor Dev for permanent residency in America, better known as a "green card." Ordinarily, foreigners could not legally work in the US without a green card. Therefore, if a company in the US wished to hire a foreigner they would have to sponsor the employee for a green card with the US government and prove that hiring this person would not displace an American. In other words, the skills of the foreigner would have to be in short supply in America.

Procuring a green card even with sponsorship was an opaque, complicated and time-consuming process. Dev, therefore, searched for an area of study, which would be in short supply in America. Dev's primary interest lay in humanities. He loved philosophy, politics, history and the arts, but he knew that these were not skills in short supply in America and therefore could not act as vehicles for keeping him in the States. He had to find something else. But find what? Dev asked a few kids that he met in International House. Many majors were suggested. Business, engineering and architecture were tossed around. Dev was confused. Godfrey Mendes, an Indian graduate student, volunteered to a detailed counseling of Dev over dinner in a nice restaurant in downtown Normal. Dev and Godfrey walked over to Cooper's, a family owned steak joint. Godfrey ordered the most expensive items on the menu and recommended the same to Dev.

"So, Godfrey, now that we have ordered, can we talk about what fields are in big demand here?" asked Dev.

"Certainly, you could go in for engineering, or business or architecture," said Godfrey.

"So everyone says, but do you have any insights into what kind of engineering?" asked Dev.

"Sure, I can tell you everything," said Godfrey. "By the way, what does your father do?"

"He is a small time textile consultant," said Dev.

"Oh, so he must be loaded, right?" said Godfrey hopefully.

"Far from it, work for him is very irregular, so, about the major..." said Dev

"We can meet next Thursday to discuss it in more detail, right here for dinner, Dev," said Godfrey.

Dev was now confused. He couldn't figure out why Godfrey couldn't discuss his insights that same evening. Anyway, dinner arrived and Godfrey started talking about all the girl friends he had at ISU and how women were just dying to go out with him. Dev looked at him incredulously, because while Godfrey seemed to talk a good game, he did not have the kind of personality that Dev thought was likely to attract a lot of women. *Maybe American girls are different*, thought Dev.

"I have to turn most of these women down and it breaks my heart to do so," Godfrey continued on his girlfriend track.

"Godfrey, I am sure a guy like you would have many women. So, what do you think of Civil Engineering as a career option?" asked Dev.

"Excellent. Very good choice," said Godfrey as he wolfed down the last of his medium-rare sirloin.

The dinner ended with Dev not any more enlightened about his career options than when it started. When the waitress brought in the check, Godfrey reached for his pocket, looked startled and said, "Oh, I seemed to have forgotten my wallet. Can you go ahead and take the check, Dev? In any case, you owe me for benefitting from my great knowledge of this country. It takes years, Dev, years, before one knows America as well as I."

Godfrey watched Dev pull out fifteen dollars from his wallet to pay the check. Godfrey also noticed that Dev had some more money in his wallet. Before Dev could return the wallet back to his pocket, Godfrey very nonchalantly said, "Let me have a hundred dollars. I will return it when we get back to I-House" (as International House was commonly known).

Dev was again a little confused. "I don't have a hundred," he replied.

"No problem. How much do you have? Lemme see," said Godfrey, casually taking the wallet from Dev's hands. Godfrey started counting the money in Dev's wallet, including the change.

"Thirty-one dollars and eighty-nine cents," said Godfrey "I really needed more, but this shall do for now." Godfrey pocketed the thirty-one dollars and eighty-nine cents, returning the empty wallet to Dev.

Dev and Godfrey walked back to I-House. It was about a fifteen minute walk and Godfrey did all the talking about how well-off he was and sometimes he wondered whether all the women were really hitting on him for his money or his good looks and charm.

"I'm certain it is because of your good looks and charm," Dev assured him. For all his positive reinforcements to Godfrey, Dev never recovered Godfrey's share of the dinner bill, nor the thirty-one dollars and eighty-nine cents. More importantly for him, however, he never learned anything of value from Godfrey Mendes.

Despite having a tuition scholarship, Dev still had financial problems at ISU. He still needed to pay for his room and board and other incidental expenses such as books and personal expenses. Dev got some limited help from his parents, but he was still well short of his requirements. Dev knew that what appeared little in the context of his expenses was still a lot for his parents, who were struggling to merely make ends meet in India. His father, Ram Singh, largely due to his own personal limitations, found irregular work and he didn't have much of an inheritance to count on. Dev's grandfather PS had run through much of the small fortune that he had inherited and now the family had literally fallen on hard times.

The teenager Dev couldn't help but notice that every teenager in America was crazy about cars. Everyone at ISU either had a car or aspired to get one. If one wanted to have an active social life, owning a car was a minimum. Dev developed a crush on a girl from Chicago who was with him in his general studies class. She was a cop's daughter—a Chicago cop's daughter—and while she was quite inclined towards Dev, she quickly turned him down once she realized he didn't have a car. Besides, not having a car severely hampered Dev's mobility, even in this small college town. Eighteen-year-old Dev badly wanted to buy a car, any car, even an old car. To meet his expenses and save enough to buy a car, Dev picked up two jobs on campus. One involved digging ditches around campus to prepare for the coming winter and the other was as a dishwasher in the I-House cafeteria. He had to wake up at 5:00 AM in the morning to work in the dish room. He hated getting up early and often times the cafeteria manager Ben had to call Dev to wake him up. Other than waking up early, Dev considered himself quite lucky to be able to go to a good university in the US, have a scholarship and have the jobs to finance his other needs.

It had been a couple of weeks since the classes had started and the deadline for dropping and picking up new classes was fast approaching. Dev still had not been able to make up his mind as to what major he wanted to pursue and he didn't want to delay that decision much longer. After doing some research at the career center, Dev walked over to the computer science department, where he found a sign-up list posted outside the chairperson's office. Dev quickly penciled his name on the list and he was now a computer science major.

Having decided on computer science as his major in order to secure a job in the US and stay there, Dev then picked western philosophy as his minor, as he loved philosophy and history. Having successfully combined a job procuring skill with his passion, Dev felt quite settled at Illinois State.

Dev soon discovered that ISU in general, and International House in particular, was an amazing place when it came to exposing students to issues of national and international importance. Despite being in the middle of nowhere and seemingly pretty much out of the academic mainstream, Illinois State provided ample opportunities for students to study, discuss and debate all the major issues of the day. In that sense, if a student truly worked at it, he could get an Ivy League education at a bargain price at ISU. Students organized lectures, events, seminars and functions on the Palestinian issue, the Cold War, American foreign policy, South Africa and apartheid, other African issues, Arab issues and the hot issue of the day—Iran. The mood at ISU campus was also quite liberal in keeping with the times and also consistent with the fact that college campuses in general were more liberal than the rest of the country.

The political science department at ISU was at the vanguard of this liberalism. In fact, there was a Marxist and even a radical Palestinian who had tenure in the department. The majority of the political science faculty was more mainstream liberal. With the exception of the chairperson, there was no one else who could be classified as a conservative. International House was a logical extension of the political science department, a symbiotic soul mate of sorts. Most international students were from Asia or Africa, part of the elite in their own countries, and were very oriented towards their own national interests. This made them quite critical of the American policies, putting them very much in sync with American liberals who were also critical of American policies, albeit for different reasons.

Most of these international students, while prescribing liberalism for America, were either stout defenders of the status quo in their own countries or outspoken advocates of more conservative and regressive policies in their own cultures. Ironically, while some expressed it openly and others did not, most of these foreign students still wished to remain in the US and were willing to go to great lengths to be able to do that. Most American students who chose to live in International House had no experience of living abroad. They, therefore, had no opportunity to emotionally experience the shortcomings of those societies and how backward some of them socially were, compared to the West. They also generally empathized with the liberal and sometimes radical views of most international students.

Having come from a country which was mired in corruption and devoid of economic opportunities, Dev instinctively reacted to the apparent hypocrisy of most international students. He became the resident contrarian of International House, causing a lot of resentment, particularly among the large African, Middle Eastern and Bangladeshi contingent that dominated the house. The East Asians (Indonesians, Malaysians, Singaporeans, Vietnamese, Koreans and Chinese) were not very many in I-House, and basically apolitical.

It was the fall of 1979—Pre-Reagan, just in the aftermath of Vietnam, Watergate and during the presidency of Jimmy Carter. America was in the midst of "stagflation," an era of high inflation while at the same time stagnant growth rates. The Fed, led by Paul Volker, had raised interest rates to more than 18%, a staggering percentage, further dampening economic growth. The American auto industry was under a great deal of stress, experiencing stiff competition from the Japanese and the German automakers. For the first time in history, the US Congress was considering bailing out an American automobile company (Chrysler). America had also just undergone an oil shock, where OPEC had dramatically raised prices, causing the gasoline addicted Americans to reel from high prices at the pump. America was in a kind of funk, which was highlighted by the famous "malaise" speech by Jimmy Carter just a few months earlier. It was an era when Americans were going through a lot of introspection, were a bit low on confidence, though they were still by and large more liberal than ever. Even as late as 1979, most Americans were either liberal or centrists. However, there was a lot of restlessness and angst at that time in Middle America and there were already signs of the beginnings of a backlash against liberalism, which had been on the ascendency in America since the election of John F. Kennedy in 1960.

One of the manifestations of the backlash was the "Disco Demolition Night" which occurred on July 12, 1979 at Comisky Park in Chicago. In between a double header baseball game, a Chicago disk jockey organized a "blowing up" of disco records. Disco was a form of dance music with influences from a variety of black music genres including funk, soul, R&B, and even the blues. It originated in black clubs in New York and Philadelphia in the early seventies and was quickly embraced by the gay clubs and communities because of its peppy upbeat sound, which was very conducive for dancing.

By 1979, disco had become a worldwide phenomenon. In the US it had completely overshadowed other forms of music, particularly the heretofore popular rock music, which was nothing but a watered down and syrupy version of R&B, sung mostly by white artists. Rock producers, artists and record companies started losing money, as disco became the new big money maker. Feeling the threat, the rock music community started a subtle campaign in Middle America to associate disco music exclusively with the black and gay community. Middle America had always been fickle on liberalism, and fortunately for the Rock music community, social and economic conditions prevalent at the time had caused unease and suspicion of liberalism in mainstream America.

The rock community tapped into this latent distrust of liberalism in 1979 and organized a "Disco Demolition Night" in Chicago in the summer of 1979. The rock community's campaign against disco music appealed to the lowest common denominator in America, to people's basest instincts of racism, homophobia and prejudice, although the organizers of this event denied that they were trying to appeal to these base instincts. According to them, they were only registering a protest against a particular form of music that they didn't like. Be that as it may, the "Disco Demolition Night" was a huge success. The organizers expected no more than 15,000 people at Comisky Park, which had the capacity to seat 50,000. Almost 90,000 people showed up and packed the stadium and police had to intervene to prevent even more people from entering the stadium. Thousands of disco records were stacked up in the middle of the field and were strapped with explosives. The explosives were lit and there was a huge bonfire. People went berserk.

The organizers succeeded in demonizing disco music in the culture-at-large by staging this event. Everything went downhill for disco from that point on, and disco as a music genre died shortly afterwards. Artists such as the BGees, who had ventured into disco, were ridiculed and several other artists who were labeled and branded as disco artists were looked upon with contempt. Soon "disco" became a dirty word in the mainstream culture and many disco artists never worked again. The event had brought back to the forefront the racism and prejudice that had receded into deep recesses of their souls for most Americans.

Another event took place in late fall of 1979 that cemented America's hard shift to the right. Back in 1953, in the aftermath of World War II, the country of Iran was headed by a democratically-elected nationalist prime minster by the name of Mossadeq. Mossadeq was a nationalist, not a Communist, and he decided to nationalize the Iranian oilfields, heretofore owned by British Petroleum, which was then controlled by the British government. From all accounts, Mossadeq had a strong case for nationalization, as the royalties that the Iranian government was receiving from British Petroleum were grossly inadequate. The British, under Winston Churchill, convinced the conservative American president, Dwight D Eisenhower, to instruct the CIA to hatch a plot to overthrow Mossadeq and install a more friendly government under the monarch Shah Mohammed Reza Pehalvi. The plot was carried out by the CIA by taking the Shah into confidence and Shah Mohammed Reza Pehalvi assumed full powers.

The Shah then proceeded to follow a pro-western foreign policy during the cold war, providing a bulwark against Soviet expansionism in the Middle East. The Shah also accelerated his father's policy of modernizing his conservative Islamic society along western lines by expanding education for all, including women, allowing for mixing of the sexes, promoting women's rights and banning the *hijab* and veil for women. He did all this with an iron fist, using his notorious secret service called the Savak, formed with CIA assistance, as the enforcers. All of this caused a tremendous backlash by the Islamists in Iran and the conservative rural population.

In 1979 there was a popular revolt against the Shah and he was forced to flee to Paris, and then to the US for treatment, as he was suffering from cancer. The Islamists led by the formerly exiled Shiite cleric Ayatollah Ruholla Khomeini then usurped power in Iran. Angered by the United States' admittance of the Shah for treatment and blaming the United States for years of repression by the Shah, a boisterous crowd of young students with radical Islamic leanings took over the US embassy in Tehran on Nov 3, 1979, and held fifty-three American diplomats hostage against all recognized diplomatic norms. The Iranian government was initially stunned by this takeover, but soon thereafter they expressed its full support for the takeover, citing United States' long support for the repressive policies of the Shah and the brutality of the SAVAK. The American media, including television and the newly introduced cable television, provided round-the-clock coverage of this event, touting the story as "America Held Hostage."

This crisis lasted for months, as all attempts by US President Jimmy Carter to secure the release of the hostages failed, including a disastrous armed rescue attempt. Although the crisis lasted for one full year, within a couple of months, public opinion in America had taken a sharp turn to the right. With all that was happening, such as stagflation in the economy, the still lingering psychological effects of defeat in Vietnam, the Opec oil shock, the general malaise, the Iran Hostage Crisis was the last straw that broke the camel's back and gave plenty of ammunition to ultra-conservatives led by Ronald Reagan to launch a frontal assault on liberalism, civil rights and women's rights. Reagan subtly implied in his speeches that anything progressive was a form of Communism in disguise—pink, if not completely red. The word "Pinko," which had already been in existence since the start of the cold war, now became part of the common lexicon. The Iran Hostage crisis was the last nail in the coffin that sealed the fate of liberalism for several generations to come, and the Reagan conservatives were right there and ready to pounce on the opportunity to make "liberal" a dirty word in the American mainstream culture. They succeeded in doing so even beyond their wildest imagination.

The first semester ended for Dev on a positive note. He did well in his classes and had saved up enough money to buy an old car from a graduating student. It was a bright red two door 1967 Chevy Impala, with a 327 engine. Dev fell in love with the car the moment he set eyes on it. He paid the full asking price of $350, which was literally the last penny he had in his bank account at the time. Dev felt on top of the world when he drove the car around the campus for the first time. There were thousands of rich students driving brand new expensive cars, but there was something about Dev's red Chevy that endeared it to everyone on campus. Dev and the car together formed an unforgettable package and Dev quickly became known all over ISU as "that guy with the red Impala."

ISU in general and International House in particular, had a typical party atmosphere all the time. With the possible exception of Mondays and Tuesdays, there were always parties around. I-House parties were typically disco parties, and were more often than not organized by the African students who had great taste in dance music. I-House was a small enough community (roughly 200 students in all) where hookups and breakups were common and gossip was rampant. Dev developed a new confidence as he had a car and a semester under his belt. While he still had a mildly contentious relationship with most of the males in I-House due to his disdain for their hypocritical political views, he found the girls quite receptive to him. Having a car further enhanced Dev's social life and he started dating more often, not only within I-House but also outside. He developed contacts in various sub-cultures at ISU and slowly became quite well-known across campus. In particular, he developed friendships with a bunch of fun- loving fraternity brothers from the Lutheran fraternity Beta Sigma Psi. This gave him access to most of the frat parties across campus, particularly the ones over at the "Beta Sig House," as it was called.

The late 1970s was a far simpler and more innocent time, particularly in small-town America. Dates were simple and inexpensive. Several Normal-Bloomington bars, private parties, Garcia's pizza and beer joint, Tien Tsin, the Korean owned Chinese restaurant, Lake Evergreen a few miles away, and the local drive in (yeah, drive-ins still existed in Bloomington Ill in 1979-80), besides the campus movie theater. These were the places where ISU students normally went to entertain themselves or went on dates. Coming from a highly status conscious society which judged people solely based on their wealth or power, Dev found ISU a refreshingly different place. While it was by no means a university of wealthy people like USC or Harvard, it had its share of rich kids from Chicago and other prominent farming families in the Midwest. While the girls sometimes preferred to date a guy with a nice car or lot of spending money, in general, ISU was pretty relaxed and classless. One's status depended more on one's personality, academic performance, excellence in sports or in music or arts or some other activity. In that sense, it was pretty much a merit-based culture. It was the first time Dev had experienced such a culture and he reveled in it.

In his sophomore year, Dev got a part time job as a computer programmer with a local company. The job paid minimum wage, but at least Dev was getting valuable experience that would enhance his career. Dev was always short of money, as he had a very small income and money from his parents was no longer forthcoming. Besides, Dev was quite liberal in spending money and was not the kind who could easily reconcile himself to tight budgets.

As usual, there was a big party in I-House at the beginning of the fall semester of 1980 and Dev met two new students. One was Khondekar Imran, a transfer student originally from Bangladesh. He was a couple of years older than Dev and was a junior. The other was Laurie. She was an attractive brunette from Peoria, Illinois. She grew up on a farm and she was a sophomore like Dev. Dev asked Laurie to dance and they hit it off quite well. Laurie seemed to be genuinely interested in Dev, and they had a good time.

Dev and Imran became great friends. Imran took some heat for getting close to Dev from a few people in I-House who did not appreciate Dev's outspokenness. However, Imran was his own man too, and he did not offer much cognizance to others on this issue. Dev was constantly short of funds and struggled with his expenses and Imran always came through like a big brother, with a twenty here and a fifty there.

The winters in Central Illinois were brutal, particularly for someone like Dev, who came from a warm climate. The winter winds would blow in from the North and pick up speeds over the flat plains of the Midwest. To Dev, it felt that the cold wind would enter his back and stab its way right through his body, coming out through the front. It was not possible to keep one's hands exposed outside in the middle of winter, as one could very quickly suffer frostbite. Everyone wore heavy coats and thick padded gloves to protect themselves from the relentless cold while walking outside on the quad or around campus.

One time, in the middle of winter, Dev dropped his gloves someplace and had to walk about half a mile back to campus without his gloves. By the time he reached I-House, his hands had turned bluish-purple and they were hurting badly. As he entered I-House and walked up to the fireplace in the lounge to warm his hands, he ran into Laurie. Laurie noticed that Dev was in pain and she set Dev down on the sofa in front of the fireplace, then she held Dev's cold hands between her own warm hands and started massaging them. Initially, it hurt like hell, but after several minutes of massaging, the blood started to circulate again in Dev's hands and the pain eased up. It was a simple act of kindness and had a profound effect on Dev. Laurie and Dev held on to each other for the remainder of that afternoon, forgetting all their worries and cares, and even skipped all their respective classes that day.

All through his sophomore year, Dev dated Laurie casually. Laurie sang in the church choir and Dev found her to be an extremely nice person. She tidied up Dev's room whenever she got a chance and also stopped by to help Dev with his laundry and things. She was a caring, kind person, not just to Dev, but to everyone. Obviously, she was particularly caring of Dev and this was Dev's first experience with a semi-serious relationship. Dev tried to reciprocate and it was a nice, easy relationship, although they never really made a formal commitment to go steady. Laurie made it easy for Dev to immerse himself into American culture and he learned a great deal from her. Dev was learning what it took to be in a relationship, and he was maturing fast. There was still a side to him, though, which was impulsive, emotional and very much in-your-face.

Things moved fast for Dev in his sophomore year. Between playing tennis on the university team, his job, attending various lectures, and socializing, Dev did not have much time to study. While Dev was learning a lot outside the classroom and maturing in all kinds of different ways, his grades suffered as a result.

In the fall of 1980, an event occurred that would shape the destiny of Dev personally, as well as many other people. The 1980 US election for president was a seminal event. Things had not gone well for President Jimmy Carter, and the US was in turmoil. The Iran Hostage crisis was continuing, with no end in sight, severely impairing national morale. Things were so bad that President Carter was facing a rare primary challenge, something that very few sitting presidents face. Senator Edward "Ted" Kennedy from the famous Kennedy clan was challenging President Carter from the left for the Democratic nomination. Ronald Reagan, the ultra-conservative ex-film actor and ex-governor of California was almost certain to be nominated by the Republicans. After a bruising primary battle, President Carter emerged victorious as the Democratic nominee, but well before the general election, Reagan's victory was a foregone conclusion.

Reagan was a master communicator. He projected the image of a kindly grandfather and spoke in grandiose terms about the past and the future of America. As great as America was, Reagan's grandiose projection of America didn't in actuality exist, even in the past. He simply spoke untruths. He was also one of the most effective demagogues in history. He used his good looks and great speaking skills to rail against the welfare system in terms that were palatable for an average American. During the campaign, Reagan told a story of a "Welfare Queen" who had embezzled more than $150,000 from the government by using eighty aliases, thirty addresses, a dozen Social Security cards, and four fictional dead husbands. A truly horrifying deed, except, that the story wasn't true. No one, including the press, could find this so called "welfare queen," despite an intense search. He succeeded in creating an image of all welfare recipients as lazy, good-for-nothings who drank beer, drove Cadillacs and wore fur coats. He spoke about welfare abuse in such convincing terms that people started believing the fabrications. The normally fair and thoughtful Americans who generally rooted for the underdog followed Reagan's lead in demonizing the weakest and the least among all Americans—the poor and minorities.

Reagan appealed to humanities' basest instincts and not only provided Americans a convenient cover to go after the weak, but also made them feel comfortable and even heroic and patriotic by going after the poor and the minorities. He also successfully convinced Americans that the best way to stimulate the economy was by putting more money into the hands of the rich so they could spend it or invest it, resulting in wealth "trickling down" to working Americans. He demonized the Soviets as an "evil empire" and basically had a retrograde image of America rooted in his youth. He *nostalgized* about an America from the past which he envisioned as some sort of "shining city on the hill" and dropped subtle hints that he wanted to take America back to the "good old days"—those glory days, whatever that meant. Reagan used another term to demagogue. He promised to promote "family values" if he got elected. For many ethnic minorities, "family values" was a code word for segregation. By constantly harping on "family values" and the context in which he used that term, he appealed to the submerged, but still strong segregationist instincts of Americans.

Like any good demagogue, what Reagan said had a great deal of truth, only the truth was mixed with small amounts of very potent and explosive untruths, particularly the part about demonizing other races, other nations, other ideologies. Dev, at the time greatly influenced by Ayn Rand and coming from a hotchpotch socialist culture, found great appeal in Reagan's idea of placing more emphasis on the free market. He fully endorsed Reagan's vision of less government. Dev also subscribed to Reagan's hawkish stand against communism. Having been attracted to Reagan because of these reasons, nineteen-year-old Dev was also taken in by Reagan's incendiary rhetoric about the welfare queen and other falsehoods. He, however, did not understand what this "family values" rhetoric was all about. *Whatever it is,* thought nineteen-year-old Dev, *it can't be too ominous.*

Dev was rather naïve and had very little firsthand experience in race relations in America and in the fall of 1980 he signed up with the college Republicans to campaign for Reagan. It seemed to him a little odd that almost all the other campaign volunteers for Reagan looked and acted the same—white, middle class and affluent. There were no blacks, no Native Americans, not even any Latinos among the ISU college Republicans in those days. Dev was one of the students in the front section when Reagan visited ISU during a campaign swing, cheering enthusiastically.

Reagan was elected by a landslide. For reasons only a *mullah* could fathom, Ayatollah Khomeini released all of the American hostages the day of Reagan's inauguration, spiting Jimmy Carter, who had worked tirelessly throughout the entire election campaign to get the hostages released. Why on earth Ayatollah Khomeini would prefer the hawkish Reagan to a more liberal and enlightened Carter is one of those inexplicable mysteries of history.

Maybe there is a simpler explanation. Ayatollah Khomeini was perhaps not the brightest bulb in the room and it is entirely possible that he did not fully understand the nuances of world politics, certainly not American politics. He may not have had the strategic thinking to understand that a liberal Carter was enormously more in Iran's interest than a Reagan who looked at American interests as a zero-sum game, i.e., in order for America to win, everybody else had to lose. In any case, Khomeini was able to do what hardcore conservatives in the US couldn't do, at least since the Great Depression. His actions during the hostage crisis caused the American populous to rally around hardcore conservative ideas of Ronald Reagan. Be that as it may, the campaign ended and campus slowly returned to normal.

Dev continued to experience a shortage of funds and Khondakar Imran did the best he could to help, but Dev constantly struggled to meet his expenses. Imran was to spend his summer on the Jersey Shore, where summer jobs were in abundance. Dev and Laurie, however, decided to move in together in an apartment in Chicago and try to find some work for the summer there. They found an apartment on the second floor of an old Division Street building which had a jazz club on the ground floor. The street was home to the most vibrant nightlife in the entire Chicago area. Division Street was only a few blocks north of the famous Rush Street, which had been the hub of Chicago nightlife up to the 1960s.

By 1981, when Dev and Laurie spent their summer break in Chicago, Rush Street had lost most of its excitement as it had gentrified and had settled into a role of hosting upscale clubs and restaurants, more suited for convention visitors and upscale tourists. Division Street had inherited the eclectic nightlife of Chicago from Rush Street. The area's bars and clubs stayed open till very late and the street was crowded, particularly at night. It was a cosmopolitan mix of people from all over US and the world. Summers, in particular, were especially "hot" on Division Street. Dev and Laurie basked in the warmth and energy of the Division Street night scene. They both found work, Laurie as a waitress and Dev as a cashier in one of the restaurants.

Dev and Laurie had a neighbor named Leroy. He was a freelance saxophone player who did gigs for area jazz bands that performed in the nightlife district of Chicago. Leroy was a black guy in his early twenties and he had an impressive personality. He was taking lessons from a guy called David Blooms, who was teaching out of his Rush Street apartment above a jazz club. Leroy, Dev, Laurie and a few other friends of Leroy's would often get together in the evenings, clubbing, discussing music, smoking pot, and just overall having a good time. Leroy introduced Dev to the music of various jazz greats, and it was during this summer of '81 that Dev developed a taste for both jazz and the blues. Dev loved the sophisticated sound and the complexities of jazz, while the simplicity and melancholy of the blues touched his soul.

Jazz and blues were pure American art forms. Leroy narrated to Dev and Laurie the story of the origins of jazz in black communities of New Orleans and how it had travelled to Chicago, where it underwent several rounds of innovation and a new cross-over sound, as more and more white artists started coalescing around it. Leroy always lamented the recent decline of jazz as a popular art form and its relegation to niche status, although the pop music of the day, including rock, had profound jazz influences, in addition to that of soul, R&B, funk, and of course the blues. Dev, Laurie and friends visited clubs of different kinds and genres all summer long and enjoyed different kinds of music. It was both an education and a musical awakening for Dev, who discovered that he was a frustrated artist, someone with an understanding and appreciation for music but no skills to play an instrument or vocalize. It was the summer of '81 which sowed the seeds for Dev to later develop a certain sensitivity and sensibility which softened him on the inside, despite all the various adversities and financial hardships he faced.

It was also a summer of awakening of a different sort for Laurie and Dev. While they had a deep understanding of each other's needs and sensibilities, they both were too young to get really serious. Had they met a few years later, their relationship certainly would have had prospects of more permanence. However, being this young and hormones wreaking havoc, they both drifted towards sexual experimentation and exploration. By the end of the summer their relationship had developed the inevitable strains that arise out of such experimentation.

While they still were very fond of each other, certain specific events caused a rift between them and by the time fall arrived and it was time for them to return back to school it was mutually understood, without it being explicitly spoken, that their relationship was over. In fact, towards the end of summer Laurie decided to transfer to Northern Illinois University in DeKalb. When Dev and Laurie parted at the end of summer, Dev to head south to ISU and Laurie in the opposite direction to head to DeKalb, it was a friendly parting, not terribly emotional, as the stresses and strains of the summer still hung over the relationship. Dev looked upon his relationship with Laurie as one of the bright spots in his life. Laurie's basic goodness, generosity and willingness to be open and learn played a large part in Dev's over-all education that taught him some very important life's lessons.

※ ※

The next year Dev decided to expand his horizons and move out of the protective confines of I-House. He was a junior and he decided to live in another dorm on campus which was more "mainstream." Despite his uncomfortable relationships with a significant number of students in I-House, he maintained a close relationship with the I-House community, particularly people like Imran, who were his close friends. He sometimes stopped by the I-House cafeteria for lunch or dinner and to socialize.

During one of these dinners Dev ran into Agnetha. She was a new exchange student from Sweden, and true to the stereotype, she was tall, blonde, had blue eyes and had a smile to die for. Dev had by then experienced many different things and developed more self-assurance and even a bit of a swagger. He soon asked Agnetha out, and she accepted. They started dating and after a while decided to go steady. Agnetha was also very gentle and caring, like Laurie, but that's where the similarities ended. While Laurie was a Midwestern farm girl, Agnetha was a very worldly, sophisticated European girl. She was well-travelled, spoke five languages, was an avid reader and very aware of the world around her. Agnetha was a delightful conversationalist and Dev could sit with her for hours, talking about a range of subjects from politics to art, from travel to skiing. Dev and Agnetha did crazy things together, like hitchhiking in the middle of winter from Chicago to New York.

In his junior year Dev realized the full extent of how much of a party school ISU was. ISU had a thousand-acre campus, literally in the middle of nowhere with twenty thousand kids between the ages of seventeen and twenty-three forming the bulk of the population. Many of the students were away from home for the first time in their lives and they were fully utilizing their freedom to experiment in all kinds of ways. It seemed like everybody was having sex with everybody, which wasn't exactly true, but it seemed that way. The Greek scene was particularly prolific when it came to sex, but the dorms too were a hotbed of sexuality. Drinking was another common pastime, which went together with sex and partying.

Dance parties were more the norm at I-House, while in general, ISU parties were just meat markets where people hooked up for the evening or the night. There was no awareness of AIDS as it had only recently begun to rear its ugly head on the West Coast. It felt to Dev like no one on campus had any care in the world and everyone was just enjoying themselves, while experimenting and learning at the same time. It is a cliché to say that the American higher education system is the best in the world, but if any cliché is almost 100% true, it is this one. On a typical college campus in America one gets an opportunity to develop in every possible way: develop their minds, develop physically, develop their soul, and even develop emotionally. Every individual has to take the initiative and work hard, not rely on teachers or administrators. The more a kid put in, the more he or she got out.

Dev and Agnetha were getting closer as the year progressed. The year 1982 saw America slip into a deep recession. After Ronald Reagan got elected as US President, Paul Volker, the Chairman of the US Federal Reserve, tried to snuff out inflation by increasing interest rates. This led to a contraction in demand and resulted in a recession so deep that the unemployment rate was closing in on 10%. Even part time and low paying jobs were hard to find. However, Dev absolutely needed summer employment to get through school.

As it got closer to the summer of 1982, Agnetha and Dev decided to spend their summer on Jersey Shore. They had heard about Jersey Shore from their friend Khondakar Imran, who had spent the previous summer there. Jersey Shore really meant the beach resort towns of Southern New Jersey along the Atlantic Ocean, in particular Wildwood and Cape May. Wildwood was where the college crowd went and it was a wild and crazy place. Cape May was more family-oriented and had better and cleaner beaches. Summer jobs there were plentiful, as one could always pick up a job in a restaurant.

Dev bought another car, simply to drive down from Illinois to New Jersey. It was an old Chevy Vega, and Agnetha and Dev packed all their belongings in the trunk and the back seat and headed east. They drove through Illinois into Indiana. Indiana was so flat and big, it seemed like it would never end. Finally, they entered Ohio, crossed into Pennsylvania and then down south into New Jersey at Camden. From there they took Garden State Parkway and reached the outskirts of Wildwood late at night. They spent the night at one of the cheap roadside motels, which was tacky and filthy. They woke up early the next morning, checked out and started looking for an apartment. They drove into Wildwood and were amazed to find a unique architecture along the coastline that was unlike anything they had ever experienced.

Dev later found out that it was the Doo-Wop architecture, which originated in California in the 1940s and then moved east across the country. However, Wildwood NJ was one of the few places that still had Doo-Wop preserved in 1982. Doo-Wop architecture was inspired by the car culture and space age and used designs that depicted motion such as boomerangs, flying saucers and atoms. Dev and Agnetha found this architecture way over the top, but gradually came to like it as they spent more time in Wildwood.

Dev and Agnetha were very fortunate to find a small cottage for rent right on the beach in Wildwood Crest. It was lovely and the view of the ocean from the cottage was just magnificent. They settled in and started hunting for work. Competition for work, even in Wildwood, was intense that summer. Agnetha found work as a waitress, while Dev had difficulty finding work. Finally, he got a job in the dish room at a restaurant called Captain's Table. The summer was intense for both Agnetha and Dev. Agnetha was supposed to go back to Sweden at the end of summer, as her one-year exchange was going to expire. Dev had to stay at the university for one more semester to complete his degree. He completed it in three and a half years as opposed to the normal four, since he had taken extra courses during the regular semesters. Dev and Agnetha didn't know when they would ever meet again, or if they would meet again. By this time they were in love and very concerned about parting.

Work for Dev was brutal. Working eight hours a day, day after day, sometimes even on weekends, in the hot and dirty dish room was taking its toll on him. Agnetha provided tremendous moral support by being very loving and affectionate. *I could have never gotten through this without her,* thought Dev. They spent the evenings walking on the beach, catching a movie or visiting the local Dairy Queen for ice cream. It was a hard summer, but also intense and melancholy at the same time. Towards the end, the stress of their impending separation took a toll on the both Dev and Agnetha and they started squabbling about little things. Finally, the summer ended and Agnetha took a bus to New York to board a flight for Stockholm. It was an emotional moment for the both of them, when Dev kissed Agnetha one last time before she boarded the bus. Agnetha kept waiving until the bus got out of sight and Dev returned back to the cottage, fighting back tears.

The cottage all of a sudden looked cold and empty and he did not sleep a wink that night. He woke up early the next morning, took a cab to the bus station, as he had sold his Chevy Vega the previous day, and took a Greyhound bus to Chicago. Thus ended another chapter in Dev's education. The summer of 1982 had made Dev mentally, emotionally and physically tougher than he had ever been before.

Dev returned to ISU and this time he decided to take up an offer by his Beta Sig friends to room at the Beta Sigma Psi fraternity house on Vernon Avenue. He continued to maintain contacts with I-House and spent his first evening back with his dear friend Khondakar Imran. After they had caught up on what each had done during the summer and Imran consoled Dev on his separation with Agnetha, they were joined by Carla, Imran's long-standing girlfriend, who cooked them a meal.

The Beta Sig house was in a perpetual party mode. Every evening, kids would gather in the basement or the living areas to drink, play music, watch MTV or just chat. "Fun" was the operative word. At the same time, Dev had to focus on his courses, as this was the last semester and the computer science courses Dev had to take were tough. Dev somehow managed to cross the finishing line and graduate in December of 1982, albeit with a low B average. Despite this, Dev had grown from a naïve, innocent boy who had arrived at Illinois State University less than four years ago to a confident, well-educated young man, with a high degree of awareness of how the world around him worked.

Chapter 20 - Story of Dev – Part 3

Dev had gone through several campus interviews, but due to the severe recession of '82 and the high unemployment it caused, he could not find a company to sponsor him for permanent residency in the US. However, he was selected by A.C. Nielsen Company, based out of Northbrook, Illinois for its executive training program to be posted in one of its European subsidiaries. A.C. Nielsen was a marketing research company famous in the US for its television ratings. It also had subsidiaries in almost every western European country which focused not only on television ratings but also other market research. Its de-facto European headquarters was in Lucerne, Switzerland and it also had a subsidiary in Sweden. Agnetha and Dev were in touch and Agnetha contacted the managing director of the Swedish subsidiary of A.C. Nielsen to see if there was a place for Dev there.

Fortunately, the managing director, Lars Nilsson (no relation to A.C. Nielsen, the founder), was impressed enough by Agnetha's eagerness and earnestness that he agreed to interview Dev for the job. Nielsen paid for Dev's airfare from Chicago to Stockholm and Dev went through a series of interviews which culminated in a job offer. The money wasn't much, and considering Sweden's exorbitant tax rates it was even more modest, but Dev had no choice and he gratefully took the job. Stockholm was a difficult place to find an apartment in. The rental laws in Sweden were heavily skewed towards the tenants and this had snuffed out the supply of apartments from the market. Dev was fortunate to have Agnetha living in her parents' apartment close to downtown Stockholm. Agnetha's parents weren't terribly thrilled, but they let Dev stay in the apartment with Agnetha until he was able to find an apartment.

After a month, Dev and Agnetha together signed a lease on an apartment in Bergshamra, an outer suburb of Stockholm. It was a modest place and they moved in together. Dev took the Stockholm Metro to work every day. The Nielsen office in Sweden was small, with only about thirty employees, and Dev reported directly to the Managing Director, Lars Nilsson. Nilsson was an older man, very kind, and was particularly kind to Dev. Lars' only son, who was about Dev's age, had recently died tragically in a sauna accident. Lars developed a soft spot for Dev. He looked after him well and gave him a travel budget so he could travel first class across Europe to visit other Nielsen subsidiaries. Dev stayed in this job for almost two years; this was another great learning experience. Dev was only twenty-two years old and already an executive in a major American multi-national company. There were corporate dinners and events almost twice every week, including some formal dinners. Dev refined his dress style and corporate etiquette while in Europe and he enjoyed all the great food, drink, and particularly the company of diverse people that he met in the corporate world. He learned a lot about his trade and corporate and business practices around the world.

Dev travelled extensively across Europe to countries that had other Nielsen offices. London, Paris, Frankfurt, Amsterdam, Rome and Oslo were his frequent stops. Lucerne, Switzerland, however, was where he spent most time outside of Sweden, as it hosted the European Headquarters of A.C. Nielsen Company. Lucerne was a lovely town nestled in the Alps. It had impressive mountain peaks, such as Pilatus and Rigi. The town was divided by a large, beautiful lake which reflected the mountains and the night lights of town. It had a wooden bridge over the lake which connected the two halves of town. The lakefront of Lucerne was lined with hotels, restaurants, bars, shops and offices.

Unlike the general image of the Swiss as rather standoffish and staid, Dev found the Swiss of Lucerne to be friendly and curious. Dev came to love this little town and its people. He normally stayed in a bed-and-breakfast in Lucerne, called Bakerstube, because it also housed a bakery school. The owners became Dev's friends and always reserved the best room for him. The room had a lovely view of the lake and Mount Pilatus from his bed, as well as from his balcony. Sometimes, when he was with other executives, he would stay at the Palace Hotel on the lakefront. It was one of the best hotels in Switzerland, known for its hospitality and style. Dev thoroughly enjoyed staying there. While in Paris, Dev normally stayed in the George V, which exemplified what Paris was all about—style, old world charm, sophistication and sensuality.

He was out almost two weeks a month, and in the winters, which were brutal and depressing in Sweden, Lars Nilsson allowed him to travel to Rome and Southern Europe on business for about three weeks in a month. Most of the time Dev travelled alone, but sometimes Agnetha was able to take a break from Stockholm University, which she was attending, and accompany Dev, particularly to Paris. Agnetha loved Paris. Its outdoor cafes, museums, architecture and energy captivated her. She used to joke with Dev that she loved Paris even more than she loved Dev.

"Maybe you have a secret lover stashed away on the Left Bank someplace," Dev used to hit back.

In Paris, Dev got an education in art from Agnetha. She used to take him around to various museums. He soon developed his own likes and dislikes in paintings and it was in Paris that he became a lifelong Toulouse Lautrec fan. He liked artists who painted to a theme. Lautrec painted the Paris society of the late 1890s. Dev loved both his paintings and the themes. Agnetha and Dev loved the Louvre, but they preferred the Museum De Paris. They felt that paintings were displayed there in a more intimate and cozy setting. As much as Agnetha loved Paris, Dev had a certain ambivalence about it, as he found the Parisians of the 1980s quite racist, rude, and overall not particularly nice. He could never understand how a people like the Parisians, who were a bit uncouth, could create a city so beautiful, so stylish and with so much charm. Dev failed to see any charm in the individual Parisians he came across.

Ironically, the best friend Dev had within the Nielsen organization was a Parisian. His name was Jean Michele Valdoua (pronounced Valdua). He was Dev's counterpart in the French Nielsen Company. He was a larger-than-life personality. The first time Dev met him, he was sitting in his office with his legs up on the desk and his two lieutenants flanking him on either side behind him, against the wall. He had the demeanor of a king presiding over his kingdom. Jean Michele and Dev clashed the first time they met over some work-related issue and their squabble got escalated all the way through their respective managing directors to the European Head of the Nielsen Company in Switzerland. However, by the end of Dev's first official visit to Paris, Jean Michele had come to appreciate Dev's competence, knowledge, integrity and ability to take a stand for what he believed in.

Jean Michele invited Dev out to lunch on the last day of that visit and they took off for Jean Michele's favorite restaurant on Champs Elysees in his little Citroen at around noon. Jean Michele drove like a mad man around the busiest traffic in Paris, swerving left and right, cutting people off and driving at very high speeds. Dev held onto his seat during the twenty-minute drive to the restaurant. Even in Europe, where wine was a normal part of any lunch—corporate or otherwise—people normally ordered wine by the glass. Dev soon found out that Paris was different. Jean Michele started off by ordering a whole bottle.

"This is my favorite, Dev," said Jean Michele. "Try it, and if you don't like it we will order a different one."

Dev tried the wine and loved the mellow taste. "Excellent," he said.

Jean Michele commented on Dev's American accent. In typical French fashion, he started trashing America, its people, and its policies. Dev started defending America. What started as a playground brawl slowly turned into a full fledged philosophical and geo-political discussion which lasted a couple of hours. A second, and then a third bottle of wine were ordered, along with several courses of sumptuous French food.

"Now it is Colheita time," declared Jean Michele after the main courses, as he ordered Crèmebrulee with some Port.

It had by now been more than two hours since they had left the office. As they consumed glass after glass of Port, the conversation turned to their private lives.

"So, about your girl friend, Agnetha," said Jean Michele, now clearly tipsy.

"What about her?" asked Dev.

"I saw her with you when I picked you up at the hotel this morning," said Jean Michele.

"Yeah?" said Dev.

"Beautiful girl," said Jean Michele, and then added with a naughty smile, "very nice derrière."

"Is that supposed to be a compliment? Should I be thanking you for that, Jean Michele?" asked Dev with a smile.

"You bet it is. I love a sexy derrière. I wish my girlfriend had one as sexy as your girlfriend's," said Jean Michele.

"I thought you were married, Jean Michele," said Dev, pointing to his wedding band. "Where did this girl friend come from?"

"Well, she is my—how shall I put it—mistress. In French we call that 'La maitresse.'"

"Oh," said Dev naively. "So you don't really love your wife then? Does she give you trouble?"

"No, no, she causes no trouble whatsoever. I love my wife. It's my maitresse I have problems with. She is a bitch," said Jean Michele.

"What on earth are you talking about? I think you have had a little too much to drink," said Dev, totally confused.

"No, no. I am totally sober," said Jean Michele, who had drunk at least two thirds of the liquor, ordered over lunch. "Simone, my mistress- she just wants, wants and wants. She consumes most of my salary."

"Why don't you drop her then?" asked Dev.

"It's not that simple. You will only understand when you are my age," said Jean Michele, looking very serious and sober, almost forlorn.

"Well, I hope it works out for you, Jean Michele," said Dev with genuine empathy.

"Merci, Monsieur," said Jean Michele.

During this and several other lunches and dinners, Jean Michele and Dev established a friendship which was both professionally and personally fulfilling for the both of them. They accomplished a great deal together for the Nielsen Company and enjoyed very much sparring with each other and ultimately supporting each other.

Back in Stockholm, Dev and Agnetha's relationship was getting to be like a roller coaster. Excellent one day and really low the next. Stockholm was a lovely place, especially in the summer. It was composed of about fourteen archipelagos where Lake Malaren met the Baltic, most connected by bridges. Stockholm was open, green, had clean waters and was sometimes referred to as the "Venice of the North." It was a beautiful setting for young romantics like Dev and Agnetha. However, there were problems. Agnetha's mother didn't much care for Agnetha dating a foreigner. Agnetha's parents lived in an idyllic Nordic town called Sigtuna, which was about an hour and a half's drive from Stockholm. Sigtuna was a picturesque little town, a storybook setting.

If one were to write a fairy tale or an ideal Christmas story, Sigtuna would be the location. It only had one main street, with charming shops, boutiques and cafes. It had a population of only about five thousand. The houses were quaint, and there was a pretty lake and lots of greenery. It was also demographically as homogeneous a place as any in the world. Everyone was upper-middle class, Swedish, same background, and same culture. Agnetha's mother had this image of a tall Swedish blond, blue-eyed boy with the tall, blonde Agnetha, living in Sigtuna happily ever after. As far as she was concerned, Dev was someone from Mars—strange and alien looking, totally not what she had imagined for her daughter.

As cosmopolitan as Stockholm was, people were not very tolerant of those who did not speak Swedish. It was okay for a few months, but eventually everyone expected a newcomer to learn the native language. Dev was very poor at learning languages, and as hard as he tried, he could not pick up much Swedish. In the office, Dev could get along quite well speaking English, since it was an American company, but working long hours, living in a totally new country, and his weakness of not being able to pick up a new language fast caused Dev to feel alienated in the Swedish society. Agnetha's mother was not good at English at all. This language barrier further exacerbated the already strained relationship between Dev and Agnetha's mother, and she literally hated Dev. That wouldn't have been so bad had she kept that hatred to herself, but she called up Agnetha every morning right after she woke up and gave her a hard time about Dev for an hour. Being subjected to this day after day, week after week, Agnetha started getting affected and her relationship with Dev started slowly dismantling.

Dev's alienation with the Swedish society due to his inability to learn the language added fuel to the fire, as Agnetha perceived it as Dev's lack of making an effort to integrate. She took this personally, as Dev not showing enough respect for her and her culture. She took it to mean that Dev didn't care enough about her to even pick up her language. Agnetha's mother's constant pressure didn't allow Agnetha the room to be compassionate and tolerant of this one shortcoming of Dev's. Agnetha's father was a passive-aggressive person. He internally didn't think much of Dev, but he had the good sense not to show it openly. He, however, covertly acted in ways that complemented his wife's efforts to break up Dev and Agnetha. Dev was claustrophobic in the rather uniform and homogeneous Swedish society. He hated the cold winters and got terribly depressed with the long nights and barely a few hours of sunlight in the Stockholm winters. The saving grace for Dev was that he stayed away from Stockholm and Agnetha half the time, when he was on tour to some other places in Europe.

After about a year and a half of this, in the fall of 1984, Dev decided he had learned sufficiently from his experience in Europe and as an executive. He grew impatient to move out of Sweden. He started applying to scores of companies in the US, looking for a job anywhere, from small towns in the Midwest to large towns and cities, to even backwater places in the Deep South. He badly wanted to be in the States.

One morning, while Dev was in London on company business, he got a call from his maternal uncle, Samir Dada, who also happened to be in London that day. Samir Dada knew that Dev was trying hard to move back to the States and he asked Dev to meet him in an apartment in Central London. When Dev got there, he found a very expensive and exclusive building. He took the elevator to the third floor apartment and he saw there a waiting area full of people. It was an eclectic collection of people, ranging from Arab sheikhs in traditional Arab clothing to American businessmen who clearly looked affluent, judging from the clothes and jewelry they were wearing. There were several young women wearing fashionable clothes, and several East Indians, in addition to a couple of British members of Parliament. Dev found Samir Dada talking to an older Indian man who was sloppily dressed.

"Over here, Dev," motioned Samir Dada as he saw Dev entering the waiting room of the apartment. Dev stepped towards Samir Dada and greeted him warmly.

"Meet Mamaji, Swamiji's secretary," said Samir Dada as he introduced the sloppy older man he was talking to Dev.

"Oh, so this is he," said Mamaji, giving Dev a thorough lookover, as if he was inspecting a horse in a thoroughbred show.

"Yes, this is my nephew Dev," said Samir Dada with pride. Dev was twenty-three years old, in the prime of his life. He looked quite attractive, dressed in a grey tailored business suit and a dark red tie, which matched perfectly with his kid leather dark red shoes.

"Ok, please wait. There is a long line waiting to meet Swamiji, but I will try to expedite your audience with him, Samir Dada. It will be at least a couple of hours though," said Mamaji.

This was the second time Dev heard a reference to "Swamiji." Mamaji moved away to talk to a short Arab sheikh who had a very traditional Arab head dress on with an embroidered gold border.

"That is Sheikh Al Kabab, second cousin to the Emir of Kuwait," said Samir Dada to Dev, pointing to the Arab man Mamaji was talking to.

Dev couldn't help but flash a smile as he surveyed the scene in the room, which looked full of B-grade comedy film characters. Having gone through years of International House experience at the university, Dev was accustomed to diverse and international gatherings of people, but this was the strangest gathering Dev had ever seen. He couldn't quite put his finger on it, but something about that room and characters in it didn't seem normal. He talked to Samir Dada as they waited, and Samir Dada filled Dev in on how Dev's parents and grandparents were doing back in India.

"Who is this Swamiji, Uncle, and why are we here?" asked Dev.

"Oh, it is Chandra Swami. He is the current rage in India. He is reputed to have '*tantric*' powers. We are here because under the guise of spiritualism, Chandra Swami brokers business deals—huge business deals," said Samir Dada.

"That figures. Now I know why all these people are here," said Dev, referring to the American businessmen, Arab sheikhs and East Indian operators.

"Yeah, it is amazing how a guy who was working as a small time cook in some private residence in Rajasthan just a couple of years ago now has all these high-powered disciples from around the world," said Samir Dada, referring to Swamiji.

"Wow, was he really just a cook till a short time ago? Amazing! Who are all these young girls? They don't look like they are here looking for business deals," said Dev.

"No, they are just Swamiji's followers," said Samir Dada.

As they sat there chatting, one of the girls caught Dev's eyes. Dev noticed her staring at him a few times. Whenever Dev would catch her staring at him she would look away, avoiding locking eyes with him. She was a petite girl, with a perfectly shaped body and a cute face. She was evidently Indian, based on her complexion and the anklets she was wearing. She was dressed in a very stylish dress which looked like it had come from one of the couturiers in Paris or Milan. She didn't look much over eighteen years of age and Dev thought she was a model. After a while the girl stood up and took a seat right across from Dev.

"Hi," said Dev.

"Hi," replied the girl eagerly.

"Are you waiting to see Swamiji too?" asked Dev trying to make conversation.

"No. By the way, I am Camilla, Camilla Kumar," said the girl.

"I am Dev—Dev Bapna," said Dev as he took the girl's outstretched hand.

"Pleasure to meet you, Dev," said Camilla.

"Nice to meet you too, Camilla," said Dev.

"Do you know London well? Have you been around much?" asked Camilla.

"Not really. I have been here a few times and have only done the tourist things mostly. What about you?" asked Dev.

"I know London well. Want me to show you around?" asked Camilla.

"I appreciate the offer, but we are waiting to see Swamiji," said Dev.

"It will be at least a couple of hours before you will be able to see Swamiji. David Miller is in there with him right now, and Sheikh Al Kabab is next," said Camilla.

"Fine then let's go," said Dev, looking at his uncle as if to seek his permission.

Samir Dada nodded his assent and Dev and Camilla walked out onto the street. They took a cab to Piccadilly and started walking. It was about 5:00 PM and the office crowd was all going home at the end of the working day. Camilla led Dev to a basement bar in one of the backstreets of Piccadilly called "Gallipoli." It had a small billboard on the outside, advertising the nightly belly dancing shows they had at the club. The billboard also showed several photographs of girls doing the belly dance. Dev noticed that some of the girls in the pictures had perfect olive colored skins in addition to absolutely perfect bodies. Dev had never seen that kind of complexion and such beautiful girls. Apparently those girls were either Turkish or Syrian or Lebanese, certainly from around the Mediterranean. To Dev's disappointment, which he didn't express to Camilla, there was no belly dancing show at 5:00 PM and they went inside.

The interior was rather dark, but elegantly furnished in middle-eastern motif. Dev and Camilla took a table in the corner. They seated themselves on the low sofa. The bar was quite full, but not overflowing, and it was quite lively, reeking of cigarette smoke, and the music system alternating between peppy love songs and international dance tunes at volumes that allowed a conversation. Dev ordered some port while Camilla ordered red wine.

"You're from India, right?" asked Dev.

"Yeah. In fact, I am Miss Congeniality India 1983," said Camilla.

"No kidding! Don't mess with me," said Dev.

"Why? You don't think I could be a beauty queen?" said Camilla naughtily, with a twinkle in her eye.

"I didn't mean that. You are quite beautiful. It's just that I…" Dev's voice trailed off, unable to complete the sentence.

"You don't think a beauty queen would wanna go out with you? You low on self-esteem?" said Camilla in a mocking tone, now really teasing Dev, almost challenging him.

"Apparently", replied Dev with a smile. "I will work on it, though, I assure you."

"Anyway, you are not from London. Where are you from?" asked Camilla.

"Stockholm," replied Dev.

"Never been there. I've hear it's real pretty, though," said Camilla.

"So, you live in London?" asked Dev.

"No, Paris," answered Camilla.

"Wow! Must be nice. How come you know London so well?" asked Dev.

"Swamiji spends a lot of time in London, so I do too," said Camilla.

"So, do you work for Swamiji, or are you a groupie?" asked Dev.

"What is a groupie?" asked Camilla, looking confused.

"Never mind. It's an American slang," said Dev.

"No, no. I really want to know. What does a groupie mean?" asked Camilla.

"Fans of celebrities, mainly girls, that follow the celebrity around wherever they go and sometimes they make themselves *available* to celebrities, too," said Dev.

"Do these groupies do it for free?" asked Camilla.

"Yeah, they are not paid," said Dev.

"I am not a groupie then, but I do travel with Swamiji part of the year," said Camilla.

"You mean you get paid?" asked Dev.

"Yeah, all of us girls, and some of the boys too," said Camilla.

"So what exactly do you do for Swamiji, besides hanging out in waiting rooms and making yourselves available to him?"

"We sometimes also entertain those who come to visit Swamiji," said Camilla.

"You mean disciples?" asked Dev, amused.

"Not all the time. There are some who visit Swamiji who are not disciples," said Camilla.

Dev looked at her with questioning eyes.

"Sometimes people just visit Swamiji on business," said Camilla.

"So there is business conducted by Swamiji as well," exclaimed Dev now sounding a little excited.

"Big business," replied Camilla.

"I thought it was only spiritualism and maybe some *tantric* stuff," said Dev.

"No, some very big business is conducted too. We help mostly to close these deals. Sometimes we also gather information for Swamiji," said Camilla.

"Okay, different strokes for different folks I guess. Although you do have a very pure look, almost virginal," said Dev non-challantly.

Camilla blushed and then smiled sweetly. Her manner suggested an innocence and purity, despite her glamorous appearance.

"Are you interested in being a male groupie, a paid one?" asked Camilla after she collected herself rather quickly.

Dev looked up, absolutely startled. He almost spilled his drink. He quickly regained his composure when he realized that Camilla was laughing at his discomfort.

"Is that a firm offer?" asked Dev smiling, trying to sound "in-control."

"Yeah, I guess," responded Camilla, now sounding hopeful.

"So, you are the recruiter? Swamiji hasn't even seen me yet. You have the authority to make me an offer?" asked Dev.

"Swamiji saw you on closed-circuit camera as soon as you entered the waiting room. He also knew that you were Samir Dada's nephew who badly wants to move to the States. He called me in and asked me to make you an offer. Swamiji will help you get a US green card," said Camilla.

"And the money. Is it good?" asked Dev.

"That depends on how much you are making right now. You will have to discuss money with Swamiji himself. There are other benefits too," said Camilla slyly.

"Like what?" asked Dev, now really curious.

"Like, some groupies can make themselves—how did you put it—*available*. Get it?" said Camilla cagily.

"How does it work? Do I get to choose?" asked Dev.

"No, it has to be somewhat mutual when it comes to employees. You are not a client, you see," said Camilla.

"That's not much of a benefit then, is it? Like who among the girls I saw in the waiting room would make themselves—how did you put it—*available*?" asked Dev, smiling.

"I can't speak for others. I can only speak for myself," said Camilla.

Dev let it go at that. He wasn't at all interested in the offer, but he was playing along to have some fun out of sheer curiosity. He really liked Camilla and didn't want to make her explicitly offer herself as a benefit to him. He developed some concern for Camilla.

"Maybe she is in over her head in this. This Chandra Swami is one mean son-of-a-bitch, a complete jerk," he said to himself, feeling protective of her. Dev hated all these fake god-men, but it sounded like this Swami was in a class by himself.

"It sounds very tempting, Camilla, particularly the benefits, really, but I will only make up my mind after I talk money with Swamiji," said Dev.

"Of course," said Camilla. "Here is a preview of the benefits." She leaned forward and gave Dev a gentle, moist kiss full on his lips.

The effect of the port, the smoke filled and slightly dark atmosphere, combined with the kiss and straightforwardness and innocence of Camilla made Dev feel warm and mellow. He started to fall for Camilla in this first brief meeting. He thought of Agnetha, and despite the strains in their relationships, he pulled himself back from the brink and swallowed his last gulp of port, then suggested that they leave.

"What's the matter? Low self-esteem again, or you haven't ever done it?" said Camilla naughtily, with a gentle smile.

Maybe what she had said was in good fun, but it was pretty hard-hitting. However, the way she said such a personal thing, it was not offensive at all, at least to Dev. Maybe it was just Camilla's innate softness or Dev falling for her or the Port doing its thing to Dev or a combination, but Dev didn't take it hard at all.

"A little bit of both," said Dev, trying to make a quick recovery.

"You mean low self-*esteem and* lack of experience—both? I may be able to help in fixing both those issues for you," said Camilla, again saying somewhat harsh words in a gentle way, making her more and more alluring to Dev.

"Shut up and let's leave," said Dev getting up and pulling Camilla by her arm.

As they boarded a cab to head back to Chandra Swami's apartment on the West End Dev pulled Camilla closer, saying, "Lemme teach you a thing or two." They made out in the cab all the way back to the apartment.

Samir Dada was waiting at the elevator as Dev and Camilla disembarked.

"Swamiji is ready to see us now, Dev," he said urgently and ushered Dev inside Swamiji's chamber.

The room was not very large, but it had expensive furniture. It looked like it had been elegant at one time. However, now it looked like a typical drawing room that Dev had seen time and again in the new-rich Indian houses. Everything in the room was expensive, but not much went together. The sofa, the carpet, the showcase, the showpieces, they were all positioned a little off from where they ideally should have been. There was a strange odor in the room that Dev found nauseating. Chandra Swami, or Swamiji, as he was constantly referred to and addressed, was seated on an unkempt bed right in the middle of the room. There were two overstuffed chairs placed about three feet from his bed, facing him.

Samir Dada went over and greeted Swamiji, with folded hands, and introduced Dev. Dev too folded his hands and Chandra Swami asked both of them to be seated on the chairs across from his bed. Dev took a good look at Chandra Swami. Chandra Swami looked as disgusting as Dev had imagined, only more so. He was a short, stocky, middle-aged man with what looked like a beer paunch, although Dev knew that Swamis generally didn't drink. All the fake god-men he had heard of would take drugs, but not consume alcohol. Chandra Swami's face was pock-marked, giving him a very bad complexion. He had small beady eyes and heavy bushy eyebrows. He reeked of sweat, which probably accounted for most of the bad aromas emanating in the room. He was dressed in a grey *kurta* and white Indian-style *pyjamas*. After surveying the surroundings, when Dev focused his attention on Chandra Swami, he realized that Chandra Swami was staring at him intently. Dev started back and the two locked eyes for what seemed like an eternity. Finally, Chandra Swami shifted his gaze to Samir Dada and said "*Chehre per tez to bahut hai,*" (meaning the face certainly has a lot of charisma), referring to Dev.

"He is working in Sweden right now as an executive in training but he really wants to move back to the States, Swamiji," said Samir Dada.

"How much money does he make?" asked Swamiji.

Samir Dada told him Dev's modest salary.

"Is that all? Really?" exclaimed Chandra Swami, and then looking at Dev he continued, "Why don't you travel with me and you will make at least four times that."

"He really wanted to move to the States, Swamiji. I am sure with your contacts you could get him a job with a good American company which can then sponsor him for a green card," said Samir Dada.

"He can travel with me and I will get him a green card," said Chandra Swami.

"How is that possible?",persisted Samir Dada, who knew Dev would never accept travelling with Chandra Swami, nor would Samir Dada want Dev to accept it.

"Oh, I know everyone in the US government. When I go to meet Reagan next I will mention it to him. Dev will have his green card in no time, don't worry," said Chandra Swami, feigning non-challance.

Samir Dada knew from the newspapers that Chandra Swami had indeed met Reagan a couple of times in the White House, but he also knew that Reagan would never entertain the idea of getting anyone a green card out-of-turn, even if Chandra Swami dared mention it to him. Besides, he knew Dev abhorred the system of patronage and would never go for it.

"Actually Swamiji, Dev really likes his profession. He doesn't want to get out of touch with software engineering. I was hoping you could get him something in his own profession," said Samir Dada, making one last attempt.

"What I am offering is far better than being an engineer," said Chandra Swami, and looking at Dev he asked, "How about it? I only make this kind of an offer to certain chosen people. No one turns down an offer like this."

Dev looked Chandra Swami straight in his eyes. He was tired of Chandra Swami's arrogance, his dirty room, his waiting room full of groupies, weirdoes and world class wheeler-dealers. Mostly, he was repulsed by what appeared to him to be the amateur manipulations and machinations of Chandra Swami. Dev thought that he had never met a man more despicable than Chandra Swami. He was about to say something impertinent, but he stopped himself at the last moment out of respect for his uncle, Samir Dada, who had brought him in to see Chandra Swami.

"No, Swamiji. I truly appreciate your offer, I really do, but I am afraid I am not a very spiritual person and I will neither be a very good disciple nor a good employee. I cannot allow your regard for my uncle to cause you to make an offer for which I find myself utterly unsuitable. I am afraid I can't accept your offer, grateful as I am for it."

"Okay," said Chandra Swami, disappointment evident in his voice. "Samir Dada, the boy is making a big mistake, as youngsters are prone to make sometimes. Please counsel him appropriately and see if he changes his mind."

"I will certainly try, Swamiji. I appreciate very much your kindness for seeing us and making this wonderful offer to my nephew," said Samir Dada as both he and Dev stood up, made a parting gesture to Chandra Swami, and they left the room.

As Dev and Samir Dada walked out of the crowded waiting room in Chandra Swami's central London apartment, both of them burst out laughing

"How do you know him, Uncle?" asked Dev, continuing "he is the most disgusting man I have ever run into."

"He is pretty bad, but not the most disgusting man I have run into," responded Samir Dada with a smile. "He has brokered some fairly large business deals for me in the past and I have to keep him in good humor. Besides, I didn't think it would hurt to take a chance on him getting you a good job with a genuine American company. It was your misfortune that he got overly fond of you and wanted you to be a part of his own entourage."

Dev never saw Camilla again. A couple of years later Dev woke up one morning, picked up the morning newspaper and found Camilla Kumar's photograph on the front page with the headlines screaming "Camilla Cordez, the modern day Matahari ." The article went on to describe Camilla as a high class prostitute who had charmed a couple of British MPs, a British junior minister, arms dealer Adnan Khashougi, a close aide of Col. Mohmar Gadafi, among others, who had secretly taped their conversations at the behest of the Indian "Godman," Chandra Swami, who was using those tapes for blackmail and extortion. Although Camilla Cordez was unmistakably Camilla Kumar, Dev thought she looked in the pictures as if she had lost all the innocence and purity that Dev thought she had possessed when he had met her in London.

Also, a few years later, Dev read in the newspapers that several countries, including US and Britain, had warrants out for Chandra

Swami's arrest, and he had fled to India where he was promptly arrested and spent a good amount of time in jail.

Back in London, after walking out of Chandra Swami's apartment, Dev and Samir Dada went to the West End and had a sumptuous dinner at a nice Indian restaurant before parting. Dev flew back to Stockholm the next day.

Dev landed at Stockholm Airport on a cold November day in 1984. He was surprised that Agnetha was not at the airport. Normally, Agnetha made an extra effort to meet Dev at the airport upon his return from his business trips, particularly long business trips like this one, which had lasted twenty days. *She may have been held up someplace*, thought Dev. He took a cab to the suburban Stockholm apartment that he shared with Agnetha. Dev found Agnetha in the living room, talking on the phone to someone in Swedish. After she hung up, Agnetha came over and gave Dev a perfunctory kiss.

"What's wrong?" asked Dev, sensing that all was not normal.

"That was Matts on the phone," said Agnetha. Matts was the guy Agnetha's mother was constantly trying to set her up with. He and Agnetha were practically neighbors from Sigtuna and had grown up together. They shared similar backgrounds and the expectations were that they would be together. Before Agnetha met Dev, that is.

Dev had come from nowhere and all the well laid plans of both the families were severely disrupted.

Dev looked at Agnetha, questioningly.

"I went on a date with him last week," said Agnetha, a little tense.

"And?" asked Dev.

"And, I slept with him," said Agnetha, a sharp edge in her voice.

Dev was speechless. He had really fallen in love with Agnetha. They had their ups and downs but he cared deeply about her. Dev had flashbacks of the great time they had had travelling through Switzerland and Paris and their days together in Illinois State. Dev had had a tumultuous life until he met Agnetha and in her he found someone who genuinely cared about him, and he experienced happiness and bliss. Despite the fact that there were dark clouds hovering over their relationship for a while, he was shocked that someone as mature as Agnetha, and as loving, would actually cheat on him in this manner.

"What happened? Shocked, are you? Don't look at me like that," continued Agnetha, with a real bite in her voice. "You will always remain a bloody foreigner. You can't even string together a decent conversation in Swedish. There is no way you can live in Sweden like this. I don't think you are planning to live in Sweden in the long run anyway otherwise you would have made an effort. Now you are applying desperately for a job in the States. I can't leave Sweden. This is my home. My mom is right. I don't have a future with you."

Dev said nothing. He was still having flashbacks about his time with Agnetha.

"What? What did you expect? My social life has greatly diminished since you came to Sweden. You have not been able to get close to my friends. You don't have any friends here outside of work. At least I didn't lie to you. These are the facts and you better face up to them, Dev," continued Agnetha, still unusually harsh.

Dev and Agnetha lived like strangers for the next few weeks, and then Agnetha started acting normal again and they resumed talking. Agnetha profusely apologized for cheating on Dev and started making a real effort at repairing the relationship. Dev still was shell-shocked and he took his job search in the US to an even higher level. In December of 1984 Dev was asked to visit Paris urgently by his company. It was to be a long visit and Dev was going to spend Christmas in Paris. Agnetha suggested that she join him in Paris after a week, when her Christmas break would start at the university. "It would be good for us. We will attempt to rebuild our relationship in Paris over Christmas," said Agnetha.

Dev arrived in Paris on Dec. 15, 1984. He checked into King George V, one of the finest hotels in the world. His good friend and counterpart in Paris, Jean Michele Valdoua, had dipped into his own company budget to put Dev up in this expensive hotel. Agnetha was supposed to arrive the following Friday and it was decided that Dev would leave the key for her at the reception desk and she could let herself inside the room, since Dev would be at work in the afternoon.

As soon as Dev arrived in Paris he was introduced to Ana, a French girl of Czech descent whose parents had migrated to France from Czechoslovakia just before the failed 1968 Czech rebellion against the Soviets. She had recently been hired by Nielsen France, reporting directly to Jean Michele. Dev shared with Jean Michele his problems with Agnetha and Jean Michele arranged a nice dinner for four for Dev on his first night in Paris. It was Jean Michele and Dev, along with Jean Michele's wife Georgette and Ana. Ana was young, voluptuous and very lively. She was also an artist and very open to Dev. The dinner was like a godsend for Dev, who was bordering on depression following the events of the past few weeks, particularly Agnetha's infidelity. Ana offered to take Dev on a museum tour of Paris the following week, before Agnetha was scheduled to arrive.

A couple of days later Dev got a phone call from his managing director in Sweden, Lars Nilsson, that the office had just received a fax from an American company called CGA Computers in Baltimore, offering Dev a job. Dev was elated. He immediately called Agnetha in Stockholm to give her the good news. Agnetha was cold and told Dev that something had come up and she would not be able to join him in Paris. Dev and Ana ended up spending their evenings together, touring Paris, and then nights together in the lovely suite Dev had at George V.

At the end of his tour, Dev returned to Stockholm just before New Year of 1985, full of hope and energy. The job offer and Ana, along with his stay at George V, had done wonders to cure his depression. Dev applied for his H-1B work visa for the US and got it within a week. In January of 1985 Dev left Stockholm—and Agnetha—for Baltimore Maryland. At the time, he didn't feel a great deal of sadness on leaving Agnetha. In fact, he had been seething inside for a while, perplexed at her behavior. Agnetha tried to be as supportive of Dev as possible during his last days in Stockholm, but Dev had had enough of Sweden. The long winters and the chill that Agnetha had been exhibiting in the previous few months had completely turned him off to this Scandinavian country, a country he would remember fondly, along with Agnetha, after the passage of some time when some of the wounds he thought he had suffered there had sufficiently healed.

As the Continental Airlines plane took off from Stockholm, carrying Dev in a crammed economy class seat, this ended another chapter in Dev's eventful life.

Chapter 21 - Story of Dev – Part 4

Dev's arrival in America on a cold winter day in January of 1985 was the start of a significant phase in his life that turned out to be completely different from what Dev had expected or hoped for. This phase turned out to be hugely eventful, at times interesting, and in some rare moments even exciting. This phase also crystallized the kind of person Dev would become for the rest of his life.

When Dev landed at Baltimore Washington International Airport, he was received by Jodi Milspaugh, a mousy HR manager at CGA Computers Associates where Dev was to work. Dev didn't have much idea about his job responsibilities except that he was to consult with the company clients and that the job would utilize his technical skills. As Jodi drove Dev from the airport to the hotel he was temporarily going to stay in, she told him more about the job. It turned out to be very different from what Dev had anticipated.

CGA Associates was one of the hundreds of companies that had cropped up in the US in the 1970s that supplied temporary technical labor to companies that required it. Temporary technical labor allowed the companies to ramp up for their projects early, allowed companies the flexibility of hiring and firing at will without going through the processes as prescribed by labor laws, and gave companies access to difficult-to- find technical skills within a short period of time. In most cases, this temporary labor worked out of the client company's site and for all practical purposes was the client company's employee. CGA Computer Associates, therefore, had a tiny office located in the World Trade Center building on the waterfront of Baltimore, even though they had more than 300 employees. Almost all of these employees worked out of a client sites and had very little connection with CGA Associates other than the fact that their paycheck came from CGA Associates. Dev was to be one such technical laborer.

Dev's first assignment as a technical labor was at a company called Blue Cross/Blue Shield of Maryland, a large health insurance company. Dev had placed a condition on CGA Associates that they would apply for his green card right after his arrival in the States and they had fulfilled their end of the bargain. Blue Cross/ Blue Shield turned out to be a bit of a nightmare for Dev. Firstly, Dev was pretty close to the bottom rung of the hierarchy and he had very little authority for any innovation. It seemed to him that he was working pretty much in a straitjacket, with no room to think or grow as a person. Coming from Europe and having worked in a very dynamic company in an executive position of authority, this was a huge change for Dev. Besides, he was temperamentally not suited to working in such a tight environment. His background and education had prepared him to think, innovate and take charge. The temporary labor assignments in Baltimore were not really up his alley.

Fortunately for Dev, within four months he got his green card. Now he was free to pursue other opportunities and not confined to working for CGA Associates. He talked to his manager about leaving, but the manager convinced him to give them another chance by offering to change Dev's assignment to another client site. The new client site was Union Trust Bank of Baltimore. This place, as it turned out, was worse than Blue Cross.

The management at Union Trust Bank in Baltimore was entirely comprised of mental cases. There was a Confederate nut who wore a Texas hat to work and had a large Confederate flag covering one entire wall in his office. He never tired of telling anyone who would listen, the virtues and benevolence of the Confederacy. Then there was an older man who was a member of the Frederick chapter of the KKK. There was a woman who closely monitored every temporary laborer, whether they were her direct reports or not. She would keep close tabs on how many phone calls each temporary laborer made, how many minutes each spent in the rest room, how much time they spent making small talk with each other, and how long each one took for lunch. Then there was one guy who insisted on taking a cut for each temporary laborer hired from the consulting company. Almost no one was normal, and the same went for the employees lower down the rung.

Baltimore had a blue collar culture and almost everyone at Union Trust came from that blue collar background—management and line employees alike. This was obviously not bad in and of itself, but it created for a very narrow-minded, stifling atmosphere at the work place, as most of the people didn't have much of what one would call a "liberal arts education." This was also the first time that Dev experienced brutal, good old-fashioned racism, which opened his eyes to a reality that he was only peripherally aware of. Arriving in America to go to University in the late 1970s, Dev experienced very little racism, if any. He was well aware, through his readings, of the legacy of deep-seated racism in America, but it seemed to Dev that the Civil Rights movement and the liberal wave of the 60s and 70s America had washed most of it away. Since he was not black, Dev never experienced the racism that was prevalent even on his university campus while he was attending college. Dev also had not by then developed the sensitivity and the sensibility to put himself in a black person's shoes to be able to understand the depth of racism present in America. Working for a progressive company in Europe as an executive also shielded Dev from much of the racism prevalent in Europe, as he only moved in more educated and cultured circles there. He did experience a bit of racism during his extensive travels across Europe, but mostly when he backpacked, as opposed to when he travelled on business, where he stayed in elite hotels. Baltimore was another thing altogether.

Dev worked in Baltimore for two years, 1985 and 1986. However, in 1985 and 1986, corporate America's exposure to Indian American technical labor was still unheard of. Corporate America was still extremely conservative and the computer industry was still dominated by IBM, or "Big Blue," as it was called. IBM was highly structured and the culture was very uptight. Blue pinstripe suits, buttoned down shirts and yellow striped ties were still the corporate uniform and American corporate management was almost exclusively white and male, with a token black or a token woman here or there.

It was in such an environment that Dev found himself in Baltimore in 1985. He had high hopes of returning to the US from Europe and he was ambitious. However, he found the going tough and he was struggling to survive, much less get ahead. His attempts to secure management positions within and outside CGA Associates were openly scoffed at. People were not shy about telling Dev that he could forget about being part of management, since he was an Indian. In addition to the claustrophobic environment of Baltimore, Dev also, for the first time, faced open hostility attributed entirely to his race.

Socially too, Baltimore was a nightmare for Dev. He had heard about a literary class in Baltimore, but found it impossible to break into. His status as a lowly temporary employee resulted in him being blacked out of the social circles where he may have found like minded people or people with similar backgrounds. He had faced no such barrier when he was in the university or when he was an executive in Europe. In Baltimore, Dev found himself in the company of people for whom the highlight of the social season was "Pollock Johnny's Hot Dog eating contest" or drinking beer in the infield at Preakness.

Professionally and personally, this was a low point for Dev. All of his dreams about making it big in America were turning into nightmares. The image of America as a hopeful Ayn Randesque meritocracy was permanently shattered in his mind. He wasn't doing much better on the woman-front either. Dev was a sensitive young man, and even at the young age of twenty-four or twenty-five, he was beginning to outgrow mere physical gratification. After Laurie and particularly Agnetha, he was used to having a partner who was intellectually his match, in addition to being physically attractive. Coincidentally, right through his two-year stay in Baltimore, Dev didn't meet any young lady that he clicked with. Frustrated professionally and socially, Dev decided to take up his family's long-standing offer to find him an Indian girl to marry. In early 1987 Dev quit his job in Baltimore and headed to India for a much needed rest and relaxation after a very eventful but satisfying two-year stint in Europe, followed by the disastrous two years in Baltimore.

April in India was the beginning of the hot season. When Dev arrived in Bombay in April of 1987, he was received at the airport by his parents, who had lived in Bombay for the past ten years. The day after his arrival, Dev's mother informed him that she had arranged for five or six girls and their families to visit Bombay to meet with them during the following week. His mother, Damayanti, had actually shortlisted two girls who came from typical "affluent families" in India. In her mind, the other three or four girls who were coming to visit were just "fillers," not really having any chance, but just there to provide Dev a good "choice."

The first girl Dev was supposed to meet was his mother's top choice. Her name was Tina and she was "well educated," had done her MBA and came from a "good" family, meaning well off and culturally similar. At the appointed time, one evening, Tina's entire family trooped into Dev's parents' drawing room. Almost from the get-go, Tina's father and a family friend who had accompanied him, clearly for the purpose of grilling Dev, started interrogating Dev about some very personal things, such as how much money he made, how much money he had accumulated, what he did in his spare time in the States, all the way down to how many drinks he had a week and what he ate. Dev was surprised at the brazenness and callousness of it all and tried his best to hedge and be cagey with his answers. Tina and Dev then took off on their own to a coffee house down the street for a one-on-one, while the families stayed back to converse with each other.

Dev found Tina to be a nice girl. She didn't have much interest in how much money Dev made or had. She kept asking Dev about his life in America and how they would live if they got married. When Dev mentioned that he had a very modest salary, Tina cheerfully responded that she could work and they could be quite comfortable together. Dev could not help but like Tina, despite her family, and after about forty-five minutes they returned to Dev's house. Tina's family took leave and Dev's father, Ramsingh, informed Dev that Tina's parents had conveyed that they would think about it and give an answer in a day or so. Dev's mother attributed this lack of enthusiasm to Dev trying to hedge on his answers about his finances. "No one is coming to check your bank balance, Dev. You could have made it sound like you have a really good salary," said Damayanti. Dev rolled his eyes at this suggestion and after some verbal sparring back and forth, Dev's parents shifted their attention to welcoming the next affluent family who were from South India.

The family from South India was not as direct, but they nevertheless were still very interested in Dev's financial situation. The girl was a chartered accountant and very ambitious. At the end of the meeting they were sufficiently impressed by Dev to where they signaled their willingness if Dev was amenable. Ramsingh and Damayanti were gracious and promised to get back to them very shortly with their decision.

"These are the two real choices we have," said Damayanti. "The rest are really no match for these two. We have to meet them, but it is a mere formality."

"Why did you have them come all the way to Bombay, Mom, if they didn't have a real chance?" asked Dev.

"Well, we wanted you to have a choice," said Damayanti.

"Okay, lemme have a real choice then. Don't write anyone off, before I even meet them," said Dev.

"Oh, I am sure the remaining girls won't even measure up. You can just tell from their family backgrounds," said Damayanti.

Dev just shrugged, not wanting to continue this conversation with Damayanti.

The next girl Dev met came from a more modest family. She was quiet, and although Dev liked her simplicity, she was far too shy and introverted.

The last meeting of the week was to take place late one night with a family from Jaipur. It was a middle-class family, where the father was a senior scientist at a pre-eminent government research lab. When the family arrived at the Bapna residence at around 10:00 PM, a tired Dev immediately sprung to life at the sight of the girl. Her name was Selena and she was absolutely beautiful. She had glowing skin, a perfect complexion, and beautiful light brown hair. She was not very tall, about 5feet 5 inches, but she carried herself with elegance, although she was dressed simply. Dev found himself praying that the girl would be as beautiful on the inside as she was on the outside.

Selena's parents were not terribly interested in Dev's finances as much as they were in Dev's field of work. They wanted to know if Dev liked his work and whether he intended to stay permanently in the US. After a brief conversation with her parents, Dev and Selena moved to another room to have a one-on-one meeting. Dev found Selena quite genuine and having no other agenda other than to explore whether they were compatible. Selena was gentle, smiled a lot, very straight forward with her answers, and an artist. By the end of the meeting, Dev was quite taken by her and the next day at the Bapna family meeting, which now included his grandparents, Dev made a case for Selena. Damayanti and Dev's grandmother were vehemently opposed to Selena. Tina's parents had called earlier that morning to confirm their interest and both the ladies started pushing for Tina. Dev's insistence on Selena resulted in a stalemate. Dev's grandfather, PS, had not said a word during the entire deliberations, surprising Dev, as PS was one person whom he would have expected to give no credence to the financial status of a girl's family.

Later that afternoon, PS summoned Dev for a private meeting with him in the guest room of the Bapna residence, where he was staying.

PS was quite tense and his face was a little drawn. Dev had seldom seen PS this stressed. It was as if PS was dealing with some kind of internal conflict within himself.

"You know, I am with your grandmother and mother on this one, Dev," said PS gravely.

"Why?" demanded Dev.

"You know better than anyone else that money doesn't matter to me. It has never mattered to me. I was never able to counsel you on how you could make more money in life," said PS, "but when I look at you, I get very worried".

"Worried? Why?" asked Dev again.

"Because, in you I see someone who is not worldly wise. You have no inheritance coming, and you don't have any money. Tina is a good girl, even you must admit that. Her family and their money would come in handy for you. You have already had a tough life. You have your whole life ahead of you. I want you to have a chance. Take a chance to make something of yourself, Dev. Otherwise, I am afraid, you may be doomed. Come on, take that chance, Dev," said PS, pleading.

"Grandfather, please calm down. You of all people should have more faith in me. I can make it on my own," said Dev, matter-of-factly.

PS shook his head and said, "It is not as easy as you think, Dev. The world is far more complex and convoluted. There is still the law of the jungle out there, whether we like to admit it or not. You have no support whatsoever from anyone. You have no backup. You are not likely to make it without some minimal backup, even in the States. Think about it."

Dev didn't relent.

Damayanti reluctantly consented to Selena, but she thought her son and her family now were destined for certain ruin. Dev's grandmother, Ratan, proclaimed that this was Selena's lucky day. Grandfather PS, however, came around to giving his wholehearted consent. For months after that incident, PS repeated this story to many of his friends, feigning fake exasperation, but everyone could easily glean the pride in his voice as he spoke animatedly of how Dev paid no heed to money. Selena and Dev got married in a simple ceremony in late 1987 at their family home in Indore.

After the wedding ceremony, the same night, PS took Dev into his room for a brief private meeting. PS pulled out a tiny silver box with a gold border. He opened the box and pulled out a ring. It was more like a thin band, and it looked golden in color and slightly faded. PS reached forward, took Dev's left hand and slipped the band on his ring finger.

"What is this, grandfather?" asked Dev, thinking that this must be his grandfather's wedding gift to him.

"This is Deoraj's ring, my most precious possession and our connection to all our ancestors. Guard it with your life," said PS.

"What is Deoraj's ring, grandfather?" asked Dev.

PS then went ahead and told Dev the story of Deoraj, their first known ancestor.

"Wow, grandfather! What a story. When did you get it from *Ba'asab* (Siremal)?" said Dev as he touched his grandfather's feet.

"A few days before his death he gave it to me," said PS.

It was a very emotional moment for Dev. He slipped the ring out of his finger and slid it into his thin gold chain that he always wore, wearing it like a pendant. From that day on Dev never separated "Deoraj's ring" from himself.

After a couple of months in India, which included a pleasant honeymoon at a friend's tea estate up on the hills of Nilgiris in south India, it was time for Dev to return back to the States. There was a year's time lag before Selena could join Dev, as it took about a year in those days for the wife to get her own green card. Selena would spend the year in Indore, with Dev's parents and grandparents, getting acclimatized to the Bapna family.

As reluctant as Dev's grandparents were about Selena being his wife, once the marriage occurred, both of them became doting grandparents to Selena. They pampered Selena no end, ensuring that every day that she spent at Bapna House in Indore before joining Dev, her favorite dishes were prepared and she didn't lack for anything. PS Saheb even hired an extra driver to escort Selena across town whenever she wished, further stretching his already meager resources. Unlike most traditional Indian families where the youngest daughter-in-law handles a good chunk of the housework, Selena was simply asked to take it easy and not bother with anything. Both PS Sab and Ratan didn't tire of praising Selena to all their relatives and stayed up till pretty late at night having pleasant conversations with her. Selena couldn't stay unaffected by this outpouring of affection and she came to regard them more as her grandparents than Dev's, and she loved them back equally. Even later on, whenever the grandparents would notice Dev and Selena having a tiff, they would invariably take Selena's side, chastising Dev. Selena often teased Dev that she would complain to his grandparents if he didn't do exactly as she wished.

By early 1988 Dev was back in the States. As he exited the baggage area of BWI airport after landing, to take a taxi, he couldn't bring himself to head to Baltimore. He decided to take the cab in the opposite direction and asked the taxi driver to take him to a friend's place in Washington DC. Dev stayed with his friend for a few days until he found work as an independent consultant at a government contracting company and then rented a small apartment at Quebec House. Quebec House was in the Cleveland Park area of Washington DC, which was a residential area, close to everything and quite lovely. There were lots of young people living in Quebec House. Some of them were students at Georgetown or GW University, others were freelance artists, yet others worked for one of the many media outlets in Washington, which was also the media capital of the world. Dev, who had starved for some likeminded company, now found himself among people he could relate to. He looked forward to a pleasant stay in Quebec House.

The political climate in the US in 1988 was markedly different from when Dev had first arrived in the US in the fall of 1979. While the late 1970s and early 1980s were a time of malaise, stagnation and uncertainty in the US, by 1988 Americans were on the march again, both economically and geopolitically. The computer revolution was at its peak and high tech was changing the way Americans lived and worked. Computer and telecom industries were generating hundreds of thousands of jobs every year and unemployment was at a historic low.

Internationally, the Soviets seemed to be on the defensive. After years of stagnation under the leadership of Leonid Brezhnev, the Soviets, under a new leader, Gorbachev, were attempting reforms through Perestroika and Glasnost. The lid was now off of the iron curtain and decades of latent dissatisfaction was erupting all across the Soviet empire. The Solidarity Movement in Poland was one of the earliest challenges to Soviet dominance, and by 1988 it looked inevitable that Poland was going to shake loose from under the Soviets.

At the time, most Americans including the intellectuals and the media, were attributing the great economy and the disarray of the Soviets to the conservative policies of Ronald Reagan. It was, after all, under Reagan's watch that the economy had stabilized. Interest rates fell, the economy grew and unemployment rates plummeted. Reagan and the conservatives very cleverly took credit and touted their policies of tax cuts for the rich as the main cause of this economic upturn.

Overseas, most people attributed the retreat of the Soviets to Reagan's policy of promoting "Star Wars" technologies. Reagan was a big proponent of "Missile Defense." Missile defense meant deploying anti-ballistic missiles, which would detect and instantly shoot down any missile launched by the enemy. While the Pentagon and the defense contracting companies that were developing this missile defense themselves claimed very modest successes, Reagan criss-crossed the country, making speeches and insinuating that such a "Star Wars" system was very close to reality. He even offered to share this technology with the Soviets, further implying that the system was very close to being deployed.

In 1988, Americans were so mesmerized by Reagan that they failed to grasp the complexities of the causes of Soviet retreat. They were so ready to believe Reagan that they became a bunch of collective simpletons and actually swallowed the hoax that Reagan's Star Wars had caused the Russians to be on the verge of collapse. In fact, Reagan and his defense secretary Casper Weinberger were the architects of this hoax, as they personally hatched and executed a plan to rig the tests of Star Wars technologies. Reagan's success in both these areas—economy and foreign affairs, had made him a folk hero in the States. Polls showed that he became the most popular president in US history and a grass roots movement started to amend the constitution to permit him to run for a third term. Reagan's hero status cemented America's hard turn to the right and by 1988, America felt to Dev more closed, more complacent and a more contented place than at any time in the past ten years.

Dev's own experiences in Baltimore and his growing maturity had turned him completely off to Reagan's style of conservatism. Dev was a proponent of the brand of conservatism that led to more dynamism, more knowledge, more enlightenment, more respect for each individual, broadening opportunities for all and more respect for hard work and enterprise. Reagan's conservatism instead promoted narrow mindedness, mind-numbing conformity, less knowledge, less respect for individualism and opportunities only for some. Dev questioned the many positions Reagan had taken, even as far back as the campaign.

Dev now became even more sensitive to the black man's plight in America. He was thoughtful enough to grasp the complexities of the reasons why the black community in America was still lagging severely behind the mainstream. He understood fully that only the black community, through its own efforts, could bring itself out of the doldrums that it was in. No amount of reliance on the goodwill of the larger community or the mandates on the larger community alone could bring about a renaissance in the black community. He also now could clearly see the pettiness and malice that America as a whole continued to exhibit towards the black community, notwithstanding all the internal shortcomings of the black community. While there was enough wiggle room in America for the black community to thrive and succeed despite this malice and pettiness, it was not lost on Dev that this pettiness and malice actually existed and that Reagan had put a complete stop to any momentum that Americans had generated over the past couple of decades towards stemming such pettiness and malice.

Reagan had not only tapped into the deep-seated resentment certain significant sections of the populace felt towards the successes of the Civil Rights movement, he was subliminally inciting such resentment in others, who without him would not have harbored such resentments. Dev had gradually come to lose all respect for Reagan and the know-nothing conservatives that ruled America. Dev also came to realize that many times Reagan blurred the distinction between truth and untruth. His pre-conceived deception to demonize welfare queens, his Star Wars hoax, his projection of the American invasion of Grenada as a war to protect the world from communism rather than an effort to distract attention from the disastrous Beirut bombing of the Marine barracks, the Iran-Contra affair, and his many highly choreographed and theatrical speeches such as Bergen-Belsen all were proof positive in Dev's mind that Reagan was personally a highly dishonest man. Either Reagan himself didn't understand the difference between truth and falsehoods or he could very comfortably lie without even a prick on his conscience.

Dev clearly saw flaws in America, but despite those flaws, he was clear that America was still the greatest experiment and experience in human history. Its greatness could stand on its own merit. America didn't need Reagan's lies, deception and make-believe to justify its greatness. Some of the reasons for its greatness, Reagan was actually trying to reverse, such as Civil Rights, women's rights, etc.

Dev was deeply dissatisfied with the work he was doing. The lack of opportunities to advance and the glass ceiling he kept running into constantly ate away at his soul. One day he made a trip to the Lincoln Memorial in Washington. The Lincoln Memorial was a temple for all who sought opportunities to make something of themselves in America. He read Lincoln's words which were inscribed on the walls. Dev then drove around parts of Washington DC that were predominantly black and ghettos. As he drove through those areas he mostly saw decay, decline and hopelessness. He issued a silent apology to the community that he was driving through, an apology for supporting Reagan—an apology for being taken in by his rhetoric on the "welfare queen." He became more and more distraught as he drove through those ghettos.

As the sun was setting, Dev went back to the Lincoln Memorial. He climbed up the steps and stood right in front of where Lincoln sat, then, he turned around and sat on the steps of the Memorial, his back towards Lincoln. He could see the reflection of the Washington Monument in the reflecting pool, the same reflecting pool around which Martin Luther King had made his famous speech. He also had a clear nighttime view of Capitol Hill, right behind the Washington Memorial. Dev started having visions of his grandfather PS. He saw a vision of his grandfather standing side-by-side with Lincoln. They both urged him not to give up. Dev felt invigorated. He felt refreshed. He stood up, sensing new energy running through his body. He felt very light as he walked down the steps to his modest car and drove back to his apartment in Cleveland Park.

When he reached home, the receptionist handed him a message from someone called Maylon Hayes over at MCI Telecommunications Corporation. The message said that Dev was to report at MCI at 11:00 AM the next day for an interview.

Chapter 22 - Story of Dev – Part 5

Washington was a pretty city with European architecture, world class museums, grand monuments, lots of history, and a great nightlife. It was not generally known as a fun town, but if one was a Washingtonian and knew the hidden spots, it had a very active nightlife, with great clubs, excellent restaurants serving cuisine from around the world, theaters and everything else that goes with it. Washington DC itself was a small town with most of the population of the metro area living in the Maryland and Virginia suburbs. The Potomac River was the natural border between DC and Virginia. Arlington and Alexandria were the nearest Virginia suburbs to DC, right across the Potomac. The US Department of Defense was headquartered in Arlington in the largest office complex in the world, better known as the Pentagon. The area around the Pentagon, although technically in Arlington, was called Pentagon City. The MCI offices were located in two twelve-story buildings across from the Pentagon.

Dev walked into the MCI building, past the security, up the elevator and into Maylon Hayes' office on the sixth floor. He sensed that the atmosphere at the MCI office was different from any other office he had been to in the US. There was a certain energy in the air and the employees looked more relaxed and animated. All in all, the office appeared to Dev as being very alive. Hayes asked Dev some general questions about his experience and background and after about five minutes declared that he was hired as a consultant and that he should report for work the following Monday.

A few days after Dev started, he was introduced to a project manager named Ken Krueger. Dev was assigned to work on a project being led by Ken. Ken looked like he was in his late thirties, had an impressive personality, and was highly professional. He was a man of few words, but when he spoke it was concise, to-the-point, and always added value. Ken made some initial assignments to Dev and his instructions were very clear. Dev and Ken developed a great professional relationship and soon Dev realized that Ken was a highly intelligent, competent IT professional, a rarity in corporate America.

Ken also was one of those rarities who only cared about how productive and competent his employees were. He had very little tolerance for "suck-ups." Ken also introduced Dev to his superior, a portly gentleman with a receding hair line and a pleasant demeanor by the name of Bruce Thomas. Bruce, a director, was a hands-on manager, who would participate actively and contribute greatly in software architecture and design meetings. Bruce was originally from Tennessee, but he was Ivy League educated and had a great sense of humor. Dev, for the first time since his days at Nielsen, was working in an environment that was calm, result-oriented and respectful of people's talents. Dev found MCI in 1988 to be as close to an Ayn Randesque meritocracy as was humanly possible. Not everyone working there was equally competent, but the reward system was very fair, with the more competent and productive being rewarded more than the less competent.

Dev often wondered why MCI was so different from any other company he had worked at. He did some research on the origins and management of MCI and found out why. MCI was a telecommunications company, the second largest in the US, after AT&T. Since the beginning of telecom, AT&T, or Bell Company as it was popularly known, had essentially enjoyed a virtual monopoly in the US until the late 1970s.

Almost all the other countries in the world also had telecom monopolies, in most cases government telecom monopolies, because if it was okay for the US to have a telecom monopoly, other countries felt validated in having their own monopolies. As a result, there were practically no advancements in telecom technologies around the world including in the US. In 1970s, Steve Jobs and his Apple Computers had just unveiled Apple 1C, the first working personal computer, but networking technologies of computers were still quite primitive, primarily because of lack of advancements in telecom technologies to support data transmission in a big way. All that changed in the late 1970s and early 1980s, largely due to an epic and a two-decade-long battle by MCI to open up the telecom market and break up the monopoly of AT&T. It was a classic American story of two Davids taking on a Goliath and winning, something that could only happen in America.

The battle was started by John "Jack" D. Goeken, a telecommunications entrepreneur who had founded a company called MCI with his four partners in the 1960s. He wanted to start a phone company that could compete with AT&T. But he soon realized that existing laws, AT&T's financial clout, its political clout and its hardball tactics created a barrier of entry too big to overcome. He embarked on a two decade long regulatory and legal battle against AT&T, to open up the telecom markets for free competition.

Bill McGowan was a big, gruff Irishman who had pulled himself up by the bootstraps. He was a venture capitalist, a self-made millionaire who owned several small companies, including a janitorial company that cleaned buildings in Manhattan. He had a larger-than-life personality and seemingly unlimited reserves of energy. In 1968 he entered into a partnership with John "Jack" D. Goeken, the founder of MCI. He agreed to finance MCI in exchange for 25% of the stock. MCI, by this time, was in court battles to try to stay afloat. McGowan's gregarious and tenacious personality kept the MCI case alive in the FCC, and in 1974 he and Goeken had some differences which led to Goeken giving up active management of MCI and McGowan assumed the responsibilities of the CEO.

Under McGowan's leadership, MCI had some small victories in the FCC case until late in the 1970s, when MCI convinced the US Department of Justice to file an anti-trust lawsuit against AT&T. The Justice Department's case was heavily dependent on the evidence gathered by MCI's legal team, and as it turned out, they used most of that evidence. The trial started in 1981 in the courtroom of the US District Court Judge Harold D. Greene. In 1982, sensing defeat, AT&T agreed to settle the lawsuit out of court, essentially agreeing to everything MCI and the Justice Department wanted.

McGowan then went on to create a near absolute meritocracy at MCI and competed aggressively in the market place, focusing on evolving state of the art technologies. MCI was one of the early pioneers of data transmission technologies that enabled the emergence of Internet as the huge cultural phenomena that it has become.

Bill McGowan was still running MCI in 1988 when Dev joined the company. Because of his ailing heart, though, he had left the day-to-day running to a man by the name of Bert Roberts. As became evident a few years later, Bert Roberts was one major mistake that McGowan made in his otherwise flawless career.

Dev recalled meeting McGowan at a party hosted by ABC news on a boat in the middle of the Potomac River a few months earlier. He had a friend living in Quebec House who was a junior reporter at ABC news who took Dev to this ABC news party. The party had several big shots and celebrities, including news anchor Peter Jennings. Dev recalled that when McGowan entered the party, the room stood still and everyone crowded around McGowan. Amidst all the celebrities, McGowan was the biggest star of the party. Naturally, with that kind of pedigree and background, it was to be expected that MCI would be as close to a complete meritocracy as one could possibly have.

Working for MCI from 1988 until 1992, when sadly McGowan died, was the highlight of Dev's career. Working under the capable leadership of Bruce Thomas and Ken Krueger, Dev was accomplishing big things at MCI. Despite being a consultant, he was now accorded management roles and he had the freedom to pick his own team, which he did, selecting only the very best and most talented people. He was happy with the work he was doing; he was happy with the company he was working for; he was happy with the monetary rewards, and he was most happy with the recognition he was getting for his hard work and talents. He was also growing a lot professionally, learning a lot from Ken Krueger, with whom he had developed not only a close working relationship but also a deep friendship.

When Dev arrived in the US in 1979, it was still the era of large mainframe computers, which cost millions of dollars, where one-tenth of the processing power of desktop PCs of 1990 took up practically one whole floor of a building, and requiring hundreds of staff to run and maintain them. By 1992, personal computers had begun to take over the work place, mainframes were already getting obsolete, the Internet had started becoming part of everybody's lives, cell phones were set to take over the world, and computers and data communications technologies had converged.

Working for MCI, Dev had a front row seat to this massive technological and cultural shift. Not only was he a firsthand witness to this change, he was an active participant, contributing to several innovations at MCI, along with Krueger and Bruce Thomas.

※ ※

On June 2, 1992, Bill McGowan, the man who beat AT&T and revolutionized telecommunications, died at the age of sixty-four. His successor, Bert Roberts, had been practically running the company since 1986, when McGowan had his first heart attack, but McGowan's presence had kept the dynamic culture that he had promoted alive and well at MCI.

After McGowan's death everything changed. Dev noticed that all of the ills that plagued most of the rest of corporate America were creeping into MCI as well. MCI became a company where a system of patronage and personal fiefdoms replaced the meritocracy, so meticulously cultivated by McGowan. McGowan had created a culture within MCI of decentralized groups, with a great deal of independence to accomplish discrete tasks, but he also ensured a hawk-like oversight and management systems that would ensure that these independent groups strictly adhere to their charter and didn't overstep them. His system ensured that there was no major duplication of effort across various groups and that these independent units act in the interest of the larger company and not become self-perpetuating units, acting in their own narrow interests. After McGowan's death that high-level oversight and system were the first to collapse.

This resulted in a lot of the independent groups within MCI acting as renegades or rogue groups who started working in their own narrow interests rather than the interest of the whole company. Cooperation and coordination between groups became major casualties of McGowan's death.

Before long, MCI became the repository of almost all different kinds of computer hardware available in the market. It also became home to an assortment of disparate software systems, both off-the-shelf and customized. It was as if MCI middle management had gone crazy and indulged in an orgy of buying anything and everything they could find in the market place. This created a huge problem, as these different hardware and software systems couldn't communicate with each other. Ironic, isn't it? A communications company could not make all these disparate systems talk to each other, resulting in massive waste and inefficiency.

The upper management had lost all abilities to regulate such rogue behavior and started focusing instead on inorganic growth via mergers and acquisitions, and even some strategic partnerships, which failed to work out. Proposed partnerships with Newscorp and British Telecom failed for different reasons, but they failed nevertheless.

Unlike other much less resourced companies such as Sprint, MCI completely missed the boat on assimilating cell phone technologies and offering a mobile product. Bert Roberts made some half-hearted attempts at cell technology, but he failed miserably as he didn't have the team or the mindset to make such an initiative a success. Not being able to jump on the mobile telephony bandwagon turned out to be a huge blunder, as regular long distance business was gradually dying, due to the fact that long distance rates had collapsed as the result of stiff competition which characterized the telecom industry. Bert Roberts preoccupied himself with soliciting mergers with a myriad of companies and strategic partnerships with others. The joke around MCI was that Bert Roberts had even approached the Hare Krishnas for a merger, but that they had turned him down.

By 1996, while Bert Roberts was busy looking for mergers, MCI had become home to a bunch of shysters, film-flam artists, pretenders, impersonators, psychotics, pathological and out-and-out liars. Suckups and sycophants were having a field day. Yapping became the new religion at MCI. Actual production slowed down to a trickle. Since the upper management didn't have the ability to distinguish between the competent and the incompetent, the ranks of middle management were filled with incompetents. Obviously, the trickledown effect down the line was even more incompetence. While Bert Roberts played the proverbial "merger" fiddle, MCI burned, and his management dutifully played the role of a cheering audience.

Dev saw innumerable examples of the unscrupulous characters that had come to dominate MCI.

There was a fellow in senior management who was a complete flake and kept talking about relocating MCI from its base in the Washington DC area somewhere else—anywhere else. He came to MCI from IBM and immediately went on this relocation kick. When his attempts to move significant MCI operations to Texas failed, he was able to relocate a significant portion of MCI operations to Colorado Springs, Colorado. His ruse was that he could advertize for IT talent in ski magazines and get IT talent more readily in Colorado Springs. Why? Elementary, my dear Watson! Because, Colorado has many ski resorts.

There was another guy in upper management who was a complete suck up and had the imagination of a water buffalo. Then there was this narcissistic witch of a VP who had created her own personal fiefdom within MCI, hiring all of her own friends. There were characters in senior positions whose only claim to fame was using a lot of buzz words and technical jargon that made no sense whatsoever. Then there were other characters who were clearly mentally disturbed, and finally, there were a fair number of the outright liars. One particularly obnoxious person who was a total nincompoop, branded people he didn't like as "diabolical" and provided a lot of comic relief by acting like a buffoon, although he himself never realized it. All these characters took center stage at MCI after the death of McGowan.

1992 was also the year Dev suffered an irreparable loss, the greatest of his life. His grandfather PS passed away peacefully in his sleep. The news shook Dev and unsettled him like nothing he had ever experienced in his life. He had faced many hardships and ups and downs in his thirty-one years, but no tragedy compared with the loss of his beloved grandfather. With his grandfather gone, Dev felt truly alone in the world. The one man in his life who gave him unconditional love was no more. Dev knew that the last bright light of the eminent Bapna family had passed away and it was up to Dev to revive the fortunes of the family, which were on a rapid downward spiral. Life at MCI after 1992 became more and more difficult for Dev. Bruce Thomas and Ken Krueger bucked the trend and kept on being promoted and thriving at MCI, despite being highly competent.

Dev was under no illusion that MCI was unique in corporate America when it came to incompetence dominating. His prior experience with a number of companies had left an indelible impression on his mind that something had seriously gone awry with corporate America by the early 1980s. Dev found that in his experience an overwhelming majority of the employees in corporate America were not happy with their jobs and their management. The morale was extremely low because the reward system was not fair. Competence had very little premium, and in some cases had severe and punitive consequences. Being a "yes person" had a very high premium. Entrepreneurship and making waves was considered a vice, and "going with the flow" and being "diplomatic" commanded a high premium. Being loyal to the corporation at large, the people that worked there and their clients was not valued as much as personal loyalty to one's immediate boss. In human affairs, some of these flaws always exist, but Dev never ceased to be amazed at the degree of dysfunction within corporate America in the 1980s and 1990s.

Perhaps with the passing of the WWII generation or perhaps because the owners of the corporations were divorced from active managements, Corporate America became anemic. In MCI, Dev felt that he had found an exception—a healthy corporation, a jewel—but after the death of its owner, Bill McGowan, MCI quickly contracted the same disease as the rest of most of Corporate America.

This disillusionment with MCI also coincided with his disillusionment with the American political landscape in the early 1990s. Bill Clinton had just been elected president after twelve years of Republican rule and almost immediately started being viciously attacked by the Republicans, religious fundamentalists, the media and several other groups within America. Eight years of Ronald Reagan, whom Dev had campaigned for in 1980 as a naïve student, was followed by the presidency of his vice president, George Herbert Walker Bush.

The invective and the virulence directed at Clinton was so far in excess of his personal failings that Dev was thoroughly disgusted by what he saw around him. His disillusionment with America due to its stupid suicidal actions against Sadam Hussain and the vitriol hurled at Clinton just because he was a liberal, combined with his disillusionment with Corporate America, left a very bad taste in his mouth. In his mind, the Republicans had made a huge mistake by weakening Sadam Hussain and thus strengthening Iran, but he was flabbergasted that thoughtful Americans and the American media failed to see this obvious mistake. This was a much greater and more far-reaching offense against the nation than any of the alleged personal shortcomings of Bill Clinton, and yet instead of the Republicans being held accountable, it was Clinton who was being pilloried for doing nothing more than receiving oral sex and then lying about it.

Dev continued to be mentally unsettled for years due to the passing away of his grandfather. In late September, 1998, Bert Roberts, the CEO of MCI, finally succeeded in his long quest for a merger partner. In his infinite wisdom he found a soul mate in one Bernie Ebbers, a Canadian charlatan who headed a company by the name of WorldCom. Already declining fast under Bert Roberts since the death of McGowan in 1992, Dev witnessed the culture and morale at MCI tanking precipitously after the WorldCom takeover. By 1998-99 his disenchantment grew, both with MCI and America in general. He started seriously thinking about leaving America and heading back to India.

PS Bapna Sb - Age 70
At the time of inauguration of River Narmada water coming to Indore
Courtesy Bapna House Family Collection

Chapter 23 - Story of Dev – Part 6

In the fall of 2000, at the age of thirty-nine, after nineteen years in the US, Dev sold his house in the Washington suburbs, packed his belongings and along with his wife Selena and children made the fateful move to India. MCI was no longer the kind of place which could fully do justice to Dev's talents. He felt like Corporate America was no place for him. Dev had left India to come to US a little before his eighteenth birthday and thus had spent all of his adult life in the US, except for his two-year stint in Europe. He had not visited India very often and his memory of India was fading.

Dev had read about and heard first hand from family members that India had, starting in the early 1990s, instituted significant economic reforms which resulted in a dramatic shift from the old socialist economy to a more market- oriented economy. The results were impressive. Economic growth had doubled from a long prevalent "Hindu rate of growth" of about 3% to a healthy 6%, and even in some recent years to 7%. The unemployment rate, though still very high in a country of one billion people, was declining. New business opportunities were opening up and markets and streets were flooded with consumer goods, both locally made and imported. Dev felt that in view of all of the above, he could put his IT expertise and education to good use in India, helping the country while at the same time make a decent living.

He was, however, not at all prepared for what he was to encounter in India. When Dev and his family landed at Indore airport, they were received there by his parents and his close childhood friend Neil. Dev's family home was all the way across town from the airport, and as they crossed the city on their way home, Dev saw some areas that he was familiar with, but a lot had changed. When Dev left India in 1979, the population of Indore was about a million, and now it was well over two million. Everything seemed more congested and the infra-structure seemed to be bursting at the seams. There were many more cars and motorcycles on the streets and the traffic was totally disorderly with no semblance of any traffic rules. No one seemed to obey the traffic lights and there was no concept of left or right on the streets. Pedestrians, hand carts, bicycles and all motorized vehicles used the same narrow streets, creating complete chaos.

The entire town was infested with small shacks, which in the local language were called *gumtis*. These shacks were kiosks selling tea, fruits, vegetables or other sundry items, and were essentially illegally setup by local strongmen or their cronies on municipal lands outside people's homes, commercial buildings or other open spaces, particularly on the roadside of every street. These kiosks were so ubiquitous and the politically connected elements that set these up at no cost to themselves were so brazen that miles of road shoulder were taken up by them, as well as sometimes significant sections of the streets themselves, and even downtown areas were encroached upon. In combination with the illegal slums that had sprung up under the patronage of the local mafia largely due to deliberate non-enforcement of laws by the government, these shacks gave the appearance of the whole city being one large slum. Dev kept asking Neil about this proliferation of slums and shacks and Neil kept referring to them as "illegal encroachments" by design. To Dev, though, it looked like nothing but out-and-out theft of public lands.

"If this looks bad to you, Dev, wait till you get home," said Neil in a very tentative tone of voice.

"Why? What's at home?" asked Dev.

Neil didn't answer, but he had a troubled look on his face.

"What? Is everything all right?" asked Dev, looking at his parents.

"Everything is just fine. What could possibly be wrong at home?" said Damayanti, Dev's mother.

The answer didn't make Dev feel much better, but Selena gave him a reassuring look and Dev did not press the issue anymore.

As the car that was carrying Dev and his family closed in on his family home, Dev did not recognize his neighbor's house as they passed it. The entire front of the house was lined with illegal shacks or kiosks which were set up on the roadside between the boundary of the house and the road. Even the neighbor's driveway wasn't spared and most of it had been encroached with barely enough space grudgingly left by the slum mafia to let one car enter the house. The last time Dev had seen his neighbor's house he could see the entire ranch-style home from the street; now it was no longer visible.

"Is the house still there?" asked Dev.

Neil nodded, signifying that the house was still there.

Then the car pulled into the outside driveway of Dev's family home. The outside periphery of Dev's house (the entire open municipal land between his house's boundary and the road, a total of about 200 ft. long x 40 ft. wide) was also encroached, but not as badly as his neighbor's. The encroachers had set up a few automobile repair shops, a few metal scrap collection kiosks, a kiosk or two selling eggs, several bicycle repair kiosks, an automobile body shop, a construction material shop and even a welding workshop or two with their backs literally supported by the boundary wall of Dev's home. The outside gate to Dev's lot was wide open and the car pulled inside the family compound, which was about a quarter of an acre lot on which there was a house of about 5,000 sq ft. There, under the porch of the house, Dev was greeted by his waiting grandmother, Ratan, and two men whom Dev had never seen before. Dev bowed down to his grandmother, as was the Bapna family custom.

"Meet Hira and Natu," said Damayanti, pointing to the two men.

Hira and Natu looked unwashed and smelled of sweat. They were shabbily dressed. They had scars on their faces and looked every bit like street hoods. Dev had seen their types when he was living in Indore, but not inside his house, and he was surprised to see them under his porch inside his lot. They both stepped forward and touched Dev's feet.

"Who are these guys, Neil?" asked Dev pointing to Hira and Natu.

"Never mind them. You haven't been to Indore in years, Dev. You have just arrived. I will slowly fill you in on everything. Let's just go inside," said Neil.

"Okay, but let's walk around the outside of the house for a little bit. Remember, Neil, how we used to play hide-and-seek around the house when we were kids? Let me check to see if my favorite hiding places still exist," said Dev earnestly.

"Okay," said Neil reluctantly.

As they walked the lot, Dev noticed that the garden was in complete shambles. The lawn was full of weeds, so much so that the grass was barely visible. Most of the fruit trees—the figs, the tamarinds, the lemons, the guavas and others—were completely gone. A couple of mango trees were left, but they looked like they were infested with ants and termites and covered in dense spider webs. The shady trees that Dev's grandfather had planted on the inside periphery of the lot were no longer there. The house itself looked sick and sad on the outside. It had not been painted in years and large black patches dotted the entire exterior. Thick cobwebs created intricate designs all across the exterior, giving it the look of a ghost house right out of a Halloween movie.

Dev and Neil walked to the backyard, where Dev found a bunch of pigs in one corner and a pack of stray dogs in another. Plastic trash and bottles were strewn across the entire backyard and it had an appearance of a landfill. Heaps of this trash was interspersed with dog, cat and pig excrement. Dev looked at Neil, who avoided making eye contact with him.

"Dev, do you mind? I have had a long day. You have all the time in the world to check out your hiding places later. Can we go in now?" said Neil who was literally squirming visibly in discomfort.

"Sure," said Dev, his heart already beginning to sink after what he saw.

They walked back to the front of the house and Dev saw the main gate that guarded the entrance to the lot wide open.

"Gimme a minute. Let me go and close the main gate," said Dev to Neil.

"No use. It's broken and it doesn't close," said Neil.

"No wonder that the pigs, stray dogs and cattle all find their way inside our lot. How long has it been broken?" asked Dev.

Neil just shrugged and quickly darted inside the house without waiting for Dev. Dev noticed that the two ruffians, Hira and Natu, had made themselves comfortable under the ant-infested mango tree in the middle of the lot. They looked very much at home, a feeling Dev did not have, despite having been born and brought up in that house.

Dev followed Neil into the house. There was chipped paint, cobwebs, and dust everywhere, and black spots on the walls assaulted his senses as he walked the narrow passage to the back veranda, where he found Selena and the kids sitting with grandma, Damayanti and Ram Singh. They were all steeped in an animated conversation.

"...had lots of affection for Dev. He was his favorite grandson. He left all this for Dev," Grandma was explaining to Selena, spreading her arms to indicate the house, tears in her eyes.

Grandma was actually trying to say that her husband, PS Sab, Dev's grandfather, was very fond of Dev and had left the house to him.

"Dinner is ready, Dev. Let's move to the dining room," said Damayanti.

The family made its way to the dining room and Dev noticed a thick layer of dust enveloping the dining table. Selena, noticing the dust herself and also noticing Dev's reaction, quickly retreated and showed up with a rag, wiping down the dining table with it. They all sat down for dinner. Dev was very quiet and the family made small talk right through dinner. After dinner Dev and Selena retreated to their bedroom, which was also in terrible shape. The fine teakwood, which at one time glistened and had a distinctive red glow was all cracked, water damaged and dull. The bathroom plumbing was non-functional. The closets were full of dust and the pictures and paintings on the walls had faded due to excessive dust and sunshine. The drapes were all teetering and the mosaic tile flooring, which was lovely at one time, had thousands of holes in it now. It was evident that the ceiling leaked and there was the foul smell of wet paint and wet cement in the room. A big puff of dust went up in the air when Dev sat rather heavily on the bed. A large slum had come up recently across the street from Dev's house and loudspeakers were blaring deafeningly loud music, despite it being very late at night.

Dev looked at Selena with a look that said, "How will we sleep in here?"

"Don't worry, Dev. Try to manage it for one night. Tomorrow we can hire someone to at least clean out this room," said Selena.

Dev spent the night sneezing and coughing and not getting much sleep. More than the physical discomfort, Dev felt mentally depressed after what he had seen that evening. The music blared almost all night.

Dev woke up early the next morning after a fitful sleep. Mercifully, the music had finally stopped. He went to the front veranda of the house and tried to take in some fresh air and soak in the atmosphere. He saw the main gate into the lot still wide open, and people walking in and out of the lot. The driveway of the house looked like a busy thoroughfare. He then saw several stray dogs and wild cats walking in and out of the lot. He also saw cattle and pigs come inside the lot from the street.

Contrary to popular belief, the cattle and pigs that roamed the streets in India were not strays. They were raised by businessmen and sold for dairy products or meat. Instead of raising them on the farms, though, it was a commonly accepted practice in India to raise them in cities and urban areas. Since there was not enough space to keep them in congested cities, where land was prohibitively expensive, the owners branded the animals and then left them loose on the street. The additional benefit the owners received was that the cattle and the pigs fended for themselves and fed themselves, either by rummaging through trash on street corners or by feeding on grass and lawns inside people's private properties and empty lots. The pig and cattle owners hired some cheap laborers to follow these animals on the streets and kept track of them. That was much cheaper than owning large tracts of land to raise these animals and feeding them on purchased feed. Of course, it created a major nuisance for everybody else, particularly for people who had nice homes or empty lots. It also disrupted traffic in a big way. The animals also performed all of their bodily functions out on the streets or inside other people's private properties. That accounted for a lot of the filth that was found in public areas in India.

"Why doesn't the government do something to stop these animal owners from letting their animals loose on the streets like that?" asked Dev of Neil, who had stopped by the house early.

"Because, these animal owners have formed a powerful lobby and associated themselves with one politician or another. No government dares take effective action against them. Every now and then the authorities go on a make-believe campaign to rid the streets of these animals, but it's all only for show and nothing ever comes of it," said Neil.

"That is unbelievable. You mean to say that the pig owners are politically connected? What possible benefit could the politicians get out of these small time hoods?" asked Dev incredulously.

"Small time hoods!" exclaimed Neil. "These guys are very rich. How many pigs do you think an average pig owner has?"

"I don't know. Maybe a hundred?" said Dev, thinking that a hundred was a rather large number.

"A hundred!" said Neil smiling. "Guess again."

"What? A thousand?" guessed Dev.

"Ten thousand!" said Neil with great emphasis. "Sometimes even

more. So imagine how much money the owners are saving on feed and land just by leaving the animals loose on the streets."

"No kidding, no wonder there are thousands of pigs and cattle roaming the streets of Indore," said Dev.

"Yup, it's all vested interests, my friend. Everything in India is the way it is because it is in someone's vested interest. The whole system in the country is very insidious. This cattle and pig thing is relatively benign compared to some other stuff that goes on around here," said Neil as if he was resigned to the situation.

"Okay, I am gonna teach them a lesson today, Neil. I am gonna go and shoot the pigs in our backyard," said Dev.

"I wouldn't, if I were you," said Neil.

"Why not? They are inside my property, my own home, for chrissake!" said Dev.

"These guys are very violent. It is well known that the animal owners have people who track these animals on the streets 24/7. They are known to exact brutal retribution from people suspected of harming or stealing animals. They are all connected to politicians too, so the police will not touch them," explained Neil patiently.

"As if it isn't bad enough that the authorities and police allow these people to run these cattle and pig operations on the streets and off people's homes… The police help them terrorize anyone who dares to oppose them too," said Dev, grasping the seriousness of it all.

"You finally got it. A better solution is to get the main gate fixed and keep it closed," said Neil.

"Fine, you know a good blacksmith?" asked Dev.

"I will look around and see what I can do," said Neil.

"By the way, I have been meaning to talk to you about something else too, Neil," said Dev.

"Yeah, I know. You are depressed about the condition that the house is in, inside and outside, right?" asked Neil.

"Oh, so now you can read minds too, huh?" said Dev.

"I am your childhood friend, remember. I have known you since we were five. It's not that hard for me to read your mind, even if we have been apart for the past twenty years. Besides the condition of your house depresses me too," said Neil.

"So, can you explain? What the fuck's going on?" asked Dev.

"Lemme see. Where do I start?" said Neil. "You want me to lay it out the way it is or should I sugarcoat it?"

"I am in one of my masochistic moods right now. Give it to me straight," said Dev.

"Well, the bottom line is that this town is essentially ruled by the land mafia. There are two kinds of land mafias in this town, both vicious, brutal and beneficiaries of political protection," said Neil. "The first is the one that consists of a bunch of big land owners, builders, developers and other rich people. They focus on grabbing large tracts of government land—valuable land—from private individuals and procuring large government contracts. These guys flout all laws, including zoning laws, and first steal the land and then overbuild on it. They are what you would call 'wholesale land grabbers.'"

"And the second?" asked Dev.

"The second consists of the slum lords and the less affluent Mafioso. They are also land mafias, but they are retail land grabbers. They grab a little land at a time, using hundreds or even thousands of surrogates. They go after small pieces of government land in good locations, grab the roadside or road shoulder and sometimes even the road itself to establish small steel shacks, usually 10 ft. X 10 ft. in size. They grab municipal land under the guise of enabling a person to be able to make a living in a country where there aren't enough jobs for everyone. Indian law doesn't criminalize establishing a shack on public lands. The worst that can happen is that the person can be removed. He can't be prosecuted or taken to jail for it. Removal almost never occurs because Indian law again gives enough leeway to authorities not to remove the encroachers, under the guise of due process. The laws are deliberately kept toothless by the politicians, as they and their *cronies are* the land mafia, and they are the same people who grab the land. It is these retail land grabbers who have grabbed the municipal land between your house boundary and the street and the neighbor's boundary and the street. That is just the first step. The next step is for this mafia to move inside people's private property as soon as they sense any weakness." said Neil.

"That's why every square inch of the road shoulder and municipal land in Indore is taken, with the exception of the land outside the politician's houses or the houses of the members of the land mafia," continued Neil.

"But there was no encroachment, at least outside our house, when my grandfather was alive. I am going to complain to the commissioner about this. I am sure the administration and the civil service officers will not tolerate this kind of nuisance outside the Bapna family home," said Dev, naively emphasizing *Bapna family home* as if the Bapna family would be immune to normal workings of the mafia.

"Good luck. You can try. While your grandfather was alive, just his personality and stature commanded respect. Even the land mafia dared not encroach outside his house. He has been dead eight years now, and lots of water has flown under the bridge since then. You are not your grandfather, not yet anyway. You can expect no help from anybody, particularly the government. I wouldn't put too much faith in the civil service either. They are all either corrupt or timid. Even an honest civil service officer will not have the guts to defy the politician, who after all is his boss," said Neil.

"Despite the fact that as per law the civil service officers are next to impossible to remove or fire, even by their bosses, the politicians?" said Dev.

"Yeah, despite that, 'cause, every officer wants a comfortable posting. The politicians may not be able to fire them easily, but they can still transfer them and give them undesirable postings. Besides, the career civil service officers are hand-in-glove with the politicians too when it comes to corruption. Why would any officer antagonize his business partner for you or the Bapna family?" asked Neil.

"So what now? Do I have to live with this nuisance? Is there no way out?" asked Dev.

"My advice is to keep on trying. Go and visit the commissioner and see. Maybe you will find an exception, that rare officer whose conscience is still alive. Just know, going in, though, that the odds are against you," said Neil.

"And what about these two guys, Hira and Natu? They seem to be a permanent presence under the mango tree right in the middle of our lot. Have my parents invited them? Do you know?" asked Dev.

"Oh, they are from the slum across the street. They work for the slumlord, the same slumlord that is also part of the land mafia. He is the guy who has established all these kiosks outside Bapna House and outside your neighbor's too. Hira and Natu sit inside your lot all day long so that one day they can claim squatters' rights over your land. Indian law says that if someone has been physically using a piece of private land for any purpose, even to cool one's heels, for one whole year, they can claim squatters' rights and they cannot be removed without something called 'due process.' Due process in India means a lifetime of court procedures. As you know, if you file a suit in India it takes decades to get a judgment," said Neil.

"So they are bloody here to occupy my lot illegally? They will slowly take over my entire house? And then where will I go?" asked Dev.

"Back to America, Dev. At least you have someplace to go where you won't be homeless. Come see my house. They have encroached on every square inch of land outside my house and they have even occupied almost one-third of my lot on the inside. Where do you think I should go with my wife, elderly parents and two children, aged four and two?" asked Neil. This time his eyes watered up.

Dev was stunned. He instinctively held his friend's hand, trying to console him. Neil was very dear to Dev. He too came from an old distinguished family. His grandfather was a doctor and his father was a highly respected teacher, now retired. They were a very decent, cultured family who wouldn't hurt a fly. They were exactly the kind of people who were totally disempowered in today's India because they did not have it in them to break the law or get associated with the politicians or join the mafia. If Dev had an alter-ego it was Neil, whom he had known since the age of five. They had been classmates and their families had known each other for generations. Unlike other friends Dev had in Indore, Neil had always been steady as a rock in his loyalty to Dev and vice versa.

"And one more thing, Dev. Your parents are very simple people. They are very scared. They will resist every move you make to fight out of your situation here. They have and will act out of fear. Please don't hold it against them. They are suffering from a form of Stockholm Syndrome," said Neil.

"And what about you, Neil? If I know you at all, I know you are fighting it. But you would fight like a nobleman, not like slimy worms, not like these land mafias. How are you holding up?" asked Dev.

"I am still alive and kicking. When I give up I will die," said Neil, smiling. It was as pure and innocent a smile as Dev had ever seen. After all these years, Neil was as childlike as when he had known him as a child.

"You won't have to fight alone now that I am here," said Dev. "I can't promise you victory, but I can promise you that I will always stand by you, Neil."

"That's what I was worried about," said Neil, very serious now. "Can't you sell your property, take whatever you can get, put it in the bank, rent a decent apartment for your parents and go back to America? Why did you feel the need to come to this godforsaken place? No one that has gone to America has come back, at least as far as I know."

"I am beginning to wonder about that myself. So you are saying you don't want me here?" mocked Dev.

"You know better than that, but in a way I am saying that. I only want the best for you. There are hundreds of cases in Indore where middle-class families have been driven out of their properties by hoods, with the police and administration taking no action. The land mafia has not even spared eminent families. You know the large plot of land very close to your house which was owned by a branch of the Holkar family? The slumlords have totally occupied it and no authorities came to their assistance. The police even tried to extort money from the Holkars. You know Ranjan Parker? A bunch of Mafiosos broke into his house, held him hostage and tortured him until he signed the papers, selling his house at ten cents on the dollar. You obviously know about my own situation, and now yours too," said Neil.

"What about all this talk about India being the largest democracy and all? And what about this new openness in the economy? Isn't the economy booming? Hasn't it created greater opportunities here?" asked Dev.

"Democracy is a joke in India. Democracy without basic law and order is meaningless. Democracy without a strong Bill of Rights and strong executive protection of those individual rights is useless. There is no law here; forget about the order. As far as economic opportunities, yeah, they have increased, but only the crooked and the connected can take advantage of them. No one allows a non- connected person any room to operate here. You will see," said Neil.

"Anyway, Neil, this conversation has gotten too heavy, and I am to blame for that. How is our good old club? Let's go there for a swim and we can have breakfast there," said Dev.

"The club has improved a lot. There are lots more facilities now. There is a new Olympic-sized swimming pool, new squash courts, new gym, a new jogging track, a new walking track and even a new cricket ground. You will like it," said Neil.

"The club" they were talking about was Yeshwant Club in Indore. It was founded during the premiership of Dev's great-grandfather, Sir

Siremal, in the late 1920s. Siremal Bapna was the main driving force behind the founding of the club.

Over the next few days Dev embarked on several projects. He started the process of getting his kids admitted in school. He applied for both of them at Daly College, his own alma mater. Indore had scores of schools and it was extremely competitive to get into a good school. There was no system of government schools and everybody relied on private schools. Despite being expensive, good schools had waiting lines a mile long, and consistent with Indian culture, you had to know someone who knew someone else who in turn knew someone just to get their child admitted in a decent school. Since Dev was an old Dalian himself, he didn't anticipate much trouble getting his kids admitted, as there was a special provision for legacy children. However, Indore being Indore, Dev had to go through hoops to get his kids into Daly College.

The lot on which Dev's house was built continued to resemble a public thoroughfare, with strangers, stray animals and livestock coming in and out at will. Neil arranged for several blacksmiths to come and fix Dev's gate. Each was threatened by hoods working for the slumlords across the street and scared away so the slum lords could continue to target Dev's home for illegal occupation. Dev attempted to call the police every time a threat was issued but the police never showed up. When Dev and Neil visited the local police station they were told flat out that the police had several other priorities and they were short-handed. They had to ration their time and they would much rather spend it on serious crimes such as murder and rape.

Actually, it was well known in Indore, and Dev quickly caught on to this as well, that police didn't spend their time on murder or rape cases either. They spent their time and resources hanging around politicians, practicing extortion and fabricating cases against people who had offended the land mafia or the powers-that-be. Dev soon realized that, unlike the US, where police normally arrived within minutes of calling 911, the police in Indore were under no such obligation. Half the time the police didn't even pick up the phone when they were called. When they did answer a phone call, they would either refuse to respond or lie, saying that they were on their way, but they would never show up.

The police in Indore acted as the enforcement arm of the politicians or the land mafia. Occasionally, when they were bribed enough by the complainant and the alleged perpetrator was not connected with the mafia or the politicians, the police would respond and file charges. Complaining to higher police officers was normally not much help. They simply refused to even see the complainant unless again the complainant knew someone who in turn knew someone else who could set up a meeting with the senior police officers. So just getting a police complaint, referred to as an FIR, filed was a tall order in Indore. Getting the police to respond to an emergency was an even taller order.

While most citizens were out of luck if they required an emergency response from the police, when it came to getting a police complaint filed there existed at least on paper, a judicial recourse. India made a big deal of an independent judiciary. The lowdown on this "independent judiciary" was that the court system in India was hopelessly understaffed. There was a backlog of cases, some going back fifty or sixty years. Cases took years, sometimes even decades, to get decided, and with appeals and reviews it took a lifetime, and sometimes more, to get a case resolved through the Indian judicial system. To make matters worse, like everything else in India, the judiciary was totally corrupt. Most of the lawyers were merely middlemen—fixers and touts for judges—and they had no clue of how to actually plead a case. The lower courts were totally compromised, but even the higher courts were significantly compromised.

Since the courts were compromised, and even in exceptional cases when they were not, it took decades to get justice in the Indian "independent judiciary", going to court was not an option for most people. They would never get justice in court. The police were totally dysfunctional and corrupt and they didn't provide the general population any relief or any law and order. The obvious question was: Why didn't the politicians who are part of the government make the police do its job? The answer is quite simple. It was the politicians who rendered the police impotent at best, and an enforcement arm of the mafia at worst. The police and courts were rendered ineffective and corrupt by design. The politicians were allied with the mafia. In a lot of cases, politicians and the mafia were the same people. The government was made up of people who were part of the mafia or allied with the mafia. It was not in the interest of the government in India to have an effective and impartial police force. It was not in the interest of the governments to have an effective judiciary. This went across party lines.

Current Bapna House Indore 2014 1
A modest structure built by PS Bapna Sb in 1963
Courtesy Bapna House Family Collection

Each political party was basically a mafia. India was a prime example of complete and utter failure of democracy. The result was that the general populace had cowered down and they lived in complete fear, a fear that was far greater than the worst dictatorships in the world. The fear was just not explicit, but had been internalized, and the evidence of this fear was that most of the population didn't rise in rebellion against their mafia government. *Most*, but not all. There were several armed insurgencies in India. Maoist insurgency, called the Naxal movement, was a misguided but direct response to this mafia government.

So, how could the people in Indore get justice? When you have a mafia government, you get mafia justice. Most people, when they get into a soup, make a beeline to a powerful local politician. The local politician then uses his influence to get the dysfunctional arms of the government, whether they are police or other institutions, to deliver on an adhoc basis. The politician acts on behalf of individuals either because he is paid a bribe or because he is known to the aggrieved party, or because of caste considerations, or because of vote bank considerations. But he acts on an adhoc basis, not to improve the system as a whole, but to dispense justice to individuals. This way he keeps his powers intact. Alternatively, where groups have strengths in numbers, they come out forming mobs, disrupting day to day life and forcing things their way through their sheer power of numbers.

The politicians knew that they could not afford to antagonize the mob, as the mob could physically harm them so they acceded to the demands of the mob, justified or unjustified. Dev and Neil talked about this all during the first few weeks of Dev's arrival in Indore.

"I have often wondered why the landscape of Indian cities like Indore looks so different from urban areas almost anywhere else in the world. The animals on the streets, the little kiosks covering the entire roadsides and even some roads, the complete lack of traffic laws, and trash everywhere makes it uniquely Indian. Now I understand. It's all by design and all to serve the mafia's vested interest," said Dev.

"Correct. As I see it, you have a choice, Dev. You can decide to become part of the system or you can fight the system. Fighting the system in India is next to impossible. You will ruin your health, lose your money, have no peace of mind and ruin your social and family life if you fight the system," said Neil.

"When you say, 'become part of the system,' what exactly would I have to do?" asked Dev.

"We have talked about it. You know, bribe when necessary, suck up to politicians when necessary, start your own business and grab resources whenever and however you can, regardless of what is right or wrong. You have to get this distinction between right and wrong completely out of your mind. No morality, please," said Neil.

"Yeah, and then be a kiss-up-and-kick-down kind of person too. Suck up to the guys who have more power and money than me and lord over people who have less," said Dev, smiling.

"Exactly, and only then do you have a chance to survive. Many people are willing to do all this and they still don't survive, it's so competitive. But with your family background and brains, Dev, you could do very well if you make peace with the system. The land mafias of Indore in general will be honored to have you join them," said Neil.

"You have a great family background and I don't see you doing very well, Neil," said Dev.

Neil looked up and smiled but he didn't respond.

"Yeah, I know. You try to fight the system. You never did tell me, what are you doing these days? I mean to make money," said Dev.

"I do private tutoring. I teach English and Math, and sometimes Science too," said Neil.

"I should have figured. You were always a great student and your father was the best teacher I ever had. Like father, like son. I am sure you are very good at it, but does it make you enough money to be comfortable?" asked Dev.

"Well, I have very limited needs, unlike you, Dev. I manage, although barely," said Neil.

"Stop pulling my leg, Neil. I thought you were my friend," said Dev.

"I didn't mean anything. You have always been a big spender, Dev. Correction—a big spender in relation to your income I meant," said Neil.

"No, I didn't mean that. I meant, a friend would not advise a friend to become corrupt. You recommended that I become a part of this system. You think I don't have the moral foundation and the strength to fight?" asked Dev.

"Not at all. I would never think that of any Bapna, least of all you. It's just that when it comes to you and me, I even forget you are a Bapna. I only know you as Dev. I would not be able to stand to see you get hurt every minute of every day. That's what is gonna happen if you fight the system here, Dev," said Neil.

"Relax, I am not going to be taking up arms against the system, Neil. I am just not going to bribe or pay obeisance to politicians, that's all," said Dev.

"I know. In some ways, it's easier to take up arms than to fight that way. But be that as it may, I know you will fight, so I won't dissuade you anymore. I just hope that after you have given it your best shot you will go back to America before you totally destroy yourself and your family. Deal?" said Neil.

"No deal", said Dev.

⊷⊶

Dev's gate had not yet been fixed. It had been over a month since his arrival in Indore and every blacksmith had been scared off by the slumlords. Early one morning a slender young man with movie-star looks came to visit Dev. His name was Bandook Khan and he was another childhood friend of Dev's. He and Dev used to go hunting together as teenagers and Bandook Khan was an excellent marksman. Bandook Khan embraced Dev warmly and complained that Dev had been in Indore a month and had not contacted him.

"I heard it through the grapevine that you are in Indore, Janaab," said Bandook Khan.

"Yeah, I am sorry. I had too many things on my mind, Bandook. I was going to call you once things eased up for me a bit," said Dev

"What's wrong? Anything I can do to help?" asked Bandook Khan.

"Thanks, but I don't think there is anything you will be able to do," said Dev and he went on to explain how he had not been able to find one blacksmith in Indore who could fix one broken gate at his house without getting intimidated by the land mafia who had designs on his house.

"You are in luck, Janaab. Your gate will be fixed before sundown this evening," said Bandook Khan.

Dev looked at Bandook Khan questioningly.

"As luck would have it, Dev, yours truly is in the gunsmithing and blacksmithing business, and everyone in Indore knows that Bandook Khan is one crazy SOB. He doesn't get intimidated by anybody," said Bandook Khan.

"I don't think I want to be responsible for my friends getting hurt, Bandook," said Dev.

"Don't worry. I won't get hurt," said Bandook Khan as he got up and headed towards the main gate to inspect it.

"Someone has jammed the hinges, Dev. It won't take very long to fix. I will be back in an hour," said Bandook Khan as he climbed into his 1940s Willy's Jeep and pulled off.

In less than an hour, Dev saw a caravan of six or seven jeeps pull up on to Dev's driveway. Out came about a dozen people from every jeep and there formed a crowd of more than fifty people. They were all wearing white *salwars* and *kameez*, traditional Afghan Muslim attire. They were carrying hockey sticks, metal pipes and baton-like sticks. Dev noticed Bandook Khan instructing the men to take positions along the perimeter of Dev's lot. He then escorted a guy pushing a cart that held an electric welding machine towards Dev's main gate. Bandook Khan, along with three of his assistants, started working on the gate and after a couple of hours of expert blacksmithing Dev's gate was fixed. Not a single hood came forward from across the street to disrupt the repair work or to threaten Bandook Khan. The slumlords knew that they had met their match in Bandook Khan, who had merely increased the cost of disrupting the work for them to unacceptable levels. A blatant street fight involving hundreds of men would have been something even the politicians would have a hard time explaining.

"*Khuda Hafiz*," said Bandook Khan, smiling broadly as he took leave of Dev, adding, "*Khuda aapki hifazat kare*", meaning "May the good Lord protect you."

Dev then hired an ex-military man as a security guard who would sit at the main gate all day long, controlling who could come inside the Bapna family house and lot. Hira and Natu were no longer fixtures under the mango tree of Dev's lot.

※ ※

Dev kept writing letters and petitions to several concerned government departments and bureaucrats, asking to have the illegal encroachments around his boundary wall removed. The efforts yielded no results. One evening, after tennis, Dev and Neil met to have dinner together at the club.

"So, have you thought about what you are going to do for work, Dev?" asked Neil.

"I dunno. I can start a software development company. That's the only thing I know," reasoned Dev.

"Software in Indore still is a rather strange concept. Companies are not yet going for computerization in a big way. There may be opportunities within the state and local governments, but then again, you would have to bribe them to get contracts", said Neil.

"What then?" asked Dev.

"I dunno. Why don't you get into media? You know, one of the biggest problems in India in general, and Indore in particular is that the media is corrupt. The newspapers who are supposed to be the watchdogs in a democracy are all being used by their owners to extort money and build their own little empires. They don't print the truth and they have allied themselves with the ruling mafias," said Neil.

"And you want me to establish a new, honest media outlet?" asked Dev.

"I do," said Neil.

"Where am I supposed to get the money? Starting a newspaper is extremely expensive and risky," exclaimed Dev.

"I have been thinking. I know these two guys who are running the local Indore branch of a national cable network called InCablenet. They are quite idealistic and clean and they may be willing to rent out a local channel to us at a reasonable rent. We could run it as our own local news channel," said Neil.

"Not bad. Perhaps we could even run it as a combination news and entertainment channel. We could even promote local artists and produce local entertainment shows, even local soap operas," said Dev.

"Cool. So you want me to set up a meeting?" asked Neil.

"Go for it," said Dev.

The men who ran the Indore branch of Incablenet were called Tito and Shakir. They were guys from the rough and tumble cable industry, but Dev was pleasantly surprised at how clean and idealistic they were. They were rarities in Indore whose conscience was still alive. They were sufficiently impressed with Dev's ideas of establishing an honest news channel. They had no reason to doubt Dev's sincerity since he came from a family that only had honesty and integrity as its claim to fame. Tito and Shakir agreed to rent out a channel to Dev and Neil at a very reasonable price of approximately $1000 per month.

Dev and Neil set about in earnest, establishing their channel. They faced many challenges—chief among them was to find honest reporters. Dev wanted to do a lot of investigative reporting but reporters working in Indore did not have the backbone to go against the politicos and the mafia. Reporters had gotten into a habit of charging money to cover events, and therefore real news never got published or aired. Dev wanted to change all of that. He found that reporters were either corrupt or scared. Over time, Dev hired journalism students from the local university, leveraging the fearlessness of their youth and grooming them into solid investigative reporters. The channel named "TV-One" soon became very popular in Indore and advertising revenues climbed to where the channel even showed a small profit.

The four years that Dev and Neil ran TV-One was another period of education for Dev. These years opened Dev's eyes to how insidious and dark Indore had become. Dev had arrived in Indore as an idealistic young man with great hopes to serve his hometown, following in his grandfather's footsteps. He felt a tremendous ownership interest in Indore. After all, it was his ancestors who had put in great efforts and performed great personal sacrifices to build the city up for almost seventy years. Through various communications he had had with his grandfather before his death and friends since, Dev had known that Indore had declined greatly since the late 1970s, but he had no idea how low it had fallen until he started his TV channel.

Corruption was rampant. Nothing got done without money exchanging hands and the entire government machinery had become callous to the point of becoming inhuman. Some say this reflected the inhumanity of the Indore society as a whole, while others blamed the government for turning the population into an uncaring lot. It was a classic "chicken or the egg" story. Every area of life had become toxic. Doctors swindled patients by ordering unnecessary tests and even extorted money from relatives while leaving patients all cut up on the operating table. Lawyers acted as brokers for the judges, arranging payoffs to settle cases in courts. Lawyers also routinely sold out their less affluent clients by accepting money from the opposing more affluent parties.

Hundreds and thousands of middle-class families who were not connected to the mafia were hounded out of their homes and lots by the land mafia, with no police, no courts and no press raising a finger to help them. Massive amounts of government funds were being embezzled by a nexus of unscrupulous business people and politicians. Even the Indian prime minister, Rajiv Gandhi, was quoted as saying that "In India, only five cents on every dollar earmarked for development actually ends up being spent for its intended purpose; the rest goes in corruption." In Indore it may even be as low as two cents.

Individual politicians, businessmen and mafia figures had amassed obscene amounts of money, easily worth hundreds of millions dollars each. There was a massive underground economy and practically no culture of paying a fair share in taxes. Only the salaried class paid their fair share, as their taxes were deducted at the source.

All of these things combined to create a society where there was no sense of community and everybody was in it for themselves. Essentially, law of the jungle prevailed. As a result, the entire city looked like a slum and a landfill.

One time Dev invited a prominent politician in town to TV-One's popular noon time talk show, for an interview. His name was Karl

Vargese and he was an up and coming star in his party on the state and even the national scene. He also happened to be a classmate of Dev's when they both attended St. Paul Elementary School in the early 70s, before Dev transferred to Daly College. Karl was very politically correct on the air, sounding very idealistic with all the platitudes about helping poor people and so on. He stayed back at Dev's place for a visit, after the shooting for the show was complete.

"You sounded very inspiring on TV, Karl. I am impressed." said Dev, welcoming Karl into his private study.

"It feels good to spend some time with you, Dev, after…what, thirty years?" said Karl warmly.

"Yes, it has been a long time. You seem to have done real well in politics." said Dev.

"Not too shabby, uh. For a son of a poor millworker to now be a minister in the provincial government." said Karl proudly.

"Yeah, I hear you. The opposition party is so threatened by you that my reporters tell me, they are gunning for you." said Dev.

"Nah…Dev, I feel in this house, I can relax and tell the truth. We are great friends with the opposition leaders. It's a small community and we are all in it together. In fact, it was Tiwari, the opposition leader who showed me the ropes on how to open and operate a Swiss bank account without getting caught and how to route money through Mauritius." said Karl.

"No kidding. So the rumors are true. That you are worth a hundred million dollars – American." inquired Dev.

Karl leaned forward, smiled brightly and whispered, "*several hundred million, and I am not done yet!*"

Dev was speechless. Sensing Dev's shock, Karl leaned back on his chair and took a sip of his iced coffee, which is called "cold" coffee in India.

"We have to do all this in politics, Dev. These are not the same times as when your family was in power. We can't survive in politics, if we don't have that kind of money to spend during elections. I take a 20% cut on all deals that go through my department and of course, I run my own land organization," said Karl.

Dev knew very well that by "land organization", Karl meant "land mafia". This hit a raw nerve with Dev.

"To be honest, Karl, I could never have imagined this about you," said Dev.

"Why? Just because I am your friend. Everyone in politics does this. Our party members, opposition party members, everyone in politics. We have to do this to survive. I am merely a regional leader so far. If I have to get to the national stage, I have to have billions-to be in the big leagues." said Karl

"Well, I don't know what to think. My mind is spinning right now." said Dev.

"Don't tell me, this is coming as a surprise for you. You are running a news channel for Christ's sake. Why do you think no middle class person ever wins any elections and the same people keep winning over and over again? This is the reason dynastic politics is so common in India. People in politics have accumulated all this money and created political dynasties. From father to son to grandson and so on. You think people keep voting for these families because they do good work? It's all based on money. Votes are bought these days. I was fortunate to have the financial support of Dayal, the famous land dealer, without who's money I could never have won the first time. Don't your reporters tell you anything?" said Karl.

"No, as you know, the channel just started a couple of months ago. Perhaps, I need better reporters. So, tell me, all these national political leaders in India, the big guys-they all have billions of dollars?" asked Dev.

"Of course. These billions are all stashed away in Swiss bank accounts or in offshore havens such as Mauritius and St. Kitts. You are not going to put this on TV, Dev, are you? This is off the record, you know." said Karl.

"Rest assured, this is off the record, don't worry, Karl. So what about these serious problems we face as a country, as a state, as a city? Who will solve these?" said Dev.

Karl breathed a deep sigh of relief.

"You seriously think anyone of us can really solve these public problems. Everyone is in it for himself, Dev. You have been around the world a few times, you know that," said Karl.

"I see." is all Dev could say.

Karl now turned to Dev and looked at him cagily.

"So, now that you have this media outlet, you and I can form a team and we can mint money together. Media is very important these days "said Karl.

"How exactly?" asked Dev.

"You are really naïve, Dev, aren't you? America seems to have retarded your brain. There are so many ways one can make money owning a media outlet such as your TV-One. We can threaten to expose people and ask them to pay up. Or we can put pressure on certain reluctant bureaucrats and policemen who are on the honesty trip and get them to look the other way, while we occupy certain prime lands-both government lands and private lands. We can directly take money from individual politicians to give them good coverage. I can go on and on and on." said Karl.

"No thanks Karl, and since you shared so many of your secrets with me, I should also speak my mind. I can't believe you will come here, to Bapna House, fully knowing this house's heritage and long history of honesty and integrity and make this cheap attempt to corrupt me. How could you ever think that I would go for a proposition like that. How dare you even say something like that to me, and say such a thing sitting inside my grandfather and great grandfather's house. You forgot that when you were a poor, young kid, who didn't even have shoes on your feet, when everyone else used to treat you shabbily, it was this house that welcomed you as an equal and with respect. You want to corrupt this house too? Have you no shame whatsoever? You can shove all your millions and billions up your "you know where". You will never have enough money to be able to compromise the integrity of this house." said Dev seething with anger.

Karl went all red. He stood up, turned around and started to walk out of the Bapna House compound. Then he stopped and walked back.

"I thought I was being a good friend. In India it is not easy to make money. You will find the going very tough. I tried to help you out by showing you a sure way to becoming a very wealthy person. You have responded by insulting me," said Karl in a hoarse whisper, his eyes all red and watery.

Then he pointed to the outside of the house and said "no one, no one out there, who I would make this offer to, would turn it down. People say your grandfather was a fool. They say your great grandfather was a fool too, for not making any money. Now I know it runs in the genes. You are a bigger fool. You don't even have their exalted position and now you have given up a chance of a lifetime. I have no use for such fools, Dev. Good bye," said Karl as he finally turned around and walked out of Bapna House.

Dev later checked with Neil, if what Karl had said was true about politicians having so much money. Neil too looked at Dev as if he had just landed from Mars.

"Of course, it is true. Every aware person in India knows the staggering sums of money these politicians have stashed away offshore and the role of money in elections." said Neil.

Dev and Neil exposed many scandals and did story after story, pointing out these outrages. They also used their channel to air serious, thought-provoking shows, trying to awaken a sleeping population.

One Sunday Dev received a phone call from a friend that their mutual friend Christopher Seth had been in an auto accident the previous evening about fifty miles outside of Indore near some village. He had just arrived at Apollo Hospital in Indore. Dev went to see him at the hospital. Christopher and his wife were both injured and in the same hospital suite.

Christopher had several broken ribs and Sheila, his wife, had a broken foot. Dev found out that Christopher and his wife Sheila were driving back from Pune after visiting their daughter there and a truck hit the car from behind. The truck driver didn't bother to stop and sped off. The car skidded into a nearby field and came to a halt. Both Christopher and his wife were in excruciating pain, not to mention in utter shock. A few minutes later the local villagers gathered around the car and Christopher thought that help was imminent, but the first thing the villagers did was pry open the car door and steal everything of value. Before they knew it, Christopher's wallet, Sheila's purse, their camera, their watches and jewelry that they were wearing were all gone. Then the villagers just stood around and waited, rather than helping them. Christopher and Sheila kept asking for water and some medical assistance but none of the villagers made a move to help them. Finally one of the villagers stepped forward and demanded money in exchange for help such as providing drinking water. Fortunately, a group of college students were driving by and noticed a crowd of people and a wrecked car and they stopped to see what was going on. They quickly transported both Christopher and Sheila to the hospital in Indore.

Dev was shocked to hear Christopher tell this story. He kept asking him if he was exaggerating what happened. Other common friends present in the room told Dev that this was a very common occurrence in India and these days it was a perfectly acceptable thing to steal and extort money even from injured people and no one was shocked by such events anymore.

How low have we sunk as a people? thought Dev, shaking his head in disbelief.

Dev was baffled at how dirty the public areas in Indore were when he first returned. After listening to Christopher's story and several other true, shocking stories like that, he concluded that all the outward filth was a manifestation of some deep malaise inside people's hearts. The people of Indore had sick souls, and the worst part was that no one even realized that this sickness existed. People seemed to be living in denial, with very few people even acknowledging that something serious was wrong and required a radical change in direction. True to what Neil had told him, Dev felt tormented every minute of every day that he spent in Indore, watching the city built by his ancestors in such sorry state. He could have dealt with the crumbling physical infra-structure and even the trash strewn across the whole city, but he could never accept the filth inside people's souls.

TV-One gave Dev and Neil enough clout that the civil service officers brokered a deal between them and the land mafia to get the encroachments outside their respective houses removed. Neil's private property, which was also encroached, was released by the land mafia. Neil quickly took advantage of the situation and sold his property and rented a large apartment in a relatively safe complex. Dev, on the other hand, was much too sentimental about his ancestral house and decided to keep it. Despite all of his media clout, the land mafia kept up the pressure on Dev all the time, wasting no opportunity to make repeated attempts to re-encroach outside Dev's house. Dev was fortunate that he was always able to find that one honest officer, either in the civil service or the police, who would provide just enough protection to Dev to prevent any slumming, at least immediately outside Dev's house.

TV-One started operations in 2001 and was on the upswing until 2004, when Dev and Neil had a head-on confrontation with the land mafia. Among the many stories TV-One covered, exposing the land mafia was an ongoing theme. Dev and Neil left no stone unturned to unearth evidence of wrongdoing by the land mafia in Indore and airing it via effective and polished in-house production. The land mafia, politicians, and the powers-that-be, were looking for an opportunity to strike a decisive retaliatory blow at TV-One. They got their opportunity when Neil stumbled upon the story of a women's shelter in Indore.

It was an ngo-run women's shelter called "hostels" in India. Its director was a middle-aged woman who looked and behaved like a bureaucrat, as she was reported to have close connections with high government officials and politicians. She was called the "matron" by her staff and the women who lived at the shelter. The shelter was meant to house women who had been abused by their husbands or in-laws. One evening a young woman came into the TV-One office which was on the first floor of Bapna House. She found Neil and told him an unbelievable story of how the matron was running this abused women's shelter like a brothel. Every evening, members of prominent political and mafia families of Indore would send their cars to have women from the shelter picked up for a night of entertainment.

Neil quickly arranged to have a cameraman assigned to take footage of every car that parked outside the shelter after sunset along with the license plate numbers clearly visible. The cameraman surreptitiously filmed for one whole week. Neil then cross-checked the license plate numbers and identified the car owners. He then aired the footage, showing each car, its license plate number and the name of the owner. The list of owners was a who's-who of Indore's powerful political and mafia establishment. Neil and Dev started getting phone calls from the representatives of the car owners in attempts to dissuade further airing of that story. Neil took it upon himself to air the story every hour on the hour for the whole week. The news story took Indore by storm. The entire political establishment across party lines had now lined up against Dev and Neil. They put pressure on the cable network, InCablenet, to cancel TV-One's lease. Tito and Shakir, the local bosses of Incablenet, flatly refused and backed the story to the hilt.

The politicians then went over their heads to the national management of InCablenet in Bombay and offered to pay up to ten times the rent if Incablenet would simply cancel TV-One's lease and rent out the channel to the politicians instead. InCablenet's national management fired Tito and Shakir and promptly cancelled TV-One's lease. On November 1 2004, TV-One went off the air, after a successful four-year run. Dev and Neil were now without any protection and were prime targets in Indore.

On Monday, Dec 13, 2004, Dev and Neil played tennis together at Yeshwant Club. Dev had noticed that Neil was terribly quiet the last several days and was probably suffering from mild depression.

He tried to spend as much time as possible with Neil so Neil would feel supported. That evening, after tennis, Dev offered to meet Neil for dinner at the club at 8:00 PM. Neil nodded his agreement and they parted after showering and changing.

Dev reached the club at 8:05 PM. He waited until 8:15 PM and there was no sign of Neil. Dev asked the captain to get him a phone inside the club restaurant. He called Neil and a staffer answered the phone, saying that something had happened and Neil had been taken to the hospital and the rest of the family was also at the hospital.

The normally hardy Dev started having a panic attack. He stormed out of the club and asked his driver to take him immediately to the hospital. It was a short ride of less than ten minutes to Apollo Hospital, but Dev had more panic attacks and acute pain in his abdomen. At one point he rolled down the car window and threw up. They reached the hospital and Dev climbed up the steps to the private suite section. There he saw Neil's mother and wife, literally wailing and surrounded by other relatives. Dev rushed to their side and Neil's mother fell into Dev's arms, sobbing uncontrollably. Dev felt numb and became disoriented. Neil's cousin tried to explain something to Dev but he barely comprehended what was being said.

A couple of hours later, when Dev calmed down enough to understand what was going on, he found out that Neil had gotten dressed to meet Dev for dinner at around 8:00 PM, then he went back into his bedroom and didn't come out for several minutes. Realizing he was going to be late for his dinner meeting, Neil's wife went towards the bedroom to see what was holding Neil up. The bedroom door was locked from the inside. His wife knocked a few times and got no answer. She then called Neil's cousin, who happened to be there, and they broke open the door. They found Neil's dead body hanging from the ceiling fan. He had hanged himself. Dev noticed that Neil's wife and mother were sitting on the floor, leaning against the wall. They seem to have gone into shock. He also noticed Neil's eight-year-old son and six-year-old daughter standing on either side of their mother, cowering in fear. Dev was also in shock. He didn't know what to do. Then he saw Selena and his own parents enter the area and approach him. Selena held Dev's hands, trying to console him. Dev's parents went over to Neil's mother and wife and started to care for them.

The next few days were surreal for Dev. He was in a daze and he couldn't walk, he couldn't eat, he couldn't even move. He refused to get out of bed and had to be forced to get up by Selena to attend Neil's funeral. He broke down like a child when the funeral pyre was lit. Dev felt like his heart had been brutally pulled out of his body.

Dev blamed himself completely for what happened to Neil. *I should have known. I should have planned to never leave him alone, not even for a minute*, he thought. "If I had not come back to Indore from America, this would never have happened," he said out aloud. Dev was still not himself for several days after that. He felt tremendously guilty for being alive, while Neil was dead. *He was more sensitive than me. He was a better man. He couldn't live amidst all this darkness, while I still can*, he thought.

One day Neil's mother and wife, and their two children went over to Bapna House. After visiting with Ram Singh and Damayanti they were shown into Dev's bedroom by Selena. Neil's mother walked over to Dev, who was sitting listlessly on his bed, dressed in a night suit, propped up by pillows. She took Dev in her arms and the two cried for several minutes, then she wiped her own tears and gently and deliberately wiped Dev's tears. Without saying another word, she stood up, kissed Dev's forehead and walked out of his room, followed by her daughter-in-law and grandchildren. Dev caught up with them just as they were about to exit the house. He took both of Neil's children in his arms and held them tightly. He made a silent compact with the children as he held them.

"You are my responsibility now. I will make sure you are all right," said Dev softly. He then released the kids to Neil's wife and walked back into his room.

It took Dev another six months to get back to some semblance of normalcy. He and everybody around him knew that he would never be the same Dev again, without Neil. Slowly, Selena started to bring up the topic of "What's next?" with Dev. The land mafia continued to breathe down Dev's neck, making frequent attempts to grab his house. Dev had by now spent about five years in Indore, and he had renewed and built new relationships. These relationships helped him thwart these grabbing attempts, but barely. He and the entire Bapna family still felt quite insecure and vulnerable.

"What are we going to do next?" asked Selena.

"I dunno. Maybe I will start another business," said Dev.

"We are out of money. Our kids are growing up. We need some minimal stability and quiet," said Selena.

Dev said nothing.

"I think we should go back to the States," said Selena.

Dev glared at Selena. "And betray my friend's memory? Neil died fighting for a cause. As it is, I feel guilty that I am alive. Now I should run away?" he spat out.

"You are not running away. Look at yourself. You don't have any resources left to fight with. You don't have any money left to fight with. At this point, you don't even have the will to fight. You need to regroup, regain your strength and then continue your fight. You can only regroup in the States. They won't let you rise again here," said Selena.

"I will not run away and I will never sell my ancestral home. I will not allow them to hound us Bapnas out of the city we built. That would be the sign of ultimate defeat," said Dev.

"Ok, don't sell the house. But as a family, we do need to have some financial security and some mental stability as well. I am afraid if we stay here we will all be destroyed. Neither our house nor our family will survive. Would you want that?" asked Selena.

Dev kept resisting, but Selena kept insisting, until one day in early 2006 it dawned on Dev that Selena was right. He had started noticing that his son, Kunal, was picking up certain aspects of Indore culture that Dev abhorred. He immediately announced to his family and friends that they were moving back to the US. Everybody cheered, knowing fully well that Dev needed a much healthier environment to regain his financial and emotional health. Ultimately, Dev could not stay in denial. He finally came to the conclusion that as bad as Corporate America was, all the negatives of America put together didn't come close to the totally perverted sick society India had become. For the first time in his life he thought of Washington as home and was very pleased to board the flight which was to take him and his family back to America.

He and Selena did agree that in view of his parents advancing age, Dev being the only child, would spend several months a year in Indore, taking care of his parents, while Selena would take care of the house and the kids in Washington. This meant sacrifices as far as his career went, but Selena and Dev decided to make that compromise.

It was during one of those visits to Indore that in October, 2010, the land mafia finally was able to successfully orchestrate a vicious mob attack on Dev in their most lethal attempt yet to take over Bapna House.

※

"Wow! What a story! I only knew bits and pieces of this, but I would have never gleaned the whole story by myself," said Ranika.

"Incredible," said Kunal.

"So, Papa, tell me something. We had so many illustrious ancestors, starting with Deoraj, then Seth Guman Chand, Seth Zorawarmal, Seth Chhogmal, Sir Siremal and PS Sab. How would you rate yourself? Would you say you are a success?" asked Ranika.

"Shut up, Ranika!" said Kunal.

"No, No. It's a legitimate question. Something I have been thinking about myself since I got out of the hospital. I have always chastised myself for clearly not having the positive impact on the world like our ancestors that you have named. And not that I want to make any excuses, but..." said Dev, trying very hard to conceal from his children the great physical pain he was in.

"But?" asked Ranika.

Dev appeared very tired and drained. He looked Ranika straight in her eyes and with a great deal of effort said, "How about if I answer that question tomorrow? I am very tired right now."

"Sure thing, Papa. You sleep well, okay?" said Ranika as she bent down to kiss Dev on his forehead.

Kunal lingered around a little longer, which was unusual for him, and just kept looking at his father as he tried to sleep, breathing a little heavily. He then touched Dev gently on his shoulders and walked out of the room, turning off the lights.

※

Kunal and Selena woke up early as usual the next morning. Dev normally slept till later in the morning, waking up closer to 10:00 AM.

"Papa finished telling us his story last night. I found it fascinating, Mom," said Kunal.

"Yeah, you were up till very late last night. I could still hear Dev talking when I got up to get a drink of water. It must have been close to 2:00 AM," said Selena.

"Yeah, we lost track of time. Ranika kept asking him if he thought he was a success, considering how hugely successful our forefathers were," said Kunal.

Selena smiled at the impetuousness of her daughter.

"What was his response?" asked Selena.

"Oh, he was exhausted by then and looking somewhat ill. He said he would give an answer today," said Kunal.

"Yeah, he has been looking really ill last few days. You guys should really give him a break and not do late nights," said Selena.

"Good morning," said Ranika as she entered the room.

"Good morning," said Selena. "I hear you gave your father a hard time last night, asking him if he considered himself a success."

"Yeah, and he is supposed to tell us today whether he thinks he is a success or not," said Ranika. "It's already closing in on 11:00 AM. It's late, even for Papa. I will go wake him up."

"Hey, wait!" said Selena, but Ranika had already disappeared into Dev's bedroom, which was adjacent to the family room in their small suburban Washington home.

Very shortly thereafter, Selena and Kunal heard Ranika's jubilant cries. "Mom! Kunal! Come here fast!"

Both Selena and Kunal dashed towards Dev's bedroom. They found Dev up and about, full of energy, almost as if he had never been sick. He had a twinkle in his eye and a glow on his face. "I have the answer to your question, now Ranika," he said confidently. "My life is not over yet. The second chapter is just beginning. Whether I am as big a success as my ancestors or not, will from now on, depend not only upon me and my actions going forward, but also upon you two. My success will be your success and my failure, yours. Just as we inherit all our ancestor's successes and failings, we are, after all, a Perennial Stream- a stream that never ends, ", he concluded by pointing to "Deoraj's ring", on his finger.

Author's Notes

This is a story of the Bapna family. It is made up of many stories, but there is a common theme that runs through each one of the stories that glues all the stories together. I did not create this story or these series of stories; I grew up with them. These are the stories of several generations of my family. These are also the stories of the times and places that the family lived in and continues to live in.

So where did I find these stories? Are they true? Yes, these stories are true stories. This is a historical family. Each of the major figures in this book was a historical figure. By historical figures I mean that there is a record of them in history books, newspapers and/or on internet archives. While the history books talk about the historical significance of the Bapna family and each of the individuals within the family, they mainly discuss their public lives and how they conducted themselves in the public arena. There is very little information in historical record of how the family and the family members lived and conducted themselves in their personal lives. For that I relied on our family folklore, which came down from generation to generation via the oral tradition and family's collective institutional memory.

Growing up, I remember my grandparents, great uncles, great aunts, elderly relatives—close and distant, elderly friends of the family, and even a family staffer or two tell me bits and pieces of these stories. No one ever sat down and told me an entire story or even a small cohesive piece of a larger story, but I picked up little portions. Most of these stories naturally came up for discussion in family gatherings-- big and small, either in the context of a contemporary situation which triggered a particular memory in someone or as a background for a family discussion. A lot of these fragments came from my grandparents, who told these to me as inspirational tales which were a part of my upbringing. A few of the stories, particularly stories of Deoraj and Guman Chand, have come down largely through family folklore. There is very little historical record of these particular stories themselves, although there is some. Their stories did not come down through generations as complete stories, and in some places I have had to use my imagination to fill in the blanks. Therefore, while I cannot claim that each and every dialogue or each and every interaction or every minor detail in this story are true; they are not. One significant fact in the book is un-aunthenticated and relies solely on a family member's interview. Therefore, it can be considered of dubious credibility, considering that Paliwals very rarely married outside their community. This is the fact of Guman Chand's wife being a Paliwal Brahmin. I thought about it a lot and chose to leave this folklore in, in order to make a larger true point, which is that not only was there an extra-ordinary level of cooperation and closeness between the Oswals in Jaisalmer and the Paliwals, but even more closeness between the Bapna family and certain Paliwal families. All said and done, however, the larger thrust of the story, the major events, the essential spirit of the story, are all true. Therefore, I have no hesitation in placing this book in the non-fiction category. The readers are free to make up their own minds, based on what I have said in this author's note, on the extensive bibliography at the end of this book containing in excess of forty sources, and other facts that some readers themselves may be aware of, as to whether this book is pure non-fiction or a novel based largely on a true story. My view is that I have done extensive research and I have attempted to stay as true to the facts and the research, as I could be and in those cases where there were gaps, I did my best to fill them with the most credible information that I could uncover.

At one level this is also a love story, or many love stories. It is one long and continuous story of love that family members had for each other and for their children and future generations. They exhibited this love by establishing a strong value system and by constantly struggling to live by it through adversity and good times, while constantly seeking to improve upon the already solid values established by Deoraj, the founder of the Bapna dynasty. There were times when each family patriarch had to make some extremely difficult and painful decisions to preserve and retain not only the family honor, but the highest ideals of humanity. There were even times when the ultimate sacrifice was required and made, as in the case of Seth Chhogmal, so the right values and messages would be passed down to the succeeding generations. These individuals would not have made these sacrifices unless they had deep and unconditional love for their children and humanity as a whole. This is also a love story of the romantic kind. The dynasty could not have founded without the pure emotional connection between Deoraj and Bhairavi and Guman Chand and Jeta and others down the line.

At another level, this is also a story of power. It is a story of how power, wealth and influence is attained in our larger human society; of the legitimacy of that power; of how it is used; of how it should be used; of the arrogance of power; of the responsibility that comes with power and how some acquit themselves well in the exercise of their power, while others do not. It is also a story of the rise and fall of various powers such as the British in India, the Rajput kingdoms of Jaisalmer and Mewar, the Maratha dynasties such as Holkar, and even the mighty Moghuls.

It is also a story of duty and a vision of how humanity can fully realize its potential. All patriarchs of the Bapna family, but Siremal and P.S., in particular, had a great sense of duty. They also envisioned humanity to live in harmonious and strong communities where each individual could develop all facets of his or her personality and not be a one-dimensional individual. They believed very strongly that human beings are special creatures of God and therefore are not put on this world merely to prey, like other animals, but to develop and enjoy the multitudes of capabilities granted to them such as music and arts, love and emotions, duty and sacrifice. So this is also a story of their struggles and sacrifices to realize this vision for all humanity.

Finally, this is a story of a constant struggle of all of humanity to find some dignity and meaning in each of our lives, as seen through the eyes of this one family. The Bapna family, from its earliest known ancestor, Deoraj, was very aware of this and has always been on a quest, a treasure hunt, for dignity. Each generation defined dignity in their own way, sought it to the exclusion of all else and mostly found it. The question is still open whether the current generation has found it. However, I would like to take this opportunity to put forward this generation's definition of dignity. Dignity to this generation of Bapnas, of course, means all the best human values such as fairness, justice, compassion and love, but also the idea of "meritocracy." It is a simple idea which conveys that each person gets a just and fair reward for their effort, regardless of who they are. Without creating a meritocracy among us, none of the other human values I mentioned above are possible. Therefore, this is also a story of the struggle of the present generations of Bapna family to seek dignity through merit.

While clearly the present generation of Bapnas have not distinguished themselves in the same way that several of our direct ancestors have, it would be fair to say that it has not been for lack of trying. There is an ancient concept illustrated in one of the most important scriptures in Hindu traditions, called the "Bhagawad Gita." The "Gita," as it is known in short, is famous, and among the many profound things it talks about is the concept of "Karma" and "Karma Bhumi." "Karma" essentially means that each person must not only think or philosophize, but also "act" as per their "dharma." In other words, a person must always be willing to act as per their duty and not be afraid or reticent or be lazy. "Karma Bhumi" is the physical location or place where a person should act. Therefore, it really is the physical location where a person chooses to live and/or exercise his or her influence. A person living in Seattle has Seattle as his "Karma Bhumi" and a person living in Washington has "Washington" as his "Karma Bhumi."

The "Karma Bhumi" of the Bapna family has shifted many times. Over the centuries they have had to migrate from Osian to Jaisalmer, to Udaipur, to Indore, and now in this generation to America. Each generation did its utmost to advance their "Karma Bhumi." The "Karma Bhumi" of this generation of the Bapnas is America. I live in the Washington DC area, and have been living here for almost thirty years. My primary interest now is enhancing my "Karma Bhumi," and I have never seen America in as much trouble as it is in right now (years 2008 through 2011, when I am writing this). Our economy is shaky, our foreign policy is directionless and our status in the world is declining. We face so many challenges, not the least of which is how we continue to live in dignity, how we continue to treat our elderly with dignity, how we continue to treat our minorities with dignity, and how we continue to treat our weak and poor with dignity.

The one value that the Bapna family brings with it to America is that the dignity of each individual amongst us, even the richest and the most powerful, is inexorably linked with the dignity of the least of us. In other words, until the least of us lives in dignity, none of us live in dignity. This is not something that the Bapna family has uniquely brought in; there are millions of Americans who I know of that already believe in this axiom. Then why do we still find ourselves talking about massive cuts in the programs for the elderly, not being able to afford healthcare for all and even cutting on essentials like defense, and education for our children? Part of the answer is because we are allowing ourselves to move away from the proposition that "dignity for the least of us is dignity for the most of us." Part of the answer also is because we legitimately cannot afford these programs. There can be no question that no matter how deeply we believe in these programs, if we cannot afford them, we cannot continue them.

So, we have to revive our economy. How do we do it? First, let us diagnose the problem. In my humble opinion, the problem is that over the years, corporate America moved away from a merit-based culture to a patronage-based culture. I have experienced it myself in my thirty years or so in corporate America. Most people I ran into were dissatisfied with their jobs, as they perceived their employers to be unjust and unfair to them. I fully acknowledge that this is anecdotal, based entirely on my personal experience and not based on any scientific study. I discuss this in the book in one of the chapters. I contend in the book that no amount of government action, no amount of any other steps, will restore our economic strength unless corporate America returns to meritocracy. It is only when we have a merit-based system that we will have justice, fairness and dignity for all. I leave the readers with one example of a meritocracy in recent times in America. It is an inspiring story and a true one.

Since the beginning of telecom, AT&T, or Bell Company as it was popularly known, essentially enjoyed a virtual monopoly in the US until the late 1970s. Americans who are normally staunch supporters of competition tolerated this monopoly out of deference to AT&T's founder, Alexander Graham Bell, the man widely regarded as the inventor of telephones. After all, if anyone has a right to enjoy a monopoly it is the founder, right? The Americans, though, were paying a heavy price for allowing AT&T this monopoly. First of all, Bell himself had been dead for decades and it was no longer a family-owned company, but a huge conglomerate controlling all telecommunications across the US. Lack of competition naturally resulted in very high tariffs and practically no advancement in technology in the telecom industry since the 1940s.

In 1979, most phones in the US were still rotary dial pulse phones--1940s technology. A coast-to-coast phone call was more than $2.50 a minute and sometimes even more, depending on the time of the call. Long distance phone calls were a big deal, even in a country as affluent as the US. Push button phones were expensive and considered quite avant-garde as late as 1979, akin to how an I-Phone would be regarded today. Steve Jobs and his Apple Computers had just unveiled Apple 1C, the first working personal computer, but networking technologies of computers were still quite primitive, largely because of lack of advancements in telecom technologies to support data transmission in a big way. Almost all the other countries in the world also had telecom monopolies, in most cases government telecom monopolies, because if it was okay for the US to have a telecom monopoly, other countries felt validated in having their own monopolies, so there were practically no advancements in telecom technologies around the world either.

In 1963, a telecommunications pioneer and innovative entrepreneur, John D. "Jack" Goeken and four friends founded Microwave Communications, Inc., better known as MCI, and began developing a microwave network. Goeken was introduced to telecommunications at an early age. He began a radio repair business in the back of a friend's vacuum cleaner shop while still in high school. Later, he furthered his knowledge in electronics as a microwave specialist in the Signal Corps of the US Army. Goeken ran into opposition from AT&T every step of the way as he attempted to develop his microwave network. He started fighting AT&T in the US Federal Communications Commission (FCC) and it became a long, drawn out battle. Five years later, in 1968, Goeken had still not been able to make much headway in his battle with AT&T. Goeken and MCI were practically broke and they needed infusion of new funds to continue fighting AT&T, now not only over at the FCC but also in the courts. It was a long-shot contest at best, with no one giving MCI much of a chance against a Goliath like AT&T.

Sometime in 1968, Goeken was introduced by a mutual friend to another brash entrepreneur by the name of Bill McGowan. McGowan was a big, gruff Irishman who had pulled himself up by his bootstraps. He was a venture capitalist, a self-made millionaire who owned several small companies, including a janitorial company that cleaned buildings in Manhattan. He had a larger-than-life personality and seemingly unlimited reserves of energy. He agreed to finance MCI in exchange for 25% of the stock, and the battle continued in the courts.

McGowan's gregarious and tenacious personality kept the MCI case alive in the FCC and in 1974, he and Goeken had some differences which led to Goeken giving up active management of MCI and McGowan assuming the responsibilities of the CEO. MCI, under McGowan, had some small victories in FCC until in late 1970s when MCI filed an anti-trust lawsuit against AT&T. McGowan again used his larger-than-life personality to convince the US Department of Justice to file its own anti-trust lawsuit against AT&T. The Justice Department's case was heavily dependent on the evidence gathered by MCI's legal team and as it turned out, they used most of that evidence. The trial started in 1981 in the courtroom of US District Court Judge, Herald D. Greene. In 1982, sensing defeat, AT&T agreed to settle the lawsuit out of court, essentially agreeing to everything MCI and the Justice Department wanted. It submitted a restructuring plan to the court, essentially breaking up AT&T into regional Bell Companies and providing equal access to MCI and other phone companies. Now MCI and other companies could have their customers access their networks by dialing 1+ from their phones.

The breakup of AT&T and Equal Access was a huge event, not only in telecom history but for the future of telecom and the computer industries. It was a great personal victory for MCI, Bill McGowan and Jack Geoken, but it also opened up the floodgates of technological innovation in the telecom industries in the 1980s and 1990s. Scores of telecom companies sprung up in the US and internationally, many countries opening up their telecom sectors to free competition. This resulted in an almost overnight drop in telecom tariffs. It also resulted in rapid advancement in technologies which resulted in a marriage between computers and telecom, culminating in computers becoming ubiquitous and the Internet becoming an integral part of the culture. It also resulted in worldwide innovation in cell phone technologies, changing the lives of billions of people around the world who are now connected. None of this could have happened without the vision, tenacity, perseverance of Jack Geoken and Bill McGowan, who put everything at risk for their dream.

This was a classic American story, only possible in America, where two Davids could take on a Goliath such as AT&T, fight it over almost two decades and then defeat it, resulting in hugely consequential evolution of human culture. An interesting fact to note is that in contrast to 1979, when a coast-to-coast long distance call could cost as much as $ 2.50 a minute, in 2011 the cost is less than one cent a minute, practically free. All of this can be attributed to giants like McGowan and Geoken. By 1984 MCI had quickly gone from being a bit player in the telecom industry to a five-billion-dollar behemoth, largely on the back of a lean mean corporate machine created by Bill McGowan at MCI. Until his death, MCI was as pure a meritocracy as one can realistically expect anywhere in the world.

Although he quit actively managing MCI in 1968, Jack Goeken continued to hold a significant portion of MCI stock. When AT&T finally broke up in the early 1980s, Goeken's stock holdings in MCI paid handsomely and he became a billionaire. He went on to found several other ground-breaking companies such as Airfone, Inflight Phone, FTD Mercury.

On June 2, 1992, Bill McGowan, the man who beat AT&T and revolutionized telecommunications, died at the age of 64. His successor, Bert Roberts, had been practically running the company since 1986 AD, when McGowan had his first heart attack, but just McGowan's presence had kept the dynamic culture that he had promoted alive and well at MCI. After his death, though, everything changed. Very quickly all the ills that plagued most of the rest of corporate America started creeping into MCI as well. MCI became a company where a system of patronage and personal fiefdoms replaced the meritocracy, so meticulously cultivated by McGowan. Eventually, MCI was taken over by another company called WorldCom.

On July 21, 2002, MCI, or WorldCom as it was called then, declared bankruptcy, the biggest in American corporate history till that date, a direct result, in my humble opinion, of the company's move away from meritocracy. Six years later, in 2008, a major economic earthquake shook America with the bankruptcy of corporate heavyweights like Lehman Brothers, AIG and several other financial institutions. Again, I feel, a lack of meritocracy in these companies was a major factor in the collapse of the American financial system.

I hope Americans can coalesce around the idea of restoring meritocracy within our society. Meritocracy is as much a means as an end. Every person should get their just and fair reward. It is a very American concept, one of the precepts that America was built on. Restoring it will also create wealth, which will enable us, as a society, to do our duty, to take care of the least among us. When we do that, we impart dignity not only to them, but also to all humans. I certainly will work wholeheartedly towards that goal, to continue my family tradition of being on a continuous quest for dignity. As a member of this generation of the Bapna family, I endeavor to seek dignity for myself and for all through an emphasis on meritocracy in my latest "Karma Bhumi"—America.

Lastly, for the record, in some cases, I have not used the real names of certain characters, to protect their privacy as most of these are still alive. The characters whose real names are not used in the book are Ram Singh, Damayanti, Kunal, Ranika, Salena, Agnetha, Laurie, Camilla, Samir Dada, Khondakar Imran, Suraj Singh, Tara Singh, Neil(deceased), Karl Verghese, Christopher and Sheila Seth, and the narrator, Dev. Bhandari Baldeo Raj is also a changed name for an actual historical figure, although he is long dead.

Penn Bobby Singh
September 2014

Glossary

Aangi: An armor for a religious idol normally made of precious metals and precious stones submitted to the God represented by the idol by either a king or a nobleman

Acharya: A religious teacher or a religious scholar

Adaab: A respectful greeting in Urdu language

Ajark: A shawl or outerwear with bright colors and designs native to Sind region of undivided India

Apfelsaft: Apple juice with gentle bubbles available in Switzerland

Atithi Devo Bhava: An old cultural tradition in India where a guest is treated the same as God

Ba'aSab: Grandfather

Baba: Father

Babu: A bureaucrat

Bahut Bada Admi: A very important person

Banjara: A nomadic tribe in Western Rajasthan which makes a living rearing cattle and famous for its folk singing and dancing

Basra Pearls: Pearls that originated in the Persian Gulf city of Basra, considered the finest and rarest in the world

Bhabhisa: Brother's wife

Bidai: In Indian tradition, when the girl leaves the father's home for the first time after marriage. It is a very emotional ceremony.

Baithak: The living room or the drawing room

Chamundi Mata: Goddess of War in Rajasthani tradition

Choli: A Midriff-baring blouse shell garment with cut out backs worn in Rajasthan

Churidar: Skin tight trousers worn both by men and women in Rajasthan

Devi: Sanskrit word for Goddess

Devata: Sanskrit word for a male deity

Dholnis: Dancing women from the Mewar state in Rajasthan where the city of Udaipur is located

Dhoti: Unstitched cloth wrapped around the waist and legs, about seven yards in size, a marker of traditional Hindu garment

Fakirs: People with no money and yet contented

Gaddi: Same significance as a chief executive's chair in an office, except that it is a cushion on the floor

Gharana: Literally means a dynasty, but in the context of this book refers to a musical dynasty with its own distinct sound or style of playing an Indian instrument

Ghoomar or Ghumar: A lively Rajasthani folk dance from Mewar, played on happy occasions such as weddings

Godrej Almirahs: Heavy steel non-attached closets made by the Godrej company, normally colored military green which were ubiquitous in middle class Indian homes in mid 20th century

Goonda: A goon or a hood

Gumti or Gumtis: Illegal shacks that dot all Indian citizens, usually setup by squatting on or encroaching on public lands or even private lands, mostly but not exclusively on the roadside, on road shoulders and often talking up significant width of the road itself. In most cases these are setup in connivance with the politicians and bureaucrats in the government and therefore, persist without being removed

Haveli: Grand mansions in Rajasthan, normally with exquisite carving and design, made with expensive materials and owned by wealthy merchants or ruling elite

Hijab: Women's head covering in Islamic culture

Hukum: Literally means, "as you command," but signifies a highly respectful response to one's elder or a person of higher status in India

Hundi or Hundis: Commercial paper in Indian tradition

Jauhar: A ritual of when Rajput or other high family women committed suicide by plunging in fire to save themselves from being mistreated by the invading Muslims. This normally followed the deaths of their husbands on the battlefield

Jharokha: Beautifully designed balconies in Indian Havelis

Ji: An honorific in Sanskrit language and Indian culture that normally follows the person's name

Kajal: Indian mascara or eye cosmetic

Kaka Hukum: A respectful greeting for one's uncle literally translated means, "Highly esteemed Uncle"

Kaka Saheb: A respectful honorific for one's uncle, except in the upper crust in Rajasthan also used to address one's father

Kalbalia or Kalbelia: A sensuous tribal snake dance performed by the banjaras of Rajasthan

Kameez: An Islamic tunic, looks like a long shirt

Karma: In Hindu tradition, performing someone's duty or taking action as per someone's duty

Karma Bhumi: In Hindu tradition, the geographical space where a person performs his duty, normally where the person resides or governs

Khadi: Rough cloth weaved on small hand operated devices in India. Gandhi used it as a symbol of India's independence from the West and its machine-made fabric

Khuda Hafiz: Respectful parting greeting in Urdu language

Kimkhawb: a Dream

Kotwal: Chief of Police or internal security

Kukri: A curved Nepali knife used both as a tool and as a weapon

Kunwar Sahib or Saheb: An honorific for Son-in-Law in Hindu culture

Kurta: A Hindu tunic, looks like a long shirt

Lapsi: A sweet paste made out of flour, butter, sugar, cardamom and dry fruits, used as a traditional offering to the Goddess of War in Rajasthan or to one's family deity

Laissez-Faire: French for unregulated free market and no government interference in trade and commerce

Lehanga: Brightly colored Rajasthani long skirt, normally made of luxurious materials such as silk and bordered with rich brocade

Maharana: Title for a highly esteemed Sisodia ruler of the erstwhile princely state of Mewar, in Rajasthan where the city of Udaipur is located

Maharawal: Title for a highly esteemed Bhatti ruler of the erstwhile princely state of Jaisalmer, in Rajasthan

Mandis: Markets

MarSaheb: Respected tutor

MaSaab: Respected elder grandmother or mother

Mujra: A gesture of high respect, usually from a younger person to an elder or from a person of lower status to a person of higher status

Mulla or Mullah: An Islamic priest

Munim: A manager of a commercial enterprise in India

Nabob: An Urdu honorific for a ruler of a small state or kingdom

Nagar Seth: The doyen of all merchants in the city or a first among equals

Nalayak: Derogatory term used to call someone good for nothing or incompetent

Naqshband Kaarigar: A designer

Nazarana or Nazaranas: A gift taken when visiting a person with a higher status (came to be used later to describe a form of bribe)

Orni or Ornee: Upper body wrap for women in Rajasthan, normally very colorful and made of delicate and soft fabric decorated with rich brocade

Palla-Failana: A ceremony when a ruler wants to make amends to his people. Highly humbling for the ruler, when he literally goes empty handed with his hands holding a piece of cloth, literally begging for alms of forgiveness. Very rare and humiliating for the ruler

Pardah or Parda: Veil to cover the face, an Islamic tradition, later also adopted by some Hindus to protect their women

Patwa and Patwon: an Honorific for a master brocade dealer, Patwon is the plural

Pedi: An office of a traditional Indian merchant, normally his headquarters in the middle of the business district within the city

Pichwada: The back portion of the house along with the backyard

Pranam: Formal initial greetings when meeting

Puja or Pooja: Act and ritual of worshipping in Hindu culture and religions

Pujari: A priest who conducts the ritual of worshipping on behalf of a person

Rana: An honorific for the Sisodia rulers of Mewar in Rajasthan

Rangoli: A traditional Rajasthani color pattern used to paint the ground or a paved area to signify an auspicious occasion

Rawal: An honorific for the Bhatti rulers of Jaisalmer in Rajasthan

Sab or Saheb or Sahib: A courteous term to address a person in India. Usually follows a person's name. Sign of respect

Sachiya Mata or Sachiya Maataa: Family deity of the Bapna dynasty, another name for Goddess Chamundi, the Goddess of War

Sakas: Indianized name for the Indo-Scythian migrants to India from Central Asia and South Georgia region. They established a powerful kingdom in North India including Rajathan in 10 BC., which lasted until 400 AD. Their descendents later reclaimed their North West Indian empire under the name of Gurjara-Pratihara empire, which was the antecedent of subsequent Rajput dynasties of Rajasthan

Salwar or Salwars: Islamic style trousers worn both by men and women

Sangeet: Music program traditionally held a day before the weddings. In affluent families this can be held for several days before and after the wedding

Sanvli: A darker skinned female in Rajasthan

Santhara: A Jain religious ritual where a person close to death, decides to fast unto death, to make amends for any mistakes they may have committed in their life

Sarai: An Indian style inn, normally but not exclusively located on way stops for caravans

Sari or Saris: An Indian dress for women, basically a body wrap

Seth: A rich and esteemed merchant

Sethani: Wife of a rich and esteemed merchant

Sherwani: A long coat in Indian tradition, borrowed from Islamic traditions

Tantrik: A practitioner of Indian occult

Thakurain: A married lady from the ruling elite in Rajasthan

Tika: A red mark normally worn on forehead, signifies a third eye. The person who applies the Tika to another person grants him or her great respect

Tilak: Same as Tika

Tirthankaras: The 24 Gurus or Shamans of the Jain religion

Vaid or Vaidya: Doctors in the ancient Indian system of medicine called Ayurveda

Bibliography - Bapna Family
Historical Record and References – Independent sources – Used to authenticate information in this book

1. 1968-69, V V Giri - President of India -. "Shree Bapna : A Great Administrator - President of India's homage to Sir Siremal Bapna." Singh, Nagendra. President Speaks: A Compilation of the Speeches Made by President V. V. Giri from May 1969 to March 1970. Delhi India: S Chand, 1970. 234.

2. 491, Clements R Markham CB FRS - Pages. "The Geographical Magazine - talks about a British Author's visit to Jaisalmer and his encounters with Seth Himmat Ram, son of Seth Pratap Mal- he describes in detail the riches and the magnificent structures and gardens of Seth Himmat Ram in Amarsagar." FRS, Clements R Marckham CB. The Geographical Magazine. London: Trubner and Company - Lubgate Hill London Also available on Google Books, 1874. 581.

3. Agarawala, Ram Avatar. "Book has evidence of 1) Zorawar Mal's friendship with Col Tod, 2) Zorawar Mal's rivalry with Jaislamer Prime Minister Salim Singh, 3) Salim Singh's misrule and cruelty and 4) A Bapna Family tree from Deoraj to Siremal - particularly footnote1 on page 30 ." Agarawala, Ram Avatar. History, Art and Architecture of Jaisalmer. First. Vol. 1. Delhi: Agam Kala Prakashan, available at Library of Congress Washington DC USA, 1978. 1 vols. 98.

4. Agarwala, Ram Avatar. "On Pages 48, 49, 50, 72, the author talks about the lavish wedding of Seth Zorawar Mal Bapna's son Chandanmal in 1925 held at Udaipur with great pomp at the expense of Rs. 1 million in those days which in todays money is worth around Rs. 1 billion." Agarwala, Ram Avatar. History, Art and Architecture of Jaisalmer. Delhi: Agam Kala Prakashan, also available at Library of Congress Washington DC USA, 1978. 98.

5. Alexander Henry E. Boileau - Pages - 3, 44, 133, 141. "Talks about Seth Buhadur Mal and Zorawar Mul, Rotschilds of Central India, phenomenally rich, mansions in Jodhpur, Ajmer, Jaisalmer, flower gardens in Amar Sagar Jaisalmer, very well thought of Diplomats, arbiters of disputes, mediators between British." Boileau, Alexander Henry E. Personal narrative of a tour through the western states of Rajwara, in 1835 (Google eBook). First. Vol. 1. Baptist Mission Press Circular Road Calcutta - also available at Library of Congress Washington DC USA and Google Ebooks for free, 1837. 1 vols. 337.

6. Bakshi, RK Gupta and SR. "1) Seth Zorawar Mal invited by Rana Bhim Singh to manage Udaipur Treasury and 2) The Entire case of Seth Chhogmal and his dispute with Rana Fateh Singh resulting in Seth Chhogmal's bankruptcy in 1890s and the role of the Viceory, Resident Agent and other." Bakshi, RK Gupta and SR. Studies In Indian History: Rajasthan Through The Ages The Heritage Of Rajputs (Set Of 5 Vols.). Udaipur: Sarup and Sons Udaipur Rajasthan, Available at Library of Congress Washington DC USA, 2008. 335.

7. Bapna, HRH Yeshwant Rao Holkar and Raibahadur Udmat-du-aula Sir Siremal. "Hand Written Correspondance between HRH Yeshwant Rao Holkar and Sir Siremal Bapna." Letters under the seal of HRH Yeshwant Rao Holkar and Sir Siremal Bapna. Indore: Bapna House Family Collection, Indore, 1939.

8. Basham, A L. "Talks about the Scythian or Saka Origin of Rajputs including Pratiharas or Parihars - Agrees with Col James Tod who also claims Scythian or Saka origin of Rajputs." Basham, A L. The Wonder That Was India: A Survey of the Culture of the Indian Sub-Continent Before the Coming of the Muslims. USA: Lightening Source Incorporated, 2009. 696.

9. Blandine Blukacz-Louisfert, Chief, UNOG Registry, Records and Archives Unit, United Nations. Sixteenth Ordinary Session of the Assembly - Sir Sireymal Bapna Indian Delegate. 09 09 1935. 31 July 2014 <http://www.indiana.edu/~league/16thordinaryassemb.htm>.

10. Budh Singh Saheb Bapna, Direct Descendent of Seth Bahadur Mal Bapna of Jaisalmer, Kota. Story of Deoraj, Guman Chand Patwa, History of Jaisalmer, Kota, Malwa Opium Trade History Interview Personal - Penn Bobby Singh - Author 1980s. 1980s.

11. Chandramani Singh, Arvind Mayaram, Rekha Gupta, Akshaya Jagadhari. "Talks about the fact that Seth Guman Chand Bapna built the Patwon Ki Haveli for himself and his five sons and is now owned by Archeological Department of India ." Chandramani Singh, Arvind Mayaram, Rekha Gupta, Akshaya Jagadhari. Protected Monuments Of Rajasthan. Jaipur: Jawahar Kala Kendra, available at Library of Congress, 2002. 404.

12. Chauhan, Mulchand. "Scythic Origin of Rajput Races - argues with evidence that Rajupts are decendants of the Sakas." Chauhan, Mulchand. Scythic Origin of Rajput Races. Ujjain, India: Rajputana Liberation Front, Ujjain, 1999. All .

13. Court, Claims Administrator - New Jeresy Circuit. World Com Litgations - talks about scores of cases filed against World Com following its bankruptcy in 2003, including cases against Burt Roberts. 26 07 2005. 25 08 2013 <http://www.worldcomlitigation.com/html/citisettlement.html>.

14. Devra, GSL. "Talks extenisvely about how Seth Zorawar Mal was invited to Udaipur, made incharge of the Treasury and how all the taxes were collected by him and the revenue first went to his Sethji Ri Haveli - Page 29 of this book talks about it in particular." Devra, GSL. Some Aspects of Socio-economic History of Rajasthan: Jagdish Singh Gahlot Commemoration Volume. Gahlot Memorial Edition. Vol. 1. Jaipur: Sri Jagdish Singh Gahlot Research Institute, available in Library of Congress Washington DC USA, 1980. 1 vols. 252.

15. Dr. Vinod Naneria, Orthopedic Surgeon Choithram Hospital and Research Center. http://www.slideshare.net/naneria/yeswantrao-holkar-266887 - Life Sketch of Maharaja Yeshwant Rao Holkar- has reference to Sir Siremal Bapna as heading the minority government as Regent during Yeshwant Rao's absence from Indore for education in England . 15 02 2008. 02 08 2014 <http://www.slideshare.net/naneria/yeswantrao-holkar-266887>.

16. Eng, William H Danforth in his tour of India in 1928 talks about having dinner with Resident Agent Reginald Glancy and Sir SM Bapna and how HH Tukoji Rao had to abdicate due to Bawla Murder Case and was living in Paris while HH Yeshwant Rao was studying in. "Random Ramblings in India." Danforth, William H. Random Ramblings in India. St Loius Missouri USA: Literary Licensing LLC, 2013 148.

374 BIBLIOGRAPHY

17. Farouqui, Amar - Pages - 59, 64, 65, 105, 125, 126, 130, 231. "1) Involvement of Bahadur Mul and Jorawar Mul in opium trade in Kota, Ujjain and Malwa, 2) Relationship between Tatya Jog Kibe and Bahadurmul and Jorawar Mul, 3) Bahadur Mal being called the Rotschilds of Malwa, 4) Bapna brother's virtual dominance-Malwa." Farouqui, Amar. Smuggling as Subversion: Colonialism, Indian Merchants, and the Politics of Opium, 1790-1843. Delhi: Lexington Books, available in Library of Congress in Washington DC USA, 1998. 263.

18. Gazette, The Edinburgh. "The Edinburgh Gazette issue 15241 Page 15 - Announces the Knighthood of Rai Bahadur Seray Mal Bapna, C.I.E., Prime Minister to His Highness the Maharaja Holkar of Indore, Central India." 07 01 1936. The EdinburghGazette Publication Date January 7 1936 Issue 15241 Page 15. The Stationary Office. 01 08 2014 <https://www.thegazette.co.uk/Edinburgh/issue/15241/page/15>.

19. Go2India.in, 32, Ganga Nagar, BhubaneswarIndia. Havelis of Rajasthan - Patwon Ki Haveli - amount of money spent to construct, that they were constructed as public works project, skilled workmen from around the world built them over 50 years - mrs gandhi designated them National Heritage Monuments-1965. 2005-2014. 01 08 2014 < http://www.go2india.in/rajasthan/patwon-ki-haveli.php>.

20. Government, Secretary State for India - His Majesty's. "Indian Round Table Conference - 2nd Session - Sept 7 1931 to Dec 1 1931 - Proceedings of the Plenary Session." 23 01 1932. India Office Archives - Sir S.M. Bapna as a Delegate. 01 08 2014 <http://www.irps.in/rtc1931.pdf>.

21. Harnath Singh Mehta Saheb, Udaipur. Story of Chhogmal, History of Udaipur (Mewar), Role of Mehta Bhopal Singh, Mehta PannaLal, Mehta Sher Singh Author (Pen Name) Interview Personal by Penn Bobby Singh. 1970s and 1980s.

22. Hingarh, Punkaj Chandmal Hingarh and Rohit Chandmal. South Asia Times / Jain Patriots Role in Freeing India - talks about five great Indian Patriots who worked towards freeing India from the foreign yolk - one of them mentioned is Seth Zorawarmal. 17 08 2013. 23 08 2014 <http://thesouthasiantimes.info/index.php?param=news/12425/India/30>.

23. Jain, Satish Kumar. "Talks at length about the Bapna family particularly Seth Zorawar Mal, Bahadur Mal and Sir Siremal." Jain, Satish Kumar. Progressive Jains of India. First. Delhi: Shraman Sahitya Sansthan, Available at Library of Congress, 1975. 319.

24. John Sutherland, Agent to the Governor General Rajputana Residency. "Seth BahadurMul-how rich he was and how he operated in Boondie and Kota in view of author and also mentions Seth ZorawarMul as brother of Seth BahadurMul and how together they controlled treasuries of Kota, Boondie and Udaipur by 1828 - Pages 94,95 and 96." John Sutherland, Agent to the Governor General Rajputana Residency. Sketches of the Relations Subsisting Between the British Government in India: And the Different Native States (Google eBook). London: G.H. Huttmann, available at Library of Congress Washington DC USA, 1837. 193.

25. Jones, Rodney W. "Talks about P.S. Bapna as Development Commissioner IAS, Government of Madhya Pradesh and also mentions Sir Siremal as Prime Minister Hokar State and also KB Bapna as Excise Commissioner Holkar State." Jones, Rodney W. Urban Politics in India: Area, Power, and Policy in a Penetrated System. Los Angeles: University of California Press, available in Library of Congress Washington DC USA, 1974. 420.

26. Kothari, DS. "Science and Ahimsa - contains an excerpt of a speech by Sir SM Bapna." Misra, KD Gangrade and Rameshwar Prasad. Conflict Resolution Through Non-Violence: Science and Ethics. Ed. KD Gangrade and Rameshwar Prasad Misra. 2nd Edition. Ajmer: Ashok Kumar Mittal - Concept Publishing Company New Delhi India - publishing@conceptpub.com, 1943. 39.

27. Lodha, Jain Chanchalmal. "History of Oswal - Gives a concise history of the Origin of Oswals and its gotras including the Bapnas." Lodhi, Jain Chanchalmal. History of Oswal. Jaipur: Google Books, 1999. 684.

28. London, Viceroy of India and India Office. "File 624-P(S)/1925-26 1. Proposal to appoint a commission of enquiry to enquire into the question of the connection of His Highness the Maharaja of Indore with the conspiracy by certain officials of the State to kidnap Mumtaz Begum." 04 08 1925-26. National Archives Government of UK - British Library Asia, Pacific and Africa Collection - Original

Papers. 01 08 2014 <http://apps.nationalarchives.gov.uk/a2a/records.aspx?cat=059-r1_1-1&cid=1-1-13-347#1-1-13-347>.

29. London, Viceroy of India representing the Crown and India Office. "File 341-P(S)/1926 1. Report on the working of the Minority Administration in Indore State. 2. Confirmation of Rai Bahadur S.M. Bapna as Prime Minister, Indore State and decision not to make any changes in the personnel of the Cabinet Ministers." 23 04 1926. National Archives Government of UK - British Library, Asia, Pacific and Africa Collection. 01 08 2014 <http://apps.nationalarchives.gov.uk/a2a/records.aspx?cat=059-r1_1-1&cid=1-1-13-266#1-1-13-266>.

30. "Indore:Two Memorials to the Viceroy against the continuance of Mr. Bapna as Diwan of the State." 2 01 1928. National Archives Government of UK - British Library, Asia, Pacific and Africa Collection. 01 08 2014 <http://www.nationalarchives.gov.uk/a2a/records.aspx?cat=059-iorlps_3-3&cid=1-1-118-7#1-1-118-7>.

31. London, Viceroy representing the Crown - British India AND India Office. "Proposed Appointment of Sir S.M. Bapna as Chief Minister Alwar State IOR/R/1/1/4001 1943." 01 03 1943. The National Archives - Government of UK - British Library, Asia, Pacific and Africa Collections. 01 08 2014 <http://www.nationalarchives.gov.uk/a2a/records.aspx?cat=059-r1_1-2&cid=1-1-1-16-92#1-1-1-16-92>.

32. Long Distance Warrior - tells the epic story or an unheralded hero, a giant who took on the most powerful monopoly in history and won, not just for himself but his victory opened up the telecom markets to revolutionary innovations in very short time . Dir. Holt Productions and Northern Light Productions. Perf. Co-Founder and Chairman of MCI Telecommunications Inc. William McGowan. 2011.

33. Lucknow, Pioneer Press. "The Feudatory and zemindari India, Volume 17, Issue 2 - Pages 653,654,657 - talk about Sir SM Bapna being a great reformer and also Seth Zorawar Mal's role in arranging treaties between the British and Rajputana States in a very evenhanded manner." Lucknow, Pioneer Press. The Feudatory and zemindari India, Volume 17, Issue 2. Lucknow: Pioneer Press Lucknow India, also available on Google Books, 1937. 672.

34. Mehta, Balwant Singh AND Jodh Singh. "1) Seth Zorawar Mal Bapna being invited by Rana Bhim Singh to manage the Treasury

of Mewar, 2) Seth Zorawar Mal Bapna being from an Oswal family that were originally Parihar Rajputs and converted to Jainism, and 3) Seth Chhogmal's Mail Cart Case w/ Fateh." Mehta, Balwant Singh and Jodh Singh. Pratap The Patriot : With a Concise History of Mewar and its missing links. Udaipur: Pratap Institute of Historical Research, Available at Library of Congress Washington DC, 1971. 110.

35. Mohanty, Subodh. Miranda House - DS Kothari - Connection to Sir SM Bapna Prime Minister of Indore. 19 06 1922. 31 July 2014 <http://www.mirandahouse.ac.in/MirandaHouse/userspace/username/admin/DynamicFolder/2008-2009/D%20S%20Kothari/About_D_S_kothari.htm>.

36. Owners, Heritage Hotel Jagadish Mahal Udaipur -. "History - narrating how Seth Zorawar Mal Bapna was invited by Maharana Bhim Singh of Mewar on the advice of Col James Tod, to take charge of the Treasury of Mewar State and rescue it from the doldrums it was into in early 1800s." 06 05 2013. Heritage Hotel Jagadish - Seth Ji Ri Haveli - Near Vidhya Niketan School, Rao ji ka hata, Jadiyon ki oll, Udaipur-313001 Rajasthan (INDIA). 01 08 2014 <http://www.shreejagdishmahal.com/history.html#History>.

37. Press, Government of Madhya Pradesh Regional. Report on the Community Development Programme of Madhya Pradesh (November 1, 1956 to March 31, 1958). Status - talks about P. S. Bapna IAS taking over as Principal Secretary Planning and Development and Development Commissioner Bhopal. Bhopal India: Government Regional Press, 1956-58.

38. Rao, R. Venkoba. "Ministers of Indian States Vol1 - Page 43 - talks about the disinterested mediation between Rajput States and the British by Seth Zorawarmal Bapna and Siremal Bapna being his great grandson and a great statesman in his own right." Rao, R Venkoba. Ministers of Indian States Vol1. London: Wednesday Review Press, 1928. 389.

39. Robinson, British Political Agent T. Eulogizes the noble qualities of Seth Zorawar Mal Bapna such as his generousity, diplomatic skills, loyalty to Rajputana States and skills as a merchant & how the Rajputana Chiefs treated him with great deference, even going against established protocol. A Report in letter form to the Maharana of Udaipur and Viceroy of India . Udaipur, Mewar State and Delhi:

Unknown - but reference taken from the book, History, Art and Architecture of Jaisalmer by Ram Avatar Agarwala, 1849.

40. S. K. Bhatt, Academy of Indian Numismatics and Sigillography. Tribal Studies Cell. "Talks about Pratap Singh Bapna (P.S. Saheb) work in Tribal Welfare and his position as the Development Commissioner, IAS Officer State of Madhya Pradesh." S. K. Bhatt, Academy of Indian Numismatics and Sigillography. Tribal Studies Cell. Tribals of India: problems and perspectives. Bhopal : Tribal Studies Cell, Academy of Indian Numismatics & Sigillography, 1990. 102.

41. Saheb, Mrs. Ratan Kumari Bapna. Story of Chhogmal, Story of Zorawarmal, Story of Siremal, History of Udaipur Personal Interview by Penn Bobby Singh Author. 1960s, 1970s, 1980s.

42. Saheb, P. S. Bapna. Story of Chhogmal, Story of Siremal, Story of Jorawarmal, Story of Indore, History of Udaipur Personal - Penn Bobby Singh, Author Interview. 1960s, 1970s and 1980s.

43. Sarma, Omprakasa. "Sir Siremal Bapna - Biography - his diaries, his meetings with world figures, his family background, family history, his administration of Holkar State, his achievements." Sarma, Omprakasa. Ek Yug Ek Purush (A Man and an Era) - A Biography of Raibahadur Sir Siremal Bapna. Delhi: Sasta Sahitya Mandala, 1969. 282.

44. Sen, AP. Indiankannon.org - Talks about how one of Yeshwant Rao's coterie, one HC Dhandha even went on to file a suit against him to extort money out of the Prince, after his state was merged in the Union of India. 04 12 1969. 24 08 2014 <http://www.indiankanoon.org/doc/1316535/>.

45. Shrivastav, P N. Madhya Pradesh District Gazetteers Indore - talks about Sir Siremal Bapna being a great administrator. Ed. Prof Dhariwal. First Edition - 1971. Bhopal MP India: District Gazetteers Department Madhya Pradesh Government Bhopal MP India, 1971.

46. Somānī, Rāmavallabha. "Talks about Deoraj, his son Guman Chand and Guman Chand's five sons, their far flung business and their havelis - particularly page 242." Somānī, Rāmavallabha. Jain Inscriptions of Rajasthan. Jaipur: Rajasthan Prakrit Bharati Sansthan, available at Library of Congress, 1982. 339.

47. Tiwari, S.N. "Seth Zorawarmal and his family's background and prominence in Rajasthan and the esteem in which the Rajputana Princess held them in - their business operations in Kota, Jaisalmer, Udaipur and Indore and their family history." Tiwari, S.N. Business Community and Freedom Movement: A Case History of Rajasthan. Udaipur: Aalekh Publishers Udaipur Rajasthan, available at Library of Congress Washington DC USA, 1991. 208.

48. Tod, Col James. "1) Saka origins of Rajputs, 2) Salim Singhs cruelty and misrule, 3) Salim Singh poisoned by own wife after being stabbed by a Jaisalmer Royal inside the Fort, 3) Saroop Singh's misrule and manner of death, 4) Rawal Mulraj puppet to Saroop and Salim Singh." Col James Tod, British Political Agent who signed treaties with most Rajputana States during his tenure in Rajputana- 1817 - 1823. Annals and Antiquities of Rajasthan Or the Central and Western Rajput States of India: ... Vols. 1, 2 and 3. London: Routledge, available at Library of Congress Washington DC USA, 1957. 3 vols. 678, 683, 754.

49. Transcriber, Bombay High Court. Bombay High Court Historical Cases - Bawla Murder Case 1925 . 12 01 1925. 04 08 2014 <http://bombayhighcourt.nic.in/libweb/historicalcases/cases/BAWLA_MURDER_CASE-1925.html>.

50. Ward, Philip. "A Jaisalmer Travelogue by Philip Ward in 1980s talking about the marvel that is Patwon Ki Haveli and also discusses the Bapna(Patwa) family - Guman Chand Patwa and his five sons - Seth ZorawarMal included." Ward, Philip. Northern India, Rajasthan, Agra, Delhi: A Travel Guide. Pelican Edition. Gretna: Pelican Publishing, available in Library of Congress Washington DC USA, 1989. 236.

www.ingramcontent.com/pod-product-compliance
Lightning Source LLC
Chambersburg PA
CBHW052009070526
44584CB00016B/1677